History, Fiction, and Germany

"Proclamation of the German Empire" by Anton von Werner, 1885. Detail.
Courtesy of akg images. Alterations by the author.

History, Fiction, and Germany

Writing the Nineteenth-Century Nation

BRENT O. PETERSON

WAYNE STATE UNIVERSITY PRESS
DETROIT

K

KRITIK

German Literary Theory and Cultural Studies
Liliane Weissberg, Editor

A complete listing of the books in this series can be found online at http://wsupress.wayne.edu

© 2005 BY WAYNE STATE UNIVERSITY PRESS,
DETROIT, MICHIGAN 48201. ALL RIGHTS RESERVED.
NO PART OF THIS BOOK MAY BE REPRODUCED WITHOUT FORMAL PERMISSION.
MANUFACTURED IN THE UNITED STATES OF AMERICA.
09 08 07 06 05   5 4 3 2 1

LIBRARY OF CONGRESS CATALOGING-IN-PUBLICATION DATA
PETERSON, BRENT ORLYN.
HISTORY, FICTION, AND GERMANY : WRITING THE NINETEENTH-CENTURY NATION /
BRENT O. PETERSON.
P. CM. — (KRITIK : GERMAN LITERARY THEORY AND CULTURAL STUDIES)
INCLUDES BIBLIOGRAPHICAL REFERENCES AND INDEX.
ISBN 0-8143-3200-5 (HARDCOVER : ALK. PAPER)
1. GERMAN LITERATURE—19TH CENTURY—HISTORY AND CRITICISM. 2. HISTORICAL FICTION, GERMAN—19TH CENTURY—HISTORY AND CRITICISM. 3. NATIONAL CHARACTERISTICS, GERMAN, IN LITERATURE. 4. NATIONAL CHARACTERISTICS, GERMAN—HISTORY—19TH CENTURY.
I. TITLE. II. KRITIK (DETROIT, MICH.)
PT345.P48 2005
830.9'358'09034—DC22
2004015829

∞THE PAPER USED IN THIS PUBLICATION MEETS THE MINIMUM REQUIREMENTS OF THE AMERICAN NATIONAL STANDARD FOR INFORMATION SCIENCES—PERMANENCE OF PAPER FOR PRINTED LIBRARY MATERIALS, ANSI Z39.48-1984.

Contents

Acknowledgments *vii*

Introduction:
How Prussian Heroes Came to Dominate
Germany's National Narrative *1*

1.
The Past as History and Fiction *29*

2.
Caste and Regional Identities *69*

3.
From Frederick the Great to Old Fritz *97*

4.
Explaining Jena *147*

5.
The German People Arise—and Marry *199*

Conclusion:
The Myth of a Common Past *267*

Notes *273* Bibliography *331* Index *345*

Acknowledgments

I WOULD LIKE TO thank the many friends and colleagues who read parts of this manuscript or otherwise encouraged me to keep going on a project that lasted too long and bridged too many personal and professional difficulties. Among those to whom I owe an enormous debt of gratitude are Kit Belgum, Anke Gleber, Sabine Hake, Pat Herminghouse, Peter Hohendahl, Todd Kontje, Alice Kuzniar, Liz Mittman, Bob Shandley, Lynne Tatlock, and Dan Watkins. The National Endowment for the Humanities funded a crucial year in my career, and I hope they are happy the investment is finally paying off. Ripon College and now Lawrence University both offered me an intellectual home, interesting students, and the chance to build their German programs. I remain grateful for those opportunities, even when they have gotten in the way of this and other endeavors. And Susan Barbour has invested more time and energy and put more meaning into my life than even she realizes.

The first chapter of this book is a longer version of my essay "Mühlbach, Ranke, and the Truth of Historical Fiction," which was first published in *A Companion to German Realism, 1848–1900*, edited by Todd Kontje (Rochester, NY: Camden House, 2002) and is used by permission.

An earlier version of chapter 2 appeared as "German Nationalism after Napoleon: Caste and Regional Identities in Historical Fiction, 1815–1830," *German Quarterly* 68.2 (1995) 287–303. It is also used by permission.

Introduction: How Prussian Heroes Came to Dominate Germany's National Narrative

[W]hat we inherit,
To make it ours truly, we've got to earn it.
—*Goethe*, Faust *(Martin Greenberg, trans.)*

The third and final version of Anton von Werner's monumental canvas *The Proclamation of the German Empire* contains even more mistakes than his first two attempts at commemorating the event.[1] For example, since Bismarck's aides had taken only dark blue uniforms to France in January 1871, the Iron Chancellor did not wear the white cavalry uniform that highlights his position at the center of the composition. He also could not have been wearing the Prussian Order of Merit, because the newly crowned emperor had not yet awarded it to him. Nor was Bismarck's friend and colleague Albrecht von Roon standing just right of center. Although he was instrumental in bringing the Franco-Prussian War to a successful conclusion and deserved to be present on January 18, 1871, the day the empire was proclaimed, Field Marshal von Roon was in bed with the flu. Unlike Roon, the painter had been in Versailles that day and had witnessed the whole affair. Werner knew what was wrong with the picture, but he still made things worse with each revision.

Or did he? Although the answer might seem obvious, the issue of truth in historical representation—whether in painting; academic and popular history; historical fiction, poetry, and drama; or in monuments—is one of the most vexing problems imaginable. For example, if

INTRODUCTION

Werner had decided to let Bismarck fade into the sea of dark blue uniforms, as he did in earlier versions of the painting, or if he had left Roon out of his cast of characters, the picture would have become false in other respects. Not only would the image of a crucial event in German history have been far less striking, but an accurate painting would also have contradicted both political reality in Germany and what most Germans probably believed had actually happened. Bismarck really was at the center of the imperial enterprise, and just as certainly, it was Roon's soldiers and leadership that won the Franco-Prussian War and made the empire possible. By getting the details wrong, Werner was able to represent a larger truth; he created an image so close to what should have been the case that it could pass for fact. Indeed, this final version of the painting soon began to displace and then replace reality. It even seems to have become true for some of the participants.

Emperor William I complained about Bismarck's uniform in this version of the painting, but after being informed that the chancellor had been entitled to wear white, the emperor complimented Werner for correcting Bismarck's mistake. Then, in 1885, when he commissioned the artist to make a copy of the painting as a present to mark the chancellor's seventieth birthday, it was William himself who suggested adding Roon to the composition. The result seems to have pleased Bismarck, and whether by accident or the Hegelian "cunning of reason" in history, only the chancellor's birthday gift survived both world wars. More important, it became a standard illustration for books on nineteenth-century Germany, because Werner had created a powerful symbol, filled with genuine heroes, whom he depicted accurately in their larger roles in Germany's nationalist narrative. The third version of Werner's "Proclamation of the German Empire" is intriguing, not just for its mistakes and hints of larger truths but because its mixture of history and fiction also typifies what historians and the authors of historical fiction produced when they tried to sell Prussian heroes to an audience of newly minted Germans.

By the time Werner painted this image, Bismarck was well on his way to becoming not only a Prussian hero but a German hero as well.[2] As early as 1872, Carl Crauer, a sculptor in the west German spa of Bad Kreuznach, where Bismarck traveled periodically for health reasons, had finished a statue of the chancellor, in uniform and holding a copy of the imperial constitution in his right hand. The first public monument to Bismarck was erected in Cologne in 1879, but by then his face in bronze

INTRODUCTION

already graced a frieze on the base of the Germania monument that rose along the Rhine near Rüdesheim (1877–83). The process of commemoration accelerated during celebrations to mark Bismarck's eightieth birthday in 1895, when over 450 cities offered him honorary citizenship. By 1914 more than 500 Bismarck towers, statues, and busts dotted the landscape from Raguit near Tilsit, in what was then far northeastern Germany, to Lorrach, in the extreme southwest, as well as in Metz, in what had previously been French Alsace-Lorraine. On the other diagonal, monuments stretched from formerly Danish Schleswig, near the site of the Prussian victory over the Danes at Düppel, to Reichenhall, now Bad Reichenhall, in southeastern Bavaria. The number of Bismarck streets and squares is probably beyond counting. For those who could afford one, starting in 1878 the Munich artist Franz von Lenbach painted more than eighty portraits of Bismarck. For considerably less money, visitors to Bad Kissingen in Thuringia could buy postcards that showed not only Bismarck and the Prince Bismarck scales but also a table of princely corpulence from 1874–93, when the chancellor's weight ranged from 216 to 272 pounds! At six feet three inches and broad-shouldered, he might have been impressive rather than fat, but the souvenir itself is bizarre if also an attempt at humanizing the great man. Although the monuments were concentrated in Germany's industrial centers, the geographical extent of Bismarck remembrances, including those overseas, demonstrates that by the end of his life the man most responsible for German unification was venerated in places and by people who had once rejected his politics. The question is how that shift occurred.

Of course, Bismarck was neither the first nor the only Prussian to attain national prominence. This book contends that during the course of the nineteenth century, Frederick the Great (1712–86), Prussia's Queen Louisa (1776–1810), and the Prussian-led coalition that defeated Napoleon in the Wars of Liberation (1813–15) also achieved pan-Germanic status. As part of this process, not only did Prussians come to think of Bismarck and themselves as Germans, but the inhabitants of territories that Bismarck helped unify also accepted him not as a Prussian conqueror but as their own genuinely German hero. Thus, along with—and probably more important than—Prussia's seizure of political power in Germany came the articulation of a national narrative, shared by most Germans, in which Prussians played almost all of the leading roles.

INTRODUCTION

Kinds of History

There would be little reason for a new account of Prussia's triumph if reading conventional history led to an understanding of how and why nineteenth-century Germans accepted Bismarck and these other Prussians as their own.[3] However, neither political nor intellectual history can show what it meant when people took Werner's *Proclamation of the German Empire* at face value. What the ordinary men and women gradually accepted as true about their past was, at best, a partial truth that depended upon omission, embellishment, exaggeration, and, occasionally, outright fraud: for example, Bismarck resplendent in his white uniform, wearing the Prussian Order of Merit and standing next to Field Marshal von Roon. But in this regard nineteenth-century Germans were no different from their neighbors or from us. As Ernest Renan, a French philologist and early theorist of nationalism, argued in 1882: "Forgetting, I would even go so far as to say historical error, is a crucial factor in the creation of a nation."[4] More recently, Homi Bhabha introduced a collection of essays, including Renan's, by talking about the "foundational fictions" upon which all nations are built.[5] In other words, to see how Germany came into existence as a discursive formation—that is, as a set of widely held ideas rather than simply as a place or a political entity—we need not reexamine German history. Instead, we ought to look at the complex set of relationships between history, fiction, and the German nation. Like people in the rest of the world, nineteenth-century Germans remembered and forgot history in an intriguingly idiosyncratic fashion, but their memories, which eventually helped produce a German national identity, were anything but random. As historian Alon Confino argues in an attempt at defining collective memory, "[T]o make a difference in society, it is not enough for a certain past to be selected. It must steer emotions, motivate people to act, be received; in short, it must become a socio-cultural mode of action."[6] I contend, first, that by acquiring a common past, parts of an otherwise diverse population in central Europe—Prussians, Bavarians, Saxons, and others—were becoming Germans and, second, that the content of their acquired memories mattered more to the shape and meaning of "Germany" than the new lines and captions that appeared on maps of Europe after 1871. Without the gradual acquisition of their supposedly common past, Germans might have treated the new state as no more than another dynastic curiosity; without an appropriate national narrative, the second German empire

INTRODUCTION

would not have resonated with the people it united. In other words, it took the transformation of Prussian heroes into Germans to make the state and nation coincide, which is why we need to trace the contours of that narrative's construction.

If the question becomes what Prussians and other prospective Germans knew or thought they knew about German history, or if we ask what it meant to talk about history in nineteenth-century Germany, the answers concern the past in all of its guises—remembered, forgotten, falsified, and interpreted. Facts are no longer the only, or even the most important, referent. Of course, what actually happened provided the framework within which such discussions took place, but no survey of events can explain either the content of historical consciousness or the persistence of selective national memory. To find out what ordinary Germans knew and what they were thinking when they talked about the past, we need access to what remains of the nineteenth-century discourse of history. Our best sources consist, on the one hand, of academic and popular histories and, on the other hand, of historical novels, because these texts can show what knowledge about the past looked like: its form, content, and mode of transmission.[7] History and historical fiction can also elucidate what was at stake in reading, writing, and talking about the past, even if some of the history they relate turns out to be misleading, false, or foolish. In fact, although much of what popular history and historical fiction contained would pass the muster of academic history, the question of truth almost disappears in the face of larger issues, such as what people believed to be true, how they came to know it, and what that knowledge meant to them.

Unfortunately, we do not possess survey data about the extent of historical knowledge or its impact on nineteenth-century Germans. We do have hundreds of texts, both fiction and nonfiction, that sought to impart some version of the facts and their own interpretations of the German past. Frequently, if often only implicitly, these same books also questioned the status of the period's historical discourse. I do not intend to summarize their arguments or plots; instead, I present a series of close readings directed at short passages and narrative sequences. The factual material can give us an idea of what Germans knew, but how these texts work invariably reveals as much as what they say explicitly. But rather than remain at the level of generalization, I want to introduce the issues raised by the interplay of fiction and popular history by exam-

INTRODUCTION

ining a brief exchange between two characters in Theodor Fontane's *Der Stechlin* (1897), a novel that deals with its own times while also illustrating the nineteenth century's fascination with the past.

The scene involves two minor bureaucrats, both of them prototypical Prussians, arguing about the significance of a roadside monument. Major von Czako explains to his friend Ministerialassessor von Rex that the object in question commemorates the battle of Cremer Damm, which had taken place in 1412, nearly five hundred years before the novel's action. Czako is particularly proud of himself for knowing that Count Hans von Hohenlohe met a heroic death near the crossroads where the two men talk. Czako's point concerns the continuity between present and past; this ancient von Hohenlohe died defending Prussia from Sweden, while at that very moment in the novel's narrated time, his descendant, Chlodwig Prince von Hohenlohe-Schillingfürst, serves as chancellor of Imperial Germany. This is supposed to be a keen observation, based on considerable knowledge, but Rex remains distinctly unimpressed: "Yes, Czako, I already know all that. It's all in *The Brandenburg Children's Companion*."[8] In other words, since Czako's background information on the monument is available in a Prussian primer, Rex claims everyone, even the most ignorant inhabitant of the land, would be just as familiar with the details of the Hohenlohe family tree as Czako.[9] He ignores Czako's larger point, because, in the fashion of so many superficially educated, pretentious Germans at the end of the nineteenth century, the two men are simply trying to outdo each other by employing their repertoire of historical tidbits. Rex not only claims to know more than his friend, but he also chastises him for drawing on such a paltry source. In Fontane's day, knowing enough history to impress your friends and vanquish your competitors seems to have required ready access to a considerably larger store of even more obscure facts than Czako commanded. Just such behavior, coupled with his doubts about the poor quality and overwhelming quantity of nineteenth-century historical writing, provoked Nietzsche's *Untimely Meditation: The Use and Abuse of History* in 1874. He complained that people knew too many facts but too little history; they invoked the past without understanding it.

One wonders what Nietzsche would make of the situation today. Unlike Fontane's contemporaries, modern readers need two long endnotes just to understand this one short passage. Nowadays, competing demands have pushed historical knowledge far from the center of the

INTRODUCTION

educational enterprise, while the issue of how much history students ought to know has become as controversial as the question of what literature they should read.[10] Just as a new generation of literary scholars has expanded the canon, so too have social and cultural historians shifted the focus of historical inquiry and teaching from the careers of great men to the lives of ordinary mortals. In Germany history remains a preoccupation, but whereas Germans once learned about the upward trajectory of the national ideal, they must now come to terms with the more recent past (*Vergangenheitsbewältigung*). Information about the battle of Cremer Damm has long since disappeared from the store of common knowledge, but rather than praise or bemoan the difference, I want to use it to ask a series of questions: First, why did nineteenth-century Germans take such an interest in the past? Second, if we believe Rex, how did even the unwashed masses come to know so much history? Third, what kinds of history did Germans know? Finally, what was at stake in their acquisition and use of this historical knowledge—in other words, why did it matter that Germans knew so much history?

Fontane poses these questions implicitly without answering them, but since the two men's conversation contains far more information than first meets the eye, unpacking the exchange between Czako and Rex starts the process of exploring the underlying issues. For example, after tracking down Rex's reference, we know that he must have read a post-1815 edition of *The Brandenburg Children's Companion,* not the first edition of 1800 or the six largely unchanged editions that followed it. After the Wars of Liberation, during which most of Europe fought Napoleon's "French" armies, supposedly in the name of national independence, the primer's author, Pastor Friedrich Wilmsen, added a chapter-long history to his increasingly popular book. Wilmsen explained the addition in a preface to the eighth edition, of 1815: "The history of Brandenburg has been added to this new edition so that this children's companion can legitimately bear the name Brandenburg. Young people will become familiar at an earlier age with the fates and deeds of their robust and honest ancestors and consequently will be able to love their fatherland more faithfully and devoutly."[11] Until 1815, the only extended mention of Brandenburg had been a sketch of its geography and a few brief excerpts from the Prussian legal code. After 1815, Brandenburg's history filled forty-one closely printed pages. It is a fact-laden and fairly dull tour, but for Pastor Wilmsen and his contemporaries such a survey had a clear purpose. As the hero of Fontane's novel

INTRODUCTION

puts it, echoing Wilmsen: "Such recapitulation always strengthens one's sense of history and patriotism."[12]

Actually, Dubslav von Stechlin refers not to a history book but to the inscription on another monument, for none of these characters would have needed to look far to find stone remembrances. The nineteenth century was a time of hectic commemorative building; statues, temples, obelisks, and columns honoring heroic Germans sprouted out of the landscape like so many mushrooms. Rudy Koshar estimates the number of "national" monuments produced in Imperial Germany at over one thousand, including three hundred devoted to Bismarck and another three hundred dedicated to Emperor William I.[13] Their purpose, in an age obsessed with history, was to invoke or, as Aleida Assmann says, to "stage the past" (*Inszenierung der Vergangenheit*), because monuments, even those not graced with long inscriptions or series of images, implicitly contain a narrative connected to what they represent.[14] However, the number of storytelling stones pales by comparison to the vast array of written history produced during the same era. By mid-century, history had emerged as a legitimate academic discipline, and historians were writing for both a scholarly audience and for interested laypeople, that is, for readers such as Czako and Rex.[15] In addition, the historical novel was the century's most popular literary genre, and it is there, in historical fiction, that the interplay of fact and fiction, along with what Renan terms remembering and forgetting, becomes particularly revealing. To be sure, Stechlin, Czako, and Rex are only characters who talk about history, but their status as fictional figures raises the issue of history versus literature as a means of promoting historical knowledge.

Although this study spends considerable time dealing with both academic and popular history, historical fiction forms its center. Novels can make history come alive. They can enliven an otherwise dry recitation of people, places, and events; they can also complicate the past by showing its contingency and ambiguity. In addition, characters and continuous narration hook readers and make them receptive to both information and interpretations. Not only does historical fiction garner a larger audience than either popular or academic history, but it also makes a particularly just claim to the ancient topos of mixing education with entertainment. For even though the history related by historical fiction is not always absolutely true, neither is it utterly false; historical fiction simply mixes historical reality with invention (falsehood), often in a far more palatable form than its nonfiction competitors. Moreover,

INTRODUCTION

whether the facts conveyed in historical novels are actually true or false, readers who believed what they read in novels set in the German past acquired there some of the shared information about history that is a prerequisite to national consciousness.

Historical fiction also allowed writers to explore themes and actions off limits to academic history. Unlike nineteenth-century historians, whose discipline forced them to concentrate on events in the lives of great men—on wars, treaties, and other acts of state—the period's historical novelists could go beyond the archives. Historical fiction could depict kings and generals up close and in private, and these same works could represent the effects of history on the lives of ordinary men and women. Novels could show what past actions meant to people similar to their readers. In looking deeply rather than broadly at their characters, the authors of historical fiction often produced a kind of social history before its time. Accordingly, a critical question addressed in chapter 1 concerns the division of labor between historians and the authors of historical fiction. In essence, I argue that fiction and nonfiction were equally implicated in the discourse of history; both contributed their own particular brand of history, for their own, often overlapping sets of readers; and both transmitted the facts, falsehoods, and half-truths that became what Germans knew about their past.

NATIONALISM

Not coincidentally, German nationalism arose at roughly the same time as historians and historical novelists were demarcating their separate rhetorical territories. In fact, history, historical fiction, and the articulation of a German national identity were often part of the same enterprise. Historical knowledge, specifically the shared knowledge that became a common past only retrospectively, helped meld an otherwise politically, religiously, and economically diverse population into Germans. Not only was a national identity part of a radical shift in orientation, but by identifying themselves primarily as Germans—rather than as Bavarians, Prussians, Saxons, or Anhalt-Zerbstians—people also laid claim to more than just a label. Their developing identity was based, first, on the belief that as Germans they had a common origin, history, and destiny; second, on a sense that they shared a single geography, culture, and language; and, third, on the conviction that all Germans belonged together in one, and only one, continuous and contiguous nation-state.[16] These three beliefs were all, if not utter nonsense, at least of questionable validity;

9

they were also new; and they were constructed—in and through history—rather than natural, given, or revealed. However, neither the vacuity nor novelty of nationalist claims did anything to diminish the political and emotional appeal of the German national myth. As we are still painfully aware, nationalism survives and even flourishes while flying in the face of reason.

A good example of the mythic nature of nineteenth-century nationalism's creed is its view of the German language, which many still regard as the core of German identity.[17] Yet, as logical as it seems to regard Germans as a people united by a shared language, anyone who travels in Germany knows that Germans actually speak a confusing array of mutually incomprehensible dialects, especially in the countryside. It is at most a slight exaggeration to say that Bavarians neither understand nor care for Berlin's "pig-Prussians" (*Sau-Preußen*), while Berliners are often linguistically lost in Munich, to say nothing of Zurich or Vienna. We can only imagine how much worse the situation was before radio and television penetrated German society and began leveling the linguistic playing field. For most of the nineteenth century, "the German language" was little more than a dream—except among regionally defined sections of a tiny, educated elite, mainly the emerging middle class of Protestant northern Germany. And the German example was far from unique. As historian Eric Hobsbawm has pointed out, linguistic disunity was the norm in preindustrial Europe: "French was essential to the concept of France, even though in 1789 50% of Frenchmen did not speak it at all, [and] only 12–13% spoke it 'correctly'. . . . Just so the Germany of the eighteenth century was a purely cultural concept. . . . It consisted of at most 3–500,000 readers of works in the literary vernacular, and the almost certainly much smaller number who actually spoke the 'Hochsprache' or cultural language for everyday purposes."[18] Linguistic and other prerequisites for a German nation were nevertheless "posited" (*gesetzt*), to use Claus Ahlzweig's term, and then gradually realized in the course of a political process *for* and then increasingly *by* "the German people," a mysterious entity that eventually became both the subject and the object of its own historical development. The articulation and successful adoption of this new, radically different nationalist orientation succeeded largely because Germans believed they already existed as a coherent whole.[19] As they accepted and acted out this identity—for example, by joining a national sharpshooters or singing club or by reading national history and literature—their identity became all the more real. Yet to ask what people's identities contained is almost too complicated a question to pose, much less to answer. German nationalism is like pornography; no one can define what everyone claims to recognize when he or she sees it. Indeed, Germans could and did agree upon the existence of a German national identity and act as if it existed, without ever being sure just what their shared identity contained. Germany could mean different things to different people, but for them all to be German they had to fill the label with content. In addition to beliefs about geography, language, and customs, nineteenth-century German identities included facts and meanings that people busily becoming German ascribed to their common past. Thus, to examine what Germans knew of German history, especially when they disagreed about its specific content, is to re-create a pivotal piece of the discursive universe in which Germany itself was invented; it is to see how myth and remembered history combined to create cultural and political reality.

Of course, German national identity was interwoven with, and sometimes contradicted by, regional loyalties, by gender roles and occupational categories, as well as by caste, class, political, and religious affiliations. Identity, then as now, is anything but an essence or a constant; no one is born with a ready answer to the question *Who are you?* We all have to learn what it means to be Protestant, Catholic, or Jewish; conservative or liberal; male or female; German or American—to name only a few of the variables. Moreover, identities are relational, contextual, and fundamentally narrative in form; they are not simply labels but stories we tell ourselves and others in specific situations. Identities change over time; they acquire new content and demand new forms of activity as circumstances change. Being German, Protestant, male, and a carpenter—to construct one possible chain of identity markers—means something different today than it would have in 1900, or in 1800. Most of the components in an individual's identity come into existence and are changed by political, cultural, and technological developments; they are not determined in any meaningful sense by biology, climate, or geography. In addition, at any particular point or situation, people can choose to emphasize one facet of their identity over another. Being asked who you are on the job elicits a different answer than the same question asked at home, in church, or abroad.

Examining national identity while bracketing the other variants of people's identities means imposing a false limit while simultaneously embarking on a gigantic undertaking. National identity markers are complex, and they appear in the most unlikely places. There are German variants of religion, family structure, class, and occupational status, and no single book can ever contain the whole disparate mass of possibilities. However, despite those caveats, and difficult though it is to elucidate the dialectical fits and starts involved in constructing a German national identity, I embark on my analysis, because the process I call inventing Germany or writing the German nation remains largely unexplored. For me, thinking about who Germans were sounds far more interesting and valuable than knowing where and under what political situation they lived. To this end I turn to what Germans read.

The Appeal of History

By the early nineteenth century an increasingly literate population was imbibing the language of literary nationalism, albeit not primarily by reading Germany's national literature.[20] For even if they were supposed to be communing with Goethe and Schiller, the era's readers actually met most of their need for narrative through historical fiction and popular histories. Particularly in this period of social and economic dislocation, when territories, occupations, and lifestyles were changing with unprecedented speed, it mattered immensely that the content of people's reading was frequently set in the past. As Slavoj Žižek argues, "'Nation' is a pre-modern leftover which functions as an inner condition of modernity itself, as an inherent impetus of its progress."[21] Germany symbolized an intact organic community (*Gemeinschaft*) at the very moment when traditional links to village, craft, workplace, and feudal overlord were coming undone. National identities allowed people to maintain an imaginary connection with the past at the same time as the retrospective, national utopias that they read enabled emerging nation-states to modernize and thus to break with that history. For individual readers the emotional link forged by reading about historical figures must have been particularly comforting as politics and society changed around them, often seeming to spin out of control.[22] In historical fiction ordinary people triumphed in the face of a historically specific form of adversity: craftsmen beat the machines and moneyed interests, and sometimes people like the readers also united to defeat an external enemy.

Winning the battle against change was plausible in historical fiction, where plots were located before contemporary threats and where heroes did not seem so distant. Bold tradesmen, honest craftsmen, and their faithful apprentices defeated bankers, merchants, and factory own-

INTRODUCTION

ers in the imaginary space of history, even though they seldom won in the readers' present.[23] And while readers succeeded vicariously through such heroes, they also learned a common language and participated in a common print culture. Print bridged regional differences not simply because of its wider distribution but also because the language on paper was standard German. The novel, and by mid-century, newspapers and family journals, linked people into what Benedict Anderson has called an "imagined community." Readers may not have had personal contact with one another, but according to Anderson they "came to visualize in a general way the existence of thousands and thousands like them through print-language."[24] Prospective Germans knew, at least implicitly, that their counterparts—throughout the nation-in-progress—were reading more or less the same texts and participating in the same discourse of identity formation.

Although the range and number of texts was expanding even faster than readership, and although history was far from the only thing that people were reading, German history was the most popular subject for authors and readers alike. Two of the nineteenth century's biggest best sellers were historical novels set on the margins of Germany; the hero of Joseph Viktor von Scheffel's *Ekkehard* (1855) was a tenth-century Swiss monk, while Felix Dahn's *Struggle for Rome* (1876) took place in Italy during the sixth century, when Germanic Goths and Visigoths overran the Roman empire. A more typical example is Gustav Freytag, who is mainly remembered for his chronicle of commercial life at mid-century, *Debit and Credit* (1855), but Freytag also wrote popular history and a commercially successful, six-volume-long, fictional survey of German history, *Ancestors* (1873–81). That narrative follows a single German family from the year A.D. 357 to the middle of the nineteenth century. Other writers produced dozens, even hundreds, of historical novels set in Germany, and libraries, particularly the commercial lending libraries that provided the masses with reading material, were filled with multi-volume German historical fiction, as were the periodicals that met readers' needs by serializing popular literature.[25] In short, German history was everywhere; both nonfiction and fiction representing this history participated in the project of inventing Germany, in other words, of writing the new German nation.

In addition to thousands of novels and history books, authors produced a vast assortment of poetry, drama, and opera with themes drawn from the German past. Historical paintings and monuments add more

INTRODUCTION

data to the wealth available in written form. My decision to concentrate on prose narratives—on history and historical fiction—is pragmatic: I would never claim that Schneckenburger's "Die Wacht am Rhein" ("Watch on the Rhine"), a classic patriotic poem from 1840, or Richard Wagner's "The Master Singers of Nuremberg," a work from 1867 that is often called Germany's national opera, were somehow less implicated in the struggle to create both a national culture and a national identity for Germans—[26] to say nothing of Goethe's *Faust* and a host of historical dramas.[27] And my discussion of Werner's painting demonstrates the potential importance of the visual arts, including the myriad images that illustrate novels and works of history.[28] However, beyond practical considerations, I claim that history and historical fiction can, by themselves, shed enough new light on the process of nation building in Germany to justify the exclusions. The interplay and the tensions between the writers of fiction and of nonfiction versions of history also raise theoretical issues that do not appear as clearly in other genres, and prose provides more than enough material for an examination of Germany's emerging national narrative. Excluding poetry, drama, and opera and drastically curtailing the discussion of visual images allows me to explore other questions in paradigmatic depth.[29]

Unfortunately, prose versions of Germany's past still present too large a category to analyze in a single book: the sheer bulk of nineteenth-century authors' writings could obscure thematic unities and overwhelm any analysis of theoretical conflicts. The question becomes, what to choose and what to exclude? Which people and events appear often enough to offer similarities and discontinuities in their representations across time and genre? Scholars have done interesting work on historical fiction set in the Middle Ages, a period whose significance lies in the frequent claim that the idea of Germany originated in the Holy Roman Empire.[30] The hypothesis is plausible, except that the novels they examine are often little more than tales of knightly adventures (*Ritterromane*), which contain little real history. Rarely do such works rise even to the level of mediocrity, let alone pose interesting questions about larger issues. Wilhelm Hauff's *Lichtenstein*, whose locally patriotic message contradicts the call for national unity, remains an intriguing but all too infrequent exception.[31] Treatments of the Reformation or the Thirty Years' War are mainly useful as a means of tracking confessional issues rather than nationalism per se.[32] The problem is quite different for figures from the nineteenth century. German scholars have done very

INTRODUCTION

promising studies of representations of Bismarck (1815–98) and Prussia's Queen Louisa (1776–1810), who both became mythical figures in their lifetimes, and whose status improved considerably thereafter.[33] However, upon closer examination, the role Bismarck played in creating and sustaining the nineteenth-century myth of Germany turns out to have been rather small. Unlike Louisa, who plays a large role in chapter 4, the Iron Chancellor was more the beneficiary of national consciousness than its symbol. The Bismarck statues and streets, the squares, shops, and ships all came later, and they rested on an established foundation of German as well as Prussian history. Thus, as interesting as the Middle Ages and Bismarck might be in other contexts, they are not very useful in examining the invention of Germany with its largely Prussian mythology.

For Germany to be invented, a complete national narrative had to emerge; individual heroism and regional histories had to coalesce into something more than the sum of their parts. Even if readers seldom realized how particular histories and historical novels fit into a larger picture, and even if relatively few readers ever acquired a coherent vision of the whole German past, they nevertheless became aware of the grand narrative of German history that was shaping German society and contributing to the identities of individual Germans. That overarching narrative allowed people similar to Czako and Rex to know which figures and events mattered and which were marginal; it can also serve as the basis for selecting and classifying texts from the otherwise overwhelming bulk of primary material.

However, contrary to what we might think (or have been taught), potential Germans were slow to realize that they shared a culture and an identity. Despite persistent growling heard during the Wars of Liberation, until the 1830s German nationalism was a dog not quite ready to bark. The euphoria of 1813–15 seems to have worn off quickly; to judge by the historical fiction produced during the next decade and a half, people were far more concerned with caste and regional identities than with acquiring a common past. The word *fatherland* remained polysemic. It could as easily refer to Württemberg, Westphalia, or Schwarzburg-Sonderhausen as to Germany, so it is no accident that Pastor Wilmsen never managed to include history in *The German Children's Companion,* as he titled those versions of his primer aimed beyond Brandenburg, including into Prussia's new territories.[34] During the first third of the century the historical novel was gradually coming into its own, while history as an academic discipline was little more than a glimmer in Leopold von Ranke's eye. The father of scientific history received his first position at the University of Berlin in 1825, but he did not become a full professor there and begin training historians in earnest until 1837. However, as chapter 2 shows, between 1815 and 1830, German readers could already choose from scores of historical novels. But the nationalist message of history developed only gradually, in fits and starts, as part of a dialectical interplay between historical fiction and academic history.

For my purposes the most useful framework, or the best heuristic device for understanding what German's thought about their history, comes from British sociologist Anthony D. Smith. After examining various national histories and contemporary ethnic revivals, Smith classified their common elements into what he calls "myths of ethnic descent."[35] He identifies six component parts in a typical ethnic myth, and there are German variations for each of them. First, Smith describes a "myth of temporal origins," which establishes the "antiquity of the community," thereby giving it a sense of long-standing legitimacy. Thus, some Germans traced the struggle for national unity back to Arminius (aka Hermann the German), a chieftain who defeated three Roman legions in the battle of the Teutoburg Forest in A.D. 9, while others waited for the unifying return of Emperor Frederick Barbarossa (1122–90), who was supposed to sleep in the mountains of Thuringia until the next German empire was proclaimed. Not without reason, therefore, did nineteenth-century German nationalists spend time, energy, and money on a gigantic monument to Hermann near Detmold, a monstrosity that was completed in 1875 and is still plainly visible from the Autobahn. The 1896 Kyffhäuser Monument to Frederick is almost as large, and its link to its context was clearer; Barbarossa awakens under a statue of his figurative alarm clock, Emperor William I. No doubt this same search for temporal origins played a role in the desire to preserve, restore, or complete various castles and the Cologne Cathedral and in the quest for authentic popular culture by the Brothers Grimm. The search for ancient forebears may also explain some of the German fascination with Greek and Roman history, because, among other things, classicism revolved around symbolic kinship with those earlier civilizations. Nineteenth-century Germans liked to imagine their own era as the fulfillment of Greek ideals, in contrast to the corrupted Roman origins of the French Revolution. In short, for enthusiastic Germans the national pedigree was more than sufficiently ancient; the nation's heirs were legitimate.

Second, in Smith's typology, is a "myth of location and migration," which assumed particular importance in the nineteenth century, when the struggle to define Germany involved either including or excluding Austria as well as drawing lines between Germany and France, Russia, and Denmark. All of the century's Rhine poetry concerned itself with the issue of borders, as did the famous first verse of Hoffmann von Fallersleben's "Song of the Germans." Its territorial claims posit *"Deutschland über alles"* (Germany above all else) stretching from what is now Belgium to Lithuania and from northern Italy to Denmark. It took Hitler to accomplish that grand vision; Bismarck's "small German" victory of 1871 produced a more limited empire. His Prussian version of Germany lacked the old imperial capitals of Prague and Vienna, the Hapsburg domains of Austria and central Europe, and, most important, excluded those territories' millions of German-speaking inhabitants. It also included numerous members of Polish, French, Danish, and other ethnic communities, who faced the same sorts of defining struggles as the Germans. In contrast to its retrospectively positive aura, Bismarck's empire did not initially receive wide support from the nationalist camp, and the exclusion of Austria helps explain why it became so important to forge a Prussian version of a common German past. Prussia's partisans were aided by literary traditions and the location of the bulk of the publishing industry in northern Germany, but it took World War II to solve the issue of Austria's belonging to Germany.[36] Only when Austrians could save face by falsely proclaiming themselves the Nazis' first victims did they finally and voluntarily become something other than Germans. At least until 1989, World War II also curtailed discussions of the mythic location of Germany that had occupied authors for much of the previous century. The Czech or German Sudetenland notwithstanding, nowadays only a few elderly irredentists still worry about the nation's lost territories. Here, the issue of location arises in chapters 2 and 5.

Smith's third myth, the "myth of ancestry," provides a different means of answering questions about membership in an ethnic community: it posits a common father or, very rarely, a common mother for the national family. Except for a few gods and perhaps Romulus and Remus, who were nursed by a wolf and then founded Rome, parental figures tend to be symbolic rather than merely imaginary. For example,

INTRODUCTION

George Washington fathered his country, not all of its inhabitants. This same notion of symbolic national families lies at the root of stories about fatherly kings and motherly queens. Parenting is a key component in the popularity of Queen Louisa, and it figures in portrayals of Frederick the Great. Father Frederick, better known as "Old Fritz," legitimizes Prussia's claim to leadership within Germany in a way that Frederick the conquering hero never could. In fact, nineteenth-century German myths of location and ancestry frequently collapsed into one another as German nationalism struggled to overcome a legacy of particularism and divisiveness that was more pronounced and lasted longer than in most of the rest of Europe. Nowhere else were there as many independent states (more than three dozen) within the nation as late as 1815, when maps of the continent were redrawn, and that was a reduction from over three hundred kingdoms, principalities, duchies, city-states, and ecclesiastical territories that had existed until then. Nowhere else were two great powers competing for hegemony within a single, still-to-be-defined national community. And nowhere else was there no urban focus or logical center for the nation's culture and its politics. This complexity and confusion make Smith's final three myths all the more important for the invention of Germany: how they developed determined the contours of the first three myths retroactively. Therefore, chapters 3, 4, and 5 incorporate discussions of location and descent, but each focuses on the construction of a single, additional myth: "the myth of a heroic age," "the myth of decline," and "the myth of regeneration."

NATIONAL NARRATIVES AS WORKS IN PROGRESS

History and myth both acquire meaning retrospectively, as part of the process of their narration over time. The significance of figures and events that we regard as mythic is seldom obvious to contemporary observers, in part because the course of events is always open. For example, had Austria somehow succeeded in uniting Germany, or if some democratic middle road to unification had been possible, Germany's national myths would have been as different as its subsequent history. Someone choosing the focus of a particular myth in 1850 would have faced a different and far more difficult task than mine. It helps immensely to know who won, as long as one recognizes the contingency of every result. Thus, using Frederick the Great to see how authors developed the myth of a German heroic age is justified by the wealth of historical novels and history books devoted to the man who ruled

INTRODUCTION

Prussia from 1740 to 1786. This austere, French-speaking monarch earned the sobriquet "Great" by embarking on a series of conquests in 1740, and his victories, as authors subsequently recounted and analyzed them, supposedly paved the way for German unification under Bismarck in 1871. Despite Frederick's annexation of Polish territories in the east and the wars he waged against Austria, Saxony, and other German states, his retrospective connection to later glories turned him into a pan-Germanic hero. Frederick's conquests connect him to the myth of location, just as his Prussian roots become part of the myth of ancestry. In the period's historical novels and popular histories the warrior king of Prussia became an avuncular man of the German people. Old Fritz was a remarkably transformed figure—wise, approachable, and utterly different from earlier representations. This revised version of Frederick II made him part of a shared German, not just a Prussian, past. Moreover, images of a king familiar enough to have personal habits and opinions gave ordinary readers a hero with whom they could identify. Chapter 3 examines how writers transformed Frederick the Great into Old Fritz, Germany's stern yet loving patriarch and the embodiment of the nation's heroic age.

Locating the era of national grandeur as recently as the end of the previous century meant that nineteenth-century authors had to compress German history considerably to include a period of decline and then one of regeneration before their own day. I argue that a single military catastrophe, the disastrous Prussian defeat at Jena in 1806, came to symbolize Germany's fall from grace. When Napoleon embarrassed Frederick the Great's heirs, Germans and the rest of Europe wondered how one of the continent's preeminent military powers could have sunk so low so rapidly. History and historical fiction soon presented numerous explanations for the debacle precisely because of its potentially mythic status. Curiously, even among historians, few authors paid much attention to the battle itself; hardly anyone discussed the opposing sides' tactics or strategies. Napoleon, they agreed, was surely a military genius, but Germans had produced his equal, scarcely a generation earlier, in Frederick II. Apparently, no one doubted they could do so again. Indeed, by the time people started writing and reading about Jena, Blücher had already vanquished the French—with considerable but less widely portrayed help from Russia, England, and Austria. Despite or perhaps because of Blücher, there was widespread agreement in both fictional and nonfictional accounts that the struggle for Germany had been

INTRODUCTION

lost at home rather than on the battlefield of Jena, which merely ratified an unexpected, yet for most writers inevitable, failure. Something had gone awry in Prussia, or in Germany, as the larger whole increasingly became synonymous with the smaller part. Jena came to stand for all the nation's humiliating defeats. The implicit question posed by the fiction and history devoted to Jena—in other words, to the larger problem of mythic decline—is *What went wrong?*

Here Smith's model again demonstrates its usefulness; his essentially structural explanation would certainly have rung true for nineteenth-century readers: "The old virtues were forgotten, moral decay set in, pleasure and vice overcame discipline and self-sacrifice, [until finally] . . . the barbarians burst through" (104). The problem for historians and the authors of historical fiction was not naming the barbarians; their difficulty was accounting for the forces and people who allowed Napoleon's armies such easy access. Chapter 4 examines authors' accounts of the usual suspects. They range from perfidious but historically identifiable individuals—poisoners and profligates—to vague, imaginary figures who symbolize the moral and ethical decay of an entire society. Villains include corrupt and incompetent officers; fatuous, dissolute, and unreliable noblemen; Freemasons and other purveyors of French ideas; the occasional Catholic, particularly Jesuits; and, no surprise here, rapacious Jews. In other accounts some of the same figures, even some of the Jews, appear among the heroes, which is what makes an examination of Jena all the more interesting and worthwhile. Specifying such a broad array of "others"—that is, analyzing the tensions between "us" and "them"—allowed writers to define nineteenth-century Germans and Germany in part by excluding various people and attitudes from the national enterprise.

Having sunk so low at Jena, Germans soon had an opportunity for mythic regeneration, Smith's final category. Renewal came during the Wars of Liberation (1813–15) as the nation supposedly united to show French barbarians the door. Young men streamed from the universities, gathered from fields and forests, and marched lustily into battle, singing patriotic songs—having just finished a round of push-ups, which Friedrich Ludwig Jahn, the Father of Gymnastics, invented expressly for the purpose of strengthening German weaklings for their struggle against French invaders and infidels. Actually, participation in the campaigns against Napoleon was rather modest. Historian Hans-Ulrich Wehler estimates that fewer than 5 percent of university students took

INTRODUCTION

part in the fighting, but the period's history and historical fiction nevertheless portrayed young German men (and a few women) as having risen en masse from their spiritual and physical lethargy to embark on a crusade for the fatherland.[37] Again, the truth or falsehood of that proposition is not the central issue here; far more significant for an account of Germany's invention is an examination of the voices deployed in representing what became a common German past. As elsewhere, neither the historians nor the authors of historical fiction ever achieved unanimity. There were always dissenting views of what had happened and what it meant. Like the chapters that precede it, chapter 5 examines the process of mythmaking and shows how diverse images still somehow conveyed a sense of commonalty. Participants in the discourse of national identity could disagree over facts and interpretations, while they simultaneously agreed on the significance of the Wars of Liberation in Germany's shared past.

These chapters also raise a number of side issues that directly bear on the construction of a German national identity. For example, one of the more surprising novels discussed in chapter 5 is Julius von Wickede's *Tall Isaack* (1863). Its central character is a Jewish peddler who sacrifices family and fortune to help liberate his fatherland from the French. From the perspective of later German history, Wickede's Isaack is a particularly problematic figure, who illustrates the liberating potential that existed within early German nationalism, along with its xenophobia and anti-Semitism. Like so many of the positive characters and villains in historical narratives, Isaack presents an intriguingly mixed message. His two daughters—Sarah, firmly in the French camp, and Rebekka, an ardent German patriot—are just two in a long list of fascinating female characters in the period's historical literature. Along with Queen Louisa these women raise questions about the relationship between gender and Germany.[38] For example, how male was German identity in the nineteenth century? Why did so many fictional women accept their husbands' German identity when they married across national boundaries? And why did such a large number of fictional women die for the fatherland, while their husbands, brothers, and lovers lived to enjoy its benefits? Given the constraints of nineteenth-century academic history, it is not surprising that novelists rather than historians explored these issues most fully. Novelists' willingness to grapple with such questions underscores the importance of demarcating the division of labor, and it makes the interplay of fact and fancy all the more illuminating.

INTRODUCTION

Julius von Wickede is not a familiar author, and no one should feel embarrassed for not recognizing his name or those of many other writers dealt with in this study. I first encountered his novel by chance in the Oettingen-Wallerstein Library at the University of Augsburg, where Wickede's novel is an oddity in this aristocratic family's rich collection of Renaissance and Baroque literature. My guess is that long after family members stopped collecting masterpieces, because it became too expensive or because their descendants no longer cared for high art, someone still bought books to read—both for pleasure and for easy edification. The same phenomenon characterized the other noble library I explored, the Princely Library at Castle Corvey, assembled by the landgrave of Hessen-Rotenburg, mainly between 1815 and 1830, and now administered by the University of Paderborn. During that decade and a half, Landgrave Viktor Amadeus bought everything his agents could find, had all the volumes handsomely bound, and no doubt savored the aura of erudition that owning so many books provided him. His heirs were apparently uninterested or unable to continue buying in such bulk, but beyond the rarities from its fifteen years of riches, the library also contains works the family read after 1830. History books deaccessioned by well-meaning librarians, historical fiction that was never good enough for academic collections, and volumes of both genres that disintegrated from frequent readings in for-profit lending libraries survive in these two collections, because princes, landgraves, and ordinary mortals read history—both fiction and nonfiction—by the yard or meter. Luckily, some of the nobility had their books so expensively bound that their heirs refrained from tossing offending volumes into the trash. In other words, works from the popular tradition of historical writing still exist, waiting to be read again, often for the first time in more than a century. Literary scholars are familiar with the masterpieces that people were supposed to read, but to see how authors wrote and invented Germany, we have to look both at the canon and beyond it.

Readers of this study might well recognize Fontane and Freytag, Ranke and Heinrich von Treitschke, but they will also encounter some totally unfamiliar names: Wickede, Wilhelmine von Gersdorf, and Louisa Mühlbach to name a few. Other writers and book titles will ring a bell, albeit softly. The latter belong to some of the more entertaining categories in Italo Calvino's imaginary bookstore: "Books That If You Had More Than One Life You Would Certainly Read But Your Days Are Numbered" or "Books That You Want To Own So They'll Be Handy Just

INTRODUCTION

In Case."[39] For most readers—even for many literary historians—Gustav Freytag's *Ancestors* and Willibald Alexis's *Keeping Calm Is the Citizen's First Duty* are classics of that vaguely familiar sort: they look too heavy to take off the shelf and too long to read in these demanding times. Scholars may know the names, but most have not read the texts. The same neglect has befallen nineteenth-century historians whose multivolume accounts rarely beckon modern readers. Ranke and Treitschke are the most obvious examples of familiar yet largely unread authors, and the shelves of older libraries bulge with their less renowned but equally productive contemporaries. All of them once mattered.

Does this mean that readers should race to their libraries' rare book rooms or burden interlibrary loan specialists with obscure requests? I would say, by all means, but I believe the question is more complicated than it seems and therefore deserves a brief exploration. These writers belong to the category "middlebrow literature"; their primary readers were neither the critics and professors who shaped the canon nor the unwashed masses who preferred what the British call "penny dreadfuls." Rather, the audience for middlebrow literature ranged from university graduates, down through the ranks of the army, the bureaucracy, and the professional classes, and on to the families of craftsmen and merchants; these books' readership ended in libraries for the working class, where Social Democratic Party activists pushed the same notion of *Bildung* (education and culture) that united the middle and upper reaches of society. Rejecting works whose message was too dark or whose ratio of work to pleasure was too high, middlebrow readers sought comfort in books that provided them "with an entrée into a fully realized world rendered with what might be called the viewpoint of the insider . . . a comprehensible story about the actions of real people." As Janice Radway continues, in her analysis of the Book-of-the-Month Club, "readers wanted to be hailed as both intelligent and as broad-minded individuals, as lovers of all kinds of books, as aficionados of the universe of print."[40] Middlebrow literature was accessible, but not without cultural aspirations; it connected leisure-time activity with self-improvement while simultaneously involving readers in an increasingly national community of literate consumers. For much of the nineteenth century, it was history and historical fiction that attracted the great bulk of such readers, men and women like Czako and Rex. However, in the field of German cultural studies, middlebrow literature remains largely unexplored.

Instead, those who look outside the canon have framed their

INTRODUCTION

inquiries in terms of popular literature. Although not as pejorative as the German term *Trivialliteratur*, the adjective "popular" still implies a negative judgment about a work's literary quality and the merit of reading it. Within the field of German literary studies, the difference in terminology between German and English signals a much larger theoretical rupture. In the German scholarly tradition, treatments of *Trivialliteratur* occur mainly in the shadow of Theodor Adorno and Max Horkheimer, whose *Dialectic of Enlightenment* (1947) subjected popular culture to a withering ideological critique.[41] For Horkheimer and Adorno, jazz, movies, and detective fiction were part of "the culture industry" whose mind-numbing products rendered the masses unable to shake off capitalism's yoke. In this light, nineteenth-century history and historical fiction were surely part of some sinister, albeit largely subliminal, campaign of diversion and enslavement. This argument has a distinct appeal: we know what horrors German nationalism wrought, and the nineteenth-century invention of Germany certainly contained the seeds of its twentieth-century excesses. But those disasters were not the only possibilities. Nazism and the Holocaust were not inevitable, nor was all popular literature implicated in their unfolding. As important as any critique might be, simply dismissing most nineteenth-century history and historical fiction as false consciousness overlooks its nuanced richness. Ignoring these texts cuts us off from what ordinary Germans read, thought, and talked about as they were acquiring a common past. We may not like the results, but its production warrants scrutiny.

In the United States and Great Britain the alternative tradition of dealing with non-canonical literature stems mainly from Raymond Williams, whose followers are ultimately responsible for what we now call cultural studies.[42] Here, the impetus has been, first, to enlarge the scope of what scholars and students read by including popular literature, nonfiction, and texts from other media: music, television, and film. Second, cultural studies offers alternative readings of the canon; it replaces an appreciation of literary quality with readings that highlight race, class, and gender. Broadly speaking, cultural studies privileges women's and feminist literature; works by gay and lesbian authors, including established authors who need outing; and a host of "minor" or ethnic literatures: African American, Chicano, and, in German studies, foreign or guest workers' literature. "Minor" has become a badge of distinction, and cultural studies often turns to supposedly minor texts to uncover the liberating potential overlooked by conventional scholarship and inherited reading lists.[43]

More than a few practitioners of cultural studies would like to replace the old canon with a newer version. While this inclination may be noble, the search for undiscovered masterpieces and liberating subtexts forces scholars to overlook works by authors who were neither radicals nor geniuses and whose messages were conventional or even reactionary. In fact, most of what ordinary people read was produced by writers of middling ability. Personally, while I shudder at the nationalist bombast I have subjected myself to over the years, I still find the debate over the shape and content of Germany's national narrative strangely liberating. Quite apart from their talents and intentions, authors were unable to narrate an agreed-upon set of facts, much less present a single interpretation, because their visions of Germany's present differed so radically. Some hoped to shape an inclusive nation, defined mainly by language, geography, or economic interests, while others sought to limit membership in the emerging German nation by using class, religion, or biology as their criteria. Although it matters immensely which side won, to understand Germany and German culture we need to follow the argument as it developed over the course of the nineteenth century. I therefore claim that some texts may be dreadful—aesthetically or politically—but nevertheless worthy of sustained analysis, while others merit renewed interest for reasons advanced by traditional scholars, ideological critics, or practitioners of cultural studies. The works in this study were mostly middlebrow texts that gave pleasure while they contributed to the larger agenda of nationalism. Their impact means I can ignore the question of quality. These texts once had numerous readers or at least publishers who thought the public was ready to buy or borrow them. Unlike many of the key texts in cultural studies, which were not popular in the commonly understood sense of the term, readers flocked to a wide array of fictional and nonfictional history. Although adherents of cultural studies too often overlook popular culture's dark side, the descendants of Horkheimer and Adorno just as often omit its heritage of dissent. Luckily, we need not choose between an ideologically based rejection on the one hand and narrowly focused affirmation on the other. Some of the texts I deal with were popular without being liberating, conservative without being monolithically reactionary, and valuable for the light they shed on one of the key questions in German cultural history. They and this study occupy that vast middle ground where ordinary readers garnered a sense of what it meant to be German.

What Is at Stake

Of course, parts of the canon remain central to this study. Fontane wrote two historical novels: one concerned with the Prussian defeat at Jena, another dealing with the Wars of Liberation. Great literature contributed to the myth of Germany, but, as the short passage from *Der Stechlin* shows, canonical literature sometimes probes the myth of Germany and raises crucial issues. In our own, supposedly postmodern age questions about the truth and relevance of history seem to have disappeared into the linguistic haze, but outside the academy millions of people still live and die for history. Not only do people still consume historical fiction, but they also invoke or invent traditions, pass them on, and then savage their neighbors over the interpretation. Indeed, except for their relentless technological ferocity and the sophisticated manner in which elites manipulate modern media to keep supposedly ancient grievances alive, battles in Kosovo and Kashmir, Bosnia and Burundi share a certain antiquarian quality. For Germany, which underwent both a paradigmatic and a particularly problematic process of nation building, authors such as Fontane can serve as points of reference in the vast sea of nationalist history and historical fiction. Besides, Fontane was there when Germany was invented; he viewed the inventors' methods, motivations, and results with considerable skepticism; and his own involvement in the nationalist project indicates just how complex the enterprise was.

Ultimately, I focus on Frederick II's life, histories of Jena, and accounts of the Wars of Liberation as these tales were told and retold over the course of a century in order to see what various iterations can tell us about the invention of Germany in the hearts and minds of the nation's authors and its inhabitants. When Fontane's Prussian bureaucrat tells his friend, "Yes, Czako, I already know all that," he means, among other things, that he knows who he is. By invoking a shared past, Rex tells his friend part of what it meant for him to be both Prussian and German. This book explores what people like Czako and Rex knew about Germany, how they came to know it, and what that knowledge meant to them. Reading the literature available to such characters offers a glimpse into the laboratory where Germany's inventors worked. Analyzing how historians and the authors of historical fiction articulated

INTRODUCTION

the content of Germany's national narrative provides access to the portion of national identity that exceeded the label "German." We need to account for the facts of German history, but like every modern nation, nineteenth-century Germany rested upon a foundation of history and fiction. Until we examine the content, form, and function of Germany's acquired collective memory as it emerged over time, we will have only a vague idea of how men and women living in central Europe during the nineteenth century became Germans and how, as a part of that process and despite their diversity, they came to accept a set of originally Prussian heroes as their own.

1
The Past as History and Fiction

The line between fact and fancy runs bold, clear, and uninterrupted until it reaches historical fiction. At least, the boundary seems clear before it bumps into novels set in the past with their curious mixture of reality and invention. For unlike both history and conventional fiction, historical novels seem simultaneously true and false, and there appears to be no means of fixing any work in this capricious genre on one side of the divide or the other. Historians find their truth in archives. They ransack bits of parchment, paper, and film; assess discarded objects; and analyze traces our forebears left on the landscape. Then they stitch the results together into a story or an interpretation of people's actions in the past. Except for those rare instances when historians wonder openly about how they put their version of truth onto the page, the reading, viewing, and listening public accepts history as a true representation of the past. Novelists, however, invent. They search for poetic truth, often in the form of generalizations about human nature, but their work seldom makes a claim upon the facts. While authors of fictional narratives may research locations or crib material from their friends, family, and, most important, their own experiences, their ultimate arbiter lies elsewhere, beyond fact checkers and footnote sleuths. Novelists' truths take shape in their heads. "Fictional truth," to use Michael Riffaterre's term, functions at the level of coherence and plausibility.[1] A novel either rings true or it doesn't; its characters and events resist both verification and falsification. The border seems clearly demarcated except for historical fiction, where the historian's facts intertwine with the novelist's fancy, leaving a product that remains puzzling.[2]

One solution would be to say simply, as Fontane did, that "literature's laws about truth [*Wahrheitsgesetze*] are different from history's."[3] And, particularly for my purposes, scarcely anyone was better positioned to make such a claim. Fontane's first novel, *Before the Storm* (1878), was a work of historical fiction, and his novels of contemporary Germany, such as *Der Stechlin*, often deal with history's hold on the present. Although his attempts at writing history failed commercially, one of the leading experts in the field of German history, the American historian Gordon Craig, concludes, "[W]hoever examines the details will find that Fontane quoted more accurately and judged more objectively than [the influential professor of history at the University of Berlin] Heinrich von Treitschke."[4] Yet, having been impressed by Fontane's credentials and persuaded, at least provisionally, by the logic of his proposition, one might well wonder what it means. Surely there must be more to this claim than initially meets the eye. On the one hand, his juxtaposition ignores the fact that history was once a branch of literature. Nineteenth-century historians were often powerful stylists, known as much for their ability to tell a tale as for their research. In fact, the first German to win the Nobel Prize for literature was the Berlin historian Theodor Mommsen, who received the award in 1902 for his scholarly, yet popular *Roman History*. In an age of narrative history Mommsen was far from an exception. On the other hand, Fontane's assertion solves nothing. It defines neither literature's truth nor history's. More important, Fontane says nothing about what was at stake in making a claim on truth, but the statement does put him in excellent company.

Gotthold Ephraim Lessing, the eighteenth-century dramatist and aesthetic theoretician, declared the poet "history's master," while the Romantic writer and philosopher Novalis claimed, "novels arise out of the shortcomings of history."[5] Friedrich Schiller, who later held a chair in history at the University of Jena, argued that the historical Egmont would be of little use in Goethe's eponymous drama, and he exercised considerable freedom in his own *Joan of Arc*. Heinrich Heine called it a "peculiar whim of the people [*das Volk*] that they demand their history from poets rather than from historians." The former, he continues, are quite accurate, "even when they resort to figures and situations that they

THE PAST AS HISTORY AND FICTION

invent."[6] Fontane's fellow novelist Gustav Freytag introduced his multi-volume saga *Ancestors* by asserting that some epochs "are more easily understood by the literary artist than the historian," and generations of historical novelists have echoed his claim.[7]

To get to the bottom of this contentious debate, one could ask what exactly is true about either history or literature? Or, if we assume for the moment that history's truth represents a smaller problem, it remains difficult to know how fiction can be either true or false. Who is to judge, and on what basis? The German word I translate above as "laws about truth" (*Wahrheitsgesetze*) could easily refer to rules, criteria, or categories of truth. Thus, Fontane implicitly asks both what is true and how it is true. He could therefore be talking about how people come to regard something as true, even if the fact is dubious, unclear, or demonstrably false. This, in turn, introduces context and agency: Who thinks of something as true, why, and under what circumstances? Among other things, these questions also concern the division of labor or territory between historians and the authors of historical fiction as both camps struggled for an audience, legitimacy, and a role in shaping national consciousness.

Fontane made his remark in 1872, in a lengthy review of Willibald Alexis's work. The relevant passage deals with Alexis's *Keeping Calm Is the Citizen's First Duty* (1852), a historical novel set in Berlin at the beginning of the nineteenth century. Specifically, the book's title quotes the governor of Berlin, who hoped to maintain order there following the disaster visited upon the Prussian army at Jena in 1806. Fontane argues roughly as follows: by using the figure of a notorious woman poisoner to symbolize the country's downfall, Alexis paints so dark a portrait of Prussian society that his novel is no longer aesthetically pleasing. The book's heroine is repulsive; she has no redeeming characteristics; and she escapes punishment for her deeds in a society that was corrupt to the point of paralysis. According to Alexis's novel, German society was too depraved and too dissolute to meet the challenge presented by Napoleon. Fontane believes that Alexis's depiction is true, that is, essentially factual, but he wonders if the novel rises to the level of art. In other words, Fontane the literary critic suggests that accurate representations of Jena might better be left to historians, whose truths are more appropriate to this particular subject. But in 1883, just over a decade after his critique of Alexis, Fontane decided to chronicle the moral decline of Prussian society in his own historical fiction, the novel *A Man of Honor*.[8]

CHAPTER 1

In the interim, Fontane must have decided he could do a better job than Alexis, but an assessment of how the two novels stack up, both against each other and against the works of historians and other novelists, will have to wait until chapter 4. Here something else matters. In order to address the question of literary as opposed to historical truth, we need not look at the facts but rather at the issues raised when Fontane claimed to separate history's truths from literature's. Again, we face a series of questions: What happened when historians and the authors of historical novels divided the rhetorical territory of history into fiction and nonfiction? Are there really different types of truth and different laws about truth, one for historians and another for historical novelists? Which of their two truths is truer, and what then is the point of the less true? Does truth even matter, particularly in literature? Where did nineteenth-century practitioners draw the lines between truth and falsehood? Were they always scrupulous about maintaining the border? What were the implications for readers choosing one genre over another?

The Object of Historical Inquiry

These questions acquired particular relevance in nineteenth-century Germany because history came into existence as an academic discipline—indeed, became the preeminent field of university study—at the same time as the historical novel emerged as the leading form of fictional discourse. Readers chose one genre or the other—or, more likely, both—in part, to acquire and then grapple with their own new, yet historically grounded identity as Germans. Thus, to understand German nationalism, it is important to consider who wrote what and how they wrote it for whom. Since historians represented no more than half the discourse of history, without knowing how they struggled with the authors of historical fiction for rhetorical hegemony, it is impossible to analyze the history both sides produced. We need to understand both the content and the mode of writing that separated academic history from its fictional counterpart before we can examine Germany's national narrative.

When Leopold von Ranke and the corps of historians he trained founded the modern discipline of history in the early nineteenth century, they deemed most people's lives uninteresting. Historians constructed the field of scientific or, more properly translated, academic history (*Geschichtswissenschaft*) as the record of past politics. Essentially, their focus meant that the entire existence of ordinary mortals as well as the private lives of public figures were not history. In fact, since scholars searched the archives only for records of men's public lives—primarily official government documents such as laws, treaties, memoranda, and speeches—what they found provided no basis for women's or social histories, even if someone had entertained the notion of writing them. There were no sources, so there could be no footnotes, no documentable truth. Just as academic libraries collaborated in collecting and establishing the literary canon, so too did the archives that interested nineteenth-century historians specialize in the written remains of decision makers. Archivists appear to have overlooked documents pertaining to people below the social and intellectual level of professional historians. Carlo Ginzburg's, Steven Osment's, and others' accounts of individual men and women of the lower classes would not have interested most nineteenth-century historians, while published documents—for example, the *Monumenta Germaniae Historica,* begun in 1819 under the aegis of Baron vom Stein in 1819—were mainly limited to classical authors, laws, and imperial acts.[9] Of course, the letters, wills, parish accounts, and tax returns now mined by social and feminist scholars were always there—in fact, in much greater quantity than today—but these traces of the past lives of ordinary mortals were irrelevant to a history concerned almost exclusively with gaining "insight into event-causing intentions."[10] The result was a doubly motivated erasure. Not only did historians show no interest in women, children, workers, and the poor, but since these people's lives appeared to be undocumented, they were also unrepresentable in academic history.

Men—more specifically, great men—made history not only biologically but also in their discursively constructed genders and as the shapers of historical consciousness. First, men made history physically and legally. Only males played the major roles: statesmen, generals, and kings. Salic law effectively prevented women in the German regions of Europe from occupying the male institutional space of the monarch, as Queen Victoria was able to do in Great Britain but not in Hanover. Even Maria Theresa of Austria needed a husband to become Holy Roman Empress, and doubts about the legitimacy of her claim gave Frederick the Great the pretext he needed to seize Silesia. Second, while great men made history politically, culturally, and metaphorically—as the putative fathers of their countries, economies, institutions, and governments—at the next lower tier, only men, in fact, mainly men from the upper and middle classes, gained admission to society's credentialing agencies—the academic high schools, universities, and cadet corps—and thereafter to the exercise of power. Third, men from these classes became historians and history teachers; despite a growing number of female authors, men wrote most of the era's historical fiction. In short, powerful men controlled the present, and they cemented their grip on contemporary events by simultaneously controlling the past.

Male hegemony resonated all the more loudly because the nineteenth century was an age of history. Witness Fontane's Czako and Rex. Educated men—and everyone else who wanted to appear cultured—had to display historical knowledge in polite company, and the culture viewed history as an important guide in the realm of public policy. Officers, bureaucrats, professionals, and other members of the educated middle class (*Bildungsbürgertum*) studied, read, and talked about history. They compared themselves to the Greeks, worried about repeating the mistakes of Roman generals, and searched for edifying traces of ancient civilizations—at home and abroad, from whence they carted treasures back to German museums. They also subscribed to fund-raising appeals for monuments to past glories, churned out local histories, and identified with the heroes and heroines of historical novels. All this history made for conversation that sounded learned, and, given the Germanic subject matter of much of the history being written, it contributed to people's growing sense of being German. If they appeared at all, cracks and interruptions within the larger field of history became visible along the seemingly solid line that purported to divide history from historical fiction.

Unfortunately, almost no one has examined either the extra-academic discourse of history or its interplay with the profession of history. Most accounts overlook both historical fiction and such celebrated works of popular history as Franz Kugler and Adolph Menzel's *History of Frederick the Great*, a lengthy and generously illustrated biography that was serialized in 1840, issued in book form in 1842, and reprinted throughout the nineteenth century.[11] We know, however, that more people read novels than works of academic history, and we will soon see that fiction's subject matter was considerably broader than history's. Yet, except at the level of individual consumers who read both genres, the few history professors who wrote novels as a sideline, and such authors and critics as Fontane who attempted to move in both worlds, there seems to be have been little contact between historians and the authors of historical fiction.[12] Historical novelists would often boast about the

THE PAST AS HISTORY AND FICTION

academic history they read, but historians seldom admitted to a passion for historical fiction. The division of labor between the two camps remained implicit, yet it is impossible to understand academic history's orientation and impact without also looking at its usually excluded other. Neither is it possible to understand historical fiction in a vacuum. Finally, and most importantly, we cannot know what history meant to readers without looking at both sides of this hitherto unresolved equation. Following Fontane, our task is to juxtapose these competing genres while comparing their respective claims on truth. Nineteenth-century historical fiction is not just another object of inquiry, not just academic history's unrelated and unloved contemporary. Historical fiction claimed to be an alternate mode of representation possessed of an alternate epistemology and in touch with truths that lay beyond the narrow confines of archival scholarship. These two modes of writing about the past were locked in a kind of structural opposition, each defined by the other, each becoming what the other was not, and each making claims that still need adjudicating.

The form of historical fiction, its readability and its focus on character rather than event, paralleled developments in the rest of nineteenth-century fiction, but it also reflected a mutually rewarding bargain that the writers of imaginative history struck with academic historians. Unlike academic history, historical fiction's task was either to represent the undocumented, human side of great men's lives, showing their motivations and portraying them in everyday situations, among their families and friends, or it served to integrate ordinary men and women into the larger historical picture, depicting how great men and their actions affected the rest of humanity. Thus, we either see Frederick the Great up close or learn what the disaster at Jena and the Wars of Liberation meant to millions of otherwise unnamed inhabitants of the German territories. Although historical fiction left the idea of greatness unchallenged and accepted the central role of powerful males and the primacy of political events, it nevertheless constituted an enormous broadening of the field of history. Moreover, toward the end of the century, novelists such as Wilhelm Raabe could build on the heritage of historical fiction and begin testing the limits of representation in ways that went far beyond their predecessors, and even farther beyond all but the most radical of today's historians, who are still beholden to the conventions of early realist fiction. They employ omniscient narrators, regard language as transparent, and view the external world as both knowable and

CHAPTER 1

amenable to representation. Rather than learn from novelists who stretched realism to its limits and then ventured further into literary modernism, as Hayden White puts it, most historians combine *"late nineteenth-century* social science and *mid-nineteenth-century* art."[13]

REALISM

Realism scarcely appears in today's literary debates.[14] Although the topic has attracted the attention of such notable scholars as Robert C. Holub, Lilian R. Furst, Martin Swales, and, most recently, Eric Downing, studies of realism remain far from the forefront of literary-critical practice and interest. Historical fiction has fared even worse.[15] Traditionalists still concern themselves with the high modernism of Kafka and Mann, while radicals search for liberating messages in popular literature but pay scant attention to its form. With a few notable exceptions, postmodernism remains uninterested in the past, while avant-garde fiction owes more to the quick-cutting aesthetic of film and MTV than it does to nineteenth-century novelists. Despite their widespread, albeit secret, passion for detective fiction, most academics regard realist fiction as a trivial, outmoded form that no longer warrants serious consideration.[16] As a result, the term "realism" lacks an agreed-upon definition. For some it simply refers to a period in literary history that, not coincidentally, corresponds to the rise of the nation-state in Europe. Realism was the form of literature preferred by the nineteenth century's self-conscious bourgeoisie, which is another reason for academics to scorn it. In Germany realism stretches from 1850, just after the unsuccessful nationalist uprising of 1848, to 1890, when Bismarck stepped down as imperial chancellor. The founding of the Second Empire in 1871 serves as a midpoint for the era of realism, and most of the high literature from those years bears the name realism. However, this temporal definition excludes the more popular varieties of realist writing—for example, historical fiction—that both preceded and followed canonical realism. Using the period to define realism therefore fails to illuminate the interplay of historical fiction and academic history, and it presumes too close a correlation between writers and political events.

A second approach regards realism as belief in both the transparency of language and its ability to reflect external reality.[17] Authors shared a conviction held by the period's painters, who believed they could capture people, places, and events on canvas without interference from the paint. Readers and viewers alike gained access to what the artist had seen; the medium did nothing to hinder representation. Accordingly, there was no need in realistic art for an instance of self-reflection. Producers and consumers alike believed in their ability to apprehend the world and were uninterested in having the matter discussed when authors could better expend their efforts developing character and moving the plot forward.

Unfortunately, this definition works better in theory than in practice. Contrary to our naive expectations, realistic writing is filled with discussions both about the manner in which the narrator came to know something and how difficult it is for him or her to reduce life's complexities to mere words on paper. For example, after noting he was "a child of clear observation," Dickens's David Copperfield wonders "how much of the histories I invented . . . hangs like a mist of fancy over well-remembered fact?"[18] Similarly, the narrator of Alexis's novel claims the perquisites of the poet (*Dichter*), that is, license to invent, whenever he "must mediate between the realms of the visible and the invisible."[19] Historians usually confine such musings to a critical discussion of sources, but their struggle to understand documents and reassure readers with footnotes reflects the same concern with representation that bedeviled the authors of historical fiction.[20] As will soon become clear, the conflict between these two modes of representing the past revolved around competing ideas about what constituted realistic depiction. Realism was central to both camps' view of truth; they simply could not agree what the term meant, either theoretically or practically. Neither side could answer Thomas Pavel's question: "In *War and Peace* is Natasha less actual than Napoleon?"[21] For Germans it was potentially just as vexing to speculate about the reality of Frederick the Great when he appeared in history versus his similarly textual form in historical fiction.

Of course, there was more to realist literature than Frederick the Great, and Pavel elides the third definition of the genre when he compares the representation of an aristocratic woman to that of the French emperor. This final view of realism maintains that its practitioners simply chose a new subject matter. In accord with their belief in democracy as a form of government, realists in the arts decided to represent classes of people who had not seemed worthy to previous generations of artists. Lessing's advocacy of the bourgeois tragedy becomes the first step along a path that leads through realism to naturalism, thus realist fiction is characterized not by formal properties but by its subject matter. As

CHAPTER 1

Linda Nochlin puts it with reference to painting, "ordinary situations and objects of daily life were no less worthy of depiction than antique heroes and Christian saints: indeed . . . the noble and beautiful were less appropriate than the commonplace and undistinguished. The very boundary-line between the beautiful and the ugly had to be erased by the advanced artist" (33).

This definition favors historical fiction at the expense of academic history, because it is only in fiction that the middle class appears—to say nothing of women and the lower orders. Thus, no matter how well documented its representations were, to the extent that history concentrated on the lives of great men, it could not, by this definition, present a realistic image of society. If history did not show how men and women like its readers lived, it could not be true, while historical fiction could base its claims on truth in the genre's implicitly democratic focus. But novelists, too, devoted considerable attention to the lives of great men, and both sides were wont to employ definitions that undercut the other. We can resolve the matter, or better understand the competing paradigms, only by looking closely at what participants in the debate said and did.

Opposing Sides in the Debate

Historical fiction needs a worthy champion to do battle with the eminent professors who populated German universities, but that person also has to represent both the genre's popularity and its high cultural aspirations. He or she needs to be theoretically sophisticated, able to write for the common reader, and concerned with German history. Sales are important, as are reflections on the status and role of historical novels in shaping national consciousness. Since no such person existed, I have chosen instead an obscure woman author, for although they were excluded from academic history, women were increasingly active as writers during the nineteenth century, very often, like their male counterparts, as the authors of historical novels. Norbert Eke credits Wilhelmine von Gersdorf with writing the first German novel to bear the title "historical"; her *Aurora Countess of Königsmark: A Historical Novel* appeared in 1817, the same year as the initial German translation of Sir Walter Scott.[22] Among other things, the coincidence means that Gersdorf and other German authors of historical fiction were not, as is often argued, simply Scott imitators. In fact, Dennis Sweet goes so far as to say that the German writer Benedikte Naubert (1756–1819) "exerted an important influence on Walter Scott."[23] And Hartmut Eggert includes more than 40 women among the roughly 250 authors of historical novels that he documents for 1850 to 1900.[24] In other words, women played an important role both in broadening and in defining the discourse of history in the nineteenth century. Thus, while I could have used any number of male authors as examples, before returning to Fontane I focus initially on a woman writer: one of the most popular, prolific, and now forgotten historical novelists of the nineteenth century, Louisa Mühlbach.

Mühlbach's life was remarkably conventional.[25] Born into the provincial middle class of Neubrandenburg as Clara Müller in 1814, she married the literary critic and liberal fellow traveler Theodor Mundt in 1839. Her initial novel, *First and Last Love* (*Erste und letzte Liebe*), appeared in 1838, when she too belonged to the progressive "Young Germany" movement, but Mühlbach soon shifted gears and turned her awesome productive capacities to historical fiction.[26] By the time she died in 1873, Mühlbach had written some 290 novels—most of them devoted to German history. Even if we divide that number by three or four, because the fashion in her day was to produce multivolume series for commercial lending libraries, Mühlbach was something of a publishing phenomenon.[27] Eggert reports that her publisher reprinted the three volumes of her *Frederick the Great and His Court* seven times after their initial appearance in 1853-54,[28] and Alberto Martino's research into lending libraries lists Mühlbach as the single most popular German author of the period 1849-88.[29] That put her in fifth place overall, behind Alexandre Dumas, Eugène Sue, G. P. R. James, and Paul de Kock, but ahead of Sir Walter Scott in the number of volumes owned by private lending libraries—and owned only because they could profit by providing them to readers. During the period 1889-1914 Mühlbach advanced to second place behind Dumas, and an eighteen-volume English-language edition of her works is still available in many libraries in the United States.

Mühlbach's novels contain, among other things, a complete history of Germany from the Thirty Years' War to the founding of the second German empire in 1871. Furthermore, even though it was fiction, hers was also one of the first full-length biographies of Frederick the Great. Mühlbach's complete Frederick cycle occupies some four thousand pages in fifteen volumes, written over the course of as many years, and they were far from the only works Mühlbach wrote between 1853

CHAPTER 1

and 1868.[30] It takes a close reading to see what was at stake in Mühlbach's version of political conflict and her unhistorical representation of King Frederick II and the maids, gardeners, and courtiers who inhabited what were the margins of his world but the center of these novels. However, before turning to Mühlbach's fiction, I propose to outline the position taken by the founder of modern academic historiography, Leopold von Ranke (1795–1886). Just as I use Mühlbach to represent the historical novelist, I employ Ranke as Mühlbach's exemplary and paradigmatic, albeit implicit, adversary in the early stages of debate between historians and writers of historical fiction. Luckily, both authors produced biographies of Frederick the Great, and although her theoretical statements are far briefer than Ranke's, Mühlbach still wrote enough on the subject to allow for an assessment of how she conceived of the profession of the historical novelist.

Ranke is mainly associated with Berlin, where he was a professor for over sixty years. His first published work, a history of the Roman and German peoples, appeared in 1825, while he was still teaching at an academic high school in the provinces, but the book's discussion of traditional historiography so impressed the Prussian minister of education that Ranke received a position at the University of Berlin. There, his most significant achievement was the development of the "critical method" of historical scholarship. He trained generations of historians to work from primary sources, which they could accept as true only after rigorous examination. More than anyone else Ranke invented and propagated the new discipline of academic history, which makes him an apt and worthy opponent for one of the historical novel's most popular authors.[31] Their contemporaries might have been stunned at the pairing, but that is precisely the problem I address here.

Ranke's famous formulation of the historian's task, "simply to show what really happened,"[32] explicitly summarizes the claim on truth made by history: nothing added, nothing subtracted, the facts and nothing but the facts, and the historian never gets in the way. If we can believe him—that is, if we can use Ranke's own archive to see how he came to that position—showing "what really happened" also differentiates the historian from the historical novelist. In a memoir of 1885, some sixty years after the previous statement, Ranke confesses that he read Sir Walter Scott "with lively sympathy," and he claims that the novelist's works "were mainly responsible for awakening an interest in the give and take of past epochs."[33] But Ranke also reports feeling disgust at

THE PAST AS HISTORY AND FICTION

what he viewed as Scott's falsifications: "I was offended in the name of the ancient princes . . . [and] I felt revulsion at the historical novel."[34] In fact, Ranke links his decision to turn to history rather than fiction to that negative reaction:

> I studied Commines and the contemporary reports that were appended to recent editions of this author [Scott], and I convinced myself that Charles the Bold and Louis XI, as they were represented in Scott, had never existed. The worthy and learned author must have known that himself, but I could never forgive him for including traits in his works that were completely ahistorical and for representing them as if he believed them himself. By comparing [the two] I convinced myself that historical remnants were more pleasing and certainly more interesting than romantic fiction. I turned away from [fiction] completely and came to the conclusion that in my work I would avoid everything that was contrived and imaginary and [decided] that I would stick resolutely to the facts.[35]

A few weeks later Ranke recounted the same episode in even more pointed fashion. He accused Scott of attributing to historical figures opinions that were different from the ones they actually held, and he calls Scott's method an "approximation of events" (*Annäherung an die Begebenheiten*). Ranke's own critical method, by contrast, "which came to be seen as the distinguishing feature of my work [was], namely, to stick to what has been passed down literally or to what can be derived with some certainty." The only caveat is that the historian avoid everything "that is significantly differed from authenticated versions of events."[36] At first glance, Ranke seems to uphold the distinction between fact and fancy, but "some certainty" and not "significantly different" are by no means impermeable barriers. By allowing the historian to work not just with "authenticated" historical reality but also with what he feels safe in deriving, Ranke may have left enough holes in the border between history and fiction for novelists to march in. Historical fiction might even displace history as the preferred purveyor of truth, unless Ranke's case against Scott remains as strong as his advocacy of academic history.

If Scott got things wrong, or if his fictional versions of events are

CHAPTER 1

less pleasing and less interesting than the facts, then Ranke's position is unassailable. Indeed, if his argument holds, no one would write historical fiction, because novels would revolt intelligent readers, whereas history would entertain and educate them. But in life, to say nothing of the marketplace, history's advantage over fiction seems less overwhelming, the boundary not so clear-cut. In fact, if we use Ranke's own statements as evidence, it turns out that drawing a sharp border between the two genres was frequently problematic. Moreover, even if it has to squeeze into the nebulous space of "some certainty," historical fiction may be better able than history to represent certain aspects of the past: the small, personal, and frequently undocumented reality that people, including historical figures and readers, usually occupy. Novelists can add what history lacks, especially but not only when documents are missing. The case for fiction is both simple and obvious. As Mühlbach's publisher put it in an advertisement for the seventh edition of *Frederick the Great and His Court*, "People [*das Volk*] cannot come to know their heroes simply through their deeds, through historical events . . . they have to see and understand the men behind the heroes. They cannot simply admire the heroes with their heads; they have to love them with their hearts."[37] In other words, without knowing the person behind the role, readers will miss some of history's truth.

Of course, Ranke realized that not everything worth knowing or telling about the past had been recorded and preserved in archives. While he was not shy about extolling the thrill of primary research—"The time one spends in the rooms of the Venetian archives is filled with astonishment and pleasure"—Ranke agonized over gaps in the written record: "What one can know with certainty is only the part of a life that has been preserved in documents."[38] Yet even more decisive for Ranke's work than the unavoidable incompleteness of archival records are the subjective limitations that he places on his inquiry. In a biography of Frederick the Great that he wrote for the *Universal German Biography* in 1878, Ranke underscores what he considers important in the monarch's life, particularly when space is limited: "The only point has to be to attain an overall view of Frederick's political activities and his military deeds and to present them to the nation."[39] Not only is Ranke uninterested in Frederick's personal life, but he is also convinced that individuals seldom matter: "What is really vital to history is the universal trend; the statesman has real meaning only to the extent that he uses his position to advance or perhaps to direct it."[40] Thus, for Ranke, archives were mainly deficient when they lacked significant documents, the treaties, dispatches, and minutes of cabinet meetings crucial to political history; it mattered little that reliable evidence about great men's private sentiments was also missing. In other words, the historian cannot derive with any certainty—and, more important, has little interest in showing—how great men related to their wives, children, and servants. Furthermore, depicting how the rest of humanity viewed heroic figures or how people's lives changed as a result of great men's actions falls outside the realm of history. Ranke not only wants to stick to the facts, but he also tries to focus solely on the big picture, drawing his portrait of Frederick with the broad strokes of larger truths on a canvas that the novelist seeks to render more complicated.

Unfortunately, even the most careful historian occasionally slips into the realm of the personal or the undocumentable. For example, Ranke characterizes Frederick's reaction to the execution of his friend Katte, which the prince was forced to witness, by writing: "The discipline of this horror steeled Frederick's soul, which thereby remained unconquered," as if the historian had access to the young man's thoughts and knew just how he reacted to the event.[41] But for the most part, Ranke skips over incidents from Frederick's life that Mühlbach describes in great, if sometimes invented, detail. Ranke begins his account with Frederick's birth in 1712, but he moves him all the way to the throne, that is, to 1740, in just four pages of his forty-two-page biography. By choice, but also by the circumstance of the encyclopedia, Ranke has room to present only what Frederick did rather than to explore who he was. Mühlbach, by contrast, begins her cycle of Frederick novels not with his birth but considerably later, sometime after 1734, at the court in Rheinsberg, where Prince Frederick lived for half a dozen years in relative isolation before ascending to the throne. For several hundred pages Mühlbach keeps Frederick in the countryside, where he writes music and philosophy, plays the flute, falls in love, and prepares himself to become king. Ranke, by contrast, covers the years in Rheinsberg in a single sentence.[42]

The Claims of Historical Fiction

To be sure, Mühlbach does not ignore the political events that were, for Ranke, the essence of history; but she embeds them in an overwhelmingly personal and private context. Her inclusion of both the personal and the common people gives readers an opportunity to identify with familiar but partly fictional characters and thus to gain the psychological benefits that identification entails. Mühlbach's inclusivity must have appealed to the rapidly growing body of literate but unsophisticated readers. For as well written as much of nineteenth-century history was, historical fiction was more accessible; it also catered to readers' emotional needs and desires. As a result, fiction enjoyed a competitive advantage over both academic and popular history. Although Ranke's life of Frederick the Great was intended for the less demanding audience of a reference work rather than for a strictly scholarly readership, as their differing treatments of Frederick's years in Rheinsberg show, his and Mühlbach's versions of Frederick's life still make different claims about what readers need to know to understand the king and his times. The question becomes not simply how they differ but which of these authors presents a truer biography of Frederick II.

Here, again, a caveat is in order: truth mattered little in the enterprise of writing Germany's national narrative. If Frederick II functioned as an "integrative figure" in the pantheon of German heroes, he acquired that status despite his aloofness, his misanthropy, and his preference for speaking and writing French.[43] Although writers could easily overlook inconvenient details in a biography aimed at the general reading public, the issue of truth remained an important bone of contention in the debate between historians and the authors of historical fiction. By establishing the conventions of what could be included and what had to be excluded both from academic history and its fictional counterpart, the genre discourse wrote the roles played by historians and historical novelists in the mythmaking enterprise of German nationalism. For example, if truth implied a scholarly tone, buttressed by footnotes in a physically substantial volume, historical truth became inaccessible to the growing mass of ordinary readers. That version of the truth was too boring and too expensive for the masses. However, if fiction could produce its own true version of the national saga, then less sophisticated readers could also access the contents of German history and acquire their share of what was becoming a common past. Their alternative was historical fiction, but fictionalized accounts of the past could function as effective purveyors of German identity only to the extent that they, like history, laid claim to a form of truth. If historical fiction had simply been another name for courtly and gothic novels, where knights clanked around meaninglessly in old castles, the genre would never have had the legitimacy necessary for it to participate in the historical and ideological

THE PAST AS HISTORY AND FICTION

discourse of nationalism. Historians would never have feared or reviled fictional accounts of past events and people, nor could novelists have laid any claims on the nation's history.

In essence, I take an opposite tack from Hayden White, who points to the necessary fictionalization of history, especially of narrative history, brought on by its use of emplotment and the other tools of literature.[44] For me, it is just as interesting to explore what happens to history when it is embedded or represented in fiction. In fact, given the popularity of historical fiction, the stakes involved in determining its truth would seem to be far higher than in questioning the truth of history. Fiction seems to provide an escape from reality, but many readers, most literary critics, and, oddly enough, a growing number of historians who use literary evidence all credit imaginative writers with special insight into the human condition. Unlike historians, novelists use empathy, intuition, or a peculiar form of understanding (Dilthey's *Verstehen*) to write "fictional truth."[45] Goethe's *Werther*, for example, contains something so profound regarding the nature of thwarted love, excessive emotions, and youthful rebellion against repressive social conventions that it captivated his contemporaries. Moreover, the novel resonated strongly enough in East Germany in the 1970s for Edgar Wibeau, the hero of Ulrich Plenzdorf's novelistic encounter with Goethe, to find meaning in his own life by reading that two-hundred-year-old text. Similarly, few now doubt that Fontane's Berlin novels present an unparalleled portrait of that city's society at the end of the nineteenth century. Even though only some of the locations and very little else can be documented, we nevertheless credit Fontane with a profound understanding of what troubled and motivated residents of the capital of Imperial Germany. However, when Mühlbach claims to explain Frederick the Great to her readers, she purports to be writing more than mere fictional truth, more than the human condition in general or the situation in Berlin during her lifetime. Mühlbach offers her readers no less than an alternative biography, and Ranke, to judge by his reaction to Scott, must have been disgusted. Indeed, warning bells probably went off through the whole profession of history. One wonders about the fuss. Why defend the boundaries with such acrimony? Is there a dirty little secret that historians are reluctant to share about their own work?

Historical fiction has always occupied a middle ground between literature and history; it necessarily and unavoidably mixes fact and fancy. Yet, except in the most egregious examples of historical romances—for example, in the Harlequin romances set in Regency England—the writer's creativity is limited by historically verifiable facts. Although recent theory has tried to reduce facts to a textual and contextual category, I say they still possess a status—not just an aura—different from that enjoyed by products of the imagination. One can argue over the definition of a fact, which means putting the dispute between history and historical fiction at its most basic, atomic level, but there are limits. Both Mühlbach and Ranke must let Frederick die in 1786; they can neither change the outcome of his battles nor invent visits to his palace by aliens from outer space. Hence, in talking about truth in history and historical fiction, it is useful to differentiate the inclusion of dates, quotations, real people, and actual events from fiction's special truth and the insight into historical people and events that literature might provide. Scott's and Mühlbach's mistakes are no more interesting than the historian's shoddy editing or botched footnotes, but their sins of interpretation lie somewhere between history's truth and literature's. Their successes, if they had any, exist only in the tension between history and fiction—along the murky border between fact and fancy, where serious questions about historical fiction reside—or not at all. Moreover, that hotly contested space is filled with other meaningful material. It is there, for example, that I locate German nationalism, which is neither a hard fact—not geography, biology, language, or destiny—nor complete fantasy, and all the more problem-laden because it occupies physically and rhetorically disputed territory. For the moment, however, the crucial issue is whether and how fiction's claim on truth stands up to history's. Where does the historical novelist gain knowledge of the past, and how does that knowledge function within the particular constraints of historical fiction?

Although Mühlbach wrote about her own culture at a distance that ranged from over two hundred to less than fifty years, the imaginative distance between author and subject matter is often greater; in novels set in the Middle Ages it amounts to centuries. It can also extend to vastly different peoples, places, and social origins. Mühlbach's novelistic insights are based on notions of universality, on the eternal verities of the human condition; they seem, at first glance, to contradict the historicity, that is, the uniqueness, of both the figures and the culture she represents. What she wrote about the private lives of great men and both the public and private lives of minor characters presupposes an underlying similarity to her own experiences. Otherwise, claims of empathy, intuition, and understanding ring hollow, just as historians who claim to understand documents that are temporally or culturally too distant from their own lives might also overstep the bounds of credibility. Additionally, even if we ignore the epistemological issues and assume that both historians and the authors of historical fiction can know across time, culture, and space, the question of representation remains. For historians, several factors limit the decision about what to represent: their notion of what constitutes history, the process of selection, and the adequacy of archives. Nineteenth-century historians were content to paint a picture that they knew to be incomplete; they sketched the broad outlines of past events both to understand them within their historical contexts and to elucidate causes, effects, and meanings for the historians' own contemporaries. Historical novelists, by contrast, hoped to fill in the spaces between the historians' lines; they offered readers a denser, more detailed image. They added the private sphere and the masses to their accounts, but at what cost? By attempting to represent more than politics and more than just the documentable outline of great men's public lives, did they necessarily falsify history and earn the justifiable scorn of academic historians? And how did the historians fare, according to their own standards?

Mühlbach was keenly aware of the difficulties she faced vis-à-vis historians, and she addressed her problems explicitly in the introduction to the final series in her Frederick novels, *Old Fritz and the New Era*. She was responding to her critics, but we can infer only who they were; precisely what they said remains unknown. For example, someone must have accused Mühlbach of factual errors, which provoked her to irony so bitter that the translator omitted it from the English edition of her works: "It would not occur to me to defend the historical novel or myself against such learned sounding quibblers [*Krittler*]. I let them have their cheap fame . . . because their own knowledge of history is so deficient that they are unfamiliar with the facts."[46] Since she wants to occupy the moral and theoretical high ground, Mühlbach also rejects those historical novels in which the past serves only as background for a pulpy plot.[47] Her concern is rather with legitimizing the idea of historical fiction, defending the genre's goals, and championing its mode of representation.

Surprisingly, given her subsequent reception, Mühlbach seems unthreatened by questions of aesthetic quality, and she makes not the faintest attempt at distancing herself from the mass of readers to whom

CHAPTER 1

she appeals. In fact, in an odd juxtaposition, Mühlbach borrows the aesthetic category of "the sublime" (*das Erhabene*) from the world of high literature and links it to the chief goal of the historical novelist—namely, "to illustrate history, to popularize it; to bring forth from the silent studio of the scholar and to expose in the public market of life, for the common good, the great men and great deeds embalmed in history," which were previously the sole property of the educated classes. Although Mühlbach's German original does not mention "embalmed," the word is a nice touch that captures her sense of how unapproachable academic history often is for the ordinary reader.[48] Her use of the words "market" and "property," especially in connection with the sublime, is as noteworthy as her criticism of academic history's elitism. Sublimity was supposed to depend on the work of art's intrinsic qualities, not on its marketability, but Mühlbach's issue is neither beauty nor literary quality. She wants to overcome the strictures that Ranke and other professional historians placed on representations of the past. "The severe historian [must make do] with accomplished facts; he can only record and describe, with the strictest regard to truth, that which has outwardly occurred."[49] In German, "severe" and "strictest" share the same root, *streng,* and "serious" might be a better translation when describing a scholarly historian. Mühlbach repeats the term, along with "outward," when she writes of "the strictest regard to [visible or external, i.e., *äusserlich*] truth." Not only is the repetition another dose of critical irony, but the positive alternative contained in Mühlbach's view of historical fiction is also easy to anticipate. Mühlbach claims that the novelist alone can penetrate to the internal truth of history, and she underscores her position rhetorically with a direct, personal appeal to the reader—three times in a single sentence using the familiar form of address (*Euch*), as if directed to friends: "The historian presents to *you* the outward face, the external form of history; Historical Romance would show *you* the *heart* of history, and thus bring near to *your heart* what, else, would stand so far off."[50] The passage might well be addressed to children, but in choosing this tone Mühlbach accomplishes something significant; she places herself in a position to mediate between the learned members of the academic community and her own dear or gentle readers. The problem with her argument is the difficulty in accomplishing its didactic goals of bringing the past to life and making history popular without simultaneously falsifying it.

Mühlbach claims to have been assiduous in her own preparations, although she seems to have meant reading secondary sources, not doing

THE PAST AS HISTORY AND FICTION

the archival work historians recognize as research. She does quote from primary material, in the Frederick cycle mainly from the king's posthumously published works, but she also insists that the novelist "must devote his whole mind and soul to the epoch that he would illustrate, he must live in it and feel with it."[51] Strangely enough, the argument resembles one made decades ago by the British philosopher of history R. G. Collingwood.[52] But Collingwood directed his idealism toward penetrating the minds of temporally distant peoples; he wanted to intuit what they thought in order to explain their actions. By contrast, Mühlbach's orientation was resolutely practical—like that of Thucydides, who invented the famous orations in his *History of the Peloponnesian Wars*.[53] Empathy rather than the archive provides material, and Mühlbach links a distinctly poetic notion of historical understanding and explanation with the difficulties—and the advantages—that historical novelists face in their representations of history. As Mühlbach explains it, the division of labor between nineteenth-century historians and historical novelists involves their differing conceptions of reality and, consequently, differing views of what they can legitimately write.

Mühlbach begins this portion of her argument with a statement that Ranke might well have supported, except for its tone. As she sees it, the historical novelist's task is "to shed light upon the dark places of history, necessarily left unclear by the historian [because the sources are not always there, and the serious historian can draw only from the sources]."[54] Since novelists accept no such academic or generic strictures, they can begin with what they glean from reading academic and popular history and then explain away gaps in the archival record using "the creative imagination of the poet."[55] The "poet"—and here Mühlbach raises her calling from "writer" (*Schriftsteller*) to "poet/artist" (*Dichter*)—understands the past creatively, in a manner that is not only unavailable but also forbidden to the historian. While serious historians limit themselves to external truth, the novelist has access to the heart of history, which Mühlbach locates within the individual. Here it becomes clear what the historical novelist can do and what, in Mühlbach's view, the historian can never even attempt: the novelist's task is "the discovery and exposition of the motives which impel individual historical personages to the performance of great historical acts, and from outwardly, apparently insignificant events in their lives to deduce their inmost thoughts and natures, and represent them clearly to others."[56] At this point Mühlbach has parted company from Ranke, not only in her differing use of evidence but also in her conception of where historical truth is located. While Ranke relegated individuals, even individuals as important as Frederick II, to supporting roles in the drama he called "the universal trend," Mühlbach pushes those same individuals and a host of lesser personalities to center stage, which means, quite literally, that Frederick and his family, friends, and servants have a great deal to say in her novels—even if they may not have actually said it.

In other sorts of novels speaking parts are only difficult to write; the dialogue must simply sound or read right. The novelist makes the written word seem like speech, knowing that real oral discourse seldom seems authentic to the reader. In historical novels, the words of well-known figures present a different problem, which is mainly evidentiary. Historians know what famous people said and, more important, what no one can prove they said. Thus, there can be no question about what to quote as speech in history books. For Mühlbach the problem is far more complex, and she adopts two very different strategies in dealing with it. The first is to quote wherever possible. Her Frederick the Great novels regularly contain footnotes with references to Frederick's published works and to the memoirs of his contemporaries, often with the straightforward notation, "the King's own words." Sometimes she simply says "historical" (*historisch*), which seems to mean accurate, true, or verifiable. Although Mühlbach's citations are an attempt to justify her undertaking according to rules laid down by academic historians, that is, to claim the legitimacy they deny her, I take these notations as a sign of just how confusing and embedded the notion of truth, particularly historical truth, had become—or always was. Too many footnotes would clutter the text and implicitly praise the enemy, but every absence calls attention to the questionable status of other statements that lie between quotation marks. Mühlbach rails against the second-class citizenship that her dependency on the historical record and the work of professional historians implies, but she seems to realize that footnotes impress her readers and may give her some traction in the battle she is waging against academic history.

Luckily, the developing conventions of historical fiction allow a second solution to the difficulties of dialogue. Unlike the historian, the novelist can claim to work "upon the foundation of history to erect the temple of poesy, which must nevertheless be pervaded and illuminated by historic truth."[57] "Nevertheless" (*dennoch*) is the key word here, because it denotes the peculiar status of historical fiction, situated between the ver-

THE PAST AS HISTORY AND FICTION

ifiable facts of empirical historiography and the notion that fiction is solely the product of an author's imagination. Here, Mühlbach places historical fiction above history; her novels transcend—in Hegalian terms, sublate (*aufheben*)—the puny products of mere professors. Yet Mühlbach also seems to have backed off from her denial of history's truth, its merely "external" status, because she wants to use that discipline's still strong claim on truth to buttress her own position. Her problem is how to reconcile the principle advantage with the principle disadvantage of the genre.

Some authors negotiate these shoals by refusing to invent speeches for historical characters; they thereby limit fiction to the minor figures— to the spouses, maids, and gardeners, who left nothing for the archives. Such choices make Scott's middling heroes attractive because they allow the author considerable freedom to comment on people and events without intervening in the historical record; but Mühlbach will have none of such hesitancy, no doubt because it would have prevented her from writing a novel of Frederick II's life—especially one four thousand pages long. Like many great men Frederick simply did not say enough publicly, specifically not enough about his private life and motivations, to satisfy the novelist. However, having read and intuited her way into Frederick's life, Mühlbach takes a huge leap into the fictional past, claiming "that it is of very little consequence whether the personages of the Historical Romance actually spoke the words or performed the [incidental] acts attributed to them; it is only necessary that those words and deeds should be in accordance with the spirit and character of such historical personages, and that the writer should not attribute to them what they could not have spoken or done."[58] While it would have been anathema for Ranke to plead for history that showed what really *could have* happened, Mühlbach apparently needed that much leeway to penetrate to history's interior, to its heart. Once she had understood, in other words, once she was satisfied that she could live and breathe an epoch, Mühlbach claims the right to invent what historical figures might have said or done. The only limit is that their actions have to be in character and not contradict the record. She also prefers to invent incidental events, although to the degree that they reveal character, these small fictional scenes are far from trivial. Indeed, they could prove central.

COMPARING THE TWO FREDERICKS

Now that we understand the terms of the debate, let us look at the

CHAPTER 1

results, with one caveat. Since discussions of literary value are even more hopelessly mired than notions of truth, it behooves us to ignore quality and limit the inquiry, first, to Mühlbach's historiographical vision as realized in her novels, and, second, to Ranke's practical work as a historian rather than as a theorist of history. Otherwise, we would have to decide what constitutes good writing, and then determine whether the criteria are both timeless and equally applicable to fiction and nonfiction.[59] In addition, we would have to assess the work of (literary) historians engaged in the project of building a national literature, supposedly using measures based on quality but often resting on a thinly veiled nationalist agenda.[60] Although important, these issues would keep us from asking, first, how and why the biographies they wrote differed and, second, whether Ranke or Mühlbach presented a more credible account of Frederick's life.

Mühlbach's view of Frederick the Great's character will be discussed in some detail in chapter 3. For now, suffice it to say that she regarded him as lonely, a man given to brooding about his fate, without the comfort of friends and family to share his burdens. But she does not depict Frederick as cold or unemotional, quite the contrary. When the newly crowned king decides to wage war against Austria for control of Silesia, Mühlbach's Frederick realizes what is at stake, both for himself and for his country. The legally questionable inheritance of Silesia by Empress Maria Theresa awakens Frederick from the torpor that had plagued him since his father's death. The young—and fictional—king declares, "My days of illness are over, and there will be life and movement in this rusty and creaking machine of state."[61] The passage, which occurs in a private conversation with an aide, must have struck Mühlbach as true to Frederick's character, because there is no citation; whereas, a page earlier, in the German edition, she claims to quote "the king's own words" when he discusses the Silesian campaign: "All was foreseen, all prepared, and we have now but to put in execution the plans that have for some time been agitating my brain."[62] In other words, Mühlbach invented the first quotation but claims she could verify the second, although it sounds as if Frederick said it in retrospect, which might make Ranke's critical historian question its validity.

Indeed, Ranke presents an interpretation of events that differs sharply from the king's own words. While Mühlbach quotes Frederick to the effect that the decision to invade Silesia was his alone, in discussing the exact circumstance Ranke leaps well beyond the written

THE PAST AS HISTORY AND FICTION

record, apparently to stress the continuity of Prussian politics: "One cannot doubt that the plan of attack, which belonged to the most secret papers passed from prince to prince, were made known to the newly crowned king."[63] Ranke's rhetoric is more interesting than his conclusion, because it shows how the historian intuits details for which he has no direct evidence but that he nevertheless believes are true. Based on his familiarity with Prussian archives, Ranke assumes that Frederick would have learned of long-standing plans to wage war against Austria. He infers the existence of evidence that either could or should have existed to confirm an event that was in character not only with this one individual but also with the course of Prussian politics. Such knowledge allows Ranke's claim that one must not doubt the transmission of information to the new king, but one might well doubt that he would have permitted Mühlbach the same freedom to draw the conclusion, especially when it contradicts a statement made by Frederick himself. In fact, except that Mühlbach feels free to invent quotations, mostly dealing with the king's private life rather than institutional continuity, the example shows surprisingly little difference between the two writers' tactics. Their competing interpretations of Frederick's first Silesian campaign suggest that Ranke's and Mühlbach's accounts vary mainly in their choice of external versus internal motivation rather than in the quality of their evidence or the stringency of their citations.

Mühlbach dwells on Frederick's private life, returning time and again to his apparent lack of personal feelings, perhaps to counter the usual image of an emotionless king. Various characters talk about Frederick's inability to love anything other than his flute; his scheming chief of protocol, Baron von Pöllnitz, repeatedly fails to interest the king in the dancers and actresses he procures for him. Frederick does invite one of these women, an Italian dancer known as Barbarina, to a private dinner, but nothing happens. Still, as he later confesses to a courtier: "Think you, that because I am a king, I have no heart, no thirst for beauty? Go! but remember that, though a king, I have the eyes and the passions of other men. I, too, am intoxicated by the perfume of flowers and the beauty of women."[64] The difficulty, and in a sense the untruth of other characterizations of the king, is that Frederick manages to keep his feelings so secret that Barbarina complains: "He has no heart; he cannot love; and shame and dishonor rest upon the woman who loves and is not beloved. Frederick loves nothing but his Prussia, his fame, and his greatness."[65] In fact, Frederick often thinks about visiting Barbarina, but he decides against his emotions and turns his attention to the war. "I dare not do what any other man might do in my place; not I—I am a king."[66] Later, the two lovers meet briefly, and when the woman starts to leave, the reader sees how difficult Frederick has made his life: "'Remain,' said he: 'I command you—I, not the king.'"[67] Of course, none of this is documented.

Mühlbach dwells on Frederick the man while omitting historical successes that she deemed merely external. She therefore skips the years 1746–49, when Prussia was first accepted in Europe as a great power, and starts the final volume in the second cycle of her biography in 1750, because she believes that the focus on public events made historians overlook the man that she, as a novelist, intuits to have been deeply troubled and supremely unhappy: "We take advantage of the liberty allowed to authors [*Dichter*], and pass over these four years and recommence our story in 1750, the year which historians are accustomed to consider the most glorious and happy in the life of Frederick the Second. We all know, alas! that earthly happiness resembles the purple rose, which, even while rejoicing the heart with her beauty and fragrance, wounds us with her thorns."[68] There is, however, more to the picture of Frederick that Mühlbach draws than the suffering of a highborn individual grappling with both his public and his male identities. She offers an alternative view of historical reality from Ranke's. In her introduction to *Frederick the Great and His Family*, the third installment of her Frederick novels, Mühlbach defines her aim: "I was concerned with the inner character development of this great man, whom many know only as the brave hero, many as the wise lawgiver, the self-controlled king, but whom few see as the noble, tenderly emotional, gentle man that he really was. I wanted to portray Frederick as a man and to generate his life from his soul and his heart."[69]

By working from the inside out rather than concentrating on external events, Mühlbach not only believes that she can define the real Frederick, but she also suggests that his character provides a truer explanation of events than the version offered by historians. A clear example of what she means comes in an episode in *Berlin and Sans-Souci*, the second installment in her series of Frederick novels. The king has refused to let his sister Amelia wed a Prussian officer, a man she loves deeply, because he needs to marry her to a prince. Although political considerations make the fulfillment of her love impossible, Frederick would like Amelia to understand and accept the burden of being a princess—just as

THE PAST AS HISTORY AND FICTION

he has resigned himself to his own fate as king. To explain himself, Frederick tries to separate the two roles: "The king was angry with you, the brother will weep with you. Come, Amelia, come to your brother's heart."[70] The reconciliation fails miserably, apparently because Frederick is the only member of the family who can countenance such cognitive dissonance. But for Mühlbach the failure has at least one significant consequence. In an effort to forget the rejection he has just suffered, Frederick returns to the official papers on his desk. There, his eyes soon brighten as he remarks to himself:

> I have just lost a much-loved sister. Well, it is customary to erect a monument in memory of those we love. Poor, lost sister, I will erect a monument to your memory. The king has been compelled to make his sister unhappy, and for this he will endeavor to make his people happy. And if there is no law to which a princess can appeal against the king, there shall at least be laws for all my subjects, which protect them, and are in strict accordance with reason, with justice, and the godly principle of equality. Yes, I will give my people a new code of laws. This, Amelia, shall be the monument which I will erect to you in my heart.[71]

Historians generally describe the deliberations that led to the introduction of the Prussian Uniform Code in 1794 as the result of one of two factors. They attribute it either to Frederick's philosophical concern with equal justice, perhaps brought on by the Miller Arnold trial of 1773–80, which supposedly convinced Frederick that he needed to end aristocratic interference in the legal system, or they cite the necessity of uniting dissimilar Prussian provinces into a single unitary state for military reasons. Ranke comes down on the side of military considerations, but he mentions only economic not legal reforms.[72] Princess Amelia and her lover never appear in Ranke's account, presumably because there is no evidence of any role she played, much less of what Frederick was thinking when he made his decision. What really happened is ultimately unknowable: Frederick's head remains sealed and inaccessible, no matter what the documents say, and here they apparently say nothing. Thus, although Mühlbach's version sounds farfetched to readers schooled in academic history, it might be true or, at least, form part of the truth along with Ranke's more conventional explanation. Neither can prove their case, but again the issue is not so much validity as the status of an explanatory model. For Mühlbach, the personal is not just historical in the sense that such seemingly trivial events occurred in the past. For her, a person's emotional life is also historical in a manner that academic historians could well have accepted—except for the tiny detail of evidence and the presupposition that political interests or great ideas, not their feelings, motivated great men. By contrast, the historical novelist claims, first, that whatever happened between Frederick and his sister is important to understanding him as a person and, second, that it may be just as critical in understanding him as a statesman. Leaping past the evidence, novelists can complicate their explanations, opening the past to interpretations that are plausible but undocumented, while they simultaneously include more of what readers seek: plot, character, romance, and figures with whom they can identify. Of course, those staples of trashy literature might make the theories advanced in historical fiction seem questionable, but they do help explain its efficacy as a transmitter of historical knowledge.

History beyond Great Men

Up to this point, the argument has mainly concerned biography. Indeed, it has revolved around the life history of the most famous man of the age. How history and historical fiction deal with the effects of great men and significant events on the lives of ordinary mortals raises similar but also different issues with regard to the truth. To look at them, I want to stage another paradigmatic debate between a prominent historian, Johann Gustav Droysen, and Fontane, asking how academic history and historical fiction differ in their explanations and representations of such complex events as the Prussian defeat at Jena. Both authors attempt to explain that disaster by using a representative figure from the past; they apparently recognized that biographies or novels focusing on a single character were more appealing to their respective publics, but their implicit agenda was to characterize an era, not to explain an individual. As a result, both of these writers focus on the so-called middling hero familiar from Sir Walter Scott rather than on men at the very pinnacle of politics and society.

Droysen, who was born in Pomerania in 1808 and died in Berlin in 1884, was only a few years younger than Ranke and did not outlive the master. He nevertheless belongs to a different generation of historians. Droysen's fame rests upon a collection of lectures entitled *Historik*, where he systematized the period's historiography.[73] While Ranke taught mainly by example, with only scattered pronouncements on the profession, Droysen explained precisely what historians were supposed to do. He also identified the dangers involved in straying from accepted methodologies, particularly in succumbing to the temptations of historical fiction. This does not mean that Droysen wrote only dry, academic history. His biography of one of Prussia's heroes, *The Life of Field Marshal Count Yorck von Wartenburg* (*Das Leben des Feldmarschalls Grafen Yorck von Wartenburg*), appears on a list of books that Fontane compiled in 1894 to answer the question "What should I read?"[74] Indeed, the tension between Droysen's well-written biography of Yorck and his pronouncements on historical methods make the historian particularly relevant to the clandestine conflict between historians and the authors of historical fiction.

While Fontane criticized Alexis for producing a novel that was historically accurate but aesthetically displeasing, Droysen disparages what he terms "poetic truth" in history.[75] For him, the first difficulty, particularly in writing biographies, is that figures from the past are seldom consistent enough for historical accounts of their lives to ring true, mainly because historians lack evidence about their subjects' personal lives. In other words, Droysen knows that historians can seldom present the well-rounded characters so familiar from realist literature and so much in demand by the readers who flocked to Mühlbach, Scott, and their contemporaries. Scholarly history simply does not allow for character development. Second, and even more troubling, is the inherent danger in letting any individual stand for his or her age. Individuals are either too "vivid" (*Anschaulich*) and thus historically false, or they are too ordinary for anyone to care. However, according to Droysen, no less a historian than Ranke made the mistake of excessive reliance on biography: "Ranke foregrounded the art of characterization, and he liked to depict not just their intellectual but also people's moral qualities. Indeed, he goes so far as to include such external elements as their clothing, their voice, and their gestures so that the reader believes he is seeing these people alive in front of him. . . . The result is that his narrative approaches the vividness [*Anschaulichkeit*] of an historical novel."[76] That last sentence is anything but a compliment, and one wonders about its effect on departmental politics at the University of Berlin, where Droysen had occupied a chair in history since 1859. In any case, Droysen put some distance between his own preferred practices and those that he ascribes to bad historians and the authors of historical fiction: "Whether Frederick blew on the flute or Caesar composed grammatical treatises is, to be sure, very interesting, but for the larger historical meaning of the two men utterly trivial."[77]

Since Ranke was also more interested in historical trends, the issue does not seem to be whether something is true or false, but whether it belongs in accounts produced by academic historians. However, the question of inclusion versus exclusion only scratches the surface of Droysen's difficulties with vivid examples, specifically with exemplary figures from history: "I do not deny that I am extremely suspicious of this kind of vivid example; the longer I live with people, the more dubious I become about understanding their characters with certainty, and the longer I study history, the more dubious it appears to me to depict people, about whom I only have the judgments of others, as if their characters were congruous with what they did."[78] In other words, drawing conclusions that reach beyond primary sources to "the judgments of others" is problematic for the historian: real people might not be of a piece, rendering their personalities unknowable. Since men and women from the past may have acted from contradictory motives, they can become vivid, illustrative examples only in the oversimplifications of historical fiction. History demands verifiable facts, not speculation based on empathy or faulty psychology. Besides cautioning his students away from that void, Droysen also worried about how historians represent the details they could account for. He seems to be searching for a form of representation whose inner logic does not force him into the "false realism" he associates with historical fiction.[79] Indeed, Droysen speaks of wanting to find a form "in which the narrative is not the most important element."[80] Perhaps to that end, he appends various documents to each of the three volumes of his *Life of Yorck*. Yet while such primary material might have given readers direct access to history, Droysen narrates Yorck's life conventionally, and he never refers to the documentary material in the main body of his text. The effect is schizophrenic, and the tension demands that we ask how Droysen's practice stands up to his theory.

The opening sentence of his *Life of Yorck* reads as follows: "Never had a state lifted itself up from a deeper fall more rapidly and more proudly than Prussia in the days after Jena."[81] By starting not with Yorck himself—his childhood, his death, or even his achievements—Droysen has fallen into the very trap that he sought to avoid: he uses his main character to illustrate the fall and rise of Prussia before and after its defeat. Yorck functions as a synecdoche both for the bankruptcy of the Frederickian system at the turn of the century and for the state's renewal in the Wars of Liberation. Droysen's theoretical difficulties are compounded by the fact that Yorck was anything but a typical Prussian. Frederick the Great personally cashiered him out of the army. Yorck also served for a time with Dutch forces in South Africa and is most famous for switching sides in 1812, against the direct orders of King Frederick William III and in violation of Prussia's alliance with France. Of course, most of these exceptional acts turned out positively, and Yorck ended his life as a count, field marshal, and hero, but scarcely as an example of the unquestioning loyalty and obedience that one typically associates with the Prussian state and army.

The second and more telling difficulty in Droysen's account is evidentiary, and the lack of documents raises the difficulty Droysen warned against in his lectures on historical methods. Note, for example, how the historian is forced into passive and agentless constructions when he discusses conditions not directly connected with Yorck and about which his hero apparently knew nothing: "Without a doubt *the army found itself* in a state of tactical perfection. . . . But in the midst of this extreme ripeness in small matters *one* began to become conscious of a certain discomfort, that *one* was utterly unprepared in precisely those areas to which Bonaparte owed his growing fame, that *one* had neither the ideas, nor the capacities, nor the passions that are a condition for greatness [emphasis added]."[82]

Yorck's silence proves doubly difficult, for not only must Droysen speculate about the global situation, but he also has to rely on the poetic truth of character, the essential unity of his hero's mind and actions, in order to guess at his reactions. "These matters could not be other than painful to Yorck's whole personality."[83] And it gets worse: "There is no evidence from which *one* could deduce how Yorck reacted to Prussia's situation in those months. *One* would, however, scarcely be mistaken if *one* assumed . . . [emphasis added]."[84] To judge from the historian's repeated cautions, *one* can imagine that the situation was also "painful" to Droysen. He may have produced a brilliant biography and an interesting interpretation of Prussia's decline and resurrection, but Droysen also had to break his own rules. Mühlbach scarcely acted differently. Working in the same manner and with the same lack of evidence as Droysen, she only took the additional step of inventing dialogue. Droysen's surrender to poetic or aesthetic truth shows just how porous

CHAPTER 1

the border between professional historians and historical novelists could become. Neither side could live with the facts alone.

CHANGING FACTS TO GET THE STORY RIGHT

Theodor Fontane was well acquainted with the tension between fact and fancy. Although he began his professional life as a pharmacist, became a journalist and theater critic, and wrote a considerable amount of poetry before finding his niche as a novelist, Fontane was also a failed historian.[85] His voluminous accounts of recent Prussian history were derided by professional historians, but some of them nevertheless convinced the University of Berlin to award Fontane an honorary doctorate in history in 1894. His *Wanderings through the Mark Brandenburg,* whose five volumes are filled with historical anecdotes, fared better with readers, but neither history nor historical fiction belonged to Fontane's strengths as a writer. He published only two historical novels, *Before the Storm* (1878) and *A Man of Honor* (1882), and his fame now rests on a series of novels set in the Berlin of his lifetime.

To judge Fontane's view of historical fiction, it suffices to sketch enough of *A Man of Honor* to illustrate its claims on truth. Like Droysen, Fontane uses a central figure to characterize Prussian society before the defeat at Jena. He based his hero on historically verifiable people and events but refracted them through his own novelistic imagination. His main character, Schach von Wuthenow, sleeps with the daughter of Mrs. von Carayon, the wealthy widow he hopes to marry. Schach is the last member of an old noble family, but unlike many officers at the time, he is not deeply in debt. Thus, a match with the mother would have constituted the almost perfect meeting of two shallow minds, not a financially expedient union. However, sleeping with the daughter while courting her mother is dishonorable, and Mrs. von Carayon eventually asks King Frederick William III to intervene to ensure that Schach marries her daughter. The king's action is almost certainly career-destroying, but as Schach sees the affair, his problem is even more intractable. Victoire, the daughter, had contracted smallpox as a child, leaving her face horribly disfigured. Schach actually finds her enchanting, but he is terrified at the prospect of socializing with his fellow officers, because he knows they would shame him for marrying an ugly woman. In the end Schach marries Victoire, but he saves himself from ridicule by committing suicide on the way home from their wed-

THE PAST AS HISTORY AND FICTION

ding. Except for the minor detail of being dead, suicide solves all of Schach's problems. He dies as he wanted to live, honorably.

Although its central character is weak, even craven, *A Man of Honor* works well as a novel. But as history the book is a disaster. Fontane gets almost everything wrong, assuming, of course, that the reports he drew on were reliable.[86] The historical Schach killed himself in 1815, not 1806; he did so not in his carriage but on the rear stairway of his own, or perhaps the mother's apartment—the evidence here is sketchy; and the deed took place before his engagement to the daughter instead of just after their marriage. The man behind the hero, Otto Friedrich Ludwig von Schack, was older than Schach von Wuthenow, a major rather than a captain, and he was deeply in debt. The mother was a banker's widow, newly ennobled, and thus not of equal social standing with the von Schack family, but she was wealthy enough to make her something of a catch. In addition—and here I limit the list of mistakes to information contained in the novel's first two paragraphs—Mrs. von Carayon's model did not live on Behrensstraße; Schach's rival, Captain von Bülow, had never been a staff officer, nor had he served the famous Regiment Gensdarmes; and Daniel Sander was not his publisher. To be sure, some of these mistakes could have resulted from the long tradition of changing names to protect the innocent, but understanding Fontane's representation of the past demands more than catching him in a few glitches and some cautious alterations. By moving the action from 1815 to 1806, before the battle at Jena, and by concentrating on Victoire's appearance as the sole threat to Schach's sense of honor rather than including money and social standing, Fontane effectively changes this tale of personal tragedy into a Prussian parable. By diminishing its facticity, he heightens the narrative's explanatory power. But what about the truth?

If the truth of fiction is essentially aesthetic, as one could infer from Fontane's review of Alexis, then truth in historical fiction becomes uninteresting. Historical novels would be no more and no less true than any other form of fiction. Indeed, if the criteria of truth were only aesthetic, Fontane could have transported the plot of his novel to 1882, when it was published, or to the American Revolution without missing a beat. However, if the novel seeks to explain, among other things, the debacle at Jena, Fontane's Schach functions far more effectively than the historical Schack as "the embodiment of Prussian parochialism," as Bülow puts it, and the translator could easily have taken the word *"Beschränktheit"* from Fontane's German text and made Schach the embodiment of Prussian narrow-mindedness or stupidity.[87] This one character's specific deficiencies let another fictional figure deliver a devastating critique of the Prussian army—dated, interestingly enough, a month to the day before the army's defeat at Jena—using the fictional Schach's death as a symbol of more significant and more pressing problems in Prussia: "It is a perfect sign of the times.... In this particular form and manifestation it could only have occurred at the seat of His Royal Majesty of Prussia's capital and court and, if beyond it, only within the ranks of our latter-day Frederickian army, an army in which honor has abdicated in favor of conceit and its soul, in favor of clockwork—a clockwork that will have run down soon enough."[88]

As dangerous as it is to conflate a character with the author, in other words, to presume that Bülow is speaking for Fontane, it is worth noting that his opinion does not differ significantly either from Droysen's or from what Fontane said in his review of Alexis. There he accuses Alexis of having depicted an "epoch of political incompetence, empty gloom, and moral decline," while claiming to view things "much more mildly" himself. But Fontane also says, "W. Alexis considered things to have been that way; hundreds of thousands agreed with him, including, no less negatively, most historical writers."[89] Here Fontane could simply be according Alexis the mantle of received historical truth, but Fontane is also casting a wider net, addressing the advantages enjoyed by the historical novel vis-à-vis history. Like Mühlbach, Fontane's implicit argument for the historical novel is that it lets authors use their aesthetic sensibilities to penetrate to the real truth of history, namely, to the lives and motives of those men and women who both cause and are effected by events.

Fontane's position comes across most clearly in an essay on Josef Viktor von Scheffel, the author of *Ekkehard,* one of the century's biggest best sellers. Scheffel's historical novel sold well despite, or perhaps because of, its extensive footnotes, which give the book a look of verifiable verisimilitude. The notes produce an aura of academic history, while the narrative advances unencumbered on the upper 95 percent of the page. Fontane himself delved into the sources, but as he says of Scheffel's work: "Such studies are not, by themselves, nearly sufficient; to them must be added historical vision and a prophetic intuition

THE PAST AS HISTORY AND FICTION

directed towards the past. Genuine poets almost always have such vision and intuition."[90]

One could, of course, argue that historical fiction is more concerned with the author's present than with the past, claiming that Fontane's questioning of Prussian virtues was directed at his contemporaries rather than a reflection on the country's history. For example, what the publisher Sander says near the beginning of the novel may have more relevance to the situation in Imperial Germany after 1871, when Prussia was forced to integrate new territory, than to circumstances in 1806: "All those who identify with the Guelphic lion or the horse rampant of Brunswick have no stomach for Prussian tutelage. And I don't blame anyone for feeling like that. We may have been equal to dealing with the Poles perhaps, but the Hanoverians are a fastidious breed."[91]

Yet to maintain that *A Man of Honor* is simply a kind of Aesopian fable, which disguises dangerous criticism of the present within the safer realm of the past, is to assume that Fontane was uninterested in history, that there is a strict dividing line between present and past. However, even in novels such as *Der Stechlin,* which he sets in the year of its publication, Fontane explores the survival or continuing resonance of the past as part of his explanation of the present. As a result, he was acutely concerned with the truth and falsehood of history or, at least, with the truth or falsehood of received historical opinion, which he did not bracket in favor of purely aesthetic considerations.[92]

Of course, the structure of *A Man of Honor* gave Fontane a distinct advantage over Mühlbach. His cast of historically minor characters, located far from the crucial battle at Jena, allowed him to explore the genre's opportunities without getting caught up in its constraints. Accurate quotation was never an issue. Still, historical novels require more than plausibility. While they limit the author's ability to invent, good historical fiction has to correspond to the history its readers already know. During the nineteenth century people knew, or thought they knew, a great deal about Frederick the Great, but what had they heard of Otto von Schack? I claim, for example, in chapter 3 that Germans garnered significant portions of their knowledge of Frederick from reading historical fiction, but readers found out everything they would ever learn about Schach/Schack from Fontane's novel. Like Scott, who famously focused on middling heroes, Fontane had the luxury of being able to get things wrong precisely because an unknown figure occupies the center of his novel. No one could check the footnotes or compare competing accounts of Schach's life. More important, Fontane's errors allowed him to deal with larger truths—truths not just of character but historical truths as well.

In contrast to Droysen's *Life of Yorck*, Fontane's text is much less clear about its loyalties. At one point Bülow poses a crucial question that might refer to both Prussia's prospects in the upcoming battle with Napoleon and, indirectly, to the legitimacy of the 1871 version of German unification: "Do you seriously believe that the breath of God is at the special beck and call of Protestantism or even of Prussia and her army?" Significantly, it is Schach, the novel's mediocre central character, who answers weakly, "I hope it is."[93] However, the novel's narrative voice, speaking directly to the reader, strikes a different note, saying, "in the final analysis only *our own* strength will be *our* security or *our* salvation. What other strength did *we* have besides the army?" (German edition, my translation, emphasis added).[94] The English translation speaks of "the country's own strength" (58), but the reader's identificatory involvement in Fontane's German makes it more difficult to locate blame for the disaster at Jena. There, neither the country nor the army, but "we"—whoever "we" may be—have failed; the inescapable conclusion is that only "we" can make things right. At one level Fontane simply presents a nuanced representation of Prussia in 1806, and, although the book contains implications for the author's contemporaries, it presents a complex case without taking sides.

At another level Fontane the critic and theoretician of historical fiction contradicts Fontane the author. By writing a more aesthetically pleasing account than Alexis, Fontane also produced an account closer to what he regarded as the historical truth. Thus, it is not so much that historical and aesthetic truths are different or antithetical, but rather that aesthetic truth allows for historical truth. Alexis's overstatement, which painted too bleak a picture for Fontane, was not merely flawed aesthetically, but rather, because the novel was aesthetically flawed, it also strayed from the complex historical truth of the matter. Alexis's lady poisoner was unbelievable as a fictional character, which made her unsuitable as a bearer of historical truth. In Fontane's practice aesthetic truth did not differ from historical truth; instead, poetic understanding served as a prerequisite for all truth.[95]

This conclusion also appears to find Droysen wanting, but the implication is somewhat unfair. His *Life of Yorck* is more a "narrative representation" and therefore closer to fiction than either the "investigatory" or "didactic" forms the historian claimed to prefer.[96] However, at least as a biographer, Droysen might admit Fontane's point with regard to Scheffel: "a great historian also has to be a poet."[97] Indeed, we now view several nineteenth-century historians as artists; the grand sweep of their narrative histories allowed for fine writing, and they found an audience. Of course, novelists, especially those who wrote historical fiction, almost always had a far larger readership than historians, and some of the dispute between the two camps might have concerned academics' resentment at their relative lack of commercial success and, consequently, their diminished role in the public sphere, where historical knowledge was a key issue in shaping national consciousness.[98] Like it or not, historical fiction rather than academic history inculcated much of what nineteenth-century Germans knew about their history; it also more readily enabled prospective Germans' identification with integrative figures from their past. It was a disadvantage that historians could never overcome, and their high-mindedness prevented some of them from even trying.

By contrast, historical novelists often wrote openly about their desire to bring history to the masses. For example, Franz Otto Spamer, who published a series of illustrated history books for children and adolescents, introduced one of his several accounts of Frederick the Great's life as follows: "The writer of this book wants to give our people, especially the fatherland's youth, an historically accurate account, but one clothed in the lighter garments of a story."[99] Spamer recognizes the difficulty that Droysen warned against, but for pragmatic reasons he makes the opposite choice. His argument shifts almost imperceptibly between the claim of accuracy and his desire to participate in the discourse of national identity, where the real action lay. In almost the same vein, Mühlbach justifies spending so much time, energy, and paper on Frederick in the introduction to her *Old Fritz and the New Era*, where she writes: "I am also fully conscious of what was and still is my greatest desire: to give the German people their history in an agreeable and popular form, to infuse them with love and affection for their particular history, . . . [and] to transform the facts of history into bits of real life."[100] Note the possessive "their"; Mühlbach wants to let the German people love and enjoy their history, in part, because making history popular flowed directly into the enterprise of giving Germans a share and a stake in what was becoming a common past. Fontane was not as open about

CHAPTER 1

his aims, partly because he was far more skeptical about nationalism, but he too participated in the elaboration and articulation of fact and fancy that shaped, reflected, and eventually became German history. Historians might have wanted to control the dialectical interplay from which Germans' sense of themselves emerged, but as a practical matter they lost the battle to historical fiction. People read more novels set in the past than works of either academic or popular history. One could argue about how much of what those readers learned was true, but novelists made a strong claim for a kind of truth that exceeded archival verification. They also challenged historians, albeit unsuccessfully, to rethink their own undertaking.

The critical moment of historical fiction is twofold: first, it insists that character is just as important as the event in historical understanding, and, second, it demonstrates that the personal is not only political but is also historical. Without individual motivation, to which the novelist claimed unique access, there can be no larger truth; in fact, there can easily be falsehood. By integrating private life and character into history, with means that historians, even contemporary social and cultural historians, have been reluctant to accept, novelists succeeded in producing accounts of the past that were both more complete and more complex, even ambiguous, than their academic counterparts' histories. If Mühlbach and the period's other historical novelists accomplished nothing else, their practical, commercial victory pushed the boundaries of historical knowledge, historical understanding, and historical representation far beyond the limits still adhered to by all but the most untraditional contemporary historians. And since novelists were the common people's teachers, it is just as important to understand the theoretical underpinnings of historical fiction as it is to grasp what Ranke and his followers meant when they founded academic history. In fact, one needs both the scholarly discipline and historical fiction to explain the larger discourse of history in the nineteenth century, particularly if the task is to untangle their combined role in writing Germany's national narrative, that is, in providing the content necessary to understand what the label "German" meant.

The point of this discussion has been to assess the sources of information about the German past that were available to nineteenth-century readers. Even if historians judged the genre harshly, people who read historical fiction and popular histories learned something from all of their encounters with the past. At the very least, they used these accounts to confirm and augment what they had already learned in school, perhaps from sources as dubious as *The Brandenburg Children's Companion*. First, readers acquired or re-remembered actual facts—some incidental, some trivial, but some that became important to their understanding of German history. Second, they learned things, both large and small, that they believed to be true but that may have been as speculative as Mühlbach's assessment of Frederick the Great's motivations. Third, they picked up or accepted overarching viewpoints about what mattered in German history: who its heroes were, where the nation had been, and where it was headed in the future. Moreover, this learning took place in an atmosphere utterly unlike the classroom. Nineteenth-century readers read popular history and historical fiction for pleasure. These works had not yet found their way into the schoolroom, the academy, or the canon; they were simply fun to read. Both genres surrounded themselves with an aura of moral and cultural uplift, but readers of historical fiction also got to see how plots turned out and what happened to the heroes. Being filled with truths from history did not prevent historical novels from including much that readers found true about their families, their relationships, and society in general. But they also found historical truth. Thus, while the advancement of historical knowledge was far from the only reason for its vast readership, the mixture of learning, pleasure, and popularity explains the importance of historical fiction as a complement to academic and popular history for an understanding of nineteenth-century German identities.

2
Caste and Regional Identities

About halfway through Friedrich de la Motte Fouqué's *The Refugee or Home and Abroad* (1824), a three-volume historical novel of the Wars of Liberation, the book's confused hero, Robert Gautier, reflects on his mixed identity: "Dear God, I praise you for making me human, and I am happy! Also for making me a German! Also for making me a Prussian!"[1] In fact, even as an officer in the midst of war, it was easier for him to maintain his humanity than to be simultaneously German and Prussian. As he reports, popular sentiment made the opposite demand: "Prussian identity can only be a German identity! And Prussian identity should disappear within German identity!"[2] The young man sees his situation as forcing a choice; to "disappear" is very different from being sublated, that is, simultaneously overcome and preserved, or whatever metaphor might have been popular in pre-Hegelian Berlin. Robert's complex origins further complicate his juggling act within the context of war-torn Germany, for this German-Prussian, Prussian-German cavalryman is not only a poor pastor's son, already an incongruous figure in the otherwise aristocratic officer corps, but as he will soon find out, Robert Gautier is also the proud scion of Huguenot aristocrats and therefore French. Thus, as if three potentially national identities were not enough, Gautier is both bourgeois and noble. In the tumultuous years 1813–15, when Napoleon's troops first occupied and then fled Germany, Gautier struggles with five incompatible identities—or six if we regard "human" as a separate category. His invoking the term implies a leveling of class distinctions and therefore a reorientation of society not unlike what had happened in France after 1789. No wonder the young man is confused.

Although exaggerated, such dilemmas were quite common in the fictional discourse of national identity recorded in novels published between 1815 and 1830, when authors and their readers began to sort out the consequences of three related developments: first, an extensive redrawing of borders within the territory that later became Germany; second, the legacy of a "national" resistance to "foreign" invaders during the Wars of Liberation, although many of the soldiers in Napoleon's armies were German; and third, strident though often nebulous appeals for German unity. In other words, demands to be German arose in a vastly different political landscape than had existed before the French Revolution. In 1815 half the population of Germany lived in different political entities than they had before 1806. Old loyalties either withered or became irrelevant; the sea change that swept through Europe produced first new hopes and then new fears. In fact, 1815 marked the onset of an era of disappointment or at least a questioning of the national agenda that had once filled the air and the works of earlier authors—for example, Ernst Moritz Arndt, Theodor Körner, and Heinrich von Kleist.[3] After 1815 Prince Klemens von Metternich was firmly in charge of the Austrian empire, and he supported the suppression of liberal nationalism throughout the German-speaking territories. Although there were numerous attempts to breach the conservative crackdown, most notably by students in 1817, the quiet retreat from politics that marked the period known as *Biedermeier* lasted until 1830. Inasmuch as 1815–30 was also the era when the historical novel was rapidly becoming the most popular genre in German literature, early German historical fiction reverberates with the conflicts and uncertainties of its age. Reading the period's historical novels closely, therefore, means exploring the complexities and contradictions of post-Napoleonic German nationalism.[4]

The officers who populate much of the period's historical fiction and their counterparts in the bureaucracy could still move freely from army to army and from court to court across borders that were dynastic rather than national. One need only think of the careers of men such as Metternich or the architect of Prussian reform, Baron vom Stein, to see how little the German nation mattered to the aristocracy. Metternich, the son of a government official in Trier, first represented the Westphalian nobility at the Congress of Rastatt; he then became Austrian ambassador to the Kingdom of Saxony and ended his career as imperial chancellor in Vienna. Only after he was hounded from government in 1848 did Metternich return to his native Rhineland, to property that had once belonged to the Hapsburgs, his employers in Vienna. Stein was born in Nassau an der Lahn, in the duchy that was home to the royal family of the Netherlands; he served various Prussian kings and was briefly advisor to the Russian Tsar Alexander II. Apparently, no questions arose about either Stein's or Metternich's loyalty. Nor were their careers unusual. They simply served aristocratic apprenticeships that mirrored the lives of mercenaries or journeymen traveling from town to town and from master to master, learning their trade. However, as the century progressed, nationalism gradually and imperfectly undermined personal, caste, and dynastic loyalties, which had allowed their bearers considerable flexibility. The nation replaced these older, often more individualistic identifactory markers with new and virtually impermeable boundaries that purported to be linguistic, ethnic, or cultural and, at some level, natural and rational. The resulting national groups were oddly inclusive—in contrast to inherited local practices—at the same time as they were utterly exclusive and absolutely rigid in their essentialism. Unlike the aristocracy, which was not so much a cohesive whole as a transnational continuum of gradations in title and pedigree, or the dizzying array of localities, where the sovereign's marriage mattered as much as the subject's birthplace in determining where someone belonged, membership in the nation was increasingly based on race or blood. As a result, aristocrats and artisans, Prussians and Bavarians, Catholics and Protestants all faced the prospect of becoming Germans, but at a significant personal cost of losing other identities. Heaven only knows how people actually sorted out these changes, but looking at the lives of fictional characters who crossed borders or were uncertain about their membership in the emerging national community can help clarify what Germany meant to the region's diverse population at a time when the term "German" was still vague and contested.

    Although accounts of German nationalism crowded the shelves of bookstores and filled the pages of popular and academic journals after the Berlin wall fell in 1989, we still know little about the actual (synchronic or diachronic) content of German national identity, especially during the early nineteenth century. Historian James J. Sheehan claims "the impact of nationalism during the so-called 'wars of liberation' was limited to a small minority of Germans, especially German intellectuals, whose memoirs and historical accounts helped to create a mythic image of the national past."[5] But we can only speculate about the precise thinness of this new veneer of national identity and about the details of how it later thickened and hardened. From the standpoint of historians there may be little direct evidence of the transformation; certainly there are few memoirs that discuss national identity with either the specificity or the doubts that affected Robert Gautier. But memoirs need not be the only source of information. Since novels exist to offer imaginary solutions to the very real dilemmas that their characters face, books like Fouqué's *Refugee* provide unparalleled access to popular discussions of the nation.

The Role of the Novel in Early Nationalist Discourse

Fiction is particularly important in the early nineteenth century. "Public" and "the public sphere" signify a realm of activity centered on, but by no means limited to, the middle class, which had been constituting itself as the subject of national and liberal political strivings since the mid-eighteenth century, partly by means of that most middle-class of genres, the novel. Moreover, even if historical fiction's readership is only imperfectly documentable, by 1820 this relatively new genre was reaching a broader audience than anyone had yet imagined—for any body of texts. The early nineteenth century also began the era of the popular, sometimes double- or triple-decker novel, whose authors wrote for the new market provided by private, for-profit lending libraries. Judging by their holdings, a growing body of readers was demanding historical fiction.[6] Before 1830 there was little popular and almost no academic history available to readers: some Ranke, but no Droysen, no Riehl, and no Treitschke. Until 1853 and the founding of *Die Gartenlaube* (*The Garden Bower*) no widely read journal spread historical consciousness. Thus, it is historical fiction, not the memoirs and historical accounts to which Sheehan alludes, that offers the most detailed insight into the initial construction of German national identity.

Of course, one could object that Fouqué's *Refugee,* a novel about the Wars of Liberation published less than a decade after they concluded, is scarcely historical. Some scholars regard the subtitle of Sir Walter Scott's *Waverley: Tis Sixty Years Since* as a genre necessity. They argue along the same lines as Hegel, whose proposition "Minerva's owl flies only at dusk" says metaphorically that the historian or the author of historical fiction requires temporal distance before past events can be understood and written about.[7] However, although Fouqué, a Huguenot baron who fought against Napoleon, had a personal stake in the events of 1813–15, for the culture as a whole 1815 marked a definite break with the past. In fact, the caesura it represented was probably an enabling condition for the rise of both academic history and historical fiction. Until the Napoleonic invasions, life and politics seemed immutable: kings died, but dynasties remained. Peasants were born and died in villages that they had little hope of leaving, while German cities were, on the whole, little more than small towns, and none of them functioned as a national center. After the redrawing of the European map, when the number of Germanic territories dropped from over three hundred to just three dozen, and after the introduction of ideas such as a national uprising, culture and politics changed forever. In effect, 1815 divided European experience into before and after, and that date allowed for history because it demonstrated to a world that had hitherto changed very little that the past was different from the present and the future. The perception that an era had ended allowed novelists to reflect on what had happened in the form of historical novels, and it is probably no accident that the genre begins in Germany after the Napoleonic wars, just as it had begun in England in the midst of those same wars with *Waverley* in 1814.[8]

This is not to say that historical novels published between 1815 and 1830 concerned themselves exclusively with German nationalism; in fact, the subject matter of early historical fiction was extraordinarily varied.[9] Texts from this period deal with everything from fifth-century Huns to eighteenth-century Swedes, from crusading knights to Bohemians during the Thirty Years' War. But there is also enough of Frederick the Great, Jena, and the Wars of Liberation to be able to see how authors were beginning to articulate Germany's national narrative. Its presence is fortunate but not accidental, because as literacy and reading increased, such works were inevitably implicated in creating the "imagined community" that would become Germany. As Benedict Anderson explains, the novel and the newspaper—and for nineteenth-century Germany, the family journal—provided the technical means both to represent that community and produce it. Concretely, the process functioned as follows: "Factory-owner in Lille was connected to factory-owner in Lyon only by reverberation. They had no necessary reason to know of one another's existence; they did not typically marry each other's daughters or inherit each other's property. But they did come to visualize in a general way the existence of thousands and thousands like themselves through print-language."[10]

Enormous numbers of texts, images, and other cultural artifacts reverberated, including some but not all of the so-called great works that became canonical. Yet the canon, despite its cultural importance, did not create the nation. Neither is national literature synonymous with the literature of nationalism. "Building a national literature," to use Peter Uwe Hohendahl's phrase, meant attempting to achieve a level of literary quality on a par with France and England, using Shakespeare and Cervantes as models, while writing the literature of nationalism involved an often conscious effort to articulate national difference. National literature implied German superiority and the renunciation of world literature in favor of the narrower compass of the nation. Thus, although the categories of national and nationalist sometimes overlap, scholarly analysis of German cultural nationalism and of the agenda behind the formation of a German national literature has frequently collapsed the distinction and obscured more of the content of Germany's national narrative than it has illuminated. Since they are satisfied to confront the canon, few scholars read the once popular bearers and shapers of national consciousness.

Hinrich Seeba, to cite a typical example of the problem, defines national literature "as the body of canonized texts into which a nation's collective sense of imagined history is believed to be inscribed in images that evoke historical continuity and social unity."[11] Seeba justifiably cites Schiller's *William Tell* (1804) as a literary attempt at reclaiming a more or less imaginary past for contemporary purposes, and one might also include Schiller's "Song of the Bell" (1800) as a work evoking social unity. Just as *Tell* reinvigorated Switzerland's foundational fiction, that poem provided a set of common images for the generations of Germans who learned it by heart. Not coincidentally, in a culture increasingly threatened by capitalism and industrial production, the poem's characters—the journeyman, the master craftsman, and the modest housewife—are all members of an intact organic community (*Gemeinschaft*). They conjure up an older, more reassuring form of social organization at a time when readers' lives had just been dislocated by political upheavals and war. Among other things, this part of the German canon posited an image of the ideal German family and household, which complemented the ideal past shared by the inhabitants of these same structures. However, I wonder if these works are symptomatic of the German canon as a whole and whether such masterpieces were the principal articulators of myths about the German nation. In other words, would we have a sufficient grasp of the content of German national myths and their discursive force if we limited our inquiry to the canon of German literature? And would we find there, to return to Seeba, a "collective sense of imagined history"?

My answer is simply and emphatically "no." As the single passage from Fouqué's *Refugee* already demonstrates, non-canonical novels also dealt with the definition and desirability of a German national identity. They raised questions and offered answers to readers who later became Germans. Yet, despite the nationalistic impetus engendered by the struggle against Napoleonic France, the popular literature of 1815 to 1830 shows no widespread agreement about what it meant to be German. Such books do, however, illustrate genuine concern with the issue of nationalism, concern we would miss if we were to concentrate on the canon or overlook literature altogether in favor of memoirs. When consensus about a German identity finally arrived, if it ever did, it was almost certainly mediated in fictional form. In other words, to the extent that historical fiction represented culturally significant events from what would gradually *become* a common German past, these texts helped shape and popularize a national myth of Germany. Despite the evidentiary problems of that assertion, one can still view *The Refugee* and similar non-canonical novels as a record of the discourse of identity formation, a process in which these texts, that is, their authors, their characters, *and* their readers, all participated.

When referring to the first third of the nineteenth century, it might seem more pertinent to speak of collective memory rather than national myth or narrative. In 1824, when Fouqué was writing his novel, the Prussian defeat at Jena and the Wars of Liberation were still relatively recent events, and Frederick the Great had been dead for only thirty-eight years. Robert Gautier is confused about his identity, but he and his creator speak from personal experience. Still, the choice of collective memory would be misleading on two counts. First, relatively few people who lived through the Napoleonic era had firsthand experience with the period's battles, to say nothing of its politics, nor would many of them have had even the vaguest personal recollection of King

CHAPTER 2

Frederick. Knowledge, legends, and anecdotes about Frederick and the Napoleonic dislocations reverberated in an oral tradition—passed on in taverns, on the job, and at home—but it was novelists and historians who exhumed, reconstructed, and popularized past lives and times in more lasting and accessible forms. Their writings, which still exist, chart the discourse of German identity formation over the course of the nineteenth century; the oral tradition, except where it is recorded in such books, is lost forever. Second, questioning memory as a category reminds us that ethnicity and national identity are always constructed, acquired, and contested—sometimes hotly. The examination of ethnic myths presumes that ethnicity, the nation, and popular nationalism are *not* biologically natural or normal states of affairs. They are, instead, learned behaviors, the effects of acquired knowledge, even if their bearers think otherwise. In fact, the evidence of historical fiction can show just how gradual, how difficult, and how tenuous the forging and acceptance of national identities actually was.

Troubled Heroes of Uncertain Nationality

This brings us back to Robert Gautier, the hero of Fouqué's novel. The boy is a refugee from the moment he first appears, running away from the nationalistic taunts of his German classmates, who are unable to pronounce Robert's family name in what he considers the proper French fashion. Their German rendition of the word "Gautier" reduces him to something like a county critter. Robert's opponent, the primitive bully Holzbecher, is as crude and ordinary as the wooden mug that is the translation of his name. When he later reappears as the leader of a particularly nasty gang of German marauders and author of a vehemently anti-French pamphlet, Holzbecher illustrates the ugliness of excessive and self-serving patriotism. To settle their schoolboy dispute, Robert suggests that the two boys fence rather than box, but Holzbecher, having already identified himself as one of the school's "good German boys," decides he will have none of this "French tomfoolery."[12]

As it happens, there is no fight—which is almost all that does *not* happen in the novel's twelve hundred pages—but two plot complications suffice as illustrations of the book's conflicted vision of German nationalism. First, Robert enrolls at the University of Berlin, which later allows him to join the campaign against the French as an officer. Second, he falls in love with Maria, Countess of Hohenstein, the sister of a friend and fellow officer. Naive readers might expect the plot to advance from there toward a happy ending, but Robert Gautier is unable to master the complex and shifting landscape of caste and national identities. His personal situation is as confused as that of Germany, and so, Robert ends up unhappy, confused, and dead.

As a Prussian soldier and German volunteer, the young hero willingly fights against the French, whom he refers to as his "former countrymen," even though they are "former" at a distance of several generations.[13] However, when he later encounters a group of women and children and hears how hated the French have become, his reaction suddenly becomes mixed: "Robert Gautier turned paler and ever paler . . . his fighting for the noble German cause suddenly seemed to him to be a kind of terrible suicide."[14] It is the schoolboy conflict all over again, except that Robert now finds himself on both sides of the conflict. If not death, schizophrenia appears to be his only option. Thus, in the novel's penultimate chapter, Robert finds himself on the banks of the Rhine—that is, in literary and nationalist metaphor at the traditional border between France and Germany—and he wonders what to do: "Oh, my beautiful native land, we cannot save you except with fire and the sword! And a son should lend his hand to the effort? . . . A son misused by the French returning home in this manner?"[15]

In addition to the problem of his conflicted national identity, Robert's love also appears destined to failure, because Countess Maria is unavailable to a poor pastor's son. Even though he is a winningly intelligent companion and a respected officer in the Prussian army, neither talent nor the brotherhood of all Germans allows these two socially distant lovers to marry. However, the reader already knows that distraught, bourgeois Robert Gautier will soon discover that he is simultaneously the Marquis de Langallerie, the proud descendant of a long line of French noblemen. The title turns him into a suitable mate for his beloved Maria, because in the old caste system neither Robert's German birth nor his French heritage jeopardizes his standing as an aristocrat. That status transcended nationality. But if my reading of the novel is correct, the aristocracy's internationalist economy, which was coming unglued in the face of nationalist uprisings, actually explains Robert's paradoxical fate.

Just as he locates a cache of papers left behind by a distant relative that would prove his eligibility to marry Maria, Robert is killed by a gang of marauding French soldiers. Not coincidentally, they also finish off the last heir of the Langallerie family, whose members had crossed

CHAPTER 2

into Germany before the border was redefined as an ethnic or national divide. Protestant Prussia had welcomed the French Huguenots as refugees from religious persecution and, probably more important, as able craftsmen and willing subjects for an underdeveloped and underpopulated principality. A few generations later and for vastly different reasons, neither France nor Germany offered the fictional Robert Gautier a home. The lines that divided nations during and after the Wars of Liberation were far less permeable than the boundaries of caste, personal, or even religious loyalty that had separated dynastic states in an earlier age. The discursive markers of identity were becoming more fixed or less open to choice or compromise, both in the literary representation of public discourse and in the world of events that realist literature strove to represent. Even the Marquis de Langallerie could no longer be both French and German, while the conflicts of an earlier age, the international struggles between Protestants and Catholics, no longer seem worth mentioning.

Fouqué's Prussian-German-Frenchman of bourgeois and noble origins is undone by the competing claims of his background and his desires. He cannot resolve the question of his identity, because in the post-Napoleonic era his situation became fundamentally irresolvable. Robert cannot lay claim to the internationalist refuge above the fray, symbolized by his own noble pedigree and by the Countess Maria, because to assume the French title would mean abandoning the German portion of his identity. Not coincidentally, Maria eventually marries another count (but a German von Sternberg), while Robert's father dies simply as Pastor Gautier rather than as the Marquis de Langallerie. The family's connection to France and the French is forgotten, and everyone else can safely become German. However, for the reader, Robert's ambiguity and Holzbecher's destructive nationalism call the Wars of Liberation into question as a part of the unifying myth of a common German past.

From the point of view of Fouqué's 1824 novel, a common past still needed constructing, not just with events but also with German heroes, such as Frederick the Great. In fact, *The Refugee* is an early example of the process of refurbishing the image of the legendary Prussian king into something he had not been during his lifetime: a national hero. One can read the beginnings of this process of reconstruction and reappropriation when Robert Gautier refers to Frederick as the man "whose burnished image once again lights our way into battle."[16] Earlier, when Robert is still unsure about joining the battle to redeem Prussia and/or Germany, he rides off to Frederick's palace in Potsdam. While sitting on the terrace or in the gardens of Sanssouci, Robert falls asleep and dreams of an encounter with the king. The imaginary Frederick encourages him and stills his doubts: "If he is an authentic son of refugees, let him prove it with deeds, let him make his way vigorously through the world."[17] Later, Pastor Gautier buys Robert, the newly commissioned officer, a horse named after the great king's favorite dog. Of course, Frederick's presence is only a sidelight in this novel about the Wars of Liberation, but even when we might anticipate seeing Frederick featured, historical novels published between 1815 and 1830 disappoint conventional expectations.

In Wilhelmine von Gersdorf's *The Conspiracy, or Treason and Loyalty* (1830) Frederick comes across as a distant villain rather than a hero.[18] As the novel opens, in August 1761, the narrator comments on the destructiveness of war in general, while reserving his or her particular scorn for the savage conflict then being waged between Prussia and Austria. The Seven Years' War (1756–63) was being fought at no small cost to Saxony, the narrator's homeland, and Frederick gets most of the blame for the conflict's tragic course. In fact, one of the novel's characters, Baron Warkotsch, becomes convinced that Frederick is the Antichrist and joins a plot to assassinate him. The real evildoer is a pastor, but Warkotsch plays on Saxon patriotism to convince one of his servants, the forester Cappel, to aid the plotters: "He [Frederick] was the conqueror, the vanquisher, the oppressor of his [Cappel's] prospering fatherland; might alone gave him the right to impose laws on a people, whose beloved princely family had otherwise seen to its well-being!"[19] Note that "fatherland" means Saxony here, not Germany, nor has Prussia come to embody German virtues.

Luckily for the Prussians, Cappel's conscience will not allow him to continue aiding the traitors, and another pastor convinces him to deliver some compromising letters to the king. The good pastor's arguments mix old-fashioned notions of divine right with local patriotism; he does not attempt to turn Frederick into a hero, either for Saxony or for all Germans: "Fly, race, the king is resting nearby. God's angels protect His anointed [representative] . . . give these letters [to King Frederick], and you will be doing God's work, saving [the king] as well as performing an important service to your country."[20] *The Conspiracy* ends after only another eight pages; Cappel becomes a master forester and marries, both steps made possible by Frederick's patronage, but the reader never sees Cappel with the king. The absence is remarkable because anecdotes about encounters between Frederick and his subjects, particularly when the people involved were from the lower ranks of society, provided much of the material from which authors were able to construct a positive image of Frederick by mid-century. To be sure, Cappel's promotion is evidence of the king's benevolence, but, unlike the long list of examples from chapter 3, no shining image of Frederick appears here; the wise and approachable Old Fritz either does not yet exist, or he is not yet firmly established as a literary topos. Early in the century Frederick's name seems mainly to denote a bygone era, not a fatherly hero potentially useful to German nationalists.

The reader does learn something of Frederick's common touch in an 1826 work by C. J. Oldendorp, an obscure author whose *Misfortune and Rescue: The Youthful Fate of an Officer in the Era of Frederick the Great* seems to have been his only literary work.[21] The book's central character is a foundling, the lost son of a Prussian cavalry officer, Captain von N, whose parents have long since died. A benevolent uncle eventually rescues young N from poverty and ill treatment at the hands of various evildoers: petty officials, cruel employers, and greedy Jews. The latter appear infrequently, but their presence is nonetheless disturbing. As represented by Oldendorp, Jews are not only avaricious, but they also cannot speak proper German: "A real businessman has to happy sell a shirt from his back, when he can an '*Profitche*' make, even one so small."[22] The sentence is syntactically false, grammatically questionable, filled with mistaken or misspelled vocabulary, and it is utterly un-German in its content. The scene shows a father literally selling the shirt off his son's back, by itself a despicable act, but by depriving his Jewish characters of the ability to speak correctly at a time when language and culture began to mark national identity, Oldendorp goes a step beyond ridicule or stereotyping. Without a proper language, Jews cease to be fully human.

Of course, the novel's hero gets a shirt in the transaction, and, no matter how badly events turn out for him, one genuinely good person always appears—a tavern keeper, a farmer, or, most frequently, a soldier, who rescues the boy. Frederick makes only one fleeting appearance. Otherwise he functions as the distant guarantor of this benign world. As a sergeant explains to young N, who is later discovered to be of noble birth and therefore destined for something better than the drudgery and despair that are the lower orders' lot: "There is justice and order in the country. Rest assured, young lord, our king is a man."[23] Admittedly, a country that prides itself on not overlooking noble birth practices an odd sort of justice, but this is precisely what the hero longs to hear. Besides confirming this orphan's legitimacy, and thus his rights of inheritance and privilege, the king also helps inspire the boy's choice of profession. As the boy, also named Frederick, puts it, tales of Frederick II and of another Prussian hero, the Old Dessauer (1676–1747), "awakened in me the wish and the desire to become a soldier, and thus, like these honorable men, to dedicate my life to my king and fatherland."[24] The use of history to justify present action and the word "fatherland" to denote Prussia rather than Germany are worth noting. So, too, is the narrative curiosity that when the king finally appears, he is more an aura than a person; in fact, he is almost beyond description. King Frederick nods to the boy at a maneuver, provoking the following comment: "What I experienced during everything that I saw and heard is impossible to describe."[25] Thus, in what the reader sees, the king neither acts nor says anything. His main function is to locate the book's plot chronologically, but in Oldendorp's novel Frederick also symbolizes a prenationalist order in Prussia and Germany.

National Identity before Nationalism

At first, one could mistake Christoph Hildebrandt's *The von Manteufel Family* (1826) for an early example of the genre of Frederickian novels.[26] Its subtitle, *A Historical-Romantic Portrait from the Era of the Seven Years' War*, implies the king's presence, but once again the period's most important figure is almost completely absent. Speaking of Frederick's Bohemian campaign during the First Silesian War (1740–42), the narrator says: "The course of this history is familiar."[27] The comment suggests, first, that the reading public already possessed a considerable fund of historical knowledge and, second, that there was no reason to show the Prussian king in a heroic fashion, for that too was familiar to readers. At this early stage of historical fiction's development, depicting great men up close seems to have been far less important than showing the adventures of lesser individuals with whom readers could identify. Here one sees two separate and only apparently contradictory functions of such identificatory figures: on the one hand, they show how historical events influenced the lives of ordinary Germans, while on the other hand, they demonstrate that ordinary life—birth, love, and death—continued outside of history, that is, despite the actions of great men and the succession of great events. The tension between these two roles for historical fiction—representing what happened in the past, while also presenting the lives of recognizable characters—is central here because Hildebrandt fills his novel, perhaps anachronistically, with individuals who face the same dilemmas during the eighteenth century that Robert Gautier confronted a few generations later. Among other things, *The von Manteufel Family* is about national identity before nationalism, but it also deals with events and people who become important in the articulation of a German identity after the Wars of Liberation. In other words, the simple statement "The course of this history is familiar" self-consciously reflects the novel's place in the nineteenth-century discourse of identity formation.

The novel lacks a preface that might have explained why Hildebrandt picked the historical von Manteuffel family—slightly altering the spelling of their name, but we can assume that these well-known producers of officers and bureaucrats immediately evoked Prussia to contemporary readers. The branch of the family celebrated in Hildebrandt's novel includes Major Eduard von Manteufel and his four children, three officer sons and a daughter. The father, who fought in the First Silesian War, characteristically differentiates his personal from his territorial loyalties when he says he "sacrificed a foot for King Frederick and the fatherland."[28] His sons fight in the Seven Years' War, which for Prussia might also be called the Third Silesian War, but the issue here is not so much what the sons fought for but rather for whom. Everyone in the book is intensely loyal to some monarch; so, when characters use the term "fatherland" it refers to dynastic states, in other words, bits of territory united by marriage, inheritance, or conquest: Prussia, Austria, Saxony, or Schwarzburg-Sonderhausen, not Germany. By contrast, modern nations claim to be based on language, culture, and ethnicity, but these ideas do not resonate for Hildebrandt's fictional Manteufels. The text identifies the family's eldest son, Hermann, as the best horseman in his regiment, "which is saying a great deal, because the regiment consisted mainly of Hungarians and Poles, who were born riders."[29] But unless they were mercenaries, these ethnically mixed cavalrymen were all Prussians; neither their origins nor their national loyalties mattered. Hildebrandt apparently recognized not only that Prussia, like Austria, was a multinational or multiethnic state, but also that many of Prussia's German inhabitants had to be viewed as distinct from one another. A good example is found in the following remark: "As loyal Pomeranians the news [of Frederick's victory at Roßbach in 1757] meant a great deal to the family."[30] The designation "Prussian" or "Austrian" was insufficient, perhaps inaccurate as a mark of identity, even for the Germans, and nowhere was its inappropriateness more pronounced than among the officer corps, whose members were fighting colleagues by birth and occupation. Only later did those brother officers become enemies by nationality rather than opponents whose allegiances could shift. By setting his novel before the Wars of Liberation, Hildebrandt was able to talk about issues that today's readers might think were already settled. The novel suggests that national questions remained open as people explored what was at stake in shifting from old to new categories of identity.

The main plot line of *The von Manteufel Family* involves a curious set of coincidences, which mostly concern conflicting and ambiguous identities. The young Prussian officer Hermann von Manteufel first captures, then is captured by, and later becomes a close friend of the Hungarian-Austrian officer Count Oskar Hallasch. To complicate matters, Hermann falls in love with Oskar's sister, Antonie, and he, no doubt like the readers of 1826, wonders if marriage is possible across military, political, and ethnic lines. Much to his surprise, Hermann learns that it is common for men of his caste to have friends and family on both sides of a conflict—or, more accurately, on all sides in an altercation that was marked by such a complex system of shifting alliances as the Seven Years' War. His commanding officer has long-standing ties to a general in the Austrian army, and Hermann's sister, Adelheid, is eventually saved from marauding Slavic hordes—literally, "swarms of monsters whose only human feature was their shape"—by a Russian officer named, of all things, von Manteufel.[31] Family and caste continually take precedence over national or ethnic interests here. Indeed, the issue of loyalty never surfaces in ethnic or national terms; caste, local, and dynastic loyalty matter, but neither the nation nor the people do. Hermann just needs to sort things out.

During the siege of Prague, before he knows anything of Oskar's sister, Hermann is shaken "by the thought of perhaps running into his friend; his heart spoke louder than his sense of duty; friendship outweighed service obligations."[32] The voice is the narrator's, but "service obligations" nevertheless represent a contractual duty rather than an affirmation of loyalty to a country (much less to a nation), which is precisely the view taken by Hermann's future father-in-law: "'I would be happy to see this marriage,' said [the elder] Count Hallasch, 'if Manteufel left the Prussian service and joined our army.'"[33] For Antonie's father and the retired General Nadasti, who soon plays an important role in the plot, aristocratic officers practice a profession independent of their employers and unencumbered by emotional bonds to the nation or its people. General Nadasti is Hungarian and loyal to Empress Maria Theresa, who is also the queen of Hungary, but he feels no obligation to Austria. He quite readily takes this Prussian officer under his wing, even offering to adopt him, so that Hermann will have enough money to marry Countess Hallasch. Nadasti gives the elder Count Hallasch, also a Hungarian patriot, the following justification for Hermann as a potential son-in-law: "A good man is always good, and whether he has King Frederick or Maria Theresa on his saddlebags is a matter of indifference . . . we won't always be at war. Our powerful leaders will also get tired of these cat fights."[34]

Much to everyone's surprise, Hermann declines the opportunity to fight for Austria and Antonie: "I will never forsake my king and my country. The two have done so much for me that I cannot reward them with ingratitude."[35] Again, "country" (*Land*) refers to Prussia, not Germany, and it is worth noting that the Hungarian connection precludes talk of pan-Germanic solidarity with Austria. Hermann's loyalty combines local patriotism with a personal bond to the king; his sense of obligation to Frederick is by far the stronger of the two beliefs. Luckily, Hermann's reluctance no longer matters, because General Nadasti replies: "Take the two properties, and stay Prussian for all eternity."[36] Unlike Fouqué's novel, there is a happy ending here—but only after the war's end, which allows Hermann to leave the Prussian army with fewer qualms than before. He marries his Hungarian countess and manages the Hungarian properties Nadasti had given him. Hildebrandt resolves the question of loyalty successfully, because, unlike Robert Gautier, whose fictional life takes place a generation later, Hermann von Manteufel can retreat from the world that made such choices necessary. Had the war continued, he would have remained on the horns of the dilemma posed by caste, friendship, and love on the one hand and by local-dynastic loyalty on the other. His choice contrasts sharply with the heroes and heroines of chapter 5, when, rather than existing in a prenationalist limbo, marriage defines the nation.

The end of the Seven Years' War lets Hermann withdraw from a nationalistically charged conflict, at least as Hildebrandt represents things in his 1826 novel, to the idyllic utopia of the Hungarian countryside. In addition to the fortunate timing, Hermann's new properties are not only literally a long way from the battleground where he and Oskar fought, but they are also figuratively far removed, because they allow for the marriage of what would soon be opposites. However, in 1763, as I would argue in 1826, neither Hermann's conflicting loyalties nor his wife's nationality matter. On his Hungarian estates history ceases to exist; the politics of 1813–15 disappear. These properties function like the "zones of retreat" that Hermann Sottong locates at the center of what he calls "historical initiation novels."[37] Sottong writes mainly of bourgeois heroes in novels set in the eighteenth century. He argues that whenever history raises its ugly head and threatens to interrupt the progress of true love or personal development, the hero can step outside of time. Back at the family castle, the world consists only of lord and peasant, which puts Hermann and Antonie on the same side. Thus, while Hildebrandt's eighteenth-century Prussian officer sometimes sounds like a prototype for nineteenth-century nationalists, the author does not force Hermann into that anachronistic role. National or ethnic loyalty would have cost Hildebrandt's hero too much in personal terms, but, unlike his counterparts from the Napoleonic era, Hermann has the luxury of not making a choice. He can retreat to the aristocratic world predating nationalism, where happy endings are still possible.

Of course, no one asks Hermann's wife about her loyalties, so we have to assume that marrying the novel's swashbuckling hero suited her just fine. Until much later in the century, women in historical fiction seem to exist only to please or reward their heroes. Men return from war and marry their comrades' sisters, who have been waiting patiently, untroubled by the conflict and the issues raised there. It apparently did not occur to the authors of these early historical novels to pose the question of national or ethnic loyalty for women: Hermann von Manteufel might agonize over the implications of marrying outside Prussia, but Countess Hallasch's only concern is love. At least the reader sees no indication that the Hungarian countess Antonie worries about having a Prussian husband. He is dashing, has her brother's approval, and bears the name *von* Manteufel; what more could she want? The problem of national versus caste loyalties was part of the public sphere, which rigorously excluded even fictional women. Change in their situation comes only with the introduction of bourgeois heroes and heroines later in the century.

CHAPTER 2

Caste versus National Identity

At first the question of the bourgeoisie seems central to another Hildebrandt novel about the Frederickian period, *The Most Remarkable Year in the Life of an Old Soldier* (1830), but the book actually raises the caste issue from a slightly different perspective.[38] This time the book's young hero—simply, Karl—is an officer in the Austrian not the Prussian army. However, as he soon learns from a general, "in the course of the war, you, too, my son, will get to know many excellent men from the enemy's army, with whom you will forget their uniform and insignia and only pay attention to their hearts."[39] On the surface Karl's personal situation resembles Robert Gautier's more closely than it does Hermann von Manteufel's: Karl is bourgeois and in love with the sister of his aristocratic friend Franz von Wallenroth. However, the novel's tension rises not between these two otherwise antagonistic castes but between officers and courtiers. Karl allies himself not with "the people," whoever they might be in Austria, but with the army in its opposition to political machinations in the capital. The object of his intentions, Theresa von Wallenroth, is engaged to the well-connected courtier Casimir von ***, but love triumphs over intrigue, aided eventually by Karl's impending ennoblement. Theresa remains an object; she is subject to Karl's plans rather than the master of her own destiny. Meanwhile, Karl needs the empress for the honor and prestige the monarch alone can bestow, but he rejects the court's values. A sympathetic general helps him by reluctantly retiring to the war ministry in Vienna rather than remaining in the field. Unlike the general, but due to his protection, Karl can stay with his friends and family in the countryside. He too retreats to an intact aristocratic world, an upper-class *Gemeinschaft* that is essentially outside history.

Like Frederick II in the novels discussed above, Empress Maria Theresa does not actually appear in Hildebrandt's novel. The subordinate position of women was certainly one reason that Maria Theresa received scant consideration as a potential German heroine. Confined to the court, with its long-established, stiff rituals, Maria Theresa also led a distinctly less narratable life than Frederick, who commanded an army and interacted with people from all levels of society. More important, although victory came much later, Prussia was already winning the ideological struggle for priority in a unified German state. It helped that Germany's major publishers resided in the north and that the Catholic Church's hostility toward the Enlightenment kept book production down in the south. In fact, minimal as her role is here, Hildebrandt's novel is one of the few from this era to mention the empress at all. Karl and his friends speak of Maria Theresa fairly frequently, but while she escapes the unrelenting criticism directed at her courtiers, the empress remains the distant representative of a world better avoided by soldiers and honest men. In these early historical novels, Maria Theresa functions like her long-term nemesis as the guarantor of an idyllic life that felt increasingly threatened, but still survived as a refuge in historical fiction.

Aside from potential victimization through intrigue at the court, the only danger to this novel's hero comes with his capture by the Prussians, who repel a foolhardy Austrian attack. More important, in thematic terms, the assault broke the rules of aristocratic combat: the Austrians charged after negotiating a truce that was supposed to have allowed both sides to occupy winter quarters in peace. Like his nominal opponents, the Prussian officers, Karl abhors "that sort of aberration from [the norms] of the military caste," and he regrets its consequences.[40] Karl's difficulty is not so much his capture as the dishonor of having been party to a breach of international etiquette, even in the service of the empress. Karl is embarrassed at betraying the principles of his caste, even though, as he puts it: "I was familiar with the animosity, with Prussian's national hatred against everything that was imperial."[41] Here again, the issue of loyalty does not emerge in nineteenth-century nationalist terms; the object of "national hatred" is "everything imperial," not the Austrians or Hungarians. Prussian hatred is a function of personal rather than ethnic loyalty, just as service to the empress transcends national boundaries while remaining almost familial.

As in *The von Manteufel Family,* one often reads of the bonds between Maria Theresa and her various subjects, particularly the Hungarians, who are devoted both to her and to her dynasty, despite the ill treatment they endure at the hands of Austria's dominant Germans. Their sense of being Hungarians is neither strong enough to inspire their own nationalism, nor, apparently, did these essentially anti-German, yet positive characters offend the German reading public. The men in Hildebrandt's novels consider war an honorable undertaking, the goals of which are of little concern to officers. Karl learns as much just as the Prussians are about to capture him a second time: "'Break! Half-an-hour's break, gentlemen!' said [the Prussian officer]. 'If you have no objections, we few men will dispense with the war! We are not going to decide the ownership of Silesia!'"[42] The reader learns that playing by the

CHAPTER 2

rules matters more than any war aims, even those advanced by one's own monarch. Soldiers could have an emotional stake in the ownership of Silesia only if they framed the issue of territorial possession in ethnic or national rather than in dynastic or professional terms. These officers do their job according to an aristocratic, that is, international, code of ethics. These ideas predate the nation, but by being published after nationalism's supposed arrival, they show that at least initially the new ideology's appeal was far from universal.

In this early period, novels depicting events from the Napoleonic wars did not so readily dismiss the politics of nationalism, but as we saw above, an author such as Fouqué could treat the nationalist agenda subtly and critically. Similarly, in E. Auerbach's *The Gypsy Theft* (1825) a character wonders whether it would be better for the anti-French coalition to win or to lose.[43] The novel is set in the Saxon capital of Dresden in 1813. With the city located precariously between the French and the allied armies, Dresden faced destruction no matter who succeeded. Nevertheless, even though it is unclear who would liberate whom, the narrator claims, "every honest German longed silently for the liberators of the fatherland."[44] From the standpoint of the "fatherland," the allies and potential liberators included Russia, Prussia, and Austria but not yet Saxony, which was still loyal to Napoleon's multinational coalition. An eighty-year-old city judge, who is one of the novel's main characters, remembers the last time they were so richly blessed with enemies. During the War of Austrian Succession (1740–48) the city had been "plundered down to its last shirt by Austrian irregulars and Croatians."[45] However, when the hated Austrians triumph again in 1813 and march into the city, the old man is reluctantly impressed by their commanding officer, who turns out to be his long-lost brother: "What a commanding, respectable man our noble guest is! He looks so German, there is just something about him, it's as if he were truly one of us!"[46] In other words, whether Austria belongs to Germany is an open question. Unlike the characters, who could be brothers *and* enemies, Austria and Saxony do not yet belong to the same family. Nor, apparently, are Austria and Germany members of the same nation. Hence, what now seems like a very strange statement: "He [the Austrian] *looks* so German, . . . it's as if he were truly one of *us*!" Since he is the speaker's brother, that is, one of *us* (Germans or Saxons), not one of *them* (Austrians), the similarity is not surprising, but the Austrian is not supposed to look German. The novel makes an implicit claim for ethnically different physiognomies among people, even though some of them subsequently thought of themselves as a single ethnic group. For Auerbach, the metaphor of the nation is not yet as inclusive as the image of the family, and novels of the period often construct difference where authors of both earlier and later eras saw similarity. Despite the supposedly crystallizing events of the Wars of Liberation, German ethnicity lacks an agreed-upon meaning.

THE IMPOSSIBLE DREAM OF NATIONAL UNITY

A similarly complicated family situation, which also transcends national borders, anchors the plot of H. E. R. Belani's 1829 novel, *The Demagogues*.[47] Strangely, in a book that I read as German nationalist fiction, the book's hero eventually leaves Europe for a villa on the banks of the Hudson River. Baron Hermann von Rosenberg flees to the United States when he is unable to find either a place or a role for himself in Germany. The novel, which is as long and as complicated as most of the period's historical fiction transports him to the new world, because it fails to resolve his identity in the old. Rosenberg, whose name, contrary to expectations, does not designate a newly ennobled Jewish family, is both an impassioned German revolutionary and the faithful son of an ancient and widely scattered aristocratic clan. Once again caste and nation prove incompatible, and conflicting demands of loyalty nearly destroy the hero. He feels bound, first, to the cause of German unity and, second, to a promise of marriage made long ago by his father. To preserve the family, Hermann, the rich German, is to marry his impoverished but far more distinguished Italian cousin, the Countess Monta Rosa. After two volumes of adventures, the cousins actually do marry, but only after Hermann has decided that the revolution and the promise of German national unity are unrealizable dreams. As he puts it: "After wandering through all of Germany and having convinced myself that in every village and in every town all the farmers and tradesmen love both their princes and peace, it seems to me impossible for the overwhelmingly cold and reasonable mass of the German people ever to be pushed into a revolutionary situation."[48] The good burghers of *Biedermeier* Germany would rather sit comfortably in familiar surroundings than be roused by the dangerous and unsettling promise of national unity.

Despite Rosenberg's disillusion, the novel contains some surprising scenes, especially considering the censorship that existed throughout Germany after 1819. Belani includes a lengthy account both of the nationalist festival of 1817 at Wartburg Castle and of Karl Ludwig Sand, the student who murdered the antinationalist author August von Kotzebue in 1819. What transpired in both instances appears in a negative light, but Belani's demagogues have ample opportunity to make their point, thereby undercutting the book's overtly conservative stance. In addition, Belani repeatedly shows how undefined, indeed how murky, notions such as fatherland, people (*Volk*), and nation still were in post-Napoleonic Germany. As Hermann and his fellow travelers cross from Germany into France, Switzerland, and Italy, friends and family members frequently assist them. But they are just as often betrayed by men and women they regard as their fellow countrymen and by their coconspirators as well. Of course, Hermann's family tree demonstrates that families and countries do not always share the same border. Hermann is attracted first to one side, then to the other, partly because his aristocratic background is intrinsically multinational. In Belani's novel caste and family trump nation, but this will become an increasingly difficult way to live. Hermann does not escape the conflict between family and folk until well after arriving in New York. He retreats from the world of nationalist politics, but he is not just seeking the safety of a conventional happy ending. On the one hand, the American utopia allows him to fulfill the contract his father made; Hermann unites the two branches of the Rosenberg family and satisfies caste loyalties. On the other hand, he pays the price of renouncing Germany with more regret than his compatriots in the works dealt with above. As in so many of these early historical novels, not only personal loyalties, family ties, and social origins triumph over what authors frequently represent as the fraud or passing fancy of nationalist politics, quite defeating retrospective readers' expectations. In fact, instead of waxing nostalgic about the nation that might have been, these same authors frequently double their condemnations by deploring nationalism's excesses.

 Two other works from this early period, Julius von Voß's *The German Don Quixote* (1819) and Willibald Alexis's *The Outlaws* (1825), share a critical view of aggressive nationalism.[49] Indeed, both authors take direct aim at the very agenda of German nationalist politics. Like all fools, Voß's picaresque hero has license to speak the truth. The narrator reports that his hero, Valentin von Edelsheim, had already begun working on the German cause before 1805, long before it was fashionable. Ironically, and unfortunately for him, Edelsheim's fellow Germans reject as ridiculous ideas that they would defend less than a decade later. Before the Wars of Liberation, his continued prattling about German virtues seems as foolish as his namesake's tilting at windmills. In effect, by attributing his hero's problems to timing rather than substance, Voß allows Edelsheim to exaggerate and thereby trivialize the ideology behind German nationalism; he does so in a series of books that constitute his life's work: "The first book that he finished was called the authentic German young man, his second was the authentic German maiden, his third, the authentic German man, his fourth, the authentic German graybeard. He was always concerned with authentic Germanness; it was an ideal that floated before him. . . . But he never published a thing; these studies were solely for his own edification."[50] Even a convinced nationalist would have a difficult time imagining positive content in Edelsheim's unpublished works; the German text leaves no doubt about their silliness. It repeats the adjective "authentic" in an outmoded form (*ächt* rather than *echt*) that was already satirical in 1819, and one only has to stretch a bit to locate authentic Germanness near ostracism (*ächten*). The authorities ban Edelsheim from Germany for taking contradictory, unpopular positions—namely, for suggesting, on the one hand, that it was "unworthy, not in keeping with the spirit of the German people," to wage war on France, and, on the other hand, that German princes should band together for precisely that purpose.[51] Banished from his native country and, to prevent his further involvement with German nationalism, conveniently, shipwrecked, Edelsheim spends nine years on a desert island. He returns home in 1817, only to find, as he puts it, "that in Germany the sense of being German is not as I had hoped it would be."[52]

This time Edelsheim's moment has passed; he no longer anticipates the future but instead tries to keep an outmoded past alive. For example, his old-German costume, which he copied from the patriotic gymnastics societies, the Turners, elicits ridicule rather than honor and emulation. A German peasant woman even mistakes him for a Polish Jew, which might be the ultimate insult. The rural population was supposed to be authentically German, and the woman should have known better—except that nationalism always had more to do with a tiny, urban elite than with the supposedly nationalist majority. Edelsheim breaks his final lance trying to educate a group of young women whom he mistakes for German maidens, but they turn out to be prostitutes. Meanwhile, the younger generation of German males denounces its patriotic fathers. The elders may still revere Frederick the Great, but

CHAPTER 2

their newly conservative sons ask: "How can you appeal to an irreligious despot whom small people still call great?"[53] Edelsheim reluctantly sums up his adventures, saying: "Everyone in Germany should be wary about appearing in the cause of truth and reason."[54] When Voß's hero retires a broken man, it is mainly to sleep off the intoxication of excessive national fervor—except that he actually missed most of the patriotic action while stranded on his desert island.

Curiously enough, the central figure in Alexis's novel *The Outlaws* also spends the years of heady nationalism virtually alone on an island, albeit off the coast of Germany. That parallel is superficial, but the two books do share an overwhelming sense of disenchantment with German nationalism. Alexis's novel revolves around a fictional character, Theodor von ***, who participates in real events and is then forced to live with the consequences. This common narrative trick of historical fiction lets readers see what happened to men and women like themselves when history intruded into lives that were otherwise unchanging. The novel begins in 1809, when the historical Prussian officer Ferdinand von Schill (1776–1809) attempts to rouse the still quiescent German people to righteous anger against the French invaders. Schill's uprising fails, and the authorities vilify him for activities that would receive almost universal praise less than five years later. Theodor and the narrator remain skeptical, calling Schill's hatred of the French "blind rage" (*blinde Wut*, 12), while patriotism is likened to an "intoxication" (*Rausch*, 14) that ends in convulsive "paroxysm" (*Paroxismus*, 14). Schill's difficulties lay not so much in the reluctance of Germans to rebel as in the refusal of Catholic Westphalians to rise against the French in favor of Protestant Prussians. Prussia had only recently taken possession of parts of Westphalia, and Westphalian troops were just as happy to fight against Schill as with him. They remained loyal to their French commanders in the battle of Dodendorf and forced Schill to retreat. In the process, Adolf von Lützow, who would later find fame for doing exactly what Schill attempted, was severely wounded, but he returned to fight another day. Schill attempted to occupy Stralsund, a northern port, where his opponents were troops from Mecklenburg, that is, supposedly friendly Germans. In addition to sharing language, culture, and religion, these men should be on Schill's side, because some members of each camp are related by blood or marriage. They nevertheless fight each other with skill and conviction, killing Schill and routing his followers. Not only is there a great deal of indiscriminate carnage, but also one of

Theodor's friends kills his own brother-in-law, with the following justification: "He was fighting against his fatherland."[55] Another character leaves his lover after saying: "Whoever loves his fatherland [can] love nothing else."[56] Theodor manages to escape from the French troops who finally put down Schill's rebellion, but he ends up spending ten years founding a family on an otherwise deserted island. He has deliberately cut himself off from news of Germany, having decided: "This fatherland was a beautiful idea, but the reality was a foolish mixture of stupidity, pride, and self-interest, not worth the efforts of a noble spirit."[57]

Actually, the novel's message is more mixed. Owing to an otherwise unremarkable genre convention, the reader learns Theodor's first name only. Theodor von *** bemoans the forgetfulness of Greeks, Romans, Wends, and, ultimately, the Germans. The young man fears that he too will be "forgotten like the other heroes who fought and died for religion, the fatherland, freedom, and their own language."[58] Of course, no one can remember the name and deeds of an incompletely identified hero. Theodor's missing last name, which in Oldendorp's and Hildebrandt's novels suggests authenticity by omitting characters only the naive reader could think real, here underscores both Theodor's and the narrator's difficulty in coming to terms with Germany and German history. Schill's rebellion, for all it cost him and his few followers, remained a minor episode, at best an anticipatory mistake foreshadowing the great events of 1813–15, but in Theodor's eyes, even the Wars of Liberation leave less of a mark than one might expect. The hero misses that era completely while stranded on his isolated island. In *The Outlaws* there are neither names nor heroic deeds to remember; the myth of Germany's common past will have to await a different sort of book.

Near the novel's end, Theodor makes his way back to civilization, where he finds that things have returned to normal in Germany. However, normalcy has come about for what Theodor considers precisely the wrong reasons: "The terrors of those long years have disappeared, the frightful names no longer register, and little more than the memory of a dream is left from that time."[59] In fact, Alexis's novel is chiefly concerned not with the memory of heroes and heroic deeds as such, but with reflecting upon and preventing historical amnesia. Alexis is painfully aware that the difficulty lies not only in fostering remembrance but also in determining, first, what to remember and, second, what that memory will mean to future generations. And it is this pedagogical dialogue between past

CHAPTER 2

and present that lies at the heart of so much historical fiction. Writing in 1825, long before anyone knew what would happen to the cause of German unity and also before he took up the cause of Prussia actively in his "novels of the fatherland" (*Vaterländische Romane*), Alexis seems unsure about the significance of Schill and his compatriots. Perhaps the tension between remembering and forgetting, especially the remembering of mistaken, premature incidents like Schill's rebellion, accentuates their decidedly ambiguous character. This tension also underscores a wider uncertainty about Germany between 1815 and 1830—an uncertainty shared by all the writers discussed here, by most of their characters, and, presumably, by many of their readers too.

In all of these works, which I take as symptomatic of texts set in other historical periods, two lessons stand out: First, as late as 1830, the cause of national unity and national identity seems to have had precious little lasting attraction, either for aristocrats or the more chastened members of the emerging middle class. Far from being an era of nationalist consolidation, 1815–30 seems characterized by profound disillusionment with the cause of German nationalism. No common myth of what it meant to be German emerges from these novels, quite the contrary. To return to Anthony Smith's terminology: Frederick the Great's era had not yet become a heroic age for Germany; Jena had not become the symbol of Germany's decline; nor did the Wars of Liberation look like a period of nationalist regeneration. Between 1815 and 1830, people in the German territories did not yet share enough of a common past for them to feel a present sense of mission; Germany's national myths still needed considerable development.

Second, most of these novels' heroes can survive the demands that national or ethnic politics force upon them only by withdrawing to the safety of inherited positions and values. Otherwise they sink into madness and despair or are killed. Not surprisingly, cast(e)s of characters who benefited from the old order seldom opted for change and the instability implicit in the new form of social organization called the nation. Yet, although the heroes reject nationalism's demands, the nation seems to have been a critical topic for authors and readers alike. Historical novels from 1815 to 1830 staged the difficult choice between caste and region on the one hand, and national unity and ethnic solidarity on the other. These shared themes strongly suggest that German society was in a state of confusion and flux during these pivotal fifteen years. For despite the abstract appeal of the nation and national identity during the struggles against Napoleon, the narrative form these ideas possessed offered only limited potential for producing the happy endings that are the staple of popular literature. Thus, if one of the tasks of historical fiction was to articulate a unifying national myth, we see just how much construction still had to occur before a consensus version of the German past could help unite the socially, politically, and regionally disparate groups of potential Germans—Prussians, Bavarians, and Saxons; aristocrats, farmers, and workers; Protestants, Catholics, and Jews. To judge from the record of historical fiction, these groups were only gradually, sometimes reluctantly, *becoming* German during the first third of the nineteenth century. In fact, many of them apparently resisted that call and remained content with earlier forms of identity.

The Arrival of Bourgeois Heroes

Of course, Germans eventually did arrive at something akin to national consensus about the meaning of the German past, albeit with any number of agreements to disagree built into that overall framework. Therefore, without getting too far ahead of the story, let us look briefly at a novel that was published just after the others in this chapter. Ludwig Rellstab's *1812,* a bulky treatment of the Wars of Liberation, appeared in 1834.[60] In it we immediately see that something remarkable has happened to the discourse of German history and identity. The change is already apparent in the novel's first sentence: "On a mild April evening in the year 1812, Ludwig Rosen, a young German, arrived with the setting sun in the town of Duomo d'Ossola at the base of the Simplon pass."[61] One notices several differences from earlier works: First, the narrator begins by identifying his hero as a German—no questions, no hesitation. Since the village of Duomo d'Ossola is in Italy, this designation might simply record a contrast to the scene's foreign setting, but Rosen is journeying home not to Germany in general but specifically to his hometown, Dresden. Thus, in accordance with the chapter's other evidence, he could be a Saxon. However, the second defining characteristic in this sentence explains why Ludwig Rosen receives the broader label: the young man is bourgeois. Although Italy was the standard destination for eighteenth- and nineteenth-century German aristocrats on their grand tours, Rosen is not returning from such an escape, and he has no zone of retreat back in Saxony. His family owns no landed estates where aristocrats like Hermann von Manteufel could hide from history. Neither will he escape the fray on a desert island or in a villa in the

CHAPTER 2

Hudson valley, nor is Ludwig Rosen part of an international caste of noble officers, who felt more loyal to each other than to an ethnic group that existed far below them in social, cultural, and political terms. Although he could have remained a local patriot, the novel's opening lines eliminate that option, while Rosen's social status cuts off the paths of retreat that were available to the aristocratic heroes of earlier historical fiction. Unable to flee into the old world of caste and region, this novel's main character has to confront German reality with all of its tensions and ambiguities.

The entrance of the bourgeoisie into the narrative of German history allowed for the development of a truly German identity, and it is worth noting that for the rest of the century figures from the middle and lower classes play a far more prominent role in historical and other fiction than they did before. They even appear prominently in books devoted to Frederick the Great. This shift was just as fundamental as Lessing's introduction of ordinary citizens into tragic drama, where heroes had previously been princes, according to the principle that high birth was a prerequisite for a great fall. However, while Lessing's Enlightenment perspective stressed the underlying humanity of every tragic figure, the entry of the middle class into historical fiction and thus into German history represents a bizarre riff on the notion of egalitarianism. When Frederick the Great is humanized into "Old Fritz," the king himself becomes a commoner. Readers can identify with him and the new image of Germany that he represents, just as they do with Prussia's Queen Louisa, who despite her high birth, morphs into the exemplary German woman. But such humanist universalism stops at the border. The middling heroes who became so popular in historical fiction after Sir Walter Scott define themselves partly by what they are not: they are not the main characters. With Rellstab, such figures begin to be "not-aristocrats" and, simultaneously, "not-French," but they almost always also take on a starring role in novels about Germany. Authors soon conflate aristocratic and French, making these adjectives two sides of the same bad penny; in the process, they effectively eliminate characters like Hermann von Manteufel and Theodor von *** from central positions in nationalist literature. Ludwig Rosen and his brethren enable a profound shift both in historical fiction and, to a lesser degree, in popular and academic history: even when dressed in court garb, bourgeois heroes and heroines make it possible for authors to invent Germany while they are writing the nation's history.

3
From Frederick the Great to Old Fritz

Adolescent girls seem an unlikely audience for history. Even in an age when stories from the past saturated the curriculum, no one would have trusted such girls' judgment, no one except Theodor Fontane. In his 1891 novel, *Beyond Recall,* Baroness Ebba von Rosenberg, one of several ladies-in-waiting to a Danish princess, bests two male opponents in a debate over the merits of European monarchs from the past. Ebba wins by remembering another heated discussion, this one from her boarding school days, when she and some classmates tried to determine which kings and queens were the most interesting, and, by contrast, which were the most boring figures in history. Henry VIII, justly famous for his six wives, was an easy winner, followed, first, by the romantically beheaded Mary Stuart and then by a long list of French kings with their assorted mistresses. German royalty brought up the rear, while the Prussians, an otherwise illustrious subcategory, finished dead last. After all, what was there in the Great Elector's military exploits or Frederick William I's stern soldiering that might have fired the imaginations of aristocratic teenage girls? Just one king made Prussian history at all tolerable to such a demanding audience, and even then, as Baroness Ebba reports, Frederick II became interesting only after "a few women authors of genius invented half a dozen amorous adventures for the great Frederick, for no other reason than because, as they quite correctly felt, without such tales his life was impossible to tell."[1]

It now seems difficult to imagine anyone thinking of Frederick the Great as one of the world's least interesting monarchs. Ebba notwithstanding, by the middle of the nineteenth century, the austere—even dour, if also undeniably heroic—Prussian monarch had been transformed into an almost folksy, pan-Germanic father figure, "Old Fritz," whose nickname connoted endearment rather than awe. Gone, or at least diminished in the popular imagination, was the military taskmaster and general who repeatedly and brutally marched through Saxony and Silesia, much to the dismay of the local German population. Gone, too, was the philosopher-hermit of Sanssouci, who preferred speaking and writing French and seemed to care more for his dogs and horses than for his fellow Germans. In his mid- to late-nineteenth-century incarnation Old Fritz was wise and approachable, feared yet benevolent, just, and, most important, prototypically German. As tales of his virtues—and some of his vices—multiplied, Frederick the Great became anything but boring.

The change was striking, and, considering the historical record of Frederick's life, probably unwarranted. Yet, as Baroness Ebba knew, fancy is often more interesting than fact. Facts are nothing more than raw material for historians and the authors of historical fiction. Facts can be selected or rejected; writers can emphasize, embellish, or gloss over them and, in so doing, turn one-sided people from the past into the well-rounded characters of nineteenth-century fiction. Facts can also appear as a series of impersonal events—dispatches, treaties, and natural disasters—that remain distant from the undifferentiated masses of ordinary human beings, or these same occurrences can loom as opportunities for the great and powerful to influence the lives of recognizable people. Facts can even provide a background against which authors narrate the lives of men and women who resemble their readers.

Given the wide variety of choices for dealing with the events of Frederick's life, both the difficulties and the stakes involved in transforming his image are worth examining. To do so one needs to look at the works of fiction and history in which the nineteenth-century shift in Frederick's image occurred. For while it is true that collections of anecdotes about Frederick II were already circulating only a few years after his death in 1786, Theodor Schieder has shown that the Prussian monarch was anything but a popular hero in eighteenth-century Germany.[2] By the time Fontane wrote his novel, Frederick's star was waning again. With the death of William I in 1888 and his grandson William II's dismissal of Bismarck in 1890, Imperial Germany had passed its own first heroic age and mythmakers had begun substituting its first emperor and his chancellor for Frederick. For Fontane, the debate over Frederick's significance therefore concerned both the historical position his heirs would occupy and the status of historical discourse in buttressing the empire. In that context, it is worth returning to the scene with Baroness Ebba to see how Fontane stages the debate over historical significance, because Ebba, her adversaries, and their listeners represent a far larger group of Germans who were as interested in the status of history as they were in reappraising Frederick.

Ebba's claim comes near the end of a longer discussion of the past between the countess, a Danish princess, three other courtiers, and their guests. Their conversation rehearses a familiar debate over the use and abuse of history in everyday life. The argument begins when a visiting clergyman promises to explain the date 1628, which was chiseled on a stone in the palace gardens. Pastor Schleppegrell, who seems fearful of offending the princess's delicate sensibilities, claims that the stone commemorates both the year and the location where King Christian IV personally paid some laborers for work they had done on the palace. According to Schleppegrell, the king was so pleased at being able to move into the magnificently remodeled structure that he dealt with the workers himself. The pastor's audience deems the story uninteresting. Even if it were true, no one but the king would think his action deserved a monument. So Ebba demands that Schleppegrell relate an alternate explanation of the date's significance, namely, that the stone marks the time and place where King Christian got into such a bitter dispute with his mistress that she locked him out of their shared bedroom. The princess terms this second version more "intricate" or, perhaps, "delicate" (*intrikater*) and declares she is not too much of a prude to weigh its validity (168). At this point, one of the other courtiers, Count Holk von Holkenäse, interjects that the story of the mistress is trivial; it has "too small a format and is, in fact, simply too minor."[3] According to Holk, even if it were true, the anecdote would be of no use in understanding as noble a figure as King Christian. The tale is beneath a king's dignity, unworthy of his office. Holk wants to differentiate between "a private and an historical point of view"; only the latter deserves a place in a people's collective memory.[4] Here is where Ebba intervenes with her assessment of Frederick the Great. For her, the king's private life explains his public actions. Moreover, these unrecorded activities round out his image and make an otherwise merely great man intriguing. Without a look behind the scenes, Frederick and his fellow heroes remain shadows or silhouettes, uninteresting and unconnected to the lives of ordinary readers.

Ebba's position echoes that of Professor Willibald Schmidt, a sympathetic character who defends his taste for the seemingly minor events of history in another of Fontane's novels, *Frau Jenny Treibel* (1892). There, Professor Distelkamp, a high school teacher with scholarly aspirations, argues Holk's position. Distelkamp rejects not so much anecdotal evidence as anecdotes themselves, because he claims: "In history only the great counts for me, not the small, the incidental."[5] For him, Frederick II was *great,* a general and a king; his private life should remain private, not so much to eliminate possible embarrassment but to avoid detracting from what really mattered. For Schmidt, the opposite is true: "That Frederick the Great, towards the end of his days, threw his crutch at the President of the Supreme Court—I've forgotten his name—and, what's even more important to me, wanted to be buried alongside his dogs, because he despised men, this *'méchante race,'* so thoroughly—you see, my friend, that is worth at least as much to me as the Hohenfriedberg or Leuthen victories."[6] Schmidt then makes a more general point: "The incidental, that much is right, doesn't count if it is merely incidental, if there is nothing in it. But if there is something in it, then it's the main thing, because it always reveals the human essence."[7] Although Schmidt has conspicuously failed to say anything about Frederick the Great's love life, his reticence might simply be the sign of a teacher's prudery rather than principled opposition to Ebba's more extreme position. Schmidt's is also a very male standpoint; his anecdotes do not extend as far into the private sphere.

Ironically, Ebba attributes Holk's taste for the great to his heritage, because the count is a patriotic Schleswig-Holsteiner who became Prussian and then German rather than Danish after the wars of 1864, 1866, and 1871, while Ebba regards herself as "a pure Scandinavian," in other words, multinational and therefore possessed of less reason to defend the Germanic king Christian IV.[8] In fact, most of the king's ancestors were Prussians, but national origin scarcely accounts for these two characters' radically different views of history. Ebba does not just prefer intimate details; she goes so far as to praise invention—by women novelists—as a means of filling in the gaps in conventional historical accounts. One could paraphrase her argument as follows: novelists include ideas they only intuit but nevertheless find both important and interesting, while historians not only suppress what they are unable to prove, but they also omit episodes they mistakenly deem inessential. Seen in these terms, Ebba emerges as a gifted advocate for historical fiction, and her position is far more radical than Schmidt's defense of anecdote. Fontane clearly sympathizes with defenders of the anecdote and the private sphere, but Ebba's skepticism about Frederick the Great was probably a minority viewpoint, both in 1860, when the novel was set, and in 1891 when it was published. However, she is refreshingly candid about the division of labor between historians and historical novelists, as well as about the peculiar tasks that the latter group faced. Perhaps only a fictional woman could make the point so forcefully and so plausibly for lay readers.

Holk, who probably represents received opinion, not only misses the importance of personal details in Frederick's life, but more important, he also fails to see Ebba's point regarding the constructedness of the king's image. He was not alone. As the century progressed, signs of the process of reinterpreting and refurbishing the king's biography disappeared. Almost without effort, the broad outlines of Frederick's life had become part of the fund of shared knowledge in Germany; it seemed as though everyone was familiar with Old Fritz, who had evolved into Germany's favorite uncle along the way. To see how this information came to be so common and how the king's image shifted over time, we need to look both at novels like those Ebba praised and at treatments of the great king in popular and academic history. To begin, a footnote in the critical edition of *Beyond Recall* mentions two "women authors of genius," Wilhelmine Lorenz, an obscure writer who lived in Saxony between 1784 and 1861, and Louisa Mühlbach, who is already well known from chapter 1.[9] Since Mühlbach did not begin publishing her fictional biography of Frederick until 1853, Lorenz's 1846 novel, *Frederick II's Only Love*, takes precedence here.[10] It starts the journey of Frederick's transformation with an almost perfect title, albeit to a less than perfect novel.

Frederick the Great's First Love

Auguste Wilhelmine Lorenz published at least sixteen volumes of historical fiction and a memoir, mostly during the 1840s.[11] Her subject matter was diverse, ranging from the sixteenth century to the recent past, and she dealt with both German and foreign heroes. Her version of Frederick's life concentrates on a single incident, but she may well have begun what proved to be a rich genre of Frederick literature. However, *Frederick II's Only Love* is a very odd, even unsatisfying work, and those who came after Lorenz had a great deal to do before Frederick became interesting. As a pioneer, Lorenz may have been stymied by the apparent paucity of events in Frederick's life that lent themselves to a romantic imagination. It was difficult to humanize him. Frederick's marriage to Elizabeth Christine of Brunswick-Wolfenbüttel was unhappy and probably unconsummated; the king spent most of his waking hours in the company of men, and otherwise he preferred to be alone. Frederick did have favorite dogs and trusted horses, and he may have been gay, although applying that modern term to him is clearly an anachronism.[12] Unfortunately for Lorenz, none of this information was very useful for inventing what Ebba had called "amorous adventures for the great Frederick." Lorenz attempts to solve the problem by writing a novel in which Frederick barely appears. She might have better titled the book *Countess Orzelska*, after the object of her fictional Frederick's attentions, but even at this early date having "Frederick" in the title may have been as much a marketing ploy as an effort to construct a positive image of the king. Of course, these two aims are anything but mutually exclusive, and Lorenz's choice need not have been conscious.

Lorenz begins her tale by introducing Anna, Countess Orzelska, and establishing her as a suitable match for Frederick the man but an impossible object for him as Prussia's crown prince. As the daughter of Augustus the Strong, King of Poland and Elector of Saxony, an arranged, dynastic union might have been possible, except that Anna was one of the king's many illegitimate offspring, so any connection to Frederick would have been illicit.[13] It mattered little that Anna was cultured and possessed of a self-confident intellect. There could have been a meeting of minds, but romance was, at best, a secret possibility. Heirs to a throne did not marry for love, particularly not in the eighteenth century. Royal heroes and heroines of nineteenth-century novels could only dream and then pine away as a result of their romantically impossible situations. This novel claims it was love at first sight for both participants, and their exchange of ideas, furtive glances, not quite casual contact, and thinly veiled promises give readers an intimate look at Frederick before he became great.

Lorenz has the two potential lovers meet in 1728, during his father's state visit to Saxony, when Frederick was only sixteen. In Lorenz's version of events Frederick is far closer to the Saxon monarch's ostentation than to his father's austerity. Augustus, known as "the strong," never felt the need to resist his passions for women and fine living, while his Prussian counterpart, the soldier-king Frederick William I, thinks only of military drills and his joyless Calvinist faith. The fictional Anna Orzelska is the adopted daughter of a French merchant, which means that she can speak to Frederick in his preferred language. Thus, during their first meeting, the narrator reports: "In the soft tones of Anna's mother tongue, which was the common language at Augustus's court, their conversation flowed, and the more it flowed, proceeding from nature to art and literature, the more interesting it became."[14] Embarrassed by his father's coarseness, Frederick is happy that Anna cannot understand the vulgar German jests, while she is relieved to see that he turns red rather than laughs. There is a bit of tension, especially in nationalist terms, when Frederick William upbraids his son for preferring French and not appreciating the German language's "vigor and vitality" (*Saft und Kraft*, 23), but under the circumstances Frederick's choice of language seems perfectly justified. After all, he has fallen in love with a French native speaker. Moreover, since Lorenz narrates this portion of the novel from Anna's perspective, the reader sees Frederick's warmth, his charm, and his intellect firsthand. The young man's shy suffering at the hands of a domineering, often brutal father becomes understandable and positive by contrast. In the course of the narration the reader learns things about Frederick that later became hallmarks in literary representations of him as king, referring, for example, to his "fiery blue eyes" (*blaue Feueraugen*, 17). Readers also get close enough to hear Frederick's whispers and to experience what he felt at moments that had to remain outside conventional history: "Invisibly, but sweetly trembling in all his nerves, Frederick squeezed the countess's finger, which lay tenderly between his own two fingers, as was the custom when a gentleman of high standing was obliged to escort a lady."[15] This is precisely what Ebba thought Frederick's image needed, and Lorenz's treatment of the prince improves as the novel progresses.

Anna and Frederick meet the next morning in a park fronting the Elbe River, each accompanied by a single trusted friend. Conversation is difficult, but their passion for each other is obvious, despite the formal form of address that hinders its expression. Frederick tells Anna that the

CHAPTER 3

Prussian delegation is leaving that very evening, adding that he could have spent years in her company: "I have to leave you, beautiful countess, you who combine everything that flies through my fevered imagination with the glory of an angel when I think of the highest ideals of noble femininity."[16] It was an age given to sentimental expression, but in the world of the novel Frederick seems truly smitten by Anna, so charmed, in fact, that he offers her his most precious possession, a ring his favorite sister had given him, along with the following explanation: "'Say that you forgive me, that you will think of me as a friend, as . . . I dare not say more,' he said, deeply pained, 'I am the son of a king.'"[17] At first, Anna, who is just as aware of the impossibility of their situation as Frederick, is speechless, but Lorenz turns the scene from renunciation into an acceptance of duty and the promise of greater things to come. Anna tacitly accepts Frederick's inability to declare his love and tells him: "Let [the ring] be a guarantee that you will always be a noble father to your people."[18] Then she kisses him on the forehead in "pure sisterly love" (*reine Schwesterliebe*, 45) and never sees Frederick again. The scene may be sad, but the reader could scarcely ask for a better glimpse of the young prince as a passionate human being. In Lorenz's novel Frederick is not the cold fish he appears to be in some history books; he is emotional but willing to subjugate desire to his station in life and, perhaps, to the greater good of Germany. In person, Frederick does not so much contradict his public image as give it a kind of sympathetic depth. Lorenz's readers learn why he appeared so remote. If this is a first step in Frederick's transformation, it is not a bad start from an otherwise peculiar novel.

Except for a heart-rending conclusion some years later, the episode in the park ends the story of Frederick and Anna—after only forty-five pages in a nearly two-hundred-page book. Running out of plot, at least as regards the main characters, must have been a problem for Lorenz. By nineteenth-century standards *Frederick II's Only Love* is very short, but without something to fill up the space between their parting and the novel's end, Lorenz would have had little more than a novella. Hence, a tortuously complicated subplot overwhelms what should have been the main action. Anna's lady-in-waiting and trusted confidante, Michalina, falls in love with a Corsican marquis, whose German father had been betrayed by King Augustus, but rather than burden my readers with these complications, I report only that Anna has reluctantly agreed to marry the Duke of Holstein-Beck. To make a fresh start, she decides to have Michalina return Frederick's ring. The novel's narrative time has advanced only a year or two, but the Prussian prince is a changed man. Frederick's difficulties with his father have escalated to such a degree that he is already planning the ill-fated attempt to flee Prussia with his friend Katte. Michalina hands him the ring, saying: "Anna returns this token of a sacred moment to the man she will honor and bless with her last breath."[19] At first Frederick accepts the ring and Anna's declaration as "balsam for the eternally bleeding wound in his heart."[20] He then changes his mind and tells Michalina to keep the ring "as a memento of her [Anna] to whom you were so true and of me, who loved her so purely. Loved her as he can never love again."[21] Since Lorenz had mentioned his escape plans two pages earlier, Frederick's excuse sounds implausible: "A [soon to be ruling] prince can have no room for such [private] pain."[22] But Frederick could simply be both gracious and dissembling.

At this point the novel jumps forward some fifty-four years to 1784, two years before Frederick's death. He is now Frederick the Great, and "his accomplishments as well as the trials and tribulations of ruling allowed him to forget the maiden who was his first and only love."[23] But time has not made Frederick happier. The reader encounters him on the terrace of Sanssouci, where he complains to a gardener that only his dogs love him. Just then an old Polish woman appears and begs forgiveness for her rebellious son, who had participated in some nationalist revolt against Prussia. Frederick reacts in a fashion characteristic of narratives about him: "His fiery eyes rolled threateningly," but the woman is Michalina, who once again offers Frederick Anna's ring.[24] The gesture softens the curmudgeon's heart, and, recalling his only love, Frederick pardons the young man. The novel ends with him returning to Corsica, where he will eventually switch sides again to join Napoleon, further complicating Lorenz's novel. Yet, as disjointed and misfocused as *Frederick II's Only Love* might be, and although it deals more with Anna Orzelska and her circle than with Frederick, Lorenz nevertheless depicts the king in an amorous adventure. That portion of the plot seems to satisfy Ebba's demand: it makes Frederick's life easier to narrate and renders him palatable to readers who might otherwise doubt his suitability as a German hero. Lorenz may not have been a "woman author of genius," but her novel began the task of making Frederick interesting to readers who were as critical as Baroness Ebba. Others would follow Lorenz's lead with better, that is, more plausible and more intriguing, results.

CHAPTER 3

FREDERICK IN POPULAR HISTORY

Of course, not just women and not only novelists took on the task of burnishing Frederick's image. One of the more substantial efforts in that enterprise was Franz Kugler's *The History of Frederick the Great* (1840), a more than six-hundred-page work of popular history that included over four hundred illustrations by Adolph Menzel.[25] J. J. Weber, a pioneering publisher of illustrated books, hired Kugler, a young historian and sometime-novelist, to replicate the success of a French biography of Napoleon.[26] Although he was only thirty-one in 1839, when he signed the contract, Kugler suggested an even younger artist as his partner. Menzel was twenty-three when he started work on the book's pictures, but they propelled him to a long and prosperous career. The two men's assignment was to mark the hundredth anniversary of Frederick's accession to the Prussian throne in 1740 and thereby to rekindle interest in the king at about the same time as Christian Daniel Rauch began working on the equestrian statue of Frederick that still occupies a prominent place on Berlin's main street. Assessing the success of their book is difficult and depends on where and how one looks. On the one hand, the copy of the first edition in the Library of Congress is bound in half-leather, and illustrations made the book expensive. Printing technology would also have limited the number of copies available, particularly because the illustrations were woodcuts. On the other hand, the book must have circulated through lending libraries, probably in a cheaper binding, and it later went through numerous printings, including some aimed directly at "the people" (*Volksausgabe*).[27] Who "the people" were is an interesting issue, as the book appeared while such an audience was still being defined. Kugler indicates as much in an "Afterword," where he claims to be "presenting the history of a man whose name causes every Prussian citizen's heart to beat faster, [indeed] causes every German's heart to beat faster."[28] The tension between regional and national identity discussed in the previous chapter was far from being resolved, as was the tension between viewing Frederick as liberal monarch or precursor of German military prowess. In 1840 Frederick's image was still up for grabs, and it may have been Kugler and Menzel who provided both the impetus and the material for a reworking of Frederick's life by other historians and historical novelists.[29]

Scholars have made much of the book's liberal tendencies, particularly when judged by the illustrations, which contrast strikingly with imposing portraits of kings, statesmen, and generals and the monumental representations of events that were fashionable at the time.[30] Menzel selected what he considered characteristic moments rather than high points, so the book is filled with images of Frederick with his friends, soldiers, and commoners. Among them he appears as the first among equals, a natural aristocrat, who dominates without relying on the perquisites of rank: no crown, chest full of medals, or exceptional clothing. Of course, Menzel's illustrations are illusions, but they are different forms of illusion from the image that Anton von Werner created in his "Proclamation of the German Empire," where Bismarck in his white uniform dominates. This is not to say that Menzel was more accurate, although he was assiduous in tracking down clothing and locations. At issue is what his images and Kugler's text, correct or not, conveyed to readers.

One example of Menzel's low-key approach is the series of nine illustrations in the chapter "The Philosopher of Sanssouci." The first picture of Frederick shows him at dinner, seated next to Voltaire (271). The king is younger and slightly taller than his illustrious guest, but his uniform is no different from those of the others at the table. In addition, neither Frederick nor Voltaire occupies the center of the picture. Instead, the space between them is central, because it represents the location of their conversation, where intellect matters, not the speakers' presence. A few pages later, Menzel shows the two men walking on the terrace of Sanssouci (275). They are alone, without servants or retainers, and the king is obviously listening to Voltaire. Again, precedence is a matter of ability and intelligence, not rank. The final image of Frederick in this chapter puts him at the center of the composition, but not in an official role: he is playing the flute for a number of guests, including two of his sisters, his flute instructor, and the court composer. Frederick is obviously the star performer, but, uncharacteristically for the eighteenth century, the audience is a mixture of aristocrats and commoners. Frederick commands the group's attention not through his position as sovereign but rather with his skill as a musician. The images evoke earned respect rather than inherited awe. Menzel's Frederick is the enlightened ruler liberals hoped for but did not receive when his great-grandnephew Frederick William IV became king in 1840. Menzel's choice of images also comprises an implicit historiography more akin to historical fiction, with its focus on ordinary people and the private lives of the great, than to the demands of academic history.

To a certain degree Kugler's text had to contradict the book's illustrations. It was impossible to write a comprehensive biography while minimizing conquests that transformed the small, backward Prussian state into a European great power during Frederick's reign. Still, there is much humanity in Kugler's version of the king's life, even if the paucity of amorous adventures would have displeased Baroness Ebba. The single love story also involves Anna Orzelska, and Kugler's account may have been the source for Lorenz's novel. The scene is again Dresden during the state visit of 1728, and Frederick is again smitten, this time by a peculiar version of Augustus's illegitimate daughter: "She was several years older than Frederick; her beautiful body, her noble manners, the exquisite development of her intellect, her typically good moods, all combined to give her something irresistibly desirable. Not infrequently, she appeared in men's clothing, which only increased the appeal of her fascinating appearance. Frederick soon felt himself seized by smoldering passions, and his wishes did not fall on deaf ears with the countess."[31]

Among that passage's many novelistic—not to say middlebrow or even trashy—elements, one should note, first, the familiar situation of love at first sight; second, the description of the heroine's costume, a standard ingredient in the recipe of romantic fiction; and, third, the suggestion of romantic fulfillment. The image of Anna in drag might be a veiled reference to Frederick's alleged homosexuality, although the person whom Frederick follows into a darkened chamber in Menzel's illustration is very clearly a woman (42). Since she has dropped a glove, Frederick is holding her bare hand, and the passage's final line leaves little doubt about what happened. To be fair, the text also portrays Frederick as above the common sort of man. He is attracted not just to the young woman's figure but also to her noble bearing, her well-developed intellect, and her cheerful demeanor. In addition, this romantic adventure suggests that the dour misanthrope familiar from conventional history harbored, at least in his youth, the potential for love, and here we have the emotion as only novelists could imagine it. Kugler leaps beyond the evidence and, just as important, beyond the realm of politics. Except for the book's title and the author's pedigree, his account and the accompanying illustration could easily pass for historical fiction. Its aim, if I may be allowed the same freedom that Kugler employed in divining how the crown prince felt, was to humanize Frederick and to make him fascinating enough as a character for ordinary readers to persevere all the way to page 623, where the book ends. In the process they would have absorbed a great deal of factual information, and those same readers would have seen Frederick as a well-rounded, even interesting figure—Baroness Ebba notwithstanding. Readers from the whole of Germany rather than only Prussia might well have felt pity or even identified with the great king when they learned of the end of his brief affair: "Frederick wrote his first poems at this time, and they are dedicated to Countess Orzelska's charms."[32] That statement is probably verifiable, but it is the tricks of the novelist rather than the resources of the historian that make this particular section of Kugler's biography appealing.

Public events dominate the rest of the biography, but Kugler and Menzel both repeatedly depict Frederick as an ordinary human being. Kugler's preference for the name "Frederick" rather than "Frederick II," "the king," or "King Frederick" brings his central character closer to readers. Moreover, Kugler often calls Frederick "father" to his soldiers and subjects, and the king is generally less a ruler or general than a wise patriarch who listens to his putative children's complaints and helps whenever he can, often with his endearingly witty goodwill. *The History of Frederick the Great* is filled with anecdotes because, as Kugler explains, such stories "are particularly well suited to place the breadth of this rare king's character in a unique light."[33] For example, in describing the battle of Torgau, Kugler omits one of Frederick's best known remarks, uttered when he saw some reluctant recruits: "You rogues, do you want to live forever!" Instead of showing Frederick as he bullied a few cowards into action, Kugler tells how the king came upon a sleeping general and refused to have him awakened, because he knew the man was exhausted (454–55). Frederick must have been just as tired, for he too sits down at the fire, pulls his cloak up around his face, and then watches as a soldier's wife puts some potatoes into the ashes to cook. She makes such a commotion that a nearby soldier, recognizing the king, sends her packing. But Frederick has the woman brought back to finish the job. According to Kugler, such actions produced an unusual familiarity between Frederick and his soldiers: "His usual morning greeting was 'Good day, children!' to which they always replied: 'Good day, Fritz!'" "All his soldiers liked to address him using just his first name, 'Fritz,' or, adding an affectionate adjective, as 'Old Fritz.'"[34]

Quite aside from their truth, it was these personalized tales, not depictions of battles or reports on the terms of treaties, that gave people more and more suitable material that they could use to fashion their own private versions of Frederick's life and German history. Obviously—and there is no reason to doubt Kugler here—the transition

CHAPTER 3

from Frederick the Great to Old Fritz had begun among his soldiers, long before nationalists turned Frederick II, King of Prussia, into a pan-Germanic hero. Unfortunately, documenting any such change as a hard fact rather than a discursive possibility would mean estimating how widespread Frederick's nicknames were at any given point. However, not only is there no survey data, but anecdotes about Frederick the benevolent Prussian also had to compete with contrary images—for example, Ludwig Pfau's anti-Prussian "Baden Lullaby" of 1849, whose refrain is: "Sleep, my child, sleep quietly / The Prussians are outside."[35] Even Frederick's positive reputation could not prevent Prussia from appearing as the bogeyman when its soldiers were busily rounding up radicals after the unsuccessful Revolution of 1848. In addition, the image of Prussian press gangs had long been used to shock children and frighten vulnerable young men.

Kugler, by contrast, saw Germany's future as Prussia's mission. While his position was not unusual, it was anything but universal either in 1840 or later. Kugler seems aware of the difficulties involved in unifying the diverse group of states, peoples, and interests in the existing German territories, and he wants to play some role in the enterprise. Thus, he links Frederick's victory at Katzbach in 1760 to events fifty-three years later in 1813, when a victory over Napoleon on the same battlefield marked a stage in what Kugler calls the "triumphal salvation of Prussia and Germany"—as if Frederick's battles were ultimately part of a grand Prussian plan to unite Germany.[36] Kugler's claim appears impossibly prescient in 1842, almost thirty years before German unification's realization under Bismarck and Emperor William I, but Kugler's contemporaries—namely, the prominent historians of the so-called small-German school, Gustav Droysen, Theodor Mommsen, Heinrich von Treitschke, and Heinrich von Sybel—all looked to Prussia to solve the problem of German unity by excluding multinational Austria.[37] This was particularly true after the failure of 1848, when uprisings in Austria's Hungarian, Polish, and Italian territories undermined the Hapsburg claim on leadership in Germany. Still, if Prussia were to play a special role in Germany, Frederick's image as an exemplary hero would have to spread beyond the borders of his homeland.

The chief difficulty in using Frederick to posit a national mission for Prussia was his status in the rest of Germany. Not only had he waged most of his campaigns against Austria, but Frederick also fought against Saxony and various other German states. As a result, Kugler frequently had to use care in what he chose to emphasize. For example, his account of Frederick's victory at Roßbach in 1757 deals more with the rout of the French than with the equally devastating defeat of the German Imperial Army. Kugler reports that Frederick himself was more troubled by the French loss, but he also speaks of "almost universal celebration" in Germany "even in the ranks of Frederick's enemies": "From that moment on, the fire of enthusiasm for this German hero, which had been tended quietly, burst into powerful flames. . . . Germans finally felt proud again to be called Germans."[38] Later, after Frederick's intervention in the War of Bavarian Succession in 1778–79, even Catholic southern Germans supposedly hung his portrait next to images of Bavaria's patron saint; Menzel's illustration, evoking a peasant household, shows a rosary dangling from the Protestant king's picture (565).[39] Clearly, something was happening to representations of Frederick. By relating facts and legends about Frederick's life to readers who never encountered the king personally, Kugler and Menzel took another step in the direction of shared history. At some level Germans who came to regard Frederick as part of their own history, and who remembered something about his life from reading this or another biography, implicitly thought of themselves as belonging to a single collective entity. They were becoming more German and less the inhabitants of disparate and diverse villages, towns, or mini-states.

This is not to say that millions of people read and retained details from Kugler's and Menzel's book, but tens of thousands certainly did. Over the course of the century the book went through dozens of editions at various prices, from various publishers, and with reproductions of Menzel's illustrations of various qualities.[40] Today the book's six hundred pages seem daunting, but since nineteenth-century historians and novelists needed hundreds of pages just to warm up, the Kugler-Menzel biography was not particularly long. Multivolume works were the norm, and *The History of Frederick the Great* had the significant advantage of its nearly four hundred arresting and well-integrated woodcuts. It is also an easy read. Whether by design or circumstance, Kugler and Menzel caught the tenor of their times. They may even have set off an expansion of literature about Frederick in a way that drier accounts by earlier historians—J. D. E. Preuß, Friedrich Förster, and Carl Friedrich Köppen—failed to do.[41]

Even though the vast majority of Kugler's text concentrates on Frederick as hero and military genius, the overall impression that he and

CHAPTER 3

Menzel leave behind is the king as fallible mortal, a man whose first interest was protecting his subjects from poverty, injustice, and external threats to their livelihood. For all the great king's flaws, Kugler and Menzel's Frederick appeals to the German peoples he fought and to the Prussians whose forebears he conscripted and taxed. Turning Frederick into the protector of those he oppressed was a neat trick, and the shift in the king's image that Kugler and Menzel signal enabled historical novelists to take up the nationalist challenge and make Frederick even more human and more popular.

MÜHLBACH'S FREDERICK OPUS

One of the most prodigious laborers in the field of Frederick's image was Louisa Mühlbach. We already know that she wrote with remarkable energy—and at almost unbelievable length—and no one, particularly not the successful commercial publishers Janke and Costenoble, would have printed so much of Mühlbach's *Frederick* if it had not sold. Her version of his life helped make Mühlbach the most popular German writer of the second half of the nineteenth century, and since sales were often to private, for-profit lending libraries, Mühlbach's works reached an extraordinarily large audience. Her Frederick opus began appearing in 1853, with the publication of three volumes titled *Frederick the Great and His Court;* it continued with *Berlin and Sans-Souci, or Frederick the Great and His Friends,* at four volumes, in 1854; and the three volumes of *Frederick the Great and His Family* followed in 1855. During 1867–68, the first four volumes of her *Germany in Storm and Stress,* which bore the subtitle *Old Fritz and His Era,* almost finished her fictional biography of the king, but Mühlbach's Frederick does not finally die until the first volume of her next series, *Goethe and Schiller: An Historical Romance.* In addition, Mühlbach wrote short stories, sketches, and anecdotes devoted to Frederick. In all, her account of Frederick's life and times comprises at least fifteen volumes and nearly four thousand pages. Having produced so much, Mühlbach could take credit for some of Frederick's popularity, but she could popularize him only because her version of the king's life answered a larger need for approachable German heroes.

Frederick the Great and His Court begins with preparations for a royal ball, which neither the king, Frederick William I, nor Crown Prince Frederick plan to attend. The king is ill, and the prince is at his palace in Rheinsberg, blissfully free from both the concerns of the

Prussian state and the court's empty ceremonies. Far from his father, Frederick has license to play the flute and read. The novel's opening scene instead revolves around the queen, who, in the absence of her odious husband, is also free—in this case to wear the royal jewels and behave like any other royal spouse preparing to attend a ball. As the narrator puts it, "a queen is still a woman [*Weib*]."[42] While recognizing how utterly normal, and therefore understandable, the queen's desires are, the narrative voice in the German original is also quite critical of her inherited position. Indeed, the narrator seems upset by both hereditary rulers and their wealth, represented by the queen's diamonds: "It was indeed royal jewelry. [It represented] millions of dollars spending their days without earning interest and able to gaze idly and contemptuously at the sweaty masses who struggled to secure a poor, worrisome, and oppressed existence. Sophia Dorothea didn't think about it."[43]

A few pages later the narrator switches sides again, and the reader sees the negative consequences of high birth. Although the queen is free to be a woman at the ball, her freedom lasts only a few hours. Meanwhile, Frederick's two sisters are also aware of the limitations under which they live. The younger of the two, Princess Amelia, declares that she "would rather wed the poorest and most obscure man, if I loved him, than the richest and greatest king's son, to whom I was indifferent."[44] Her unrequited love for one of Frederick's officers occupies a significant portion of the next few volumes of the novel, along with Prince Augustus William's similarly hopeless love for a lady-in-waiting to the queen. Their older sister, Princess (Wilhelmina) Ulrica, would like nothing more than a propitious marriage, but she is cynical enough to recognize how little control she has over her fate: "Are we not born to be handled like a piece of goods, and knocked down to the highest bidder?"[45] The novel also portrays Frederick as both victim and victimizer in his own loveless marriage, but before examining that more complicated situation, a few minor figures warrant our attention.

Before Frederick even appears, the reader meets Fritz Wendel, one of the gardeners at Rheinsberg and a character for whom there is almost certainly no historical documentation. At least by one definition Wendel makes the novel more realistic, but he is not simply a fictional representative of the common people surrounding the crown prince. His situation parallels that of Ulrica and Augustus William, who did exist. According to Mühlbach, Wendel is in love with a noblewoman who reciprocates his illicit attentions. Moreover, all three love affairs mirror

CHAPTER 3

bourgeois relationships represented in canonical literature at least since 1774, when Goethe published his *Werther*. By the nineteenth century much of society regarded emotional bonding in a companionate marriage as the norm, albeit without the political and social consequences that Enlightenment theorists had hoped for. However, as broad-minded as Frederick might otherwise have been, Mühlbach's version of him still regarded the heart as a subversive element, so he keeps these couples apart at great cost. At their brother's insistence both Augustus William and Ulrica eventually marry for political reasons, while Fritz Wendel lands in prison for his affront to the nobility's dignity, which was all the more egregious because he tried to win Frederick's approval for his own relationship by betraying Augustus William. All of these affairs show how the nobility suffered from the same personal problems as those endured by ordinary mortals. In fact, highborn individuals in novels are not infrequently worse off as a result of their status, whereas commoners endure innumerable difficulties because of their superior's actions. To be sure, the problems Fritz Wendel might have experienced in one of Frederick's military campaigns were worse than his frustrated romance, but crossing the great king in private was no blessing.

Not that Frederick lived a wonderful life—quite the contrary—and Mühlbach shows him trapped in a situation that he only gradually accepts. Frederick's first appearance in the novel comes when he learns that a publisher has agreed to print his *Anti-Machiavelli*. The news arrives while his father is still living, that is, while the crown prince is free of other responsibilities. Frederick rejoices at what the book means for his self-image, which gives the reader a glimpse of both his emotions and values: "I shall no longer be unknown, or only known as the son of a king, the inheritor of a throne. I shall have a name. I shall acquire renown, for I will be a poet, an author, and shall claim a place in the republic of genius. I shall not need a crown to preserve my name in history."[46] Unfortunately for Frederick, his idyllic life changes quickly once he accedes to the throne. As king, Frederick no longer has time to play the flute; he must work incessantly as "the first servant, the first worker, and the first administrator of a people and a country."[47] The quotation elaborates one of Frederick's most memorable phrases, as does the final sentence in the first volume of *Frederick the Great and His Court*: "In Prussia each man shall be saved in his own way" (*muß ein Jeder nach seiner Façon selig werden*).[48] The only exceptions are Frederick himself, his friends, his family, most of his courtiers, servants and soldiers, and, eventually, a considerable number of central Europeans, once the new king launches the series of internecine wars that followed Prussia's first seizure of Silesia in 1740. As a historical novelist, Mühlbach seeks to chart this mixture of public and private anguish, but she invariably focuses on people rather than events.

The struggle to wrest Silesia from Austrian control allows her to raise the issue of German nationalism, while she simultaneously personalizes the consequences of the extended conflict it entailed. On the one hand, Mühlbach uses these wars to show how beloved Frederick was among his troops—for example, after the battle of Sohr in 1745. The Austrian army has plundered the Prussian supply train, and besides losing his books and his favorite dog, Frederick faces a hungry night without so much as a crust of bread. The officers who try to buy a loaf from a more fortunate soldier are rebuffed until the man learns they want his food for the king. He then divides the loaf in two and says, "I will give you half of my bread, that is really all I can do for the king."[49] Significantly, Frederick receives nourishment from an admirer similar to the book's readers, who might imagine themselves ready to perform the same noble sacrifice. On the other hand, Frederick's wife learns she lost one brother who fought in Frederick's army, while another was severely wounded fighting on the Austrian side in the same battle. The narrator uses the anomaly to draw attention to contradictions in Frederick's meaning for Germany: "The Prussians have gained the day, but it was a fearful victory, a murderous battle between brothers, German against German, brother against brother. . . . Poor Queen Elizabeth Christine, your husband has conquered, but you have both paid dearly for the victory. . . . His is the fame and honor. You, poor queen, you have only a new grief. Yours are the tears and the pain."[50] Mühlbach's mid-nineteenth-century Frederick is well on his way to becoming the kind of integrative figure that the historical king could not have been during his lifetime, but he has not yet arrived.

Since Mühlbach begins her narration of Frederick's life in the early 1730s, Countess Orzelska is absent from this version of his biography. However, Mühlbach either invented or embellished several amorous adventures for readers with Baroness Ebba's tastes. The first combines an insignificant courtesan, Madame von Morien, a series of intrigues related to Crown Prince Frederick's nearly constant need for money, and his difficulties in relating to his new wife. Although Frederick appears to pursue a life of pleasure in Rheinsberg, his father is unwilling to finance the

CHAPTER 3

parties, concerts, and plays that are the main occupations at the prince's court. Frederick is actually not short of money, as "loans" are pouring in. England, Russia, Austria, and a few private bankers all hope to curry favor with the man who will soon ascend the Prussian throne. Mühlbach sets the scene by introducing the spies and agents of the various "lenders," chronicling at least three other illicit love affairs, some with political consequences, and including regular bulletins about the king's health, that is, about the prospects for a speedy change of rulers. At the same time, she gives her readers their first glimpse of Frederick's character. Although the Austrians hear from their spies that he "loved his flute alone," they suspect that Elizabeth will not become queen, that Frederick will leave her for Madame von Morien once his father dies.[51] As Frederick's supposed lover, Morien becomes a key player, and her relationship with the young prince reveals Frederick's values: his sense of loyalty and propriety, his style of government and finance, and, most important, his future priorities. In an era of dynastic politics, the personal is anything but trivial; it is not just a sop thrown to women readers.

Meanwhile, the action shifts for a moment to an encounter between Frederick and an elderly Jew named Ephraim, probably Veitel Heine Ephraim (1703–75), the court jeweler who later helped Frederick finance his wars by debasing the currency. Ephraim demands immediate repayment of a substantial, long overdue loan. At first, the prince tries to bluff the moneylender into an extension, but upon hearing that the man needs capital for his business, Frederick relents. Ephraim, seeing that Frederick is not about to cheat him, also backs off, but he does accept some money that has just arrived from St. Petersburg. The scene is worth noting because both men, prince and Jew, play their roles nobly. In an age when readers would scarcely have been shocked by a burst of anti-Semitism, Mühlbach's account might have come as something of a surprise:

> Ephraim bowed silently, and turned slowly toward the door. The eyes of the prince followed him with a kindly expression. He stepped to the table, and took up his flute. Ephraim had reached the door of the antechamber, but when he heard the soft melting tones of the flute, he stopped, and remained listening breathlessly at the outer door. The piercing glance of the prince rested on him; but he continued to play and drew from his flute such touching and melancholy

tones that the poor Jew seemed completely overcome. He folded his hands, as though engaged in fervent prayer.[52]

Beyond Ephraim's honesty and humanity, proven because music moves him, the exchange also shows him speaking standard German rather than the ungrammatical pidgin that frequently constituted Jews' speech in nineteenth-century fiction. And Ephraim's statements, filled as they are with Enlightenment idealism, are almost as remarkable for their unaccustomed, easily overlooked eloquence as for the ideas they contain: "'My prince,' said he, 'I am a Jew, that is to say a despised, reviled, and persecuted man! no—not a man, but a creature—kicked like a dog when poor and suffering, and even when the possessor of gold and treasures, scarcely allowed human rights. It is better for the dogs than for the Jews in Prussia!'"[53] No wonder Frederick embraces religious tolerance.

Having paid this particular debt, the prince decides it is time to forget "the burdens, the gravities and cares of life! Come, now, spirit of love! spirit of bliss!"[54] The object of this outburst is "the little Morien, that fluttering, light gazelle, that imperious, laughing fairy—that *Tourbillon* [whirlwind] of caprice and passion."[55] His only obstacle is Princess Elizabeth Christine, who loves her husband with secret passion but also suspects there is "an impassable gulf between them."[56] Frederick married her to mitigate the punishment his father had decreed after a failed attempt to escape the old man's tyranny. In Mühlbach's portrayal of the situation, Frederick never returns his wife's affections, no matter how deserving she may be. At best, Frederick is courteous but distant; he seems to believe that Elizabeth is just as constrained by the circumstances of their union as he is. In fact, this inability to see his wife's true feelings is one of Frederick's few weaknesses, but in Mühlbach's version of his life Frederick is not without emotions. As Morien reports: "He secretly presses my hand; he occasionally whispers a few loving, tender words in my ear; and yesterday, when I met him accidentally in the dark corridor, he embraced me so passionately, and covered my lips with such glowing stormy kisses, that I was almost stifled."[57] The passage is not quite up to the standards of Harlequin romances, but had Baroness Ebba and her friends read the English version, they would have been shocked by its directness, especially by its beginning: "It is true that he makes love to me" (82).

In the German original Frederick only courts Morien (*"Er macht mir den Hof,"* 1: 111), with whom he hopes to spend the evening danc-

CHAPTER 3

ing. However, just as the ball is about to begin, Frederick receives word that his father is near death, so he hurries off to Berlin. Two days later, the court at Rheinsberg learns that Prince Frederick has become King Frederick II, and everyone, including Morien, expects a reward. Indeed, they plan to live in an entirely different moral and political universe, one filled with theater, song, and art, but without Frederick William I's tight grip on the royal purse strings. They will be sadly disappointed. Frederick does not divorce Elizabeth, and in the middle of a masquerade staged for the sole purpose of deceiving the Austrian ambassador, the new king departs for war in Silesia. While others thought that he was simply amusing himself, Frederick had actually been planning a surprise campaign: "All was foreseen, all prepared, and we have not but to put in execution the plans that have for some time been agitating my brain."[58] He now seeks a very different sort of fame than that connected with mere authorship, and he also recognizes its cost: "Princes are condemned to live solitary and joyless lives."[59] Mühlbach's Frederick is very much the state's first servant; for him duty always comes before pleasure. Thus, while she includes the episode involving Madame von Morien and a much longer affair with the dancer Barbarina, Mühlbach relies primarily on means other than romance to make Frederick attractive to her readers.

Like Kugler, Mühlbach frequently turns to anecdotes that both idealize and humanize the monarch. For example, in a novella titled simply "Old Fritz," she depicts the elderly king as someone who has come to terms with his own mortality.[60] Frederick reluctantly realizes that "an old man can no longer play the flute," but he can still rule with paternalistic benevolence.[61] This version of the king turns him into a symbol for an old order that promises hope and stability once men who share Frederick's values finally unite Germany. Whatever sympathies Mühlbach might have had for "Young German" liberalism in her pre-1845 novels, these ideals seem to have disappeared from passages such as the following: "I am here to listen to the complaints and grievances of my subjects and to help them whenever possible."[62] By 1865, and probably a lot sooner, she must have come to trust the ruler who would become Emperor William I—or noticed where the money was.

In fact, Mühlbach's fictional Frederick does not have to listen at all. So insightful and penetrating is his gaze that the supplicants in the novella relate their stories only for the reader's benefit. Once again Frederick's eyes characterize him, providing a window to his soul: "The king fixed his eagle eyes on the face of [his adjutant], and a friendly smile flew over his features."[63] When a palace official from Breslau shows the king how he intends to house the royal family, Frederick studies the man's plan "with an examining [*prüfendem*] eye" (14). Then, dissatisfied with what he sees, "The king's fiery eyes aimed their flaming bolt at the chamberlain's face."[64] Later, a young woman too impoverished to marry an equally poor junior officer implores Frederick for help. The narrator twice mentions the king's "large blue eyes" and his "gaze," which is at once "firm" and "mild," and the reader knows that Frederick will give the deserving woman a dowry.[65] He will not, however, be fooled by an exceedingly vain man whom he tricks into accepting the coveted title of privy councilor on condition that he never use it in public. Mühlbach's Frederick has become an almost fairy-tale monarch and folk hero, characterized by his wise, nearly omniscient insight.[66] The values he represents coincide with those of the ordinary people who occupy the margins of Frederick's charmed world, while these same beliefs promise a conservative utopia to the books' readers. If the love interest falters in Mühlbach's magnum opus, its replacement is no less useful in transforming a stern and distant Frederick II into a far more lovable Old Fritz.

Frederick Goes A'Courting (and Stops Being French)

Of course, as Kugler and Menzel have already shown, it was not just "women authors of genius" who made King Frederick more interesting by depicting his amorous adventures. Males were just as capable of producing romantic fluff. Indeed, in 1857 Julius Bacher published *Frederick the Great's Search for a Wife*, one of the strangest contributions to the genre by any author.[67] In this account the heroic King Frederick the Great is not yet a distant possibility. Instead, Bacher relates a tale of domestic bliss that utterly contradicts Frederick's biography while remaining completely consistent with the project of turning him into an approachable, even ordinary human being. To be sure, Prince Frederick still occupies a privileged world, but the novel transports him to a thoroughly bourgeois drama of family conflict. Again, the issue is not quality or accuracy. What interests me here is how malleable Frederick's image had become and the consequences I can infer from what the author chose to emphasize. Bacher raises the stakes by portraying Frederick not simply as a man in love but also as an exemplar of new,

CHAPTER 3

and for Frederick, incongruously bourgeois characteristics that the text deems explicitly German. It remains difficult to decide which of Bacher's inventions was more daring.

The narrative begins with its central figure in Kustrin, the northern city to which the young Prince Frederick was banished after his ill-fated attempt to flee his father's harsh regimen. By starting the plot after Frederick's flight, Bacher actually minimizes the struggle between father and son, while also allowing King Frederick William I to define their conflict in terms of national identity rather than personal failings: "As long as those confounded French ideas are rattling around in the prince's head, . . . nothing good can come of him. The most important thing is that he become German, that he enjoy hunting and a hearty peasant meal."[68] The king's ranting continues for the next few pages, where he reproduces many nineteenth-century prejudices about both the Germans and the French. And the king's manner is just as revealing as what he says. Almost invariably he mentions only one term of the opposition, because Bacher can assume his readers will fill in the missing element, at least subconsciously. For example, in Frederick William's opinion Germans are "sturdy," "manly," "orderly," and "natural" in the sense that they love "forests and fields," which makes the French weak, feminine, wasteful, and interested mainly in urban pleasures.[69] Similarly, he calls the French "slippery" and "dishonest" and accuses them of being "ready to steal a person's faith," so, by contrast, Germans must be trustworthy and steadfast in their religious views.[70] When Frederick William learns his son has been baiting wild boars, he is pleased because the activity shows Frederick "has realized that Germans' essential nature is better" than that of the French.[71] Frederick's conversion from Francophile to stalwart German makes reconciliation between father and son possible. Frederick can resume his position as crown prince and marry a princess suitable to his station and to his father's dynastic interests. Everyone is happy and the book could end, but without a more careful reading one could easily miss what is really happening here.

Since the novel accomplishes Frederick's transformation from a French sissy into a solidly German and resolutely male hero in fewer than three dozen pages, it is safe to assume that he will be involved in a variety of plot twists and turns before marrying the princess. But instead of chronicling that story or simply turning to the last page and its happy ending, let me consider how this novel defines its characters. What I would like to call the nationalist identification in Bacher's text is a particularly obvious example of a narrative strategy employed by many nineteenth-century historical narratives, both fictional and nonfictional. The process works at two levels: First, the portrayal of a sympathetic character such as Prince Frederick draws people into the text so deeply that they share his hopes and fears. Readers come to care about what happens to Frederick and, in so doing, they take on his identity while reading the novel. In other words, readers *identify with* the protagonist, who, in the case of Frederick the Great, happens to be both a national hero and a national exemplar. Second, characters such as Frederick are formed from traits that not only define them as individuals but that also *identify* both the nation and its enemies. Indeed, the one demands the other or, as recent theory would have it, the "Other," a label that suggests fundamental and irreconcilable difference. In historical terms, as Michael Jeismann argues in his analysis of Franco-German antagonism from the French Revolution to World War I, "national self-understanding necessarily implies separation and opposition [*Abgrenzung* and *Entgegensetzung*]," and early on, German nationalists focused on the French as their chief foil.[72]

In the discursive universe in which he operated it is no accident that Bacher constructs Frederick as a German through his being increasingly not-French, while he characterizes the French not simply by what they are but rather by what makes them not-German. The contrast strengthens and fleshes out the meaning of both halves of any semantic pair; it adds a contrary reflection of the first element to the qualities of the second. Thus, what Bacher means by "sturdy" becomes clearer when *not* "slippery and dishonest" are added to the first word's connotative field. And more important than the narrative economy that an author achieves with this shorthand is the effect of promoting intragroup unity where there might otherwise have been diversity. There is only one "us" when "we" come into existence, which "we" do mainly through our opposition to "them." In other words, although one could, in theory, define Germans by their shared beliefs and behaviors, it is easier and less divisive to turn them into a cohesive group by identifying what they are not. In such a scheme Germans may not all be Protestants or boar-baiters, but no true German is weak, feminine, or godless—those are French traits. Germans, without it being necessary to say so explicitly, are united by their strength, masculinity, and faith. The latter can then safely seem to be simply Christian, undifferentiated except in Germans' opposition to French atheism. Of course, religious antagonism remained powerful in Germany throughout the nineteenth century, but if Germans were to coalesce into a single people, religion would have to become less of a defining characteristic. Thus, to the extent that Bacher and others could contrast German beliefs with French questioning of religious values during the Enlightenment and the Revolution, they could elide the split between Protestants and Catholics in Germany. Similarly, in representations of Frederick and, in the next two chapters, in portrayals of Germany's decline and rebirth, the French represent more than the nation's real enemies on some battlefield. Their values, especially when espoused by potential Germans, signify what went wrong after Frederick's reign and what would have to change in order to achieve national renewal, which makes it all the more important for authors to make sure that Frederick himself was thoroughly German, whatever that may have meant in particular circumstances.

At this level, Bacher's novel deals with Frederick II only tangentially. The norms and values that clash here add a psychological dimension that transcends any German longing for beer and forests or French preference for haute cuisine and cities. For Frederick William I, as Bacher portrays him, the French simply enjoy themselves too much: they eat too well, dress too fashionably, and think too deeply. He deems their behavior unnatural and excessive; he also hates them for it. As Slavoj Žižek explains the same feature of modern nationalism: "The hatred of the Other is the hatred of our own excess of enjoyment."[73] In other words, Frederick William I combines dishonesty with envy; he couples a denial of his own vices with a belief that others are getting away with sins he either has committed or would like to commit. In this light, an otherwise insignificant incident in Bacher's novel warrants a closer look for what it says about the process of national identification. The scene involves the king's decision to close Berlin's taverns at 9:00 P.M. so that workers will not be hung over the next morning. This logical if also excessive order prompts a tavern keeper's daughter to ask the king how he and his ministers can drink until after midnight and still carry out the state's business the following day. The woman's fearless Berlin lip lets her declare not only that the emperor has no clothes but also that he resents the Other's finery. Frederick William I's order dramatizes an inability to control his own desires.

In fact, desire and loathing often go hand in hand, as do difference and similarity. Thus, as Bacher's novel makes clear, the French were not simply other than the Germans but rather, to use Anne Norton's term, "liminal": "The recognition of the liminal marks the conscious differentiation of the self and other, the body politic from other's bodies politic. The differentiation of subject and object, self and other, requires both an object of likeness and object of difference. Liminars provide an object that is like, though demonstrably other than, the subject. They thus provide an object with which the subject can identify even as it differentiates itself."[74] The attraction and danger of Frederick the Great for chroniclers of his life lay in the fact that he was simultaneously French and not-French, German and not-German. Just as revolutionary France served both as a model to Stein, Hardenberg, and the other Prussian reformers and as the hated enemy whose enviable military success resulted from the very modernization that they feared, so too was Frederick complex and open to widely varied depictions. As the king of Prussia and known Francophile, Frederick was utterly different from his subjects and their descendants, while as Old Fritz (or, for Bacher, as Young Fritz) he was becoming both more familiar and more similar to the readers of works about him. His usefulness as a figure in literature and history lay in his letting authors and their readers think through variations in German identities, which means that the stakes were actually high in what might otherwise seem to be trivial depictions of his tastes.

For Frederick to function as a national hero, every writer who dealt with him had to take on his relationship to things French. Kugler, for example, excuses the king's preference for French literature by claiming that French drama, verse, and prose had reached their highest peak of sophistication during Frederick's formative years, while "German literature at that time was at the lowest level of degeneracy."[75] In other words, Frederick's tastes were more astute than French. In Mühlbach's first Frederick novel King Frederick William I decries "this sentimental boy, this hero of fashion, who adorned himself like a French fop,"[76] but by his actions—for example, by leaving the masquerade to invade Silesia—Frederick proves his German mettle. In Bacher's novel, Frederick William calls his son's attempted flight from family and duty an aberration; "too much French foolishness misled him into various stupid acts."[77] Frederick redeems himself in his father's eyes by consenting to a suitably German marriage. Had Frederick not begun by being French, these excuses, transitions, and transformations could not have served so well in clarifying what it meant to be German. To authors engaged in the project of narrating a national identity, Frederick's ambiguity turned out to be not so much a problem as an opportunity. It is a process that will shift into overdrive in descriptions of Prussia's Queen Louisa in chapter 4.

Meanwhile, back in Kustrin—and back in Bacher's novel—young Prince Frederick has heard about his father's choice of a daughter-in-law, the very German Princess Elizabeth Christine of Brunswick-Wolfenbüttel. However, the queen, who favors a match with an English princess, has arranged for Frederick to receive an unflattering portrait of his intended bride, and the potential for conflict between father and son escalates on the basis of a rumor that Elizabeth Christine is as dumb as she is ugly. Frederick wants to see for himself, so he decides, against his father's express prohibitions, to travel incognito to Berlin to have a look. At this point the tavern keeper's daughter, who loves a poor but loyal soldier, recognizes the crown prince, but rather than betray him, she and her intended husband help at crucial moments, for which Frederick later rewards them. These plot developments illustrate how historical novels show great people or momentous events affecting the lives of ordinary mortals and, conversely, how the common people can affect history. Besides augmenting more scholarly accounts of the past, such figures have the additional advantage of being closer to readers than the powerful—even when otherwise distant figures like Prince Frederick experience familiar personal travails.

The key scene in Bacher's novel has Frederick secretly listening in as Princess Elizabeth explains to her lady-in-waiting what she has done in an effort to please her prospective husband, whose reputation as an intellectual and a bon vivant preceded him to the court of Brunswick-Wolfenbüttel. The young woman has read French literature, learned to play the harp, and taken dancing lessons, but she still worries about her shy nature. Elizabeth need not be concerned, because Frederick, hidden in the next room, hears her confession, "is completely taken by the princess's inner worth," and wants to see what she looks like. He is barely disappointed: "The individual features of her face did not reveal much intelligence and spirit, and they could not be deemed particularly beautiful, nevertheless, the overall impression that her appearance made was quite pleasant."[78] Elizabeth, as Frederick decides, is good enough to accept in exchange for his father's forgiveness.

Actually, the scene is wildly implausible and almost certainly an invention, but it nevertheless shows what popular historical novels can reveal about the discourse of history and identity formation in nineteenth-century Germany. One sees how difficult it was for writers to maintain the semblance of veracity that historical novels demand while simultaneously inventing amorous adventures for Frederick II.[79] Bacher solves the problem by ending his novel as the king presents the happy couple to her parents, the court at Potsdam, and the queen, whom he has decisively outsmarted in the selection of a mate for the crown prince. The book's final image extends only to premarital domestic bliss, including that of the tavern keeper's daughter and her soldier fiancé, whose dereliction of duty is forgiven in the interest of true love—both his and Frederick's. The reader assumes this happiness continues, even though the facts of Frederick's life tell a contrary story. The two couples' relationships, told in tandem, are roughly parallel; linking Frederick's courtship to the lowliest of his future subjects, with whom the crown prince easily interacts, makes him approachable. Through his supposedly companionate marriage Frederick also becomes more German than French and, just as important and part of the same overall image, more bourgeois than aristocratic.

Bacher even manages to reclaim the tyrannical Frederick William I as an appropriate German father figure, in as much as the novel justifies the harsh punishment his son received in nationalist terms. As the king explains: "I want him to become an authentic [*ächter*] German prince, so I am giving him time in Kustrin to gather his wits."[80] At this point, an odd coda seems to contradict the reconciliation between father and son. The novel concludes by reporting that Frederick remained in Rheinsberg instead of returning to Berlin, and Rheinsberg was where the crown prince read philosophy, enjoyed the theater, and played the flute. However, as far as Bacher's reader knows, the prince's life in the countryside was happily domestic. Perhaps Frederick was secretly drinking beer, eating sausages, and fathering children. Of course he wasn't, but such an odd and historically impossible conclusion fits Bacher's Frederick perfectly, and the book's implied happy end certainly makes its "Young Fritz" attractive to the widest possible audience. It even won the approval of the court, which permitted Bacher to turn his novel into a play that was performed in Berlin.[81] In 1857, when the book appeared, public portrayals of the royal family needed the explicit permission of the king, which suggests that the royal family was also interested in using Frederick's image for its own purposes.

CHAPTER 3

Frederick the Great for Adolescent Boys

Children's literature was another genre that expanded the audience for books about Frederick. While that fact now seems unremarkable, segmenting the marketplace for literature by age is a relatively new phenomenon. The first children's books appeared in Germany near the end of the eighteenth century, and there is still considerable confusion about who read them. Franz Otto [Spamer's] *The Great King and His Recruit* (1865) shows why: the book's subtitle reads, in part, *Adapted for the People and the Army, Particularly for Adolescents*.[82] Spamer may have mixed his categories because he thought children and the unwashed masses had achieved roughly the same level of literacy; he simply attempted to pitch Frederick to as broad a readership as possible. He must have known how such books sold, because during the period 1860–80 Spamer was the most successful purveyor of adolescent literature in the German-speaking world. His Youth and Home Library series contained another Frederick novel, set during the prince's boyhood, *The Tobacco College and the Age of the Powdered Wig*, while his Illustrated Adolescent Home Library, which leaned toward nonfiction, included a volume titled *The Old Fritz Book,* intended, according to the subtitle, *For Adolescents and the People*.[83] One need not examine all of this material to see how Spamer treated Frederick, but to appreciate what had changed in the world of children's literature in the intervening fifty years, we need to return briefly to Pastor Wilmsen's *Brandenburg Children's Companion* (1815).

Wilmsen devoted eleven pages (239–49) of his forty-one-page history of Brandenburg to Frederick. No one else receives as much coverage, but in Wilmsen's version of his life the great king is little more than a stick figure. Rather than showing character in a manner that might have appealed to its young readers, the text summarizes facts, often reducing events to a sentence or less. Wilmsen's preferred mode is the lecture. His entire description of a battle from the Second Silesian War in 1757 reads as follows: "Glorious was the victory that was achieved at Leuthen in five hours; with a small force of 30,000 men Frederick defeated an Austrian Army of 90,000 men, capturing 21,500 common soldiers and 307 officers. The booty included 59 standards and 134 cannons."[84] Obviously, Wilmsen felt constrained to be as brief as possible, so he identified the most important events in Frederick's life. His choices were mainly political and military: battles and their results. With few exceptions the Frederick of the *Brandenburg Children's Companion* is simply the king, rarely the man. Schoolboys and the few girls who went to school in those days read that "people regarded their great king with the most intense love," but there was no way for the book's young readers to find out why Prussians embraced their king so devotedly.[85] Indeed, there are only four personal touches in Wilmsen's portrait: two sentences devoted to Frederick's attempted escape from his father's harsh regimen, an aside saying that the king "did without the joy of fatherhood," half a sentence about Frederick's sadness at the death of his favorite sister, and an indication that he was depressed during the Seven Years' War (239–47).[86] In all, scarcely six sentences show Frederick up close, and Wilmsen's book has none of the anecdotes that are otherwise so common in treatments of the king's life. Spamer must have thought he could do better, particularly for an audience of adolescents.

In contrast to Wilmsen's brief account, *The Great King and His Recruit* devotes almost four hundred pages to the Seven Years' War, and the book depicts its two main characters, Frederick and Felix Wunderlich, in considerable detail. As important as events are to the narrative, they serve mainly as background, while the two men function as foils to illustrate each other's strengths. (There are no weaknesses here. At most, Felix's occasional naiveté shows how wise Frederick is by comparison.) As the son of a widowed weaver, Felix is perfectly situated to let readers see the great king through a commoner's eyes; the king's recruit functions as a kind of identificatory Everyman, who rises to the odd heroic deed through and for Frederick, his acquired father figure. The two men's possessive, almost familial relationship begins when Frederick encounters Felix in Potsdam one Sunday after church. Although the young man's mother wants him to become a weaver, mainly to support her, Felix would rather be a soldier. He confides his troubles to an elderly gentleman, not knowing he is speaking to the king. Frederick tells him they should meet again the next day. By then Felix's mother has been offered a job in the royal kitchens, which obviates any need for Felix's support, and Frederick has recruited this soldier all by himself—no draft and no press gang, just a son's loyalty and a father's solicitude.

The year is 1756, and Frederick is already middle-aged. Still, "his eyes were large and blue; his gaze was penetrating."[87] In other words, Spamer gives his version of the king's typical physical attributes, while Felix is a strapping recruit whose principal talent is an inability to do anything less than what Frederick commands. The two men share enough adventures to make Prussian history and Frederick come alive,

CHAPTER 3

albeit mainly to boys and young men. One looks in vain here for romance. Yet, despite the novel's distancing third-person narration, its readers could almost become Felix while reading, and they could also share Felix's feelings for Frederick.

Again, unlike Wilmsen, who covers the battle of Leuthen in the two sentences quoted above, Spamer takes twenty pages to show how Frederick, with Felix's help, defeated the daunting Austrian and French forces assembled there. To be sure, Spamer's text includes a laudatory summary, rather like Wilmsen's: "Frederick the Great had observed the position of the enemy army exactly, and his genius enabled him immediately to find the correct means of successfully advancing his own small army against an enemy that was three times stronger."[88] Apparently, Frederick's stroke of genius was that his opponents left their fortified position to meet the Prussian army in the open. Spamer's description of the battle occupies only four pages, but he uses Felix to explain at great length why the Austrian commander was foolish enough to attack in the first place. The account is typical of Felix's adventurous service to his king. Frederick spots his recruit, by now a corporal, and sends him and a dozen other riders behind enemy lines with a letter to a friendly nobleman. This secret admirer of the great king is supposed to tell the Austrians how meager Frederick's forces are, thus provoking an attack, but Felix does him one better. After a French general's daughter recognizes Felix and unchivalrously betrays him, the very man who once rescued her from a burning castle—"our hero," as the book refers to him—is captured and brought before the Austrian Field Marshall Daun.[89] Felix feigns an interest in deserting and informs Daun that Frederick's army is even weaker than the report in the planted letter suggests. This deception seals Frederick's plan, and Felix regrets only that he is unable to capture Daun when he escapes and returns to the Prussian camp. During the ensuing battle Felix manages to capture another Austrian general, but he is so modest that he leaves it to a Prussian general to tell Frederick about his recruit's exploits. The king takes Felix aside and says: "I am pleased with you, Sergeant Wunderlich! Did you hear? Sergeant in the Guards [an elite regiment that stayed close to the King]!"[90] Incidentally, Felix's last name means miraculous, as well as odd, and his promotion is almost as much a miracle as Frederick's victory, except that the king is again as close to his recruit as God apparently was to Prussia. Spamer reports that as the fighting ended, the entire Prussian army joined in singing the hymn "Now Thank We All Our God [*Nun danket Alle Gott,* 1: 156]." It is a proud, Protestant, Prussian moment.

Frederick next sends Felix to London, where in only two days he persuades King George II to intervene directly with Prime Minister Pitt and grant Frederick a much-needed subsidy and some troops. The Prussian ambassador had been less successful, but Frederick trusts in Felix's good fortune and his wits: "In principle you are certainly missing a lot of what makes a genuine diplomat, but you will understand as much of the business at hand as you need to, which mainly requires common sense and your presence of mind."[91] Of course, Frederick's advice proves sound, but for Spamer Felix's spectacular success contains the potential for a complex and telling narratological disaster. First, every time he succeeds, Felix runs the danger of detracting from Frederick's own achievements, for even if the king is ultimately responsible, it is still his recruit who carries out the brave deeds. Second, Felix becomes so successful and so central to the novel's plot that he can no longer perform the task that Harry Shaw ascribes to the "disjunctive hero," namely, "to frame and illuminate their novel's true subjects."[92] Ever since Sir Walter Scott's *Waverley* (1814), the heroes of historical novels tended to be supporting figures of only middling abilities; they observe rather than act. Felix clearly oversteps that boundary. Indeed, his repeated triumphs make it difficult for Spamer to explain how and why Frederick nearly lost the Seven Years' War. The logic of the novel demands that Frederick and Felix both be personally responsible for the victory rather than having it result primarily from the timely death of the Russian Tsarina Elizabeth and her replacement by an outright admirer of the Prussian king, Tsar Peter III. However, as important as accurate details of Frederick's ultimate triumph were to more demanding readers, my point here is not to condemn Spamer's history but to illustrate structural difficulties in the genre of historical fiction, particularly when it involves as towering a figure as Frederick the Great.

To Spamer's credit, he seems to have constructed Felix in an attempt to minimize the problem of the hero's subordinate position. But as far better writers than Spamer have discovered, the Sancho Panzas of literature can easily steal too many scenes. Although Felix always attributes his own success to Frederick's eagle eye, the excuse works better as an explanation of the king's strategic brilliance rather than his tactical virtuosity. For example, unless readers are credulous enough to believe that Frederick knew in advance that the woman Felix had saved from a burning castle near Gotha would be looking out the window of a fortress near Leuthen at the very moment the young recruit passes by, then the hero's protestations of paternal foresight ring hollow. Felix's individual efforts almost invariably overshadow the king's distant leadership; his extraordinary achievements also make it difficult for him to play the role of an ordinary mortal caught up in historical events or affected by larger historical figures. In addition, since by this point in the novel Felix is mainly off swashing buckles, there is little opportunity for the king to confide in his recruit for the reader's benefit. Thus, as close as Felix is to Frederick the king and general, Frederick the man almost disappears. Felix's exploits may have made him attractive to young, less critical readers. His exploits may also have swelled their pride in the fatherland, but because he often overshadows Frederick, Felix remains a problem for Spamer's novel and others like it. If Frederick is to be the repository of national consciousness, then he—not some historically minor character—must occupy the novel's center. At least, he should not have to compete for the reader's attention with a character who turns out to be more appealing.

On a larger scale, the difficulty with Felix's role is even more intractable and more serious. Ultimately, it concerns the dividing line between history and historical fiction and illustrates a danger inherent in literary representations of the past, a problem that transcends the legitimacy of inventing dialogue for the king. Although Mühlbach and others have shown that it was fairly easy to portray a fictional Frederick up close and in private, in Spamer's novel Felix becomes so instrumental to the king's success that he almost has to cross the line from fiction into fact. Anyone who accomplished as much as the king's fictional recruit does in this novel should have made it into the history books. But a real protagonist would have undercut Spamer's freedom to invent adventures. In other words, except in fictionalized biographies of the great, a middling central character, who is a hero only in narratological terms, is not just a useful device, it is almost a necessity, especially once such a figure steps into or even near the public sphere. Felix's visibility at court and in the army, his close relationship with Frederick, and his many successful exploits strain the genre conventions of historical fiction precisely because of its dependence on historical reality.

The authors of purely inventive fiction have an easier task; the plausibility to which they aspire is mainly a matter of internal consistency, and they also make a less specific pretense of educating while entertaining. The knowledge that novels typically claim to impart relates to the human condition rather than to details of the battle of Leuthen. In conventional fiction the mere presence of the hero cannot call the background and setting into question, whereas Felix comes perilously close to undercutting the history he should only be bringing closer to young readers. Spamer probably gets off easier than he deserves by writing for adolescents, whose knowledge of the rules and the boundaries of history and fiction is limited. Still, the past seems to have intruded on the process of composition, and Spamer's novel comes unglued shortly after Felix's return from London.

At this point, Felix inherits a sizable fortune from an uncle in Moravia, then part of the Austrian empire, and Frederick allows him to accept it because a report on conditions there could prove useful in upcoming campaigns. Fortunately for Spamer, the historical Frederick was never able to make use of the information, so this and Felix's subsequent adventures remain unconnected to any developments in the king's life. As a result, Felix and the king rarely encounter each other in the last third of the novel, and Felix's capture, Siberian exile, and escape from Russia all fail to let him do anything useful for the Prussian cause. While Felix is off fighting Cossacks, wolves, and blizzards, the reader suffers through dry stretches of history and random anecdotes about Frederick. None of them, as was appropriate in a book intended for male adolescents, involve his amorous adventures. The book's only love interest is Felix's affection for a rich brewer's daughter, a woman he sees just once during the Seven Years' War. After the war is over, her father rejects Felix as a suitor until Frederick himself intervenes and tricks the man into accepting a marriage proposal for his daughter. Having already made Felix into a manufacturer as part of his plan to rebuild a devastated Prussia, securing a bride is the final service the fatherly king performs for his recruit and protégé. Frederick does attend the wedding, but Felix disappears for another twenty pages of anecdotes that take the novel to the end of the Frederickian era. An initially promising plot ends disappointingly, although the fault is as much the material's as the author's. Old Fritz, as Baroness Ebba warned, was a tough story to tell.

A Liberal, Anti-Austrian Frederick

In the late nineteenth century, amorous adventures for Frederick the Great remained in short supply, but authors were no less inclined to

CHAPTER 3

polish his image as a German. A good if also peculiar example of that project is Hans von Zollern's *A Political Chess Move by Frederick the Great* (1883).[93] Actually, this title is misleading. After taking center stage for the first two chapters, Frederick vanishes for hundreds of pages; the novel ends up being little more than the long-winded explication of a single anecdote. At 727 pages I regard it as too much of a good thing, but the book does show how novelists dealt with Frederick in the years after 1871, when Prussia had unified Germany politically but was still trying to consolidate the nation ideologically. As the disparity between title and content suggest, Frederick's name still sold books, just as it had in 1846, when Wilhelmine Lorenz was writing about Countess Orzelska. Zollern could easily, and more accurately, have called his novel *How Danzig Remained Independent* or *Love Saves the Free City of Danzig*, but one can scarcely imagine books with those titles leaping off bookstore or commercial lending library shelves. And the novel does contain an embedded explanation of Zollern's choice. When an aide to the Prussian consul in Danzig entertains a few of the city's beleaguered citizens, the narrator reports, "the young diplomat spiced the meal with a number of terrific anecdotes related to the latest inventions about the great Frederick. Fortunately, since this was a distant and somewhat rural area, the stories were unfamiliar, and their teller was rewarded with happy and constant laughter."[94] Readers must have expected more and better information from a novel with Frederick in its title, but to see why its characters were so amused requires a closer look at the text. Luckily, explaining the solitary Frederick anecdote does not demand a replay of the entire plot, even if readers of the present book deem the account below so long that there could scarcely be more. Those who doubt me should tackle Zollern's novel themselves.

The story opens in Berlin in 1778, as the king assembles his cabinet to discuss Prussian intervention in the War of Bavarian Succession. Here and elsewhere Zollern weaves considerable factual information about Frederick into the novel. As Kugler and Menzel represented it in 1842, that easily forgotten war mattered because it supposedly caused Bavarian peasants to hang Frederick's portrait next to images of the kingdom's patron saint. However, as important as the War of Bavarian Succession might have been in making the Protestant king of Prussia palatable to Germany's Catholic south and west, that history was not intrinsically interesting. To his credit, Zollern frames the conflict in a manner that shows how Frederick's deeds were open to various, contextually determined interpretations. The plot and narrator's commentary actually make more sense in 1883, a dozen years after Bismarck's anti-Austrian unification of Germany, than they do as an explanation of Frederick's motives over one hundred years earlier: "Austria was viewed as the hereditary enemy [*Erbfeind*] of Prussia and Germany."[95] This turn of phrase indicates that for the narrator Prussia and Frederick are no longer separate from Germany, but rather have become the quintessential embodiment of everything German, while the text relegates Austria to some non-German outer darkness. Indeed, since *Erbfeind* is a common name for the devil, the term makes Austria into the ultimate other for the German national cause. By contrast, Frederick represents goodness, and Zollern uses the familiar leitmotiv of his gaze to demonstrate Frederick's effect those around him. Although the king is now an old man, "his posture still revealed the powerful ruler's thoughts; more than ever his eagle-like gaze commanded his surroundings."[96] For two chapters it seems as though readers will witness Frederick once again leading his troops to victory, but just as the campaign is about to begin, he abruptly disappears until page 357 of the novel's second volume! Although what Frederick represents to the book's characters is never far from view, the scene shifts to Danzig, where the action remains for most of the novel. At issue is whether Danzig should remain a free city or be annexed by an expanding Prussian state, that is, by the political entity identified with Frederick and, subsequently, with German unification. The goal of maintaining the city's inherited rights and privileges has come into conflict with the demands of territorial modernization. As a result, the novel ultimately revolves around Frederick's relationship to power, justice, and the idea of Germany as it developed after the king's death.

The plot pits a minor Prussian diplomat, Ernst Normann, against Max Bertling, a Danzig businessman who fought on the American side during the Revolutionary War and is therefore sympathetic to Frederick's Enlightenment ideals. The novel uses Max, a non-Prussian, to represent Germany and what the nation might become under an enlightened leader, while Ernst stands for everything wrong with the Prussian state, both in 1778 and in Zollern's day. In other words, the novel's version of Frederick turns into an ideal embodiment of Germany rather than Prussia, and the king appears prototypically German in the guise of Old Fritz in the novel's central anecdote. The situation in the novel gains complexity through the familiar conflict between regional and national interests, and that conflict shows how authors could use historical fiction to discuss contemporary issues at a temporally safe remove. For example, as Günther Hirschmann has demonstrated, it was easier to discuss the struggle between the new German state and the Catholic Church (*Kulturkampf*, 1871–87) in novels set during the Reformation or the Thirty Years' War than in political tracts about the present; a transparent disguise served well enough to keep the authorities from intervening.[97] Zollern employs the free city of Danzig to argue the advantages and disadvantages of German unification under Prussia, no doubt because for the inhabitants of Hannover and other territories that had been swallowed up or relegated to less than their former status in 1871, the question of Prussia's role in Germany remained a contentious topic of debate a decade and a half later.

As a result of the first partition of Poland in 1772, Prussia controls virtually all of the territory surrounding Danzig, and Frederick's government has decided to force the city's inhabitants to accept annexation by means of a blockade. People from Danzig can scarcely take a walk without being searched and required to pay various duties, while autocratic and arbitrary Prussian soldiers and customs agents harass the city's inhabitants further with their exceptional petty enforcement of other regulations. Ernst Normann arrives in Danzig just as his government's agents are tightening the screws, and he witnesses a particularly grievous example of intentional nastiness: some soldiers threaten forty-eight hours of incarceration with only bread and water as punishment for a civilian's questioning a Prussian officer. The book treats such behavior as unexceptional; Ernst even calls it a "genuinely Prussian scene."[98] By using such phrases, Zollern associates the label "Prussian" with its tyrannical, power-hungry bureaucracy and army, while reserving "German" for Frederick's loftier aims. However, since Frederick was also Prussian, and since national and regional identities were still in conflict, the novel's semantics soon turn more complex. The opposing terms are actually Prussia, Germany, and Frederick on a positive axis versus Prussia, the Prussian army, and its bureaucracy on a negative axis. In other words, "genuine Prussian" evil coexists with Prussia's and Frederick's "grand German mission."[99] The multivalent status of "Prussia" allows one of Frederick's ministers to appeal to a delegation from Danzig by asking them to join Prussia in Germany: "You are thinking German, gentlemen, but you still steadfastly resist becoming part of the German body that you praise. But what is Prussia if not the vanguard of the German Empire in the East?"[100] Indeed, at the book's conclusion its narrator looks forward to 1793, when Prussia finally did annex the city, and he makes an even more fulsome claim: Danzig was and would remain "the strongest rock and refuge of the German Empire and the German mission in the east opposing the cravings of greedy Slavs."[101] This ominous phrase shows just how complex and dangerous nationalist imagery could become, and how difficult it must have been to keep various, overlapping portions of Prussia's image separate. The inevitable confusion also shows why Frederick's stand-in, the proud Danzig patriot Max Bertling, can claim "to be at home everywhere in Germany or Prussia."[102]

Along the way Bertling makes two other arguments that are useful in characterizing the novel's view of Prussia, Germany, and Frederick the Great. First, he realizes that independent city-states are medieval relics. As he well knows, Danzig would actually prosper under Prussian rule. Having fewer borders, tolls, weights, measures, and currencies to deal with and, more important, being protected rather than attacked by a strong Prussian state would help the city more than the nominal support of the Polish Crown. In the long run, Max realizes that Danzig will have to face the reality of Prussian power and accept some form of incorporation. The city is also important to Prussia with its expanding eastern provinces. The benefits are mutual and virtually inevitable, but the text raises an issue larger than economics and power politics.

Implicit in the entire narrative is the idea that Prussia and Germany have "natural" boundaries. Accordingly, part of the novel's project is to depict the historical accident of Danzig's continuing independence as somehow "abnormal." The argument is roughly as follows: since nation-states supposedly consist of continuous and contiguous territories, once Prussia becomes identified with Germany, the incorporation of German-speaking Danzig into Prussia, even against the will of the city's citizens, is "normal." Annexation on such grounds becomes natural, rational, even moral. Moreover, once this key idea behind the nation-state has acquired legitimacy, creating and sustaining such states is easier, practically and intellectually, that is, ideologically. The paradigm has shifted, and in the process, normalcy, nature, and reason become powerful arguments against the particularism that seemed so sensible to earlier generations.[103] In Zollern's novel, Danzig is returning home to Prussia and Germany; its other choice was maintaining what the text represents as a misguided, outmoded, and even delusional policy of separation. To Danzig, stylized

CHAPTER 3

as the German prodigal son, Frederick's Prussia can say, "come back," just as twentieth-century Germans could justify their conquests with the battle cry, "Come home to the Empire!" (*Heim ins Reich!*) But returning home to a symbolic space, where one was never at home in the first place, requires a conceptual shift of considerable magnitude. Zollern's novel shows how that process began working in nineteenth-century historical discourse.

Max's second argument, lest one think that nationalism is simply rearing its ugly, repressive head here, concerns his reluctance to aid the city's patrician elite in putting down a Prussian-inspired rebellion. It correlates to the hero's belief that the working class, albeit misguided, is suffering real need and injustice. As much as he disapproves of the heavy-handed tactics of the local Prussian authorities (the bad Prussians of the bureaucracy and the army), Max realizes that a new economic system and different leadership (the good Prussians associated with Frederick) would benefit the poor. As one worker says, "for the common man it would be better to have a good chunk of Prussian bread and some of their meat instead of the long, dry fasts of Danzig's magistracy."[104] Here Frederick symbolizes economic and political egalitarianism, while Max's refusal to have the rebellious workers arrested draws attention to contrary policies in force at the time Zollern's novel appeared. In 1883, five years after the passage of the Anti-Socialist Laws, the author might well be using Frederick to criticize Bismarck's repressive regime at the same time he is advocating the incorporation of smaller states into the Prussian-German whole. The image of the Frederick the Great embodied in the nickname "Old Fritz" had become so multifaceted that it could simultaneously represent both liberal paternalism and conservative nationalism. In other words, learning about Prussian or German history in historical fiction was no guarantee of a unitary German identity. As long as the vision of the nation remained in flux, works of history, both singly and as a group, were constantly negotiating and renegotiating the parameters of what it meant to be German.

Meanwhile, despite the utter illogic of their position, the people of Danzig remain independent until 1793, long after Frederick's death in 1786. According to the novel, a benevolent Old Fritz allows them to remain free for reasons found in the novel's concluding anecdote. Unfortunately, to understand why requires just a bit more background. Unbeknownst to Max, who is off representing Danzig's interests abroad, his beloved Magda, herself a daughter of Danzig, has become an actress of European stature. At a conference in Vienna, where the city's fate is to be decided once and for all, the two lovers are reunited, and Magda uses her considerable charms to obtain an audience for Max with Austria's Emperor Joseph II and Russia's Empress Catherine the Great. Max succeeds in pleading the city's cause, and Magda decides to move with him to Berlin, where he serves as Danzig's ambassador to the Prussian court. This is good news for Frederick, who has been trying for some time to entice Magda to the city's stages, but at the last minute she refuses to sign a contract. Her reason is simple: Frederick has not yet approved the treaty guaranteeing Danzig's independent status. Magda therefore declares: "To defend the towers of my hometown [*Vaterstadt*] I say 'Check' to the King." Not for nothing is Zollern's novel called *A Political Chess Move by Frederick the Great*; it is now his turn: "Just so my beloved Berliners won't have to wait for this stubborn diva, I'll have to sign my contract at once."[105] Old Fritz, wise father to his people, symbol of freedom and justice, and lover of the arts, gives in, albeit for the wrong reasons. This is a powerful and attractive image of the limits of royal power, and it could have threatened Frederick's successors in Zollern's day. If two longish volumes seem like a great deal of prologue for a single anecdote, the novel nevertheless contains a great deal of interest to readers along the way. Once again, the past was not dead; rather, it remained a forum for the discussion of current events, including the still unsettled question of German identity.

Along with works like Zollern's, in which Frederick plays a positive if also minor role, one would expect to find novels in which the Prussian king is the villain. But if they exist, such books are difficult to find. Part of the problem may be that Protestant northern Germany published most of the era's books in an industry centered in Leipzig. The north also had more readers. For example, in 1884, according to Hagen Schulze, "Berlin alone had more bookstores than the whole of Austria."[106] Although published in Berlin, Levin Schücking's *The Cavalry Colonel* (1858) looks like an anti-Frederick book.[107] Schücking was a Catholic from Westphalia and thus doubly predisposed to hate Frederick: he could have resented Prussian domination of his homeland and also rejected the Protestant premise of nineteenth-century German nationalism that Frederick increasingly represented. Moreover, anyone familiar with eighteenth-century German history knows that Schücking's book concerns the infamous Trenck family, long a thorn in the side of Frederick's Prussia. The Austrian Colonel Franz von der

Trenck fought against Frederick with distinction in the first two Silesian Wars (1740–42 and 1744–45), while his cousin, Baron Frederick von der Trenck, was an equally distinguished officer in the Prussian army—until charges of treason and rumors of an affair with the king's favorite sister brought him into disrepute. Despite Frederick's professed belief in the rule of law, the Prussian Trenck spent almost ten years chained to the wall in a dungeon in Magdeburg, without benefit of trial, and he later described his adventures in a notoriously self-serving memoir. In short, Schücking had plenty of material for a fictional look at the underside of Frederick's kingdom, but he omits it from his novel. The book's hero, another Austrian officer, Joseph von Frohn, has prolonged contact with both Trencks and finds them repellent. As represented in Schücking's novel, the Trenck family produced men united mainly by their bombastic and unscrupulous egotism. They might have regarded Frederick as a tyrant, but the king looks positively angelic in comparison to such detractors. Even Empress Maria Theresa, that most Catholic of monarchs, comes across as narrowly moralistic rather than good in Schücking's treatment. She inflicts little damage by calling Frederick "the heretic King of Prussia" (*Ketzerkönig*) (138). But, surprisingly, in this potentially damning book, subtitled *Historical Novel from the Age of Frederick the Great,* the Prussian king is virtually absent. It seems the era took its name from Frederick, and he probably sold more copies of a book originally subtitled *From the Days of the Great Empress.*[108] Still, the book is a disappointment to anyone hoping for a contrary view of the Prussian king and his role in the invention of Germany.

Since Schücking's novel was published in 1858, it includes passages that praise pan-Germanic unity, although if their author had been Austrian, these same sentiments might have been simply anti-Hungarian. For Austrians, the other was located in Eastern Europe rather than in France. Thus, when a Hungarian countess asks Frohn to define patriotism, he replies, "in German it means love of the fatherland, while in the Magyar tongue it expresses more hatred."[109] The question is unusually direct, and it is also strange that a woman poses it. Politics remained a largely male preserve even for fictional women, so this Hungarian countess is something of an exception. She marries an Austrian baron, presumably without any nationalist qualms, and her husband is the same man who helps Frohn foil a plot against Empress Maria Theresa, because he is, in Frohn's words, "a good German" (*ein guter Deutscher*) rather than a loyal Austrian or supporter of the

Hapsburg dynasty (267). For these characters, and perhaps for Schücking, the label "German" transcended Austrians' regional and ethnic diversity, as well as the Hapsburg's religious particularism. One senses, even from a Catholic author, that Frederick's legacy of religious tolerance could best serve the nation. He proves again that the agenda of historical fiction was always political, if often as confused as German politics.

Frederick in Academic History

Returning to politics is a means of returning to history, specifically academic history. For a last look at the century's image of Frederick, the most useful portrait is that sketched by Heinrich von Treitschke. His *History of Germany in the Nineteenth Century,* whose five volumes (seven in English) had reached only to 1847 by the time Treitschke died in 1896, was one of the most widely read histories of its day, and Treitschke was a popular lecturer and influential teacher of generations of historians.[110] That his Prusso-centric version of Germany history, including its notorious anti-Semitism, was controversial goes without saying, but his work also sums up a century's interaction with Frederick the Great.

Unlike Kugler and Menzel, Treitschke was not writing a biography of the Prussian king, and he aimed his work at more literate, more intellectual readers. Hence, his *History* contains none of the anecdotes that had become a fixture in most narratives of Frederick's life. Treitschke's method is also to tell rather than show, and the magisterial historian apparently felt no compunction in judging events and people from the past. For example, his Frederick steps into a power vacuum and immediately fills the decades-old empty space at the center of the German stage. In Treitschke's view, for the first time in well over a century, Frederick was "a heroic figure upon whom the whole nation could gaze with wondering admiration."[111] Note how Treitschke's formulation assumes that during the eighteenth century a nation ready to gaze in Frederick's direction already existed. Since he published the passage in 1879, when Germany had finally achieved a political and geographical form, the gazing nation presumably included the Saxons, who suffered considerable devastation during Frederick's campaigns for Silesia. However, it must have excluded the Austrians, who were outside the German empire after 1871. Thus, while discussing Frederick, Treitschke twice refers to Maria Theresa, the empress of Austria, as simply "the Queen of Hungary."[112]

CHAPTER 3

The title is accurate as far as it goes, but by not mentioning Maria Theresa's numerous German titles, including Empress of the Holy Roman Empire of the German Nation, Treitschke commits a serious sin of omission. In effect, the image of people gazing "with wondering admiration" at the "heroic figure" of the Prussian king, while not looking at Frederick's Austrian adversary, shows how history, in both its fictional and nonfictional formats, helped constitute and define a narrowly specific version of the German nation. United through the single focus of their vision, Frederick's partisans become Germany; his uniting presence anticipates the Prussian-dominated, post-1871 incarnation of Germany. By using Frederick to justify the present rather than to explain the uncertain path by which it was achieved, Treitschke narrows the king's range as a character. In his version of events German history was never open to alternative trajectories; instead it seems as if Frederick, fate, or God had planned every step along the way.

By 1885, in the fifth volume of his *History*, Treitschke's own gaze becomes godlike. In a single passage he links the formation of the German Customs Union of 1834, which was dominated by Prussia and excluded Austria, to both Frederick the Great and the battle of Königgrätz in 1866, in which a Prussian army decisively defeated the Austrians, paving the way for Germany's subsequent unification. In Treitschke's version of events the Customs Union was not just ratified on the ground: "The eagle eye of the great king looked down from the clouds, and from a remote distance could already be heard the thunder of the guns of Königgrätz."[113] Frederick's spectral presence not only ratifies 1834 and 1866 as decisive points in German history, but Treitschke also uses Frederick to limit the meaning of these events to foreshadowing 1871. In addition to being utterly implausible, the passage makes a huge leap beyond the evidence—all the way to the sky; it is all the more remarkable for its novelistic mention of Frederick's gaze, which almost all the authors in this chapter have used, but, in contrast to Treitschke, as a leitmotiv to signal the king's keen insight, not his approving presence. The passage also shows that the dividing line between historical fiction and academic history remained far less well-defined than one might expect. Treitschke makes no pretense of objectivity or distance from his material, nor is he afraid to invent images that would have rung hollow in fiction.

In Treitschke's hands Frederick not only prepares the way for German unification under Prussia; he also becomes thoroughly and narrowly German. For example, only at the end of Treitschke's account does the reader learn of Frederick's preference for French literature, French customs, and the French language.[114] Treitschke's initial portrait is quite different: "The central characteristic of this powerful nature was his pitiless and cruel German realism."[115] Curiously, Treitschke transforms "pitiless" and "cruel" into positive attributes by linking them to "German," and a distinctly masculine quality underscores Frederick's supposed ability to make difficult choices. Why his realism should be German, a category that has become ethnic and essentially biological, remains as unclear as it is silly and dangerous. It is also not an isolated slip, as Treitschke's Frederick "displays his German blood, that from the first he knows how to control his ardent love of action by cool and sober consideration."[116] Frederick, hero of the German nation, embodies Germany's destiny as well as the character traits of the ideal German. The mixture is powerfully self-reinforcing, with little room left for the contradictions and ambiguities of earlier accounts. Treitschke's Frederick has a few relatively minor character flaws: a preference for things French and too strong a reliance on the nobility. There is no more of the openness that allowed Zollern to invoke the king's Enlightenment ideals or permitted Spamer to show Frederick indulging common soldiers. For all his bombast, Treitschke sketches a radically diminished portrait of Frederick, an image in black and white without shades of gray, contrast, or contradiction.

Treitschke's Frederick is also resolutely Protestant, and his Protestantism represents the ideal choice not only for Germany but also for an enlightened humanity. One could ascribe Treitschke's vehemence to more than fifteen years of public struggle between the new German state and the Catholic Church, but the position still sounds extreme. For example, after various Prussian victories in Silesia, Treitschke declares Frederick "the official protector of Protestantism" in Germany, as if there were such an office, while the "establishment of the Protestant-German power was the most serious reverse that the Roman See had experienced since the rise of Martin Luther. King Frederick had in truth, as the English ambassador Mitchell phrased it, been fighting for the freedom of the human race."[117] With Frederick on the side of truth and justice, Treitschke can demonize his opponents. For example, he disqualifies the Wittelsbach dynasty of Bavaria from a leadership role in Germany because the family was "estranged from German life by its hereditary association with France as well as by the rigidity of Catholic unity."[118] In

CHAPTER 3

Treitschke's hands Maria Theresa's husband, Emperor Francis I, is not only "brainless" (*hirnlos*) but also becomes "this Lorraine-Augustus" to emphasize his French roots, while on his other borders Frederick faces "the savage mob" of Eastern Europe and "the barbarians of Moscovy."[119] In sum, Treitschke uses Frederick to define real Germans as not-French, not-Russian, not-Austrian, and not-Catholic; the Prussian-dominated state of Germany after 1871 becomes the ideal incarnation of Germany's destiny, while Frederick is its exemplary predecessor. In mythic terms the difficulty is that at the time of Frederick's death in 1786, Germany had only arrived at its heroic age. That means there was less than a century left for the nation's decline and regeneration. Having achieved such heights with Frederick, Treitschke and others faced a daunting task in explaining the precipitous decline that propelled Prussia toward Jena.

From Frederick the Great to Old Fritz

However, before moving on to the next of Germany's national myths, let me summarize what had happened to Frederick's image since 1830. First, by the end of the century Baroness Ebba's claim that "a few women authors of genius" were responsible for reshaping perceptions of Frederick the Great was no longer true. Most of the novelists and all the historians who wrote about him were men, and they demonstrated precious little interest in Frederick's private life, perhaps because they sensed that he had none. There are no amorous adventures in Treitschke's *History,* even though the narrative stance that allowed him to see Frederick in heaven gazing down on the German Customs Union would have let him invent them. Except for Treitschke the most common phenomenon in works about Frederick is an abundance of anecdotal evidence that turns the originally austere king into an approachable father figure for his individual subjects. Frederick II has become Old Fritz, a hero with the common touch, and the successful effort to humanize him also broadcasts an image of the monarchy as a caring institution and guarantor of the old order. In fact, Frederick has become a stable anchor, firmly connected to a proud past, who lets Germans accept or overlook the radical changes that were occurring in their lives in the present.

Second, during the nineteenth century Frederick gradually became more German than Prussian, a shift that was necessary for the king to play the role allotted him in the national myth. Curiously, both Bismarck and Emperor William I represented an older version of identity and thought of themselves as Prussians first and Germans, if at all, only later. Bismarck, for example, regarded the Polish inhabitants of Silesia as his fellow Prussians, an option closed off by the essentially racist nationalism of Treitschke's late-nineteenth-century *History*. Other works fall between these two poles, but the overwhelming tendency, demonstrated as much by the widespread availability of books about Frederick as by their overt content, was to make the once-Prussian king attractive to the largest possible audience, which was necessarily German rather than Prussian. And books were published in German, not in regional dialects, a fact that by itself promoted unity among an increasingly literate population. Still, given the regional diversity that characterized Germany far beyond 1900, most authors recognized the difficulty in the nationalist undertaking, and they frequently addressed it, more or less openly. For example, Kugler's "Afterword" vacillates when it speaks of Frederick as "a man whose name causes every Prussian citizen's heart to beat faster, [indeed] causes every German's heart to beat faster," while Spamer claims in his "Introduction" that "our book is written not only for Prussian readers alone [but also for] Prussia's neighbors or all good Germans."[120] Some of Spamer's floundering stems from his dual role as publisher and author hawking his own book, but it also shows the tension and the effort involved in representing Frederick to putative Germans. Every version of Frederick implied its own definition of Germany, just as different visions of the nation demanded their own corresponding images of its most illustrious king. However, the issue was increasingly framed in German not Prussian terms, because for many nationalists Prussia, like its illustrious king, had come to represent the nation's essence.

Third, given the enormous labor—and the enormous stakes—involved in constructing a German version of Frederick, authors aimed their works at a broader audience than Ebba's circle of judgmental teenage girls. Romance might have attracted female readers, but Treitschke, Zollern, Bacher, and their counterparts were at least as interested in an adult male audience as they were in attracting women, whatever their age. History, particularly Germany's national history, was a public and therefore male realm. Even Lorenz and most certainly Mühlbach hoped for a larger and therefore partially male audience, for although Mühlbach spent much of her vast energy narrating Frederick's private life, she did so with an eye toward its public consequences. Her Frederick was more the monarch up close than a private person who behaved differently among his friends and family. Mühlbach's king

CHAPTER 3

combines the public with the private sphere, largely by letting the latter atrophy in the service of the former. His dinners with Voltaire and the flute concerts are little more than a respite; they enable Frederick to return to battle or aid his beleaguered subjects. Mühlbach and most of the other authors here regarded the real Frederick as the public person. Thus, their intimate views of the king show him perpetually engaged in public activities; his acts of private kindness serve only to further the war effort or to effect a paternalistic style of governance. By the end of the century Frederick may have become a lovable king, but he remains the king and little else.

Fourth, Frederick's image increasingly resists multiple interpretations; in large part he had become the property of conservative ideologues. Even Zollern, who hints that a true follower of the Prussian king would favor the working class, makes him into the proponent of Prussia's and Germany's naturally expanded borders. Frederick is not available to opponents of German unification; neither does he figure in socialist literature.[121] Except for Schücking's veiled reference to Frederick's religious tolerance, the great king no longer resonated so powerfully with liberals. After the failure of the Revolution of 1848, Frederick the pathfinder of German liberalism gradually made way for Frederick the prophet of German national unity. However, there is no reason to believe that Frederick was destined to be the ridiculous figure he became with the help of his great-grandnephew, Emperor William II, who attended a costume ball dressed as his famous ancestor in 1897. A portrait from the event survives. In it William's clothes are fair copies of Frederickian originals, as is his powdered wig, but the emperor's trademark mustache is only part of what spoils the overall effect. It required a considerable portion of antic goofiness, and a well-sublimated longing for love and acceptance, for William to think he could pass as Frederick.[122] His hat is foolishly ornate, and we see no evidence of the tobacco stains that often covered Frederick's well-worn uniforms. William looks pudgy, a stark contrast to the rather gaunt Frederick, and his bearing is posed and haughty, again sharply different from that of Frederick, who usually looks as though he resented being painted. While Frederick often appears hunched, leaning on a cane, William rests his withered arm on a long sword to disguise the deformity; his attempt at strength was bluster, but all the more dangerous because he constantly had to prove himself. This Frederick is a caricature, yet strangely similar to Treitschke's portrait. Its content is no more accurate but no more false than Ebba's call for romantic invention. What this costumed portrait of William II demonstrates is how easy it had become to insert an image of Frederick into a German nationalist myth, to use him as a prop in the German identity kit.

Oddly enough, William II's prototypically German Frederick is no longer Old Fritz. The avuncular king lived on, particularly in fiction, but to play the part of a German hero Frederick had to be great. To appeal to the reading public of post-1871 Germany, writers increasingly turned to Bismarck or Emperor William I, or they presented a version of the Prussian king whose wisdom and heroic qualities made him an example to all true Germans. Of course, historians and the authors of historical fiction could disagree about Frederick's truth, because as we will see there was still no broad agreement about Germany and what it meant to be German. Ebba's claim that women refashioned Frederick into an interesting monarch is partially a demand for women's inclusion in the nation, including in its Prussian form, but Fontane's use of her as a character calls the process of reinterpreting Frederick into question. Writing in 1891, near the end of the trajectory traced here, Fontane had reason to be skeptical, but he also recognized that Ebba's counterpart, Holk von Holkenäse, was closer to the majority position in Germany. Holk stands for all those patriots and nationalists who accepted Frederick's heroism without question and who believed that the king's being Prussian was another sign of Prussia's destiny with the fatherland. Despite preferring the big picture, for Holk and millions like him, anecdotes about Frederick make the king more fully human while simultaneously showing him as the ideal ruler of his country and father to his subjects. Why the nation, when confronted by Napoleon at Jena, fell so quickly and so far from the heights of Frederick's reign was probably difficult for most Germans to understand. But few Germans doubted that the Prussian king, both as Frederick the Great and Old Fritz, embodied Germany's heroic age. Ebba notwithstanding, the great bulk of narrative devoted to him proves Germans found Frederick not only useful in coming to terms with their newly common past but interesting too.

4
Explaining Jena

On October 14, 1806, not quite two months after the twentieth anniversary of Frederick the Great's death, it became clear to everyone who noted such coincidences just how much had been lost in the preceding two decades. On that October day Napoleon's troops annihilated the Prussian army at Jena, and within the year Frederick's heirs ceded effective control over their few remaining territories. French forces even occupied Berlin. If tragedy requires its heroes to fall from a great height, the battle of Jena gave historians and the authors of historical fiction an almost perfect opportunity to posit a tragic phase in Germany's national narrative. Just as Frederick the Great came to embody the myth of a heroic age, Jena was a defeat so total that it could stand for all of Germany's humiliations at the hands of an upstart emperor. Viewed more broadly, the disaster at Jena became the dominant symbol of the nation's fall from grace.

Paradoxically, explaining Jena was seldom an exercise in military history but rather the mythic low point of Germany's moral, political, or social decline. Once it had been transformed from an event into a symbol, the Prussian debacle at Jena also became a necessary precursor to the nation's equally mythic regeneration during the Wars of Liberation. Depictions of Jena therefore tend to be far more concerned with the mistakes and failures that preceded the defeat rather than with the actual

CHAPTER 4

battle. One reason might be their timing. Texts dealing with Jena began appearing after the Revolution of 1848, which one could view as another era of national failure. For many, 1848 was a turning point when Germany failed to turn. It too was marked by a loss of nerve at all levels of German society, and those who wondered just what had gone wrong could easily turn to Jena in their search for precursors and parallels. Was Frederick William IV as ill suited to the task of being king as his father, Frederick William III? Was he surrounded and misled by the same sort of corrupt and incompetent advisors? Had the disease of revolution once again spread to Germany from France, or were the difficulties experienced from Berlin to Vienna homegrown? Why did the reformers fail? Most important, how deep-seated were Germany's problems? Were they the result of inept or evil individuals, or were they symptoms of some profound national malaise? Jena might not provide answers to these and all the other questions that arose in the aftermath of 1848, but it did let authors and their readers talk about what had gone wrong.

Inevitably, the search for miscreants also gave authors a chance to identify some people who were less guilty and others who were innocent. From that latter group these same writers could begin to speculate about heroes who could undo the disaster. At least by implication they could use villains and their faults to create positive alternatives that were then fleshed out in books about the Wars of Liberation. In fact, Jena produced a heroine whose virtues reverberated in the national cause for the rest of the century. Like the versions of Frederick the Great's life discussed above, accounts of the Prussian defeat at Jena gradually gave the disaster national status, and Jena came to serve as a shorthand reference for the myriad German hopes and aspirations that seemed utterly dashed in 1806, only to resurface with renewed vigor in 1813. If 1848 was a subtext in many of these narratives, it was because Jena and the unsuccessful uprisings of that year combined profound fears with dashed hopes, just as they demonstrated that there were more incompetent generals and politicians than real heroes in Germany. Thus, even though the defeat at Jena inspired fewer writers than Frederick the Great's heroics, narrating the battle and its prologue became essential to the project of inventing Germany.

To understand what "Jena" signified to nineteenth-century Germans, one has to remember not only the glory that was Prussia under Frederick but also what the French Revolution and its aftermath meant to the inhabitants of the German territories. During the eighteenth century, intellectuals regarded France as the pinnacle of European civilization. French was the language of diplomacy, philosophy, and literature throughout the continent, while French fashion set the standard for the aristocracy's tables, dress, and palaces. From Vienna to Potsdam, from Brussels to St. Petersburg, rulers wore silk knee breeches and powdered wigs; they read or watched Racine's and Moliere's plays; and they built their own versions of Versailles, surrounded them with French gardens, and viewed themselves as no less central to the universe than Louis XIV. Frederick the Great, as we have seen, was neither an exception nor the worst offender. He named his own favorite residence Sanssouci, which is French for "without worries," and his most prominent guest was the French philosopher, historian, and playwright Voltaire. In short, even before the Napoleonic wars engulfed the continent in twenty years of sustained, costly combat, what happened in France mattered immensely in the rest of Europe. Between 1789 and 1815, life in the German-speaking territories of Europe changed forever, and most of the changes originated in France.

In 1803, after Napoleon's representatives had redrawn the map of central Europe, an estimated 60 percent of the German population had different rulers than before the Revolution. In fact, much of German Europe changed hands several times between 1789 and 1815. For example, the ancient bishopric of Münster was secularized in 1802, and the city soon became the capital of a newly created Kingdom of Westphalia, ruled between 1807 and 1813 by Napoleon's younger brother, Jerome. After the "restoration" of 1815, Münster was no longer one of the hundreds of more or less independent entities within the Holy Roman Empire; instead it became the capital of Protestant Prussia's westernmost province. Münster's inhabitants now lived in one of the roughly three dozen states that managed to survive the transition from the eighteenth to the nineteenth century. The reduction in the number of independent political entities from well over three hundred to fewer than forty shows that Münster's situation was typical. Throughout Germany people owed allegiance to different rulers—sometimes to princes who practiced another religion at a time when faith still mattered immensely; they also lost many of the laws, customs, and institutions previous generations had inherited without question. In addition, the residents of those redistributed territories had been subject to extraordinary taxes, requisitions, quartering orders, and conscriptions in order to finance,

CHAPTER 4

provision, house, and man armies that had marched from one end of Europe to the other, leaving death, destruction, and impoverishment in their wake. Territorial reorganization meant not only that the German-speaking population of central Europe had to become acquainted with new states and different dynasties, but the inhabitants of these new territories were also cut off from centuries of tradition. No wonder, then, that nationalism, which appealed to a supposedly better and more settled past and offered the promise of a more glorious future, found so many adherents, especially when Germany's emerging nationalist narrative became common currency.

Along with these momentous, albeit often small-scale, territorial realignments instituted at the beginning of the century, events summarized under the heading "Jena" included at least one major change within Germany. In 1806 the Holy Roman Empire of the German Nation ceased to exist. That first Reich, which had lasted for over a thousand years, was no more, and Emperor Francis II of the Holy Roman Empire became Francis I, Emperor of Austria. After 1806 there was no longer even the illusion of a unified German state. Thus, although it was little more than a fortuitous coincidence, that the empire ended in the same year Prussia suffered its ignominious defeat effectively doubled the symbolic weight of Jena. In a very real sense Jena marked the end of "old" Germany.

The battle itself pitted badly led and vastly outnumbered Prussian soldiers against an entirely new kind of army. While the rest of Europe relied on relatively few professional soldiers, ever since the *levée en masse* of 1793, which introduced universal conscription, the French could overwhelm almost any opposition numerically. Unlike their opponents, the French army was also a national army fighting for a uniting cause rather than for pay or plunder, and their leader was Napoleon, the most brilliant military commander to emerge in Europe since Frederick the Great. The contrast could scarcely have been greater. By 1806 the Prussians were bereft of allies, and in political terms, they had long been essentially rudderless. An incompetent king relied on men who failed to see that the world around them had changed. They were comfortable with the glory that had been Frederick's and unwilling to listen to those who suggested reform or redirection. As historian James Sheehan puts it: "The difficulty with Prussian foreign policy after 1795 was not its neutrality, but rather the weakness of will and obscurity of vision this neutrality attempted to mask."[1] Novelists and historians sought to explain precisely this drift and, in retrospect, the seeming inevitability of the disaster at Jena.

FANNY LEWALD'S ROYAL NE'ER-DO-WELL

One of the first attempts at explaining this failure of both imagination and nerve was Fanny Lewald's 1849 novel, *Prince Louis Ferdinand*.[2] It was her sole work of historical fiction, probably because the novel aroused such controversy. Its central character is the disreputable but nevertheless appealing nephew of Frederick the Great, and Lewald's contemporaries were apparently unhappy about her fictional portrait of the prince for a variety of reasons: First, Lewald had chosen to represent a member of the royal family whom King Frederick William IV would rather have forgotten. Louis Ferdinand might have been a hero, but he was a notorious spendthrift and womanizer, who fathered at least two illegitimate children. In addition, he opposed the present king's father, King Frederick William III, and made him look foolish and timid. Second, Lewald's depiction included Louis Ferdinand's platonic but nevertheless romantic involvement with Rahel Varnhagen von Ense, a Jewish woman who presided over a well-known Berlin salon. Since according to popular opinion he should have shunned Jews, just as she should have had less frivolous friends, there was reason to overlook their relationship. As a result, the book offended both the monarchy's supporters and Rahel's dedicated fans. Third, Lewald, who was herself Jewish, dared to subject Prussian politics to a devastating critique, and that was a task better left to male Protestants—or, more likely, better left undone altogether. Also, it was easy for Lewald's initial readers to find echoes of the Revolution of 1848 in her novel. As in 1806, an indecisive and incompetent ruler, who was also badly advised, very nearly ended Prussian history. In all, it is easy to see why Lewald never returned to historical fiction, but her choice does nothing to diminish the novel's import.

The book opens on New Year's Eve 1799, with Louis Ferdinand lamenting the end of an era: "How much has happened in the last century! What men, what deeds the Fatherland has seen! And now!—the eagle's flight is obstructed by clouds! Delusions, humiliating weakness—that is what we have now! And I stand here doing nothing, helpless, chained! I—"[3] That final "I," the end of the prince's outcry in the text, suggests that Louis Ferdinand might have achieved something more substantial had he been born into a meritocracy, but he and Prussia

CHAPTER 4

are both constrained by the institution of hereditary monarchy. For all his potential, Louis Ferdinand has no role other than watching his irresolute cousin dither in the face of Napoleon's threat to Prussia's heritage and sovereignty. Louis Ferdinand realizes that the king is the wrong man, at the wrong time, in the wrong place; but as a prince far removed from the royal succession, he can only speculate about what might have happened under different circumstances. He can neither act nor urge others to action in a system that demands loyalty to a single sovereign, however inept the occupant of the throne may be.

Lewald's Louis Ferdinand actually keeps busy, but he is mainly killing time rather than doing anything useful. However, since the prince becomes a focus for popular discontent with Prussian neutrality, Lewald uses her hero to examine a range of possible causes for the country's malaise. For example, Louis Ferdinand's life dishonors him and his acquaintances; his debauchery undermines proponents of active resistance to the French, because his allies are as dangerous as those they seek to replace. For all his brilliance Louis Ferdinand is so disreputable that he calls into question the very possibility of reform within a monarchical system. Still, the novel's central character permits a nuanced appraisal of a complex situation. If the book has a weakness, it is that the narration sometimes seems as scattered as the catalog of evils it dissects.

In one of the opening scenes Louis Ferdinand happens upon a young soldier who has just killed his lover. Denied permission to marry, the man had deserted only to return when a promised pardon would have given him the opportunity to wed. In fact, corrupt officers had lied to him, and the young soldier's fiancée asked him to kill her because she could not endure the even longer separation that she now faced. Ordinarily, murderers are not sympathetic characters, but this particular soldier was driven to his deed by an unreformed Prussian army. Louis Ferdinand cannot help, because the situation transcends their personal tragedy, just as it plays on and involves his own promise and weaknesses. While reformers were calling for universal conscription and an officer corps open to all talented members of the population (as they did in 1848), traditionalists maintained that since long-serving soldiers commanded by noble officers had been good enough for Frederick the Great, the inherited army could certainly defeat Napoleon. Readers begin by seeing what this army does to its soldiers, but as the narrative progresses Lewald not only discredits the military in human terms, but its usefulness in war also begins to look questionable. At one point

Louis Ferdinand overhears several officers talking about their miserable recruits, which was an endemic problem in conscripted armies: "Nevertheless, these fellows are jewels compared to the dandified officers and generals. [A junior officer] told me that the commander of his regiment always had a groom place a footstool by the side of his horse because the man had become too fat to climb in and out of the saddle."[4] Soldiers singing about Frederick the Great prompt a comment from the narrator about their far more enthusiastic French counterparts, whose passions are roused by the "Marseillaise" and its bloodthirsty promise of lasting patriotism: "The enthusiasm that is associated with the genius of a sovereign dies out everywhere with the death of the genius."[5]

Louis Ferdinand argues that the *real* Prussian army still exists, despite the foreigners and miscreants who fill its rosters: "The army consists of natives of the country, and these love their land, they are loyal, and will know how to preserve their national autonomy if they are threatened with losing it."[6] It is a plausible theory, devoutly believed or wished for by those characters in the novel who urge the king to war, but there are doubts. The manufacturer to whom Louis Ferdinand is speaking in this scene replies: "Did your ancestors believe in national autonomy when they helped to partition Poland, and wanted to change this pure Slavic people into Germans? Did Frederick the Great respect the national rights of the Austrians when he annexed Silesia to Prussia?"[7] Of course, the answers are all no. This representative of the bourgeoisie believes that people must be free before they can feel genuine patriotism. While his arguments, including his enthusiasm for Polish independence, might well relate to the time of the novel's composition in 1848, they also constitute a telling critique of the situation before the disastrous defeat of 1806. Twenty years after the death of the great king, the Prussian army appeared content to rest on its ever more-faded laurels; Frederick's legacy had turned into a burden. Jena, or something like it, had become a necessary but costly purge, not just for the military but for the whole society—from top to bottom.[8]

As in 1848, when the national assembly in Frankfurt tried to agree on a German emperor, there is considerable talk in the novel of Prince Louis Ferdinand as an alternative to his cousin, Frederick William III. Pitting the two characters against each other allows Lewald to examine Prussian society and politics in some depth, especially since her protagonist is not a particularly plausible replacement for the king. In fact, while she shows the king as timid and inflexible, Lewald's Louis Ferdinand symbolizes wasted potential and moral decay. The prince's most notable failing is his womanizing, but he also has no sense of money and carries the additional stain of French aristocratic manners. The contrast could scarcely be sharper. Among other things, Frederick William III and Queen Louisa present a convincing picture of domestic propriety, and as we shall soon see, they come to stand for those German virtues that should not only defeat Napoleon but also lead to the remaking of Germany.[9] Marital bliss, for all its limitations as a political creed, at first seems to be what Louis Ferdinand wants too, albeit in his own inappropriate fashion. As the novel opens he is rushing off to visit Henriette Fromm, the mother of his two illegitimate children but a woman whose station in life prevents their marriage. Since he cannot be king, Louis Ferdinand complains to Rahel, who is by then his confidante and passionate admirer: "Then give me the freedom to be a middle-class citizen; give me the freedom that is rooted in the equality of mankind! Let me choose a wife according to the dictates of my own heart."[10] Of course, things are never that easy. Louis Ferdinand moves to a cottage in the countryside with Henriette and their children, but he is soon bored and begins visiting a former lover on her husband's nearby estate. That woman is one of many. More telling, however, is the fatuous emptiness of Louis Ferdinand's high-minded protest. While he might illustrate the need for change, as Lewald constructs him, Prince Louis Ferdinand cannot carry the nation's hopes. At his best, he serves as mouthpiece and ear for those Germans whose complaints are legitimate.

Louis Ferdinand knows, for example, that the young soldier who murdered his fiancée will be executed, the victim of corrupt officers and an impossibly harsh military organization. Similarly, a manufacturer's son commits suicide after running the gantlet, a punishment imposed because he too deserted to marry the woman he loved. The second case is complicated by the bride's Jewish origins; neither family sanctions the proposed union, and the Prussian state also intrudes. As Rahel explains to Louis Ferdinand, it is the "insane laws of your country which, to wipe us out from the earth like poisonous reptiles, permit only two children of every Jewish family to marry in their own native town and settle there."[11] Lewald underscores her complaint by the reference to Prussia, or perhaps Germany, as "your country" rather than "ours." As the narrator notes, overcoming legal and military hindrances to this couple's marriage would have given the young man more reason to fight. Prussia could have been *his* country, too, and his wife's. In essence, the irrationality of such persecution and Louis Ferdinand's desire for rights that do not exist, either for him or the bourgeoisie, emphasize both the woeful inadequacy of the Prussian army and the increasing illegitimacy of the society that it was supposed to protect. If the state is so corrupt as to be indefensible, no wonder it cannot defend itself; for Lewald, Louis Ferdinand is a perfect symbol for both sides of its failure.

Ultimately, Prussia's malaise went far deeper than Lewald could represent with a single individual, so she inserts a number of other weaknesses, unconnected to her unfortunate hero. A chief target is the government and its incompetent ministers, particularly Count Haugwitz, who was in charge of foreign policy. The narrator compares his home to Versailles before 1789: "people close their eyes and ears, they do not want to see what is going on beyond the borders, do not want to hear what the voices of the people demand."[12] The speaker, a Frenchman in Berlin, seems surprised that Prussia has not already had a revolution. Later, the respect the narrator feels for Napoleon and the French army contrasts with the prerevolutionary torpor of the foreign minister. At a time when the king and queen have made a public show of purchasing German fabrics, the reader sees Haugwitz "wrapped up in a housecoat of Persian silk, his scarf untied, jabot opened, and his feet enveloped in warm slippers."[13] The man charged with keeping the country safe appears soft, even effeminate, with a taste for foreign luxuries—in short, the exact opposite of what Prussia needs for the approaching war with France.

As was so frequently the case in treatments of Frederick the Great, in *Prince Louis Ferdinand* France and the French always carry a double meaning. That country's norms and values, precisely because of their complexity and ambiguity, function as a liminar for the text's Germans. On the one hand, Lewald associates Haugwitz and the rest of the old ruling class with an aristocratic tradition whose appeal dates from the age of Frederick. The association makes it difficult for the country's generals and bureaucrats to abandon French customs, and it puts Louis Ferdinand on the wrong side of the equation. On the other hand, both the devotion that the national cause continues to inspire in France and the grudging admiration that some Germans have for Napoleon—the dynamic general, resolute negotiator, and newly crowned emperor—serve as models for those who would arouse the populace and reform the Prussian state and its army. The question is whether Prussia and, by implication, Germany need their own Napoleon. In broader terms, will they have to abandon older, aristocratic French customs and then adopt

CHAPTER 4

newer, revolutionary French values in order to survive as Prussians or Germans? And who will lead, if not embody, the transition from one form of social organization to the next?

When a group of officers ask Louis Ferdinand to urge the king to replace Haugwitz and to prepare for war, the prince demurs, claiming that dissent within the officer corps or the royal family amounts to treason. That night, however, Louis Ferdinand dreams about a future in which he possesses Napoleon's courage and sense of purpose. "He saw himself at the head of an army, the best men of the Fatherland streamed toward him, he advanced toward Bonaparte, the spirit of the Great Frederick hovered over his banners."[14] In reality nothing happens, because neither Louis Ferdinand nor Frederick William III can match Napoleon, nor do they aspire to the mantle of Frederick the Great. As sympathetic as the narrator sometimes is to the book's hero, this is a very bourgeois novel, so Prince Louis Ferdinand does not emerge as the answer to the country's misery. Queen Louisa, whose saintly image finally causes the prince to renounce his insubordination, also proves insufficient. In Lewald's version of events the nation apparently needed Stein, Hardenberg, and Humboldt, Prussian reformers who were not themselves middle class but who nevertheless championed the broadly based meritocracy that Louis Ferdinand advocated, at least in theory. Unfortunately for him and for those who would have liked to see a successful version of 1848 occur in 1806, Lewald's narrative is undone by its hero's lack of real virtues, as well as by the complexity of the situation it examines. Louis Ferdinand cannot make good on the hope that his fellow officers see in him, and those readers who identify with the prince are just as likely to be disappointed. By itself Jena cannot produce a happy ending, and one wonders to what degree the difficulty is inherent to the subject matter and ultimately its limiting weakness. For as important as defeats and lost causes might be to the national myth of Germany, they make for problematic and less than popular fiction.

Instead of promise, Lewald shows Prussia in 1806 with an indolent king, an incompetent government, a thoroughly corrupt society, and a wastrel prince. And while Louis Ferdinand does not stay alive long enough to participate in the disaster at Jena, his death a few days before the disaster prefigures that grand defeat. Louis Ferdinand dies during the battle of Saalfeld in an attempt at preventing a small mistake from turning into the subsequent debacle. However, not only is Louis Ferdinand's effort doomed by larger social and political forces, but his fate also depends on the actions of an individual soldier, whose own small tragedy once again illustrates what is wrong with Prussia more clearly than any factual analysis could do—at least for ordinary readers. While trying to rally his troops, Louis Ferdinand happens on a man whom careful readers might remember from the beginning of the novel. He is the foreigner pressed into Prussian service who refuses to fight, thereby condemning an entire battalion, including its commander, to death. Louis Ferdinand's heroic end is senseless and in vain but neither arbitrary nor accidental. As the novel represents the situation, from the lowest levels of the army all the way to the king, Prussian society is rotten and about to collapse. Still, Lewald manages to extract a moment of consolation from her hero's demise: "Fate which had denied him the experience of seeing the revival of 1813 had at least spared him the deathly pain of witnessing the hopeless defeat of the Fatherland, or so it seemed at the time."[15]

That last phrase, "or so it seemed at the time," underscores Prussia's nearly miraculous recovery during the years 1813–15, which must have been impossible to imagine in 1806. But it also throws readers into a kind of double present—into the period of the novel's composition and into the reader's own time, whenever that might be. Unlike Louis Ferdinand, contemporary readers knew what happened next, but they still had to become aware what that particular past meant to them. As acutely conscious as Lewald seems to have been of the project of narrating a common past, the phrase "or so it seemed at the time" indicates she also recognized the unfinished nature of her task. If the novel's lack of focus is a weakness in narrative terms, it is also a potential strength, because it allowed her readers to compare various interpretations of what was not yet a common heritage. In fact, Lewald's jarring final phrase suggests that in 1849 the task of narrating Jena as part of a German national myth had barely begun. As a group writers would have to explain the nation's decline before they could posit its rise, and, for all its difficulties as a source for middlebrow fiction, Jena gave a surprising number of authors the perfect subject matter to use in exploring what had gone wrong.

Poisoners and Profligates

Willibald Alexis's treatment of Jena, *Keeping Calm Is the Citizen's First Duty,* appeared in 1852, three years after Lewald's novel. His work is even more sprawling—1,247 pages in the modern edition—but Alexis spends even less time than Lewald with actual battles. Like her, Alexis is not interested in warfare or the army but in the society he holds responsible for the military disaster. Best known as the author of eight "novels of the fatherland," the subject matter of which ranges from the fourteenth to the early nineteenth centuries, Alexis was not patriotic in any conventional sense.[16] For him, the fatherland was Brandenburg Prussia rather than Germany, and at times his critical historical fiction seems ill suited to Germany as a whole. Despite what commentators as knowledgeable as Fontane have claimed, Alexis's work never indicates whether he believed that Prussia had a German mission, or even if he thought that the Prussia he represented in fiction was up to the task of unifying Germany in a desirable manner.[17] If nothing else, Alexis understood just how messy the history of his fatherland was. His achievement—as well as the chief difficulty in dealing with *Keeping Calm Is the Citizen's First Duty*—is that the novel chronicles the entire amorphous mixture of mediocrity, mendacity, and evil that characterized Prussia at the beginning of the nineteenth century. Moreover, it does so without the narrative luxury of a central figure such as Louis Ferdinand.

Contrary to Fontane's critique, Alexis does not focus on Madame Lupinus, the privy councilor's wife, who poisons her husband, her sister-in-law, a niece and a nephew. In fact, she is only one of two poisoners among the novel's many delinquents. That long list includes noblemen, ministers, courtesans, and merchants, who harbor in their midst not just murderers but thieves, louts, cowards, and incompetents. In Alexis's representation of 1806, there are no heroes and nothing to minimize the gravity of Prussia's inglorious and nearly total defeat. The novel's characters are linked by a series of overlapping friendships and business connections, and by their shared corruption and moral decay. The resulting series of plots combines to present a damning portrait of a ruling class not only unworthy of its position and dangerous for the people it purports to govern but also incapable of defending itself. Ultimately, readers must have wondered how such people managed to stave off defeat for so long.

The answer, the one thing that seems to have kept Prussia afloat in the sea changes brought about by the French Revolution, was the memory of Frederick the Great. But his legacy was costly. Not only did the Frederickian system demand a leader as capable as the great king had been, but it also froze Prussia's society, government, and army in their eighteenth-century forms while the rest of Europe was undergoing rapid and almost unprecedented change. One character even asks "if Frederick's genius itself would be capable of parrying [Napoleon] on every front."[18] The question is rhetorical. Of course he would, but compared to their illustrious forebear, Frederick's heirs appear puny and timid. Thus, the reader overhears discussions within the general staff about introducing conscription on the French model, a suggestion that is rebuffed in the great king's name: "Frederick would never have conquered Silesia with theories; our army is the way it is and not different . . . would it still be good, if a new recruiting system were imposed? For God's sake, no new patches on an old coat. [There may be] disorder beyond our borders, but calm, calm, calm within them! Don't touch a thing!"[19] In effect, keeping calm becomes the reason for Prussia's failure, and the book's title, taken from a proclamation issued by the governor of Berlin a few days after the defeat at Jena, sounds like an unlikely prescription for success after 1806, or, for that matter, after 1850. For Alexis, the phrase is more likely an ironic demand for change in a society whose ruling class had wasted Frederick's legacy.

In part, the book chronicles a series of generational conflicts, but, ominously, the sons and daughters seem as incompetent as their elders. No one is up to the challenge that Napoleon and revolutionary France present. As an example I choose Privy Councilor Bovillard and his son, Louis. The former is a government official of considerable power and influence, while the son has spent much of his time in prison for drunkenness and inopportune patriotism. Louis Bovillard is one of the hotheaded young men demanding war with France to preserve the fatherland's honor. His father counsels peace, because he knows that Prussia cannot take on Napoleon and win. At first glance, the father seems completely rational, while his son appears to be a dangerous lunatic, but for Alexis things are not that simple.

Following years of estrangement and separation the two men meet again at the privy councilor's home, but that potentially happy scene occurs only after another telling delay. According to the butler, who turns away a number of visitors, the elder Bovillard is discussing significant government business, but one of those rebuffed is doubtful: "If only this terrible helplessness would really lead to advice—and if that would only produce deeds!"[20] In fact, the privy councilor and three friends are planning to embarrass an opponent by involving him in an affair with a married woman. They are also about to open their fourth bottle of wine. Not surprisingly, when a courier arrives with the urgent

CHAPTER 4

news that ninety thousand French troops have crossed the Prussian border, the butler tells him to go away: "Nothing is accepted after ten o'clock. [Come back] tomorrow morning at eight. If it's really important, you can ring at seven."[21]

At this point Louis Bovillard comes up the back stairs, not as the prodigal son but as a fiery student patriot: "Father! Forget for a moment the son whom you have forbidden to cross your threshold. Behold a son of the fatherland. This concerns [the fatherland's] honor, perhaps its existence."[22] Contrary to the reader's expectations, the father suddenly turns reasonable, although reason and with it moderation are precisely what the son hates. With the freedom to be honest normally accorded children, fools, and drunks, this consummate politician warns his son: "There are hotheads like you, dreamers, patriots, unfortunately some in very high positions and very dangerous, who want to risk the fate of the state on a single card."[23] Lowering his voice, lest he be overheard, the elder Bovillard continues: "We are not armed; there you have the truth that one is not supposed to express."[24] When the son asks about the millions appropriated every year for the army, his father answers: "They have been spent to preserve the appearance, the exterior semblance of Frederick's army. Everything is polished and freshly painted, but the wood is rotten and brittle . . . Our fortresses have collapsed, our generals are old men, our system of leadership has decayed, most of our troops have never been in battle, their drill is antiquated, and we are facing an enemy who is a swift as the wind."[25] As accurate as this assessment might be, the son sees caution that has become cowardice, and he wants no part of the truth that seems to have paralyzed the Prussian state. In effect, Louis Bovillard speaks for an entire generation when he asks his father to disinherit him. He is indifferent to financial loss, for unlike his father, the younger Bovillard is too high-minded to worry about money or inherited position; rather, he wants to seize the opportunity that freedom from the old order, from the mistakes of the past would give him. He hopes for a fresh start, personally and politically. In mythic terms, the young men of this novel are preparing the ground for Prussia's and Germany's redemption. For them, Jena will not simply be a disaster but a cleansing fire from whose ashes the new nation can arise.

Those who called for such a conflagration were reacting both to the old order's criminality, ranging from corruption to murder, and to its adherence to French norms and values. While Frederick the Great's tastes in literature and philosophy made it easy to represent him as, at worst, a liminal figure, Alexis, unlike Lewald, finds no need for ambiguity in dealing with the Prussian ruling class at the beginning of the nineteenth century. Although the novel sometimes treats a taste for French refinement ironically, it ultimately scorns those whose manners undermine their politics. Their treasonable habits point to the root causes behind Prussia's weakness and irresolution. Among the many examples of spiritual malaise, characters' discussions of fashionable writers allowed Alexis to unmask the book's true villains. Not coincidentally, he also makes a case for his own work.

At a reception attended by Madame Lupinus, the evil woman wonders why people are still discussing the merits of Goethe and Schiller, as if Schiller's preeminence were not already well established. Her real interest is contemporary literature, and Privy Councilor Bovillard seems to be an expert. His office contains "elegantly bound [copies] of the most recent works of French literature," but he proclaims—in French—that only "the classical is eternal! Racine and Corneille."[26] As for German literature, by which he means the Romanticism then popular in some circles, Bovillard asks, rhetorically, whether either of the brothers Schlegel will ever get a university post. "And this young man, this Monsieur Tic or Tique, who wants to turn the world on its head with his muddled fantasies, . . . will anyone give a hoot about him in ten years?"[27] Ludwig Tieck, whose name is so badly botched here, is the subject of considerable abuse in the novel, and he probably represents the anti-Alexis. When some middle-class parents think about the content of their daughter's education, they readily agree on geography, history, Goethe, and Schiller "so that one isn't stupid in society," but the father wants to draw the line at "Tiedge, who is supposed to have extravagant ideas and preaches a new litany of immoral principles."[28] He is dissuaded only when his wife notes that Tieck also wrote a number of moralistic tales for children but nothing, readers are left to conclude, as relevant as the novel in which they find the above exchange.

For the elder Bovillard, however, the most dangerous notion, which motivated both the collecting and writing of fairy tales by the Romantics, was their sense of national mission. He rails against writers who want to bring heroic figures from the German past to the stage or the page. "They should let Hermann [the hero of Kleist's dramatic call for German unity and liberation] sleep on his bearskin."[29] The privy councilor prefers to write French verses as a means of political expression, and he publishes them under female pseudonyms, thereby marking his taste for French manners and literature as decadent, unpatriotic, and lacking in manly virtues. No wonder the nominal males who run the Prussian government fear Napoleon. How much better off they might have been reading Alexis, who points to the real problems, thereby paving the way for genuine solutions.

In contrast to these weak male Francophiles, Alexis portrays women as strong, and some of his female characters are even patriotic. The much-maligned Madame Lupinus, for example, turns to crime only because she can find no legitimate outlet for her ambitions in a society dominated by effeminate men. Under other circumstances she might have become Germany's Napoleon and saved the nation from its humiliating defeat. Instead she marries for wealth and social position and has only endless, meaningless social engagements to occupy her talents. Bored, unfulfilled, and politically impotent, Madame Lupinus starts poisoning her oppressors.

Mercifully, no aristocratic superhero saves the day. Alexis breaks with the conventions of popular criminal fiction begun in the 1840s by Eugène Sue and leaves all the book's wrongs unrighted—including, of course, Prussia's defeat at Jena. The few positive characters manage to expose the evildoers but never to bring them to justice. The book's message must be that no one in Prussia possessed either the strength or authority to clean house. That role is certainly too large for its apparent claimant, Adelheid Alltag, the young woman whose parents worried about her reading Tieck. Her failure is particularly unfortunate, because she would have been better suited to performing great deeds in this eminently bourgeois novel than a woman bearing the surname "everyday."

Instead, Alexis turns to Prussia's Queen Louisa, but in contrast to her later admirers, his portrait is decidedly ambiguous. On the one hand, he calls Louisa the "patron saint [or goddess] of the fatherland" as well as the "mother of the country."[30] On the other hand, Louisa's banality and sentimentality undercut the political potential of her vaunted virtues. Again, the telling issue is literature. Louisa considers Novalis, the brothers Schlegel, and Tieck to be "eccentric reading matter that stirs up the blood; [they are] inappropriate for a young woman who wants to cultivate her heart and mind for conversation with virtuous people."[31] She prefers the escapist fictions of August Lafontaine, like Fouqué and Fontane a German of Huguenot descent: "how many warm and happy hours do we owe to him, how much comfort for those evenings when we retreat to the sofa after a vexing day?"[32] Since Alexis did not write the sort of book that the queen liked to read, one cannot assume that he is sympathetic to her argument. In fact, Adelheid Alltag's defense of books like his own may anticipate Fontane's criticism that Alexis painted too dark a picture for it to be art: "It seems to me that the writer's task is to portray people as they are. Since he is an artist, he can use his wonderfully crafted mirror to enlarge and improve what is beautiful and grand, and he might also be permitted to make what is ugly and evil somewhat more ugly." Lafontaine, she continues, growing less tentative with every sentence in what is, in the novel, a much longer passage, "is familiar with our weaknesses and tries to comfort us; he holds our hand and plays seductive chords . . . [but] when we wake up, we are ashamed because he has made us weak, where we should be strong."[33]

A less engaged writer than Alexis might have dropped the debate at this point, having just presented both sides of a long-standing controversy concerning the use and abuse of literature in life. But the notion that art can make readers strong was apparently too important for Alexis to let it go without further comment. He turns from literature to the similar place of history in society when a character who fears war with France alleges that Frederick William III wants to ban history from the classroom: "Where do all the misfortunes that nations suffer come from? From examples that we carelessly take from antiquity, from the irrational application of ideas that were true then to conditions today."[34] History, particularly the memory of Frederick the Great, might legitimate Prussia's Hohenzollern dynasty; but the wrong sort of history—for example, Kleist's dramatic presentation of Hermann the German resisting Roman invaders—could just as easily undermine Frederick's heirs. Better, from the perspective of the peace party, to leave the past alone. It is therefore not surprising when, a few pages later, Prussian troops who are about to march off to war refuse to sing patriotic tunes of past glories, and one of their commanding generals doubts that history has any effect at all: "No soldier is going to be invigorated by someone croaking the history of the Seven Years' War. Did Papa Gleim [Johann Wilhelm Ludwig Gleim, the author, in 1758, of *War Songs of a Prussian Grenadier*] help the great king win his battles? Let them sing of schnapps and buxom maidens."[35] Readers might also begin to wonder just why they are slogging through more than twelve hundred pages of fictional history rather than enjoying a bawdy romance, but if they make it to the novel's final chapter, the narrator reveals his purpose, which he differentiates from the task of academic history.

CHAPTER 4

Returning to the book's title, the narrative voice reminds readers that after the disastrous defeat at Jena the king's ministers ordered the citizens of Berlin to keep calm in order to mitigate the effects of a French occupation. Most Berliners were "well-meaning" (*gutgesinnt*) and obeyed, which is the faintest praise imaginable, particularly when that weak adjective is repeated just before a lengthy discussion of those who were not so "well-meaning":

> There were men, and women, too, who addressed that evil by its name. . . . These few were the flints upon which steel could strike sparks and ignite a small fire that grew into the conflagration [of 1813–15]. . . . History has identified many of them, or is now beginning to identify them, but how many others are now asleep, whose headstones are covered with moss that history will not scrape away. . . . Literature, which cannot pass over wretchedness and evil in silence, can nevertheless remember brave individuals, and if, in order to be truthful, we have to present images of cowardly defeatism in the Prussian capital, we are also obligated to note a few developments that appear like distant clouds on the horizon presaging better times.[36]

That injunction lets us return to Louis Bovillard, a hero who would be forgotten except for the genre of historical fiction. After an infatuation with Napoleon, the younger Bovillard turns patriotic, renounces his wanton ways, and declares his love for Adelheid Alltag. The narrator repeatedly describes her as a "German maiden" (*deutsches Mädchen*, 1: 272, 370), and the name Alltag links the couple to the German people in a manner that would be difficult for Louis Bovillard, the noble son of a disreputable privy councilor whose name is French. Adelheid directs Louis onto "the only path to a new life, the fatherland," but only after she convinces him that Germany has a future rather than just a glorious past. At first, the young man is doubtful. "The people will never again awake, they are not one [i.e., a single] people. Germany is only the dream of poets."[37] But Adelheid, who has just read Schiller's *History of the Thirty Years' War*, reminds him of that era's courageous fighters, men whose hopes and dreams kept their honor and a noble cause from ruin. The upshot is that Bovillard joins the Prussian army just in time to witness Louis Ferdinand's death at Saalfeld, an event that seems less pointless in the context that Adelheid Alltag has given him. Meanwhile, she accompanies Queen Louisa to the front, where, much to Napoleon's dismay, the queen is rousing the troops to action. Napoleon accuses her of everything from secretly receiving English money to conspiring with the Russian Tsar Alexander: "She is the hope or the puppet of the German fanatics. She egged [the king] on, she stoked the fire." Napoleon then offers to make peace at the last moment, but says there should be "no women [using the pejorative word *Weiber*] between us. The queen has to leave."[38]

In addition to his misogyny, Napoleon appears to be genuinely afraid Louisa could unite Germany, and in this role the Prussian queen almost becomes the heroine of Alexis's novel. Louis Bovillard, captured as a spy, has been listening to Napoleon's rantings, so when he is set free as a messenger, the young man decides to warn the queen rather than take Napoleon's offer of peace to the king. His constructive disobedience mirrors that of General Yorck von Wartenburg in 1812, when he broke with Prussian politics in anticipation of the Wars of Liberation, but the younger Bovillard is too stained by his past misdeeds to set foot in the promised land of German unity, at least in this life. Nevertheless, he finds redemption in a passage where realistic description crosses into the realm of hokey symbolism. Louis arrives at the queen's quarters wounded and so exhausted that he falls from his horse. Someone carries him into a nearby chapel, where God in his Prussian Protestant guise must have been smiling: "Sunlight fell through the yellow panes onto his face as Adelheid entered."[39] She arrives not a moment too soon; there is time for only a quick marriage ceremony and a kiss before the young man dies.

Queen Louisa also dies before the patriotic upheaval of 1813–15, but her attempts at rousing both her husband and the Prussian army appear to have been just as worthy of divine approval: "A sunbeam that fell on her hair through the treetops set a golden crown on her head."[40] Although he was critical of the queen's reading habits, writing in 1852, Alexis might have thought that Prussia and its royal family once again needed the kind of steeling that Louisa had offered her compatriots in 1806. Louisa's image has not yet solidified into saintly perfection, but for Alexis she remains patriotic and practical: "I say that my husband, my children, the succession to the throne, everything that I hold dear was in danger. . . . Yes, I thought that war was necessary, and if that was a crime, then I hoped for it."[41] As corrupt, immoral, criminal, and inept

CHAPTER 4

as Alexis depicts the Prussian ruling class to have been, this novel's sympathetic figures—Queen Louisa, Adelheid Alltag, and Louis Bovillard—represent the hope that Prussia will rise again. For all of its darkness, *Keeping Calm Is the Citizen's First Duty* nevertheless uses the disaster at Jena to point to the future, and Alexis employs Queen Louisa and her helpmates to symbolize hope in a manner that would prove symptomatic of a rash of books and images devoted less to the battle and more to the queen's memory during the rest of the century.

Queen Louisa Turns Bourgeois

Not surprisingly, Louisa Mühlbach devoted some of her vast energies to Prussia's queen, and it is in her novels that readers began to see Queen Louisa's potential not only as Germany's mother but also as the prime example of the new nation's values. To be sure, Mühlbach continued a trend that had begun as early as the queen's death in 1810 and that received particular emphasis when the first Iron Cross was issued in her memory in 1813, but once again the novel proved its special worth in providing narrative content to mythic representations that were only implicit in fountains, hospitals, and schools for girls dedicated to Louisa.[42] As usual, Mühlbach exceeds expectations. Eight of the sixteen books of her 1858 cycle, *Napoleon in Germany,* revolve around Louisa, and they make up two substantial volumes in English translation, *Louisa of Prussia and Her Times* and *Napoleon and the Queen of Prussia*.[43] Readers first encounter the royal couple just after Frederick William III ascended to the throne in 1797. The queen's mistress of ceremonies rebukes the king, telling him that his actions undermine civilization as she knows it: "Having often heard your majesty, in conversation with her majesty the queen, contrary to etiquette, use the vulgar German language instead of the French tongue, which is the language of courts throughout Germany, they [the other courtiers] believe they have a perfect right to speak German whenever they please."[44] Since Frederick William is used to the woman's complaints, which he terms "unnatural and mere affectation," he is more amused than angry.[45] Alone with Louisa, Frederick William vows that they will remain a "Christian family," and he also promises that they will use royal palaces only for state functions, otherwise remaining in their more modest home, content to eat the same number of courses at dinner as before, even though their meals should now be fit for a king.[46] The royal couple's conversation takes place in private, because, contrary to all etiquette, the king has slipped into the queen's chamber through a side door, while her mistress of ceremonies, carefully traversing the six reception rooms that guard its main entrance, has not yet arrived. Historians, as Mühlbach was fond of pointing out, would remain as unable to break through to Louisa's essence as this poor courtier.

Observant readers might remark that if the queen's portion of the royal residence has six reception rooms, any reference to the simplicity of their home is either disingenuous or a sign of how completely out of touch Mühlbach has made her characters. Still, however mistaken or ironic the situation may be, its terms are important. It is not sufficient to notice that bourgeois values have begun to permeate nineteenth-century novels. When the king and queen claim to prefer simplicity and quiet pleasures to luxury and ostentation, they stand in sharp contrast to the French norms long associated with Europe's aristocracy. By embracing romantic unions rather than arranged dynastic marriages, by valuing comfort over pomp, and by endorsing the nuclear family, where husband and wife use the familiar "du" instead of the linguistically formal, emotionally distant "Sie," Frederick William III and Louisa set themselves apart from Germany's traditional elite. The inherited caste identities discussed in chapter 2 have now become vaguely treasonous, and the aristocracy has lost its claim to represent the nation. Louisa remains the queen, but Mühlbach employs her and Frederick William III to begin the process of relabeling middle-class traits as fundamentally German.[47] Frederick William III might slip in through the queen's side door, but he arrives in the middle of a large and important enterprise.[48]

In Mühlbach's treatment of the era neither Frederick William III nor Queen Louisa display any of the liminality associated with Frederick the Great, and it is beginning to become clear—especially in these fictionalized and essentially liberal versions of the larger national narrative—that renewal will come from the people. It will therefore incorporate popular language and customs. Queen Louisa's role in that larger story is to function as a transitional or mediating figure between Frederick the Great and the mass of ordinary Germans who supposedly united to fight the Wars of Liberation and who could still unify Germany, even in the decade after 1848 when Mühlbach was writing. The historical queen of Prussia may have spoken German, loved her husband, and even preferred beer to wine, although the latter seems particularly unlikely, but there is far more at stake than accuracy in any representation of these qualities. The issue is what Queen Louisa stood for rather than who she was. It is, to be sure, ironic that a queen helped make the terms "German" and "bourgeois" synonymous, but once Louisa had passed into the national pantheon, to be truly German one had to espouse middle-class values, while the bourgeoisie was increasingly viewed as the one true source of nationalist sentiments.

As the novel's title indicates, *Louisa of Prussia and Her Times* contains more than a teasingly egalitarian portrait of the queen. Mühlbach's personalized version of German history teems with strong women who are just as involved as Louisa in the struggle to free Germany from French oppression and unite its disparate territories in a single nation-state. Like the queen, they broach the twin issues of German identity and women's role in the nation, but some of these women raise the stakes involved in what it meant to be German in 1858 to an even higher level. Two of the most conflicted figures in the book first appear as Jewish beauties from Berlin, albeit with very different social positions: Fanny Itzig is the daughter of a prominent banker, and she is destined for an arranged marriage with a Jewish man. Marianne Maier, by contrast, is alleged to have been one of Goethe's lovers, and in the novel she is the mistress of the Austrian ambassador to Prussia, Prince von Reuß. He cannot marry her unless she converts to Catholicism, and even after she consents, their marriage must remain secret, which makes her the object of public ridicule. Marianne Maier nevertheless inherits both a title and a considerable fortune after her husband's death. As Princess von Eibenberg she moves to Vienna, where she is active in the cause of German unification. She even attempts to assassinate Napoleon, and she finances Friedrich Gentz's notorious anti-French pamphlet, *Germany in Her Deepest Depredation*. However, these are small successes, and they come at the cost of Maier's religious if not her national identity.

Fanny Itzig's life also raises the issue of German-Jewish relationships. When her father decides to marry off his three daughters, he decides, "they should wear exclusively the productions of German industry, and that not a single piece of their new household goods be of French manufacture."[49] The idea causes such a stir that he is forced to exhibit their trousseaus to the curious citizens of Berlin, including Queen Louisa, who remarks, "How glad I am to see that Germany is really able to do entirely without France."[50] Not that the situation for Fanny and her sisters is entirely happy; their father has arranged all three marriages. As Fanny puts it, "We rich Jewesses are treated in the same manner as poor princesses; we are sold to the highest bidder."[51] Fanny's husband, Baron von Arnstein, whom she does not love, is both Jewish and a Viennese nobleman, but her admirers include a Prince von Liechtenstein, who offers the following insulting but not unexpected proposal of marriage, should she divorce her husband: "You will cast off the semblance of a religion which in reality is yours no longer. . . . You have ceased to be a Jewess, owing to your education, to your habits, and to your views of life." Although she loves the prince, Fanny replies, "Never," and Mühlbach's plot kills him in a duel the next day.[52]

These characters demonstrate that nineteenth-century representations of Germany were not resolutely anti-Semitic. In fact, several works dealt with here contain serious discussions of the difficulties faced by Jews who remain committed both to their faith and Germany, particularly to German culture. In Fanny's case it is Marianne Maier, uncomfortably rechristened Princess von Eibenberg, who offers solace and a sense of purpose: "You shall be the mediator between the aristocracy of blood and of pedigree and the aristocracy of money—the mediator between the Christians and the Jews."[53] "And you shall assist our despised and down-trodden Jews, too, by proving to those who scorn us and contemptuously treat us as aliens, that we feel like natives and children of the country in which we were born [greater Germany], and that we do not seek for our Jerusalem in the distant Orient, but in the fatherland we share with all other Germans."[54] This is a tall order, but its representation in the novel indicates that Mühlbach's keen awareness of the problems involved German-Jewish assimilation, which necessarily includes the juggling of difference and similarity. However, knowledge of the dilemma does not translate into an ability to solve it in realistic fiction; Mühlbach fudges the issue by consigning the end of Fanny von Arnstein's story to a footnote, where it belongs not "to romance, but to reality."[55] Feminine grief over the deceased prince overshadows the impossibility of her political situation. The lesson seems to be that even Mühlbach found it difficult to construct a happy ending for strong women, particularly because she felt obligated to remain faithful to the historical record.

She has an easier time dealing with less prominent figures, people about whom little documentation survives. Readers probably also identified more readily with their peers than with the queen of Prussia, however normal she is portrayed in historical fiction. One of many charac-

CHAPTER 4

ters who exemplifies Mühlbach's search for the common touch is Anna Palm, the wife of a Nuremberg bookseller, a man who was executed for treason two months before the battle of Jena for publishing Gentz's pamphlet. Mühlbach spends far more time detailing the wife's efforts to locate her husband and intercede on his behalf than she does on the man's arrest and trial. She also takes her time depicting the other women of Braun, where the French have ordered the population to witness and thereby legitimate Palm's execution: "But while all the men were giving way to cowardly fear, while they timidly swallowed their rage and humiliation, the women arose in the genuine and bold enthusiasm of their grief and compassion. They could not threaten, nor arm their hand with the sword, like men, but they could beseech and supplicate, and in the place of weapons in their hands they had tears in their eyes."[56] Nothing these women do can save Palm, but the sight of them kneeling in the town square unnerves the general. In addition to indicating how widespread Mühlbach thought anti-French feelings must have been, their gesture shows the moral force women could exert. It also involves them in a national narrative they could not enter as easily as men did; their actions give women readers a stake in the nation.

Unfortunately, despite these demonstrations of female strength and resolution, Mühlbach still has to deal with the disaster at Jena without compromising either the queen or the nationalist project. Her solution is to contrast popular enthusiasm for the war with the opinions of a few "prudent and sagacious men," with the clear implication that Prussia's ruling class was actually neither careful nor perceptive.[57] In two or three pages, Mühlbach covers the entire range of difficulties that these unnamed observers saw as undermining the Prussian army: the generals were old, lazy, and too used to the comforts of their quarters; their soldiers had grown "hoary" (*ergraut*) and had no experience of war; the army's organization was outmoded, its arms defective, if well polished, and the supply system was chaotic; most important, relentless harsh discipline had "cudgeled ambition and self-reliance" from the troops. Faced with Napoleon's generalship and his well-equipped, enthusiastic soldiers, "The apprehensions of the prudent were but too well founded, and the anxiety visible in the king's gloomy mien was perfectly justified."[58] Queen Louisa is still confident, but she seems totally unaware of the military situation. In any case, her function in the novel is not so much to embody popular enthusiasm as to express the unwavering conviction that a renewed and bourgeois Prussia will triumph in the face of all odds.

In the second installment of her novel, Mühlbach shows the queen's long trail of suffering, humiliation, and eventual justification. In contrast to the image Alexis conveys, readers of this work do not sense that society was corrupt from top to bottom; rather, the Prussian army and a few ministers disappointed both the queen and the overwhelming majority of Prussians who enthusiastically supported both her and the national cause. Mühlbach omits the battle of Jena altogether, which makes it easier for her to show a renewed Prussian spirit rising already from the ashes. A few days after the event, while Napoleon is occupying Berlin and stealing mementos from Frederick the Great's study in Potsdam, Louisa is already able to foresee victory in defeat: "'Ah! my sons, you are old enough to comprehend and appreciate the events now befalling us; at a future time, when your mother will be no more among the living, remember this unhappy hour. Shed tears for me, as I do for the ruin of our country! But listen,' she added, and her eyes beamed with enthusiasm, 'do not content yourselves with shedding tears! Act, develop your strength. Prussia's genius, perhaps, will favor you. Then deliver your nation from the disgrace and humiliation in which it is at present groveling!'"[59]

Although Mühlbach fashions Louisa into an inspiration for her sons, in keeping with the biblical precedents that echo through most biographies of her, the queen does not live to set foot in the promised land of German unification. In fact, she does not even survive to witness the string of Prussia's victories that began in 1813. The king and queen return to Berlin in 1809 in muted triumph, but Louisa has already fallen victim to the disease that will kill her. Like many nineteenth-century heroines, she is unaccountably weak. She seems to realize that she will not survive to see Napoleon's fall, and she knows why: "This man [Napoleon], who is to be married to a German princess [Maria Louisa, the daughter of the Austrian emperor] tomorrow, has wounded my heart so that it will at last destroy me."[60] The implication is that Louisa died a martyr for Germany. Indeed, it would not unduly stretch the biblical parallel to say that she perished for Germany's sins. The battle gets short shrift in Mühlbach's multivolume novel, because Louisa's sacrifice is so much more important to the work's overall point. Queen Louisa's death expiates Prussia's failure at Jena; her martyrdom enables the German nation's rebirth.[61]

CHAPTER 4

Nonfiction Versions of Louisa

In 1858, when Mühlbach published her novel, Louisa's second son, Prince William, took over as regent for his mentally ill older brother, Frederick William IV. Three years later he ascended the Prussian throne in his own right as William I, and with that same name became the emperor of Germany in 1871. No wonder it became so easy to link the defeat and humiliation of Jena with Germany's complete reversal of fortune when Prussia vanquished Napoleon I's nephew, Napoleon III, in 1870. Only one long generation separated the two events, and mythmakers seized on the continuity. Emperor William I was living proof that Jena had been a cleansing experience, a decline and fall that enabled Prussia's renewal and Germany's ascent to undreamed heights. With Louisa's son on the imperial throne, authors poured ever more energy into chronicles of her life. A prime example is a four-part series, published in 1876 in the most widely circulated magazine in Germany, *The Garden Bower*, to mark the hundredth anniversary of Louisa's birth.[62]

The series begins by contrasting Louisa with other famous queens, Elizabeth I of England and Russia's Catherine the Great, and it notes that unlike those notable rulers, "this genuinely German princess made herself immortal through her authentic feminine virtues, through moral purity, selfless love, and self-sacrificing loyalty."[63] The author stresses that Louisa's marriage to Crown Prince Frederick was the product of love rather than dynastic considerations. Moreover, like her equally German husband, she preferred the simplicity of country life to the corrupting influences of the court and city. The details are significant, because by the end of the century, urban life was increasingly viewed as a threat to the German and bourgeois values the queen represented: diligence, frugality, sincerity, and domesticity. Thus Louisa, as she appears in novels and the popular press, was not simply the repository of positive traits; she embodies opposition to the corrosive influences that both led to Germany's downfall and still threatened the nation in 1875.

At the time of her marriage, Louisa's father-in-law was infatuated with Countess Lichtenau, whom the author calls "the Prussian Dubarry" after the mistress of King Louis XV of France. By contrast, when Frederick William III ascends the throne, he and his wife decide to "restore the royal family life, which has been undermined by French values, to suppress elegant immorality, and to set an example for all through bourgeois frugality, strict morality, and discipline."[64] Of course, the text notes that the royal couple speaks German—then a "forbidden" or "despised" (*verpönte*) language, even when the servants are present—and it makes exaggerated claims about Louisa's political acumen (7). For example, although she died three years before the Wars of Liberation began, *The Garden Bower* reports, "Only the queen with her prophetic vision recognized the importance of the popular uprising."[65] Through Louisa, Germans can lay claim to a near monopoly on civic as well as personal virtue, while Prussia as a frame of reference for the queen almost disappears in favor of Germany. Thus, the series concludes by claiming, "Louisa, as long as she lived, was the purest German housewife, the most loving wife and mother, [and] the incarnation of the family, but after her death she became the patron spirit of her people, who still honor her as a saint and to whom she remains unforgettable as the ideal image of perfect femininity."[66]

Lest this be dismissed as the hyperbolic rantings of some trashy magazine, one should note that *The Garden Bower* was a family journal dedicated to providing quality entertainment and enlightenment—high culture—for men and women alike. Its editor was a noted liberal, and its stable of authors included some of late-nineteenth-century Germany's best writers, along with a few clunkers. In addition, the magazine's praise was far from uncharacteristic for its times. In 1876 Heinrich von Treitschke held a similarly effusive public lecture in Louisa's honor in the imperial chamber of the Berlin city hall, to mark the centenary of her birth.[67] Treitschke must have sensed not only that Queen Louisa was a historical figure of some consequence but also that something larger was at stake in any account of her life than the fee or medal that he no doubt received for his services. Part of the attraction of Queen Louisa was the ease with which her persona could be used to invoke continuity with the past. As Treitschke put it, "she lives on in the memory of her thankful people, a luminous figure who pointed the way for combatants in our war of liberation shimmering high in the heavens."[68] Conveniently in his account, Louisa remains untouched by the failures of her age: "The dissolute, yet refined depravity that filled Berlin was hidden from her . . . This happy woman had no idea just how rotten everything in the state had become, how the eye of the great king [Frederick II] looked down on his heirs in anger."[69] The imagery of decline and fall helps explain Jena in familiar terms, but Treitschke's rhetoric is more complicated than it appears at first glance. Frederick the Great died in 1786, so he could scarcely have known Louisa, but since the queen was, according to Treitschke, "blessed by the same heroic spirit whose presence *we* felt in *our* most recent war," his mythic version of Louisa turns the eighty-five years that separated Frederick's death from William's coronation into a single historical era with Louisa at its center.[70] Her bridging function lets Treitschke pass over the chasm that was Jena without peering into the abyss. Louisa's image sanitizes the German past, and she becomes not so much the queen who experienced defeat and humiliation as the mother to both the new emperor and his subjects. Finally, invoking her spirit of female domesticity, Treitschke concludes his lecture by warning against any use of Louisa's image to instill hatred for the French. Now that the nation's once-reviled enemies have done penance for their sins, Louisa's legacy can be a kinder and more feminine ethos for Germany, "which alone gives a guarantee of permanence to the fame and power of nations."[71] For a country unified by "blood and iron," Treitschke's peaceful invocation of the saintly Queen Louisa presents an odd contrast to Bismarck.

Of course, Treitschke may have felt constrained by the occasion to render Louisa's life in such glowing terms; he barely mentions her in his more scholarly *History of Germany in the Nineteenth Century*. Still, even in Treitschke's more professional estimation, Louisa's role in Prussian politics was considerable: "Through the cheerful cordiality of Queen Luise, the relationship between the Hohenzollerns and their loyal people acquired that homely characteristic of confidence which was elsewhere displayed only in the quiet life of the petty states."[72] By establishing a personal link between the people and the monarchy, Louisa helped enable the popular uprising of 1813, saving the Prussian state from Napoleon and thereby paving the way for German unification. But she was not officially connected with either politics or the army, and since she also left few traces of her influence in the archives, Treitschke passes over her in his more academic history.

The one consistent element in Treitschke's two accounts is his focus on personality. For him, the debacle at Jena indicates how powerful men rather than great men—and very few women—make history: they are not the bearers of larger trends or the unwilling victims of events but rather the authors of their own fates. Treitschke's tsar, Alexander I, for example, appears ill prepared for the job, bereft of suitable advisors, and ultimately "left to the fancies of his restless imagination."[73] His counterpart, Frederick William III, is also weaker than his predecessors and surrounded by irresponsible and incompetent advisors, although on occasion it was "only the sober good sense of the king which saved the state from a disastrous step."[74] Francis I serves Austria just as poorly, so when the three great powers of the east fail to form an effective alliance against Napoleon, it is "the fault of the two emperors" and the hapless king of Prussia.[75] In rhetorical terms, this focus on personality forces Treitschke to ascribe personal motivation to political decisions, almost like a novelist employing an omniscient narrator: "it was with honest regret that he [Frederick William III] saw the empire abolished. ... The king no longer believed a single word or the smooth flatteries which Napoleon had continued to shower upon him."[76] Plausible as this account sounds, the historian cannot test the validity of such statements; they arise necessarily from personalizing politics. By contrast, the politicizing of personal life championed by feminists has long been the mark of historical and other fiction.

Also unlike the novelists dealt with above, Treitschke treats Jena primarily as a military event with discernible, proximate causes: the defeat, he says, "was mainly due to bad leadership."[77] Thus, although he is certain the battle had profound consequences for Prussia and Germany, Treitschke does not view the defeat as the product of something tragically amiss in society as a whole. In fact, he minimizes the battle by claiming that Jena marked the beginning rather than the end of a process; after Jena the period of decline and decay among the ruling class is over. The defeat sweeps away the old guard, making way for "a new generation [that] suddenly rallied round the throne. There appeared men of powerful character, enthusiastic spirit, and clear intelligence, an unending abundance of them, a crowd of persons brilliant in camp and in council, who could take equal rank with the literary great ones of the nation."[78] In short, it is not so much Jena—the battle and its causes—as Stein, Hardenberg, and the other ministers who orchestrated the post-1806 movement for reform and renewal in Prussia who are the real focus of Treitschke's attention. And since in his view these men served the nation in both practical and spiritual terms, Treitschke pays them an intriguing compliment by linking them to Goethe, Schiller, and the Romantics.

Two things are happening here. First, Treitschke's praise accords the Prussian reformers a role otherwise ascribed solely to literary artists; they become the bearers and shapers of a German national tradition, while at the same time the idea of Germany moves one step closer to fruition. With that shift from the imaginary life of the spirit to the realm of politics, Treitschke seems to argue that the vaunted German *Kulturnation* was well on its way to becoming reality. Hence, it was no longer necessary to relegate national aspirations to the stage, poetry, and the novel. Second, Treitschke uses Jena to snatch victory from the jaws of defeat. In so doing, he demonstrates his belief in historical progress, specifically in the upward trajectory of the national idea in history. Thus, Jena becomes neither a symptom of national malaise nor a tragedy and sign of national decline but rather an aberration that nevertheless produced a cleansing catharsis. The battle's importance lies not so much in the individual suffering and humiliation portrayed by novelists as in its inscription into the larger narrative of Germany's triumphal march toward unity. In order to speculate retrospectively about Germany's coming glory, Treitschke reduces the battle to a prologue. It is a telling but typical example of Treitschke's willingness to gloss over the problematic aspects of German history. Of course, Jena was a calamity, but it was mainly an event made important by its clearing the way for great men and momentous developments. Implicitly, Treitschke claims Prussia's defeat at Jena had no lasting impact and therefore warrants little of his attention. Novelists might delve into the pain and suffering felt by ordinary Germans or the moral decline of Prussian society before 1806, but Treitschke is content to chronicle the nation's victories.

Most of Treitschke's colleagues shared his view of German history as progressive or even triumphant. Since military history sold well, they often include accounts of combat, but they spend more time with victories, even with those of lesser impact, than with the disaster at Jena. As a caste, professional historians seem to have regarded Jena as a transitory event, not as a separate, distinct, and tragic stage in Germany's development. Two examples, both as eminent as Treitschke, illustrate the point.

One of the first historians to deal with Jena was Johann Gustav Droysen. During the winter semester of 1842–43 he held a series of *Lectures on the Age of Wars of Liberation*, which he published in two volumes in 1846.[79] Droysen's project differs from standard histories of Germany in that he deals with 1813–15 in the context of the fifty-year period from the American Revolution through the end of the Napoleonic era. In his view, there were numerous wars of liberation, so he looks only briefly at Jena and its meaning for Germany and waits almost two hundred pages into the second volume of his lectures to do so. Droysen was writing before the end of Germany's national strivings, but his lectures nevertheless anticipate "the re-establishment of a Protestant German state," about whose future he can only speculate.[80]

However, Droysen is convinced that history is not an accidental process. It is not one damn thing after another but rather the unfolding of a divine plan for humanity. As he says: "The science [or academic discipline, *Wissenschaft*] of history has no more important task than justifying that belief; it is a science for that reason. It apprehends and finds in the wild sea [of events] a direction, a goal, a plan; it teaches us to understand and to marvel at God's ways."[81]

In light of his theological presuppositions it is particularly significant that Droysen begins his account of Jena by noting that "Germany was not yet sufficiently humiliated; it still had to be completely trampled and scourged before it could raise itself up."[82] "Humiliated" or "degraded," which are both plausible translations of *"erniedrigt,"* echo the title of the pamphlet that caused Palm's death in August of 1806, two months before Jena, and Droysen may have taken the term from that unfortunate publication. By August 1806 Austria had suffered its own humiliating losses; the thousand-year tradition of the Holy Roman Empire had ended ingloriously; "Now it was Prussia's turn."[83] However, with Prussia there is an important difference, made possible by the acuity of Droysen's hindsight. While Prussia deserved a devastating end to its Frederickian hubris, its defeat marks a pan-Germanic turning point. Droysen may not be particularly interested in the fate of ordinary Germans, but he does accord mythic significance to Jena: "Never," he writes in a telling phrase, "was a defeat more total."[84] In other words, after Jena the cup of German suffering was filled to overflowing. The nation's degradation is finally complete, and the process of rebirth and unification can begin. Since Jena represents the final fall, the end of the line for Germany rather than for Prussia alone, renewal can proceed for the entire nation under Prussia's leadership. Specifically, Jena allows the Prussian eagle to arise phoenix-like from Germany's ashes, which means, paradoxically, that Prussia's most inglorious defeat becomes the enabling event for a version of German history dominated by this once and future great power. After Jena, Frederick the Great's state returns to the European playing field chastened but once again headed for greatness.

Yet, for all of its symbolic importance, Jena occupies very little of Droysen's account. Like Treitschke, he treats the battle primarily as prologue. The momentous defeat cleared the way for what followed, so its significance lay not in the event itself but in what—and who—was purged in that battle's cleansing finality. To be sure, Droysen's account of the not particularly great men of Prussian politics forces him to conclude

CHAPTER 4

that their collective weakness lay behind that state's inability to meet Napoleon's challenge: "There were enough ideas present, but they were never able to overcome the morass of indolence, complacency, and self-indulgence that characterized men grown gray with age in service to the cabinet and the throne. Bitterness, immorality, and eccentricity united with weakness, indecision, and the perquisites of rank [*Gamaschen- und Tabellenwesen*]; together they defined [Prussia's ruling caste]."[85] According to Droysen, the king was personally beyond reproach but too weak to intervene. Although the moral and intellectual life of Prussia had not deteriorated to the degree found in Vienna, St. Petersburg, and Paris, the examples set by Prince Louis Ferdinand and, curiously enough, Friedrich Schlegel's novel *Lucinde* (1799) were nevertheless debilitating. Prussia, as Droysen writes, "vacillated between offense and defense, deliberated without reaching a conclusion, and maneuvered without a plan," all of which makes it impossible for the historian to assign more than a vague and undefined sense of responsibility.[86] There is no guilt, particularly not at the level of the Prussian state or the German nation. The most significant fact about Jena is the extent of the destruction it produced, not its causes. In Droysen's account the battle of Jena occurs between paragraphs as he jumps—without so much as a glance at the actual battlefield—from Napoleon's ultimatum on the eve of the event to Prussia's military and political devastation once it is over. Of course, all is not lost: "under the calcified exterior of the old Frederickian state a new Prussia had already begun to grow."[87] In metaphorical terms, Germany is about to metamorphose from caterpillar into butterfly. Jena simply marks the end of the chrysalis stage, the time before the German nation emerges from its cocoon of defeat, disgrace, and despair. The defeat may have been a harrowing transition, but for Droysen its importance lay in the renewal that followed defeat, not in the reason that change proved necessary.

By contrast, one of the major historical works of the 1850s, Ludwig Häusser's *German History from the Death of Frederick the Great to the Foundation of the German Confederation* devotes considerable space to Jena, but its focus is similar to Droysen's far briefer treatment.[88] Häusser was trained in Berlin and then occupied an influential chair at the University of Heidelberg, and his *History,* despite its four lengthy volumes, went through three editions between 1855 and 1861. The chapter on Jena weighs in at nearly fifty closely printed pages. Häusser's work benefited from a wealth of material that had become available since the

1840s, for while Droysen complains in the introduction to his *Lectures* about the lack of German archival material, Häusser quotes from numerous memoirs and thanks the director of the Prussian State Archives for access to documents held there. Like Droysen and Treitschke, Häusser was a Prussian partisan, and as James Sheehan writes, he intended his *German History* to demonstrate that "by taking the lead in the national battle against the French, Prussia at once anticipated and legitimized her eventual domination of German Europe."[89] Jena plays a crucial role in that narrative.

Häusser sets the stage for his discussion of the Prussian defeat in the very last sentence of a chapter on the Confederation of the Rhine, which immediately precedes his discussion of Jena. After recounting the fate of the unfortunate bookseller Palm, Häusser concludes by saying, "But the outer limit of German humiliation had not yet been reached."[90] Here, too, the argument is that Jena sealed Prussia's German mission. Without Jena there might have been wars of liberation, but Prussia could not have become Germany's savior with the same moral legitimacy; she could neither have suffered for Germany's sins nor expiated them. Yet, having joined Droysen in ascribing such centrality to the defeat at Jena, Häusser is curiously confused about what went wrong.

He begins with the assertion that "no one" in Prussia "realized just how rotten the inherited system of government had become," but a page later he contradicts himself by praising one of the country's eventual heroes, Baron vom Stein, for possessing just that knowledge: "Under these conditions men such as Stein thought above all else about improving governmental machinery that was, without a doubt, one of the causes of the decline."[91] Häusser largely ignores both the monarchy and the social factors that figured so prominently in earlier accounts; his litany of incompetence centers on the military, where he finds "aristocratic-soldierly insolence," weaponry that was "very deficient," "miserable" uniforms, and leadership that "barely understood, to say nothing of imitated," Napoleon's tactical and strategic innovations.[92] In short, according to Häusser, "one did not realize that the Prussian military system had outlived its usefulness. One believed, as Kleist expressed things at the time, that we only had to show ourselves, and the French would run away."[93] Häusser faults what he sees as widespread and officially tolerated arrogance, but the way he presents the indictment undercuts his argument. "One" is forever unaware, uncertain, caught up in false assumptions, and attempting the unwise or the impossible, but rarely does

Häusser name any "one" or hold him accountable.[94] In Häusser's account, despite its length and attention to detail, the mistakes and failures that led to Jena are disembodied, and without agents his accusations lose their force. The sole exception occurs at the level of tactics, once the scene shifts to the battlefield. There, Häusser describes the duke of Brunswick, who commanded the Prussian army, as a seventy-one-year-old long past his prime. He also repeats the duke's assessment of his subordinates: he "called Rüchel a blusterer, Marshall Möllendorf a worn-out old man, General Kalkreuth a clever intriguer" and so on, naming names and specifying weaknesses.[95] The reader is left with the impression that a change in plans or a mistake on Napoleon's part might have made considerable difference in the outcome. Success depended upon "beating the enemy to the punch."[96] "Possession of this place determined the outcome of the battle."[97] Surprisingly, Häusser ends his account by declaring not only that the army had been defeated but also that "the ancient monarchy had been destroyed," a sweeping conclusion that seems incommensurate with the series of paltry explanations that precede it.[98]

At the end of the chapter Häusser returns to the rebirth that he, like Droysen, implicitly prophesied. Jena was the necessary and sufficient condition to sweep away the old order, putting Prussia at the center of Germany's return to national unity. But there is something about the genre of history, particularly military history, that frequently lets the effort fall flat. On the one hand, historians tend to forget the lesson distilled from watching Napoleon by the era's most notable observer, Baron von Clausewitz, who famously said war is the continuation of politics by other means. Since avoiding defeat at Jena would not have solved the social and political malaise that Häusser identifies as its ultimate cause, he must have realized the debacle would have come another day. Politics renders military history irrelevant. On the other hand, without the human dimension that the nineteenth-century discourse of history theoretically reserved for historical fiction, something always seems to be missing, so historians are forever venturing beyond the archives to make up for that lack. Häusser's rhetorical strategy is to retreat into the impersonal in an effort to recuperate the emotional resonance he believes every ordinary German must have felt: "Wherever German shame and patriotic sentiments were still alive, one now, finally, began to survey the fatherland's immeasurable distress; the last, self-made illusion of solace had disappeared . . . The nation itself had to show if its continued existence was worthwhile."[99] The passage slips from "one" to an "illusion" that disappears without agent, only to conclude with "the nation," an impersonal replacement for a people that had not yet coalesced under its banner. As much as Häusser would like to explain the mythic significance of Jena, generic conventions limit his options, forcing him to spend most of his narrative detailing verifiable events. At crucial junctures, often at the beginning and end of chapters, the facts prove insufficient, so Häusser, like so many nineteenth-century historians, reaches beyond what he can prove. No wonder historical fiction seemed so attractive to readers and writers alike.

A Novelist Tries His Hand at History

However, before returning to novels, Gustav Freytag's *Portraits from the German Past* merits a brief examination, because it represents a mixture of narrative history and fictional attention to character.[100] In essence, Freytag's book is a hybrid, an attempt at bridging the gap between history and fiction. The *Portraits* are part of a series of popular historical essays that first appeared in a journal Freytag edited. In 1867 he put them in chronological order, making the essays chapters in a grand historical narrative that covers almost the entire time span of German history. It begins in Roman times and ends, almost eighteen hundred pages later, just before the outbreak of the Revolution of 1848. Typically, chapters open with a fairly conventional survey of events, done almost entirely without footnotes and therefore marked as extra-academic; the real innovation is Freytag's inclusion of a more personalized version of events, generally located at the end of the chapter. For example, the Jena chapter, "From the Era of Destruction," contains ten pages from the unpublished autobiography of a mid-level Prussian civil servant, Christoph Wilhelm Heinrich Gethe.[101] Freytag thanks the man's family for the document, which he introduces with a few biographical details, and the narration then shifts to Gethe's first-person account, with no indication of any editing. The narrator recounts Gethe's birth in 1767, in the Prussian province of Kleve on the lower Rhine; Gethe himself tells of his posting to a more recent Prussian acquisition, Münster, in 1803, after French troops had occupied his homeland. Münster was staunchly Catholic, but, much to the dismay of its citizens, this formerly independent bishopric had been secularized and acquired by Protestant Prussia in 1802. Although Gethe, like Freytag, was a Prussian loyalist, his account offers a rare glimpse of local patriotism and popular resistance to Prussia's expansionist politics. This view of the tensions in the Prussian state before Jena also serves as a window on Freytag's historiography.

Gethe's autobiography lets Freytag personalize an otherwise dry narrative. The text is a far cry from tabloid journalism, but Freytag must have learned early that history comes alive when seen from the standpoint of an involved individual, particularly one with whom readers can identify. To be sure, Freytag's characterization of the malaise that preceded Jena does not differ greatly from those of his counterparts among academic historians: "The Prussian army suffered from the same shortcomings as politics and the bureaucracy. Here, too, there were isolated improvements, [but] much that was old had been carefully retained; things that once were progressive remained now as hindrances."[102] However, Gethe's autobiography allows Freytag to illustrate his conclusion in a more understandable fashion. Gethe relates the story of a long feud between several Prussian officers and three respected canons of the Münster cathedral. He tells how the soldiers, bound by an aristocratic code of honor, challenged the civilians to a duel, while the clerics, whose code of conduct forbade combat, refused what they considered an outmoded, even foreign form of satisfaction. All the grievances felt by the citizens of Münster coalesce into a morality play that pillories aristocratic arrogance and judicial manipulation.

The three clerics take the officers to court and win, only to see the soldiers make a mockery of the nominal punishments meted out by the Prussian legal system. The conflict then escalates with a series of property confiscations, and it becomes obvious to Gethe, as well as to town observers, that Prussia's vaunted civil service is anything but impartial. As Gethe writes: "This unfortunate episode, occurring as it did in a province that was not yet favorably inclined towards Prussia, had to outrage people . . . and our Prussian legal system, about which we had bragged so effusively, came away with an ugly black mark."[103] Hence, Gethe is not surprised when news of the defeat at Jena causes public rejoicing. When Dutch and then French troops occupy Münster, Gethe reports that prominent citizens vied with one another to curry favor with the new government. He understands their reaction but cannot avoid a shift in tone to bemused condescension when the French commandant leaves before accepting an expensive sword that the town's citizens had ordered for him: "At this point they were sorry for their overhasty groveling, and they had no interest in forwarding the sword, because they never found the compliance they had expected. I have been unable to learn what happened to the sword; the affair was kept secret."[104] Essentially, Freytag the historian has returned to the novelist's mode of representation, in which the fate of identifiable individuals substitutes for larger concerns. The behavior of the three officers helps him illustrate what went wrong before Jena, while Gethe, who functions like a fictional narrator, reports that a solid healthy core of reliable men is ready to move Prussia and Germany into the future. For all of his critical impetus, Gethe, who mirrors Stein, Hardenberg, and the other reformers, puts a positive spin on this disastrous chapter in Prussian history. Once again, the tale behind Jena points toward the future.

Among other things, *Portraits from the German Past* served as a preliminary exercise and source of material for the cycle of novels that Freytag began publishing in 1872. Unavoidably, because the six volumes of *Ancestors* narrate almost fifteen hundred years of German history through a single family's story, they sacrifice coverage to character. The final volume of the series, *From a Small Town,* barely mentions Jena.[105] The book mainly deals with the triumphs of 1813–15, but it does contain a milder version of Freytag's indictment of German politics and society before 1806. The army and the aristocracy appear in a particularly bad light when the novel's hero, a young country doctor, treats an otherwise unremarkable fellow who was severely beaten for wanting to marry a woman servant of a local count. She needs the nobleman's permission, which he refuses, and the count's inherited authority also allows him to punish her suitor. After hearing the man's story, the doctor says, "Conditions that allow that sort of thing are tyrannical and flagrantly contradict the laws of humanity."[106] The man hopes to escape the count's wrath by joining the army, but he is anything but an enthusiastic soldier. Meanwhile, a lieutenant who witnesses the whole affair calls the doctor a "Sansculotte," a lower-class adherent of the French Revolution's most radical wing. The officer corps and the aristocracy were the closest of allies, so it is no surprise when none other than the unfortunate recruit relays the news of Prussia's defeat at Jena to the doctor. The soldier welcomes the prospect of a French occupation for the freedom that new order promises; the doctor, who is neither peasant nor aristocrat, is appalled at the man's lack of patriotism, although he understands its origin. Luckily, the rest of the community is more than willing to rise to the fatherland's defense.

One might not have expected them all to be patriots. The novel is set in Silesia, another majority Catholic province that Prussia had annexed in the relatively recent past. Although the book appeared at the height of the new German state's struggle with the Catholic Church, it contains little evidence of the era's official anti-Catholicism.[107] To be sure, the doctor is Protestant, and he falls in love with the daughter of a village pastor; but where the novel could have shown a lingering fondness for Empress Maria Theresa, Freytag represents the ordinary inhabitants of the countryside as contentedly Prussian. Most of them, he writes, have a portrait of "Old Fritz" in their living rooms. Freytag has eliminated the confessional tensions that marked the Jena chapter in his *Portraits*. There he characterized Münster and Würzburg by noting their "rampant clericalism" (*wuchernde Pfaffenwesen*, 761); the Rhineland earns the sobriquet "the empire's long priestly alley" (*große Pfaffengasse des Reichs*, 762). By 1880 such language might have dampened sales, so Freytag's rhetorical retreat should not suggest that confessional tensions in Silesia or the rest of Germany had diminished. His novel does imply that some of the struggle over the new state's past at least raised the possibility of religious tolerance in the service of national unity. To judge by the evidence of *From a Small Town*, Freytag might have preferred a culturally, politically, and economically unified Germany to Bismarck's policy of continued confrontation with the Catholic Church. The contrast between his two works shows how difficult it was to deal with the issue of religious division within Germany, even when the locus of the argument had shifted to the past. The difference also shows how much such history mattered—even the details.

A Conservative, Anti-Semitic "Jena"

George Hesekiel's *Before Jena* (1859) should have preceded Freytag, but chronology has temporarily fallen victim to two other considerations: first, to relationships of genre, historians versus the authors of historical fiction, where Freytag played a transitional role, and, second, to continuities of theme, namely, Queen Louisa.[108] Although Louisa makes a brief appearance in Hesekiel's novel, his work is more interestingly linked to Fontane's *A Man of Honor* (1882): aside from the central question of what went wrong at Jena, both books deal with the fashionable Berlin Regiment Gensdarmes; they share a female character disfigured by chicken pox; and Fontane reports having preferred Hesekiel's title to his own.[109] The two men were also friends and colleagues. Most important, *Before Jena* is a prominent writer's disturbingly anti-Semitic explanation for the crisis of Prussian society. For this reason alone, it warrants a closer examination, even if the analysis comes out of sequence.

Hesekiel (1819–74) was the long-term editor of Berlin's influential and, needless to say, conservative *New Prussian Newspaper*, better known as the *Iron Cross Newspaper* from the symbol that graced its masthead. He and Fontane were both members of the city's famous literary club, "Tunnel Over the Spree [River]," and in 1860 Hesekiel offered Fontane a position as the journalist responsible for English affairs at his paper. Fontane needed the money and stayed until 1870. During this decade he also wrote the opening volumes of his *Excursions through the Mark Brandenburg* and began work on his first novel, *Before the Storm*. Hesekiel was considerably more productive. In addition to editing the paper—and writing all of its stories about France under a pseudonym—he authored an early biography of Bismarck. Moreover, Fontane reports owning over fifty volumes of Hesekiel's fiction.[110] *Before Jena* is only the opening installment of a four-part series of novels—in twelve volumes—treating German history from 1806 to 1813.

Before Jena includes the familiar litany of problems in Prussian society: antiquated ideas, incompetence, and greed figure prominently, but with the difference that Hesekiel concentrates on the corrupting influence of money. Selfishness has even invaded the countryside, where the landed aristocracy, once the backbone of Prussian society and its state, faces inevitable decline. As one nobleman complains to another, using their generic East Prussian name, "You poor Junkers are becoming poorer all the time. You cannot turn back, because the God-forsaken serfdom of your peasants hangs around your neck like a hundred-pound weight." The cities, he continues, are filled with "a damnable mixture of pretty turns of phrase, Jewish cleverness, and French-revolutionary impertinence."[111] The old order, characterized by organic communities and personal relationships, is gone forever, replaced by cash, bills of exchange, and the marketplace. Similarly, in the novel's opening scene, the aristocratic parents at a children's ball agree on the reason for the evil that has befallen not just humanity but also the army: "From top to bottom [people] are devoted to money, and they regard its acquisition and a comfortable life as the purpose and goal of their endeavors."[112] In other words, the old Prussian virtues of hard work, frugality, and the acceptance of harsh military service have fallen by the wayside. No wonder the

CHAPTER 4

country seems destined for collapse, including an ignominious defeat from virtually the same French forces that Frederick the Great had defeated a generation earlier.

Except for the mention of "Jewish cleverness," Hesekiel plows familiar ground, although, in contrast to Lewald, Alexis, and Mühlbach, his nostalgia for Frederickian Prussia seems excessive. But the novel's relentless anti-Semitism sets Hesekiel apart from those authors. For example, although plot considerations do not motivate such outbursts, Hesekiel lets a prominent officer claim, "Jews have absolutely no affinity for animals, not even a rational, honest affection, no pleasure in a horse or dog, no understanding of nature. We enjoy ourselves in a rustling forest; the Jew, however, trembles."[113] Instead of wondering why his countrymen were so corrupt and so reluctant to embrace the proven political and military innovations that the French army brought to Germany, Hesekiel is content to blame others. His Prussians may be feeble, but Hesekiel minimizes their weakness with the implicit claim that external forces poisoned or infected them: Jews imported dangerous ideas from France and caught the poor Prussians off guard. As the same officer remarks, at a Jewish salon where Rahel Varnhagen is a guest, "the Jews and the French have more similarities with one another than one thinks . . . we lose our German thoughts, our German emotions on those intellectual gaming tables; our female conquerors force us to accept un-German thoughts and emotions . . . these Jewish women intellectuals are the advance guard of revolutionary French world domination in Berlin."[114] Thus, while Jewish men allegedly undermine German society by injecting the cash nexus into an otherwise intact community, their wives and daughters prove equally dangerous. Hesekiel lets this same character interrupt the plot for pages on end, saying, for example, "I've noticed for a long time that Jewish men, with few exceptions, only know how to earn money, lots of money, while Jewish women have made themselves intellectually sovereign; this gives the Jews here a double power."[115] Meanwhile, the Germans or Prussians—Hesekiel conflates the two while simultaneously regarding Saxons as foreigners—get off easily. They may duel over trifles, but Germans come to real grief only when Jews become embroiled in their affairs.

The book begins when a Prussian lieutenant, Hans von Leist, the typical hero from an old noble family, falls in love with Elizabeth von Reinbeck, the daughter of a corrupt official in the Ministry of Finance. Not surprisingly, money lies behind her father's difficulties, but his susceptibility to dangerous—that is, foreign—influences becomes obvious in that most German of institutions, the family. Elizabeth grows up in a state of linguistic and therefore nationalistic confusion: "No one allowed her to use the beautiful name that she had received at baptism; her French-speaking German father called her Babette, while his German-French wife, who preferred English, referred to her as Betty."[116] Figures this flawed must fall, so Reinbeck soon finds himself implicated in a financial scandal involving a Jewish businessman, Privy Councilor Ephraim. Here, Hesekiel gets himself caught between two incompatible facts: On the one hand, the acquisition of a title that only the king can bestow represents a considerable accomplishment for the character, and Hesekiel is probably referring to Benjamin Veitel Ephraim (1742–1811), the son of the eloquent moneylender in Mühlbach's account of Frederick the Great's life (see chapter 3) and the first Jew to receive that coveted title. At least in theory, Ephraim is a valued—and confidential—advisor to the court. On the other hand, narrative conventions to which Hesekiel subscribed require Jewish moneylenders to speak pidgin German, however exalted their social position. Thus, when an officer accuses Ephraim of theft, the stereotypical Jew but utterly anomalous privy councilor replies, "What means? Stealing? God should me another fifty little years give, then will we in this city the noblemen be and the noblemen goyim who our servants are!"[117] By both his grammar and actions Privy Councilor Ephraim confirms the prejudices of the book's "authentically" German characters. Within the novel Ephraim is ultimately responsible for the bureaucrat's corruption, just as Jews are to blame for the Prussian defeat at Jena.

Actually, after a series of complications and coincidences, Reinbeck declares his innocence, and the novel's hero should be free to marry Elizabeth. However, in a scene that echoes the machinations of Madame Lupinus in Alexis's novel, Reinbeck's explanation includes a confession that his present wife poisoned her predecessor. The second wife then decamps with her brother in the hope of avoiding scandal, while Reinbeck commits suicide. The question of whether Elizabeth and Lieutenant von Leist marry remains unanswered. Curious readers need to buy or borrow the next installment of Hesekiel's series of novels.

Meanwhile, in contrast to Fontane's novel, the pockmarked woman is reconciled with her erstwhile lover; they marry and, presumably, live happily ever after. However, one wonders just how long the book's harmonious conclusion can last, given its avowed purpose of representing German society on the brink of disaster. Later in the novels Hesekiel devoted to the Napoleonic era, the narrator notes, "Unfortunately, there are still authors who are not shy about serving up the old falsehoods again and again, and they tell how the Junkers and aristocratic officers, whom they call cowardly, stupid, and brutal, brought on the fatherland's misfortune."[118] In *Before Jena* the narrator's tone is fatalistic: the catastrophic decline of Prussian society seems inevitable, albeit temporary. The novel's implicit good news is that change will come once the country's inhabitants are no longer tempted by the mixture of greed, free thinking, and immorality that the Jews have been importing from France. If the conspiracy seems nebulous and frighteningly familiar, it is. The enemies of the German people are readily identifiable, and the need for cleansing and renewal is clear, if dangerously misguided. In this novel's universe Germans need to return to German values; the Prussians, who are about to take up the cause of Germany's rebirth, are guilty, but only of succumbing to the temptation of foreign ideas. By shifting blame for Jena to an external enemy, Hesekiel offers a comfortably xenophobic means of identity formation. The catastrophic defeat is proof that speculation, murder, revenge, and moral decay have consequences. But since none of the Germans in this novel are really guilty of anything more serious than allowing themselves to be misled, *Before Jena* allows its author to draw a clear dividing line between them and us. If we were merely deluded, then the old order, which normally flourishes only in dreams of unreconstructed conservatives, offers genuine hope for the future. Unlike the alien Jews, Germans love animals, do not fear wind in the forest, and will triumph—even after Jena.

Louisa, the Clueless Saint

Fontane's world is far more complicated. Perhaps because he saw in Berlin of the 1880s and 1890s the same arrogance, greed, and incompetence others had found there before Jena, he was less likely to view the Prussian defeat as either the end of Germany's decline or the event that enabled its future triumph. Although he could have set *A Man of Honor* in contemporary Germany, without Jena looming over the horizon, this story of thwarted love and cowardly suicide would have mattered less. History gives the novel depth. And if Fontane was not solely concerned with an imaginative recreation and retrospective explanation of past events, he nevertheless cared deeply about the survival of historical knowledge, its transformation into myth, and the past's hold on the present. A seemingly casual remark by Schach's friend Bülow raises precisely this issue of false memory or a misunderstood past: "Imagine how Frederick the Great would have rolled up his eyes if he'd been called the 'good Frederick.'"[119] In fact, Germans frequently referred to the good Frederick; it happened whenever they spoke of Old Fritz. Thus, to judge by Bülow's statement, the legendary king must have spent much of the nineteenth century turning in his grave in a state of angry disbelief as supporters and detractors argued over his legacy. However, with *A Man of Honor* Fontane joined a different fray from debates about Frederick. This novel, in which Bülow's pronouncements function as a meta-discourse, provides both an alternative reading and a paradigmatic questioning of the myths surrounding Jena. Since chapter 1 has already dealt with the theoretical issues, only a brief second look at this short but rich work is now necessary.

Fontane belongs to the camp that found Prussian society as a whole responsible for the defeat. According to *A Man of Honor*, the king and queen were not solely at fault; nor were the country's generals, bureaucrats, and businessmen primarily responsible; neither, certainly, were the Jews to blame. Nor, most surprisingly, is Schach von Wuthenow, the novel's central character, guilty of complex and devious villainy. He is neither corrupt nor particularly decadent. He is merely weak. Schach lacks character; he is a man without a moral center. His single flaw is a morbidly dependent vanity. Schach prefers death to dishonor—not on the battlefield, where soldiers face adversity, but in the court of public opinion. Schach is caught between his aristocratic origins, which include an exaggerated sense of honor, and his bourgeois inclinations, which seek domestic comfort and the safe haven of a companionate marriage. Even though he knows Victoire von Carayon is witty, charming, and intelligent, a cartoon showing her pockmarked face is more than Schach can bear. What Victoire sees in Schach remains profoundly unclear, but by concentrating on his solitary, albeit socially complex, weakness, Fontane transforms Schach into a Prussian Everyman. In contrast to Hesekiel's xenophobic rantings, Fontane makes his central character so ordinary, so familiar, that readers have to regard Schach and his problems as indigenous rather than foreign. In Pogo's famous words, "We have met the enemy, and he is us." Fontane depicts a character so paralyzed by the fear of ridicule and a society so devoted to outward appearance that neither could stand up to the French. Indeed, his version of Prussian society is scarcely worth saving.

Unlike those who bemoan a decline from the glories of Frederick's age, Fontane is anything but nostalgic; in fact, his critical reckoning with the myth of German decline goes so far as to include an attack on good Queen Louisa and her bumbling husband. Near the end of the novel, Victoire's mother appeals to the king as Schach's commander, the man ultimately responsible for both the military and the moral conduct of the officer corps. Simultaneously, Queen Louisa intervenes in her own fashion. Mrs. von Carayon's action moves the plot along, but without knowing what an icon Queen Louisa had become, we could not appreciate the mythic significance of scenes involving the royal couple. Most authors show Frederick William III both as a loving husband and a man hopelessly out of his depth as monarch. The portraits are sympathetic if tinged with regret. Fontane eliminates any sentimental veneer and reduces the king to a parody of the era's telegraphic military speech: "And the daughter! Know about it of course, know it, poor child. . . . All the same, must have found her attractive." Faced with the alternative of marriage or resigning his commission, Schach opts for Victoire; he is too weak to do otherwise. He also silently obeys the order to meet with Louisa: "Have spoken about it to the Queen; wants to see you; woman's notion."[120]

That final phrase, "woman's notion," both undercuts what Louisa will have to say and indicates that the king, while denigrating the idea, cannot resist her demands. At least Louisa speaks in complete sentences: "Certainly, there's little that would so please me just now as the settling of this dispute and the union of two hearts that seem to me to be meant for each other. . . . And now quickly go home and spread happiness and be happy yourself!"[121] How noble, the reader might think, but everything about the statement is wrong. First, in the context of Prussia's impending social, political, and military collapse, Schach and Victoire's affair can scarcely be the most important threat to the queen's happiness. Second, the myth usually has Louisa deeply involved in the affairs of state rather than dispensing advice to the lovelorn. Moreover, in Fontane's representation of her efforts, Louisa fails miserably. To say, as she does, that these two people seem meant for each other is either a slip into wholly unexpected sarcasm or a sign of her complete misreading of their characters. As the narrator remarks, rather than returning home to spread joy, Schach "had to devise a scheme that would combine obedience and disobedience in one."[122] He goes through the motions, submits to the marriage, and shoots himself on the way back to his apartment—scarcely a happy ending. And it foreshadows worse news for Prussia, although not without a lesson. One moral of Fontane's account has to be that if Queen Louisa cannot accomplish such a trivial undertaking as matchmaking, she is even more unsuited to the task of atoning for Germany's sins. Nor can she legitimately inspire a national renewal and redirection following the penance of Jena.[123] In short, Prussia's demise is so thorough, and its weaknesses are so widespread and banal, that no one, not even the country's saintly queen, seems up to remedying the difficulties. Thus, although the novel at first seems understated and indirect, it is difficult to imagine a harsher reckoning with either the causes or effects of Jena than the one contained in *A Man of Honor*.

The jump from 1859, the year Hesekiel's *Before Jena* appeared, to 1882 for Fontane's novel indicates that after mid-century, novelists seldom dealt with Jena. Not that their output ever matched the number of books devoted to Frederick the Great or the Wars of Liberation. Freytag's decision to mention the defeat only in passing in *Ancestors* (1880) is more typical than Fontane's attempt to reassess the era of Prussia's failure. Decline is an inherently difficult subject, at least for popular consumption; it is far easier and presumably more lucrative to recount the heroic elements of a country's past. So far as I can determine, after Fontane the only work to deal with the period is Wilhelm Jensen's *At the Turn of the Century (1789–1806)*, which appeared in 1899.[124] As the title suggests, Jensen's text is broader in scope, but it still illustrates the discourse surrounding Jena as Germany moved into the twentieth century.

JENA'S VICTIMS

Nowadays, Jensen (1837–1911) is just another obscure author, but during his lifetime he enjoyed considerable popularity, even prestige. Like so many writers of the period, he published over forty novels, numerous short stories, a few plays, and volumes of poetry; he was also a long-time friend of Wilhelm Raabe, whose literary talent Jensen could not match.[125] His most famous work, *Gradiva* (1903), is known not for its author's skill or promise but as the subject of Sigmund Freud's first extended commentary on literature. *At the Turn of the Century* has little psychological interest; its characters and settings are so overdetermined

CHAPTER 4

as to suggest parody, but Jensen's exaggerations are nevertheless in keeping with the questioning tone his forebears devoted to Jena.

The story takes place in the tiny state of Falkenberg-Hochberg, where Count Wolfgang von Falkenberg rules his few subjects in the manner of Louis XIV. The count's palace is a miniature Versailles; its gardens and entertainments are French; and the court's lackeys use French to write birthday greetings to Count Falkenberg's mistress, Baroness von Bettendorf (Bedvillage). She arrives at the palace in a richly decorated coach, but the reader sees only her dainty foot in a golden slipper. The baroness epitomizes refinement and the triumph of form over substance; the overall effect is artificiality. The reader soon senses that life in this sovereign mini-state is pathetic and unnatural, as is, by implication, life in all the German mini-states that Falkenberg-Hochberg epitomizes. The cultural dominance of the French language, style, and manners, appears to be as repugnantly un-German as France's political hegemony under Napoleon. And once again, the villains are all aristocrats.

Jensen's elaborately detailed picture of aristocratic decadence contrasts sharply with his image of the commoners who pay the bills. Thus, when the count notices that, like his mistress, statues in his park have unnaturally small hands and feet, who should appear but the pastor's daughter, Dieta Bodmer, whose feet were not "doll-like and dainty but rather correctly proportioned for her size, as were her ungloved and well-formed hands."[126] The difference between this wholesome peasant and the count's doll-like but aging mistress could scarcely be greater. The girl is free and natural, and she is forever hearing larks, the uncaged bird of the German countryside. Dieta loves and is loved by the adopted son of a cabinetmaker, Berno Lindenblatt, who eventually rescues her from the count's immoral designs, only to be banished for his troubles. It all happens one eventful night when Dieta appears at a birthday celebration for the count's mistress, where she overshadows the reigning paramour and precipitates Berno's rash actions. If the novel were shorter or less like a fairy tale, the two lovers could marry at this point, but Berno must still be tested. He needs to wander in the wilderness and return to further complications. For example, unbeknownst to Berno, Dieta is severely burned when a replica of Mount Vesuvius meant to cap the festivities explodes, killing or wounding many of the partygoers. Berno escapes and eventually joins the French army, drawn to its antiaristocratic ideology, but in so doing he becomes alienated from his German roots. The novel's Francophile aristocrats display a penchant for luxury, ostentation, and unnatural forms of feminine beauty, while the Germans, mainly farmers and craftsmen, prefer plain food, hearty laughter, and big feet. They also believe in the family and honest work, but Berno is torn, that is, ambiguous, as a character. He is not interested in cabinetry, fails as a scholar, and turns out to be the count's illegitimate son. Flawed from the moment of his conception, Berno seems to stand for a Germany that is good at heart but corrupted—culturally, politically, and militarily—by years of foreign domination. Berno and his newly found father battle repeatedly, but their antagonism revolves around competing versions of the German polity rather than traits that separate two well-rounded characters.

One could complain about Jensen forcing his figures to carry so much symbolic weight. This is not great art, but because they are so burdened, these characters can show how forging a German identity was not simply a matter of rejecting French norms and values. According to the novel, Germany and its history were multilayered, so any explanation of Jena needs to address that complexity. Berno confronts it in the form of a neighboring nobleman, Baron von Velberg, who rules his own mini-state, but in the enlightened tradition of Frederick the Great. Velberg has also modeled himself on the fabled Prussian king. For example, although he speaks "the half-French language" that was typical among "imitators of the court at Versailles, it sounded completely different on his tongue; one did not think of anything foreign, [his language] made a solid impression, as if it were a blunt form of German, straightforward and able to hit the nail on the head."[127] Not surprisingly, the only picture in Velberg's study is a portrait of the great king, and it hangs so that sunlight falls on Frederick in an otherwise darkened room. Frederick's radiance makes French ideas liminal instead of merely evil, and it raises the possibility of German renewal through a return to older values. But any new Germany, even one based on an older model, can arise only at the end of the nation's current troubles.

A few years after his hasty departure, Berno comes back to Falkenberg at the head of a squadron of French troops. In a quixotic attempt to revenge himself on the hated count, he briefly declares his native village a republic. He also visits Velberg. The baron is gladdened by his overbearing neighbor's misfortune but shocked at Berno's French uniform: "Whoever raises his sword against his nation is a crook and a *Cujon*. If you've been in France, you know what that means, but I'll tell

CHAPTER 4

you in your mother tongue. In German the word is scoundrel [*Hundsfott*, literally, a bitch's cunt]."[128] Berno is chagrined but not quite convinced. He breaks his sword in half, and with it his connection to France, and then he flees to Holland, far from concerns that might animate a patriotic German. As the narrator notes, "A deep lethargy lay over the German people."[129]

Berno does not return home until his father's death in 1806. The Prussian defeat still lies a few months in the future, but the date is scarcely a coincidence. It links personal and national tragedy, indicating just how costly the quarter century of indolence and indecision since the novel's opening pages has been. Returning before Jena also allows Berno to participate in the nation's fall. Baron von Velberg is a shadow of his former self. Nevertheless, he urges Berno to join the Prussian army, and he marches off, but not before seeing Dieta for the first time in years. She has become the baron's trusted servant, in part because the position shields her from society. The accidental explosion that precipitated Berno's flight from Falkenberg burned and badly scarred half of Dieta's face. Berno still proposes, but she turns him down. In her view, the two of them are too poor and too damaged to live happily ever after. They—and Germany—have almost hit rock bottom, but here the issue is not so much the need for the ultimate humiliation of Jena as the requirement that both characters and country admit their faults as a prelude to redemption.

Aristocratic Prussian officers, who mistrust all volunteers, initially reject Berno as a commoner with a well-developed sense of independence. When he finally talks his way into a cavalry regiment, the narrator comments—almost quoting Queen Louisa—that the army is still resting on the laurels it gained under Frederick II. Berno fights at Auerstadt, the companion battle to Jena, is wounded, and believes he is about to die. Again the narrator intervenes, just in case the reader has been asleep through all the heavy-handed symbolism that precedes this weighty assessment: "Prussia fell with him."[130] However, Berno is only wounded—and left with a noticeable facial scar. Returning home, he learns from Dieta that he has inherited Baron von Velberg's castle. The two characters can finally marry and retire to comfortable obscurity. Germany's fate, as they represent it, is somewhat more complex.

The good old days, which were actually quite terrible, have not returned. Indeed, the count and all he represents have disappeared, at least temporarily, and a renewed Germany becomes visible, albeit in a dim haze. Berno and Dieta inherit Velberg's castle but not his independent mini-state, because Frederick the Great no longer offers a model for the future. The novel apportions blame, but the guilty aristocrats are far from the center of the book's action. The reader mainly sees how an ordinary German hero and equally German heroine suffer, atone for, and ultimately overcome the sins of the fatherland. Berno has to accept the disfiguring scar that aristocratic frivolity left on his beloved's face, just as Dieta must welcome home a scarred but chastened victim of Prussian military incompetence. For them, Jena represents an inescapable burden, the lasting mark of a flawed but still promising past—once they learn its complex lessons. Perhaps speaking for Germany, Dieta closes the novel by saying, "I bless that evil sword that struck you, because it brought on my happiness."[131] One can almost imagine their brood of big-footed children romping happily in some rural utopia, a prospect marred only by its lingering antimodernism. Jensen closes the century with an almost progressive work. For all of its artistic flaws and narrative implausibilities, his vision of Germany no longer depends on Frederick or Louisa looking down from on high to inspire future greatness. Here, the German people, not their leaders, take responsibility for the nation. The novel's final image is vaguely democratic and hopeful, but without the Wars of Liberation it can offer only a truncated version of how Germany developed. That myth will have to wait for the next chapter. For the moment it is time to sum up the lessons of Jena.

Villains, Victims, and a Saint

If explanations of that momentous defeat function as the emerging German nation's myth of decline, then the issues it raises in all these texts are guilt and the possibility of an enabling redemption. Someone must be at fault, but for Germany to rise from the ashes there should also be potential saviors. In fact, the two phenomena are closely related—as well as being utterly different. A disaster of Jena's magnitude demands a thorough housecleaning, while excessive guilt disqualifies the adjudged party from future positive actions. From the clear perspective of hindsight, writers have to condemn those they hold responsible but not mourn either their failure or eventual disappearance from the national scene. At the same time, they must be careful to minimize or excuse the actions of those they will later deem heroes. Germany loses, that much is unavoidable, but there can be no complicity by the father-

CHAPTER 4

land's future champions. If not minor heroes, they should be victims or remain distant from the battlefield. There is simply too much at stake and too little time separating defeat in 1806 from the victories of 1813–15 for personal guilt to be expiated, but neither is there space to create a wholly new group of redeemers. The narrative dilemma here is that Jena brings good and evil into uncomfortably close proximity; the defeat forces an essentially affirmative literature to deal at great length with villainy in the context of a historical event that leaves little space for heroism. Thus, as important as Jena was in mythic terms, it presented authors with an extraordinarily difficult task, particularly if they wanted to sell books.

In the broadest possible terms, depictions of Jena's villains divide the evildoers into two categories: "them" or "us." Depending upon the works selected, the first group includes the French, Jews, moneyed interests, Francophile aristocrats, corrupt and incompetent officers, the upper levels of the civil service, and the court. By contrast, the German people, purged of these few outsiders, constitutes "us," and that "us" also has room for all of those not implicated in the defeat at Jena. "They" simply must be someone else if "we" are to save Germany. Thus, if "they" are Jews or some different, easily defined other, "we" can still be the old elite; but if an author decides "they" were members of the traditional ruling class, than "we" need to be different from that group. "We" might even be the common people, with all the revolutionary ramifications that "we the people" implies, should no one else be left unsullied. However, quite aside from the political implications in every choice of heroes, not every set of villains works equally well. If, for example, the problem were simply the tactical superiority of French forces, aided by Napoleon's skill as a general, it becomes difficult to explain Germany's broader decline. Such explanations might work for historians sequestered in dank archives, but it has little promise as a myth for the national cause. In such a scenario there are no rascals to throw out and no one to take their place once the guilty parties fail. In addition, however convenient they might seem at first glance, under the circumstances of national mythmaking, competent foreign enemies only confuse the issue; they do not explain Jena. Small wonder, then, that only one of the authors dealt with here blames the French or discusses Napoleon's military prowess. For Jena to acquire mythic significance, "we" or some part of "us" must be guilty rather than some distant "them."

Aristocrats, officers, and government officials are more useful evildoers. When writers focus on groups that were at once the elite bearers of power, their failure not only accounts for the Prussian defeat, but it also permits the argument that they needed replacing—and not generally by a competing elite, but by the German people or those who claim to represent them. Thus, when authors characterize villainous groups by their adherence to French norms and values, they can easily argue that the evildoers were outside the German body politic and that they therefore have no legitimate claim on the future of Germany. In this version of the myth, people who wore silk knee breeches and powdered wigs, who preferred their gardens ordered geometrically, and who spoke French even to the servants were outsiders, "them" not "us." "We" remain relatively unsullied and can renew the fatherland.

For all of his weakness as an author, Jensen's implicitly democratic views were the most radical; he points to national regeneration from the middle or lower classes. Except for a charming remnant from the age of Frederick the Great, Jensen has no need for positive figures from among the former rulers. Hesekiel, by contrast, creates a different group of outsiders, the Jews and their few adherents among the aristocracy. Since his political agenda calls for the old order's renewal, he cannot logically allow the aristocracy to be corrupted beyond hope for improvement. Otherwise, the Junkers and officers he defends would be incapable of leading Germany into a national future. Earlier authors offer some hope for the traditional power structure, but they were also willing to accord it some share of blame for Jena. After 1848 democratic reform also seemed less likely. Perhaps because he was writing in the 1880s, Fontane is less sanguine about the aristocracy, the officer corps, and the monarchy as forces for national renewal. His elites, including Queen Louisa, hold out little promise for the nation, and he presents no alternatives.

Fontane is virtually alone in rejecting the good Prussian queen as a symbol of hope in the midst of Germany's greatest degradation. Otherwise, whenever Louisa figures prominently, she dies for Germany's sins. By expiating the nation's guilt, she allows authors to avoid specifying what went wrong; they can also use her bourgeois orientation to sketch a genuinely different Germany. The queen functions as a link between the past and the future—first, as the transitional representative of a more German elite and, later, as the mother of united Germany's first emperor. Louisa requires Jena for her role as the nation's savior-mother, but the injustices Napoleon inflicted upon her personally let guilty Germans off lightly. However grave the aristocracy's sins, at least they

CHAPTER 4

did not force the young queen to flee with her children through ice and snow to Königsberg. In narrative terms, Louisa is the perfect answer to the problem of explaining Germany's decline; her noble suffering limits the nation's humiliation and points toward its rising from the ashes of disgrace. In this light, Fontane's critical view of the queen represents a radical reversal of the accepted myth; just as he makes the villains "us" and no one else, so too does he render Louisa powerless in the face of corruption and incompetence. Thus, he does not offer "us" any reason to believe that "we" could right Jena's wrong. In 1900 "we" were still governed by Schach von Wuthenow's heirs, not yet by Berno and Dieta's children. William II, not his Anglophile father, Frederick III, was on the throne.

Fontane's critical stance was all too rare. Historical fiction, particularly in its popular incarnations, tended to affirm the culture in which it was read. In fact, retrograde politics is one means of identifying literature that does not quite measure up.[132] Without entering into that fray, one can still appreciate the difficulty faced by many of the authors dealt with in this chapter. They needed to explain Jena, which necessarily involved examining weakness in the German body politic. At the same time they were hoping to use the myth of decline to point toward the nation's renewal. That task remained, and the final chapter of this text shows how writers were more comfortable and more successful when they turned to the Wars of Liberation to fashion positive narratives of national resurgence while remaining conscious of Jena's ambiguous legacy.

5
The German People Arise—and Marry

For Germany to become a nation, Germans had to think of themselves and act as though they were a single people, a *Volk,* rather than the disparate inhabitants of the villages, towns, counties, duchies, and principalities in which they lived and to which they owed linguistic, cultural, and political allegiance. At first, it seemed enough to have a common enemy or, at least, to cherish the belief that Germans had once united to drive French invaders from the fatherland. However, as historians and the authors of historical fiction elaborated the past that potential Germans were supposed to share, differentiating the inhabitants of Prussia, Saxony, Bavaria, and Baden from the French proved insufficient. Germans needed to be more than simply not-French; some "we" had to emerge from the conflict between "them" and "us." So, after selecting Frederick the Great as the nation's benevolent uncle and declaring Queen Louisa the martyred saint and symbolic mother of its people, writers took up the task of describing the rest of the national family. They settled on the Wars of Liberation as the unifying background for their attempts, because that conflict appeared to show Germans working together on a shared task. Germany could rise, phoenix-like, from the ashes of the national disaster at Jena and emerge renewed, ready to turn military success into cultural, social, and political reality: tales of the men who fought Napoleon would prefigure the nation's trajectory toward unity.

CHAPTER 5

Readers must have expected tales of battlefield heroism, punctuated by scenes of brotherhood, as Germans rather than noblemen, Hessians, or Catholics overcame differences of region, caste, occupation, and religion and defeated their common foe. However, the myth of regeneration proved even more difficult to articulate than either the myth of a heroic age or that of decline; for not only did the nation's history remain contested territory, but also the stakes in every account rose to new heights. Representations of 1813–15 invariably combined a depiction of what had happened with a prescription for what should follow. Thus, it mattered immensely whose tale was told and how: whether the militia or the army carried the day, whether the troops' leaders were aristocrats or men of the people, and whether the men and women who remained home participated in the struggle or merely awaited the soldiers' return. As Germany's nationalist narrative emerged, the Wars of Liberation became both the first act performed by a newly united German body politic and a symbolic enactment of the nation's ultimate destiny.

Yet, for all their potential as the space where Germans first practiced national unity, military campaigns and battles fill relatively few pages in the histories and historical novels that focused on 1813–15. The absence is startling, a lack not just of quantity but also, and perhaps indicative of the conflict's ambiguous aims, of quality too. No one in nineteenth-century German literature approaches Stephen Crane's images of war in *The Red Badge of Courage* or Tolstoy's depiction of the battle of Borodino in *War and Peace*. German writers either felt themselves incapable of such scenes, or, for reasons to be explored in this chapter, they chose to concentrate on other aspects of the conflict. As a result, since there are few accounts of combat, there is almost none of the proto-fascist male bonding that Todd Kontje locates in Körner's poetry or that Klaus Theweleit sees permeating images of World War I.[1] Instead, particularly in the novels, readers encounter tales of domestic romance as heroes return home to marry.

Locating the action on the home front allowed writers to concentrate on the national family that was supposed to have emerged from the unifying struggle. Who marries whom became more significant than who fought where, and these romantic entanglements were probably more entertaining to readers, both male and female, than endless tales of troops scurrying up the side of one hill only to run down another. How generals make decisions is not intrinsically interesting, nor does the fate of the

THE GERMAN PEOPLE ARISE—AND MARRY

nation rest in any easily demonstrable fashion on the outcome of a particular battle—Jena notwithstanding. However, if the cause of national unity lets the soldiers in history and fiction look beyond their caste, religious, or regional loyalties, the implications are stunning. As chapter 1 demonstrated, the aristocrats of early historical fiction seldom wed across class lines. The entry of bourgeois soldiers and officers—not just into the militia but also into novels—changed the equation dramatically. Writers who wanted to envision a new Germany faced the relatively simple task of uniting people in marriage; but since they often wanted to unite couples across gaps that had been unbridgeable and to do so plausibly, their narrative task proved almost as difficult as the dilemma that the era's politicians faced: how to unify a disparate population whose memories and experiences may not have matched the national myth.

In retrospect, it mattered little that many Germans, and not just those conscripted into battle on the wrong side, cooperated with the French until 1812. Until Napoleon's debacle in Russia, people were probably motivated by a combination of self-interest and cowardice, so they collaborated. There was also a widespread belief, particularly among intellectuals, that the French emperor offered the best hope for progressive change in Germany. Napoleon had, after all, presided over a thorough redrawing of Germany's old borders, eliminating clerical territories and drastically reducing the number of mini-states; he also ordered an end to the antiquated Holy Roman Empire. Coupled with the introduction of the Code Napoleon, which freed Jews and made the rest of the citizenry equal before the law, these changes did more for the liberation of the fatherland than anything attempted by reformers, who mainly tried to rid Germany of the French by copying the enemy's military and bureaucratic innovations. Moreover, the same officers, bureaucrats, diplomats, and kings whose squabbling and incompetence allowed Napoleon to triumph remained in power after 1813, and there is little reason to believe that nationalist sentiment was common—despite Körner's patriotic effusions and the rousing poetry of Arndt, Schenkendorf, and their compatriots. Except in hindsight—that is, in some of the histories and historical novels that dealt with the Wars of Liberation—the German people had not yet coalesced into the subject of their own history: the myth of universal resistance to the French arose gradually, and its scope was never as inclusive or as unquestioned as naive readers might expect.

CHAPTER 5

Naming the Conflict

To begin, even the term "Wars of Liberation" (*Befreiungskriege*) came into general use only gradually, and it arrived with a political agenda firmly attached. The label was part of what Christopher Clark calls the "dynastic" interpretation of the conflict; it privileges the notion that Prussia freed Germany from the French and could therefore lay claim to leadership within the nation.[2] The dynastic narrative minimizes the contribution of the *Landwehr*, a reserve militia often under local control, and concentrates instead on the regular army and its victorious generals, most notably on Gebhard Leberecht von Blücher, the Prussian hero of Waterloo (June 1815). However, these accounts often turn most revealing not when the war is winding down toward Napoleon's final defeat but at the battle of Leipzig (October 1813), when the allied armies of Prussia, Austria, and Russia handed Napoleon his first significant defeat. According to some writers, this "Battle of Nations" (*Völkerschlacht*) was where the popular militia first proved its worth, presaging a more democratic Germany. Others see Leipzig as the first decisive act in a coalition led by Prussia. Although proponents of the "small German" solution used the label "Wars of Liberation" to exclude Austria from the ideological territory of Germany during the first two-thirds of the nineteenth century, the term acquired new weight as writers employed it to justify Prussian hegemony in the German empire of 1871. The novelist Louisa von François went so far as to title her popular version of events *The History of the Prussian Wars of Liberation* (1873).[3]

Those who advocated a liberal or democratic future for Germany favored the locution "Wars of Freedom" (*Freiheitskriege*), which connoted popular participation during the conflict and a longing for its subsequent exercise. Clark calls this approach "voluntarist," and he sees its first expression at the Wartburg Festival of 1817. On October 18 of that year, several hundred students gathered at the castle where Luther had translated the New Testament, to celebrate the three hundredth anniversary of the Reformation and the fourth anniversary of the allied victory at Leipzig. Their celebration stylized the religious revival of the sixteenth century into a popular movement and linked Luther to the people who triumphed three centuries later. Adopting the black, red, and gold colors of Lützow's legendary, anti-Napoleonic volunteers, these students claimed that Germans had joined together of their own free will to fight both for national unity and freedom. Thus, one of the books they burned—setting a none too salubrious precedent—was a pamphlet written by the rector of the University of Berlin, in which he claimed Prussians had taken up the cause of liberation not in a spontaneous outpouring of national enthusiasm, much less as incipient democrats, but as loyal subjects of the king. When the authorities intervened to suppress the celebration and forbid its repetition, they were also renouncing the students' interpretation of events and the political agenda it contained.

Writers' interventions tended to be less direct, but their choice of names was never neutral. For example, in 1836 the *Universal German Encyclopedia for the Educated Classes* presented its version of events in a long article titled "Russo-German War of 1812–1815."[4] Not only is the name far less inspirational than either "Wars of Liberation" or "Wars of Freedom," but the name also gives prominence of place to "Russian" rather than "German." More important, by dating the conflict from 1812, the anonymous author does not treat Prussia's entry into the anti-Napoleonic coalition, much less the popular uprising that it purportedly unleashed, as a distinct and decisive phase in the struggle for the fatherland. Instead, Germans appear as latecomers to an event both begun in Russia and carried all the way to its conclusion with the aid of Russian troops. To be sure, the article mentions King Frederick William III's "Appeal to My People" of February 1813, an event that subsequent accounts use to mark the beginning of the Wars of Liberation, but here the author disposes of the king's appeal in a single long and curiously ambiguous sentence: "He [the king] still did not reveal his purpose, yet his people understood him, and with an enthusiasm the likes of which had never been seen before, they gathered at the assembly places by the thousands from every region; thousands who were too old to fight gave the last penny of their savings."[5] The effect is threefold. First, the author accords the king every initiative; "his people" assemble, but only after they hear the monarch's call. This is not the dithering king who is familiar both from the previous chapter and from standard historical accounts. There is also no mention of those who welcomed General Yorck's disobedience in December 1812, when he defected to the Russians, taking with him an entire Prussian army corps of fourteen thousand men. What these omissions mean is that the German people were not yet actors on the stage of history. They are barely even spectators until the king calls upon them to respond. Second, the phrase "his people gathered . . . from every region" not only contains the common (and usually problematic) Prussian focus in German history, but it also suggests diversity rather than homogeneity among Frederick William

III's subjects. He neither addresses nor hears from the German people as a whole; the phrase also leaves out the Austrians, Saxons, and other Germans who later joined the allied forces arrayed against Napoleon. Third, once assembled, these thousands disappear from the narrative. The author concerns himself with the series of battles fought by regular troops that culminated in Waterloo. Thus, for the era's most authoritative encyclopedia, these wars were another dynastic struggle whose outcome had everything to do with kings, princes, and generals but was of little lasting concern either to the soldiers who did the fighting or to their families. National unity does not figure in the agenda of an article titled "The Russian-German War," while popular sovereignty, which might be evidenced by images of widespread participation, is not even a distant possibility.

By contrast, Droysen's *Lectures on the Age of the Wars of Freedom*, which appeared in 1846, a decade after the Brockhaus article, interprets the Napoleonic wars as a popular uprising. As he writes in the summary that precedes these lectures: "In Germany we are accustomed to use the name Wars of Freedom to designate those three unforgettable years in which, for the first time in centuries, the German people, jointly and exhilarated by a feeling of unity, fought and were victorious."[6] But for Droysen to say this is the customary usage is to imply that he will use the name differently, and in fact he begins with an extensive treatment of the American Revolution. Then, after a lengthy account of that first "war of freedom," Droysen spends several hundred pages treating the French Revolution in a manner one might not expect from a German academic: "What a contradiction between the [absolutist] French state and the French people. When Louis XVI finally attempted to mediate . . . the ideas of freedom, human rights, and equality overwhelmed him like water from a thousand floodgates."[7] Droysen also deals with the dark side of the French Revolution, and before turning to Germany, he also looks at the "wars of freedom" directed against Napoleon in Spain and Portugal between 1808 and 1812. Not until he has worked his way four hundred pages into the second volume of his lectures does Droysen turn his attention to Germany.

However, before examining the causes, course, and effects of the conflict, Droysen wonders what to call it. After quoting a contemporary dispatch that claims "the second Polish War" broke out on June 23, 1812, he asks rhetorically in what sense the war was Polish: "Was its point the [re]building of Poland?" Of course, the answer is no;

THE GERMAN PEOPLE ARISE—AND MARRY

Germany would fight a war of freedom, and Droysen underscores his interpretation by saying "The statesmen's war [*Kabinettskrieg*] became a people's war [*Volkskrieg*]."[8] Unfortunately, he has difficulty representing the people. Genre conventions force him to focus on the actions of great men as they participated in significant events. When the mass of ordinary Germans put in an appearance, Droysen reduces them to an abstraction, almost to a general will: "The full glory of a great and grand fatherland arose before the German people. Without a doubt Prussia, its king and people, appeared as an edifying example."[9] If anyone is free to act in such formulations, that actor is the king, and he alone has a name. Soldiers seem to exist only on the battlefield, where their sole function is to obey orders. Thus, when Droysen describes a military engagement, we need to look at what is missing.

What follows is his complete account of a supposedly decisive encounter between French troops and their German opponents on August 23, 1813: "Not far from Berlin, near Grossbeeren, a decisive battle occurred; [General von] Bülow risked it against the advice of the crown prince of Sweden [the former Napoleonic general Bernadotte]; only the Prussians were present for the fighting; it was the first day of glory for the militia; blows from their cudgels [*Kolbenschläge*] forced the victory; Berlin was saved."[10] The historian's style has become almost telegraphic, not, one suspects, to save space but to avoid the pitfalls an expanded narrative might produce. To begin, Droysen faced the inherent difficulty of compressing the ebb and flow of battle into a coherent whole. He needed a focus and selected one of two people he could readily identify (and with whom German readers might themselves identify). He accords initiative to a member of an ancient and well-known family, the Bülows, and then underscores the (great) man's heroism by implying that General von Bülow acted alone, against the counsel of his superior. Since the educated reader recognizes Bernadotte as one of Napoleon's most accomplished commanders—before he changed sides—Bülow's action seems all the more significant. Second, Droysen chooses to emphasize an engagement in which only Prussian troops participated. He certainly had other choices, for not every account of the campaign mentions Grossbeeren. Yet, ironically, as Droysen narrates the action, the battle does more to strengthen Prussia's claim on hegemony within Germany than to emphasize broad-based support for such a result. Third, Droysen's description of the day's crucial moment reduces the soldiers' and volunteers' undoubtedly heroic efforts to the savage actions

CHAPTER 5

of untrained and ill-equipped irregulars who fought with cudgels. To be fair, giving the nameless inhabitants of Germany a role in the struggle against Napoleon is a task for which history is not well suited. Novelists alone can turn the German people into characters with names, faces, and destinies; only in fiction can ordinary mortals overcome the strictures of archival memory and emerge as full-fledged characters. This is not to say that historians shrank from the task of representing popular participation in the Wars of Liberation—quite the contrary—but they almost always leave a blank space where the German people might have appeared.

Ludwig Häusser's *German History from the Death of Frederick the Great to the Formation of the German Confederation*, already familiar from the previous chapter, provides a revealing example of the people's absence. The book's many readers found an account of the uprising in Prussia that begins with the actions of a single man, General Yorck von Wartenburg, but Yorck has to do double duty in Häusser's text. On the one hand, the general's indisputable courage, paradoxically displayed in the act of capitulating to the Russians and then changing sides, merits considerable attention, as does the personal cost of his disobeying orders to serve the larger cause of Germany unity. Disobedience was not a Prussian virtue, and Häusser, who had access to a number of pertinent memoirs, shows how Yorck agonized over his decision. In essence, this is the story of a great man who made history, which makes Yorck into a standard figure in nineteenth-century academic history. On the other hand, Häusser employs Yorck as a stand-in both for the ordinary soldiers under his command and for the German people as a whole:

> What silently struck hundreds of thousands at the first news of the Russian disaster was a premonition that now or never was the moment to shake off their chains, and here [at Tauroggen] it had already happened unexpectedly. Yorck's deed realized an idea whose time had come. Millions far and wide felt it. Not just in Prussia, . . . not just in Austria, . . . but deep in the Confederation of the Rhine, . . . And even in France . . . one believed absolutely that this was not the isolated action of an individual but rather the first symptom of an uprising by the German peoples.[11]

The narrative device of letting a single individual represent the masses is a fairly common trick, especially in historical fiction, but Häusser the historian has clearly leapt beyond the evidence. He has no way of knowing what average people in Prussia, Austria, and the Rhineland thought about Yorck's actions, and by speaking of "the German peoples" Häusser implies that the German people had not yet constituted themselves a unified whole. Without naming the conflict, Häusser cites Stein's call for a "people's war" (*Volkskrieg,* 4: 29), but since the people remain unavailable, his book focuses on the efforts of a single—presumably for him, representative—soldier, Friedrich August Peter von Colomb. As a nobleman and a cavalry officer, Colomb was more typical of the Prussian elite than the majority of the army. Faced with a crop of motley volunteers, he wonders "how he will be able to produce a competent force from the young men of the educated and well-to-do classes, to whom discipline was foreign." Contrary to his expectations, Colomb is surprised at what good soldiers he is able to train from the ranks of "farm managers and bureaucrats in training, students, businessmen, and apprentice attorneys."[12] Meanwhile, "the population [*die Bevölkerung*] exhibits the warmest enthusiasm and on many occasions demonstrates its sympathy for the noble cause in a truly moving fashion."[13] Yet, as positive as his judgment initially sounds, Häusser essentially reduces ordinary Germans to spectators at the same time as he makes the bourgeoisie bearers of the national idea. Then, in a gesture that may well reflect both the political liberalism behind demands for a popular militia and their mixed record in the Revolution of 1848, Häusser's young heroes need the nobility to teach them the finer arts of war.

The book's lengthy description of Lützow's volunteers also seems to aim at establishing a middle-class basis for German nationalism, while Häusser's account of the battle of Grossbeeren devolves into a confusing argument that tries to decide whether Bernadotte or Bülow deserved more credit for the victory. Häusser does remark, albeit at the very end of his narration, that the Prussian militia passed its first test with flying colors, but he diminishes their achievement with an implicit comparison to the more substantial and somehow more significant deeds of trained soldiers: "When it came to hand-to-hand combat and when weapons failed, [the militia] applied their cudgels to the bloody work like the natural children of war."[14] Such praise damns with both its faintness and ambiguity. "Natural children" projects an image of savages, particularly in German, where the phrase "*natürliche Kinder*" suggests illegitimacy. In a sense, Häusser is saying that neither the nation's ideal parents nor its legitimate heirs could be found among the masses who made up the militia. Volunteers, who play such a prominent role in German mythology, remain offstage. At first glance, they seem to be present in Häusser's account, but they turn up missing if we read closely and look for their actual participation in events. As much as Yorck's presence, this absence demonstrates again the difficulty historians faced in dealing with the issue of popular nationalism.

Prussians, Bavarians, and Germans (and Austrians?)

A few years after Häusser, another prominent historian turned his attention to the Wars of Liberation. Heinrich von Sybel, who held chairs in history at the universities of Bonn, Marburg, and Munich and was also the founding editor of Germany's most prestigious journal of academic history, the *Historische Zeitschrift*. He joined the fray in 1860, with a series of three lectures titled *Europe's Uprising against Napoleon I*.[15] Since he spoke in Munich, Sybel had to account for the sharply divergent behaviors of Bavaria and Prussia during the Napoleonic era without offending either against local patriotism or the larger national narrative. The tension is apparent in his introduction, where Sybel is quick to differentiate between the advantages that accrued to Bavaria while it was allied with Napoleonic France and the larger national stakes involved in the Wars of Liberation. Bavarians fought valiantly and profited substantially, but considering the grand sweep of German history, they were on the wrong side. Fortunately for Sybel, there is an explanation that minimizes the Bavarians' mistake at the same time as it unmasks the true villains: the Austrians, particularly Prince Metternich, their long-serving chancellor.

The argument is fairly simple, but it carries a great deal of weight in determining the shape of a united Germany based on shared as well as disparate histories; for if Austria and her ministers were responsible for Bavaria's error, one can legitimately exclude them from the German body politic while simultaneously excusing and thereby including Austria's Bavarian victims. Sybel can therefore reassure his Munich audience and the other proponents of a small German answer to the question of unification that they view matters from a properly German perspective, whereas the Austrians, even though they, too—like the Bavarians, Saxons, and Prussians—fought as often with Napoleon as against him and are not to be trusted. Thus, when he ends his third lecture by proclaiming "God bless Germany!" (*Gott segne Deutschland!* 146) Sybel has drawn a subtle but nevertheless recognizable map of the Prussian-dominated nation that is to be sanctified.

However, having claimed that "even Napoleon's towering genius as a military commander would not have been able to overwhelm us had we not fought, crippled, and defeated ourselves," Sybel is left to explain how Germany was able to rise from the ashes of corruption, incompetence, and immorality that characterized eighteenth- and early-nineteenth-century German states.[16] In Prussia, for example, the same weak and irresolute Frederick William III who presided over the debacle of Jena still occupied the throne in 1813, while his saintly wife, Louisa, had been dead since 1810. Sybel's answer is that the German people forced their rulers into action, but like other historians, Sybel has difficulty identifying the people and narrating their achievements. On occasion, he reduces Germans to the anonymous forces he claims motivated them: "Meanwhile, the uprising and enthusiasm of feelings [*Begeisterung der Gemüther*] spread themselves unstoppably through the land."[17] At other times, Sybel resorts to representative types: "Young and old alike, fathers of families and old men presented themselves, and more than one girl stepped disguised into the ranks of men in order to offer her blood and life to the fatherland."[18] And in an almost novelistic turn, one peasant, who comes very close to acquiring a name, joins the volunteer forces: "A shepherd from Anclam sold his herd, used the proceeds to buy himself weapons and a uniform, and proceeded to a regiment."[19] Still, Sybel seldom accords such individuals more than a sentence, in contrast to the pages he devotes to politics and the activities of various generals. His account culminates in the battle of Leipzig, where the people are visible mainly as statistics—for example, in the number of troops commanded by various officers. The one exception is a final anecdote that transforms individual suffering into national pride through the wise interpretation of the king: "An old Prussian officer who had brought four sons to the army was asked by the king how he and his sons were doing. 'We're doing well,' the man answered and hesitated for a moment, 'my sons all died for Your Majesty.' 'Not for me,' said the king, visibly shaken, 'not for me, who could bear that, but for the fatherland.'"[20]

To his credit, Sybel seems to be using his lectures not only to justify Prussian hegemony in Germany but also to refute those who would limit popular participation in the national enterprise. He contrasts his own view with that of the nation's leading poets and thinkers from an

CHAPTER 5

earlier age when "patriotism was thought to be a mark of limited intelligence while a real man was called solely to aesthetic education and humanistic world citizenship."[21] The shepherd and the old officer show that even the lowliest inhabitants of the land were capable of understanding and, therefore, of participating in political life, but like so many nineteenth-century historians, Sybel talks about the German people while almost never describing their activities. He invokes ordinary Germans but omits them from history, which remains an activity carried out by great men. Notwithstanding Sybel's liberal pretensions, the genre of academic history almost does him in.

Heinrich von Treitschke was scarcely a liberal. In fact, the last historian in this brief survey of academic opinion was unhesitatingly and openly conservative. His *German History in the Nineteenth Century* makes an unabashed case for Prussian leadership in and beyond the new German empire in the form of the following lofty claim: "The struggle for the liberation of the world remained, therefore, in the first place, a struggle for the re-establishment of Prussia."[22] And Treitschke signals his aim when he calls his long chapter on what happened after 1813 "The War of Liberation" (*Der Befreiungskrieg*).[23] Making the term singular allows him to argue more easily that one state took precedence in Germany during the Napoleonic era, thereby earning rights for the future. He therefore depicts the new German empire as the inevitable and morally justifiable culmination of historical forces rather than the aberration that it appeared to other equally ardent but differently oriented nationalists. The difficulty in both narrative and evidentiary terms is that Treitschke cannot simply show what happened. His nation-building agenda forces him to leap over facts in order to arrive at his conclusion.

Of course, Treitschke tries to control his account, but people and events sometimes slip from his grasp. Not surprisingly, the German people produce a rupture in the text as the historian struggles to combine the myth of universal participation in the uprising against Napoleon with the facts as he discovered them. He begins expansively: "Next to the old soldiers, it was the educated youth who grasped most vividly the seriousness of the time. There glowed in them an enthusiastic yearning for the free and only German fatherland. Not a single student who could wield a weapon remained at home."[24] Then, having ventured so far, Treitschke spends the next few pages backtracking: "It was only the Poles in West Prussia and Upper Silesia who did not share the devotion of the Germans; and in a few towns which had hitherto been free from liability to military service the new laws encountered resistance."[25] "It was only the old Goethe who could take no pleasure in the new time."[26] "In its first and more difficult half, the German War of Liberation was a war of Prussia against the three-fourths of the German nation that was ruled by France. . . . it was not until two generations later [in 1870] that the south had the happiness of taking part in the struggles of the victories of the great fatherland."[27] "Yet something of the German-patriotic ideas which filled the minds of the armed youth of the cultured classes gradually came to permeate the lower strata of the Prussian people."[28] By the time he is finished, Treitschke has conspicuously failed to represent the German people uniting to throw out a foreign invader. His version of the imagined community that would become Germany ultimately includes only the soldiers who were already in the Prussian army or who had once served there and the relatively few students from north German universities who joined them. Apparently, there is an enormous conflict between the notion of objective history, to which Treitschke is formally and professionally committed, and the task of writing the nation.

Treitschke has no more luck portraying those he regarded as villains, namely, the petty princes and their courts. Austria and Saxony bear the brunt of his abuse, because he wants to claim that these two states' leaders ignored the legitimate demands of their subjects. However, since he has just depicted, albeit reluctantly, a widespread lack of interest in German unity under Prussian hegemony, it must be the case that these rulers failed to foster support for what perhaps should have been, but was demonstrably not, a universal longing among their subjects. Accordingly, the blame Treitschke wants to apportion to the leaders of Austria and Saxony ought to be shared by rulers and ruled alike, but that would complicate the nationalist project that lies at the heart of his undertaking. Treitschke attempts to solve his dilemma by making three separate narrative moves. First, he openly invokes a national religion: "The old German God, to whom they [the awakened students] prayed, was the God of the Protestants."[29] Writing at the height of Prussia's struggle with the Catholic Church, it must have been particularly comforting to invoke God's past and present blessing on the empire of 1871. The gesture undercuts the legitimacy of resistance to Bismarck's version of Germany by Catholics both within the new state and in Austria; it also sanctifies the small German solution to the question of German

CHAPTER 5

unity. Second, Treitschke vilifies the opposition. For example, he calls a Saxon minister "one of those inflated mediocrities of whom there are so many in the diplomatic history of the middle states," and he speaks repeatedly of "the criminality of the German princes."[30] They served particular interests rather than the Prussian/German cause upon which Treitschke focused his attention. Third, he portrays other German leaders in a manner that allows readers to identify with his heroes and thereby with the national goal as Treitschke imagines it. General von Blücher is the most salient example, and in contrast to the short negative characterizations of various scoundrels, Treitschke spends half a dozen pages on the general's biography before he allows him to lead the troops.

For Treitschke, Blücher is exemplary in two senses. On the one hand, he appears as a warrior and leader par excellence. In fact, Blücher cuts a figure almost destined to grace an equestrian statue: "To the soldiers he appeared as glorious as the very God of War, this handsome, tall, old man, sitting [on] his gray charger with youthful energy and grace."[31] On the other hand, the text emphasizes Blücher's lack of education, his disdain for convention, and his coarse sense of humor. These were qualities that Treitschke could easily have overlooked had he been interested in a different version of the Prussian general, but here these potentially negative attributes make Blücher "a true Teuton, whose rough greatness could be comprehensible in its entirety only to men of Teuton blood."[32] The one jarring exception, which might make Blücher sympathetic to some modern readers, is his flouting of gender conventions. "The *petits-maîtres* [little masters] were disgusted with the gray-headed youngster at the court balls who still sometimes danced a quadrille with the elegant young officers of the guard; but those of deeper nature soon felt that this unrestrained activity was no more than the natural expression of the unlimited fervor of his vital energy."[33] Unlike Blücher's small-minded opponents, Treitschke seems unconcerned with the general's behavior or his sense of decorum. In fact, by calling Blücher's critics *petits-maîtres,* Treitschke implicitly sanctions the commander's gender-bending as "German," an action no more remarkable than eating sausages or drinking beer. And as odd as this behavior might seem to the modern reader, for Treitschke's account to succeed, Blücher must be both heroic and typical, because the general represents the otherwise missing ordinary inhabitants of Germany. Treitschke's only other choice would be to chronicle the deeds of some representative militiaman, while still providing a clear view of the larger struggle for Germany. But not only were such figures beyond the scope of academic history in the nineteenth century, Blücher, the man rather than the military leader, also possessed enough narrative resonance to fulfill the demands Treitschke placed upon him.

Treitschke seems to have been well aware of the stakes involved in his narration of events; his text even includes a passage in which the historian, perhaps inadvertently, foregrounds his own mythmaking enterprise. At the end of his chapter on the War of Liberation the reader learns that the Prussian minister, Baron vom Stein, charged Ernst Moritz Arndt with assembling "all the historical recollections and romantic images which were at his disposal to influence the nation, thinking out a view which was then new, but was soon to become one of the driving forces of the century—the idea that, in the last resort, language and the historical peculiarities of the nations must determine the frontiers of states."[34] Essentially, Treitschke recognizes, first, that a language community can constitute itself as a nation—culturally and politically—only with the help of nationalistic propaganda, notably, with appropriate accounts from the ranks of historians and, as we shall soon see, from historical novelists. Otherwise, prospective members of a united Germany could easily overlook the supposed congruence of language and national identity. Second, since Treitschke remains a proponent of Germany without Austria, he has to add "historical peculiarities" to the qualifications for inclusion; for to the extent that Germany was not populated by speakers of mutually incomprehensible dialects, Austrians shared a language with Prussians. However, in Treitschke's version of events, Austrians were historically and culturally different from the people united under Bismarck's leadership: "The great gulf between the mental life of the Austrians and that of the other Germans, was not bridged by the War of Liberation."[35] No wonder the fledgling nation needed Arndt and his heirs to explain the real history of 1813–15. Small wonder, too, that the concept of nationality proves so elusive and so slippery in the hands of historians.

Novelists Imagine the German Family

As chroniclers of the Wars of Liberation novelists enjoyed considerable advantages over both academic and popular historians.[36] Historical fiction almost invariably focused on individuals in whom readers could see themselves, and authors who made use of Sir Walter Scott's middling heroes could imagine a future German nation while simultaneously hooking readers on plots and characters. Potential Germans had little difficulty identifying with the ordinary men and women who populated novels of national regeneration, and, once identified, it was also easy for readers to think of themselves as partners and participants in the emerging national community. Fictional accounts of the Wars of Liberation link entertainment with a political agenda, even—or perhaps especially—when the outcome is not just victory but marriage and the founding of a new "German" family. As Martin Swales has argued, a characteristic feature of German realism was the lack of tension between the public and private sphere.[37] Through their portrayals of courtship and union these novels almost invariably posed and then attempted to answer a set of interrelated questions: Who was included in the national family? Who was excluded? And how did texts legitimize these choices? The answers are particularly revealing whenever novels focus on marginal groups—Jews, women, and men of divided loyalties—but the fictional image of German identity remains both tentative and conflicted even when the heroes are stolid males. Looking closely at a dozen examples allows us to see these tensions and note the means authors employed to resolve them, as well as to appreciate what was at stake in historical fiction that was both disparate and oddly homogeneous; for while not every romance led directly to marriage, every romantic inclination contained the promise of its own future Germany. Novelists' difficulties were seldom structural; their problems arose when imagination confronted or outstripped German reality thereby threatening plausibility.

Although it was published in 1834, Ludwig Rellstab's *1812* appears here rather than in chapter 2 because the novel's focus on bourgeois men and women results in a substantially different image of Germany than its predecessors. Unlike authors from the period 1815–30, whose aristocratic heroes and heroines ultimately chose caste over country, Rellstab presents readers with characters whose identity is national, rooted in descent or ethnicity, that is, in blood. Of course, *1812* is long and complicated. The book proceeds through myriad plot twists and turns before its half-dozen heroes and heroines finally unite in national groups, and Rellstab needs more than a few unlikely coincidences to keep the whole intricate structure from collapsing under its own weight. But despite the author's clumsy plotting and his recourse to an implausible happy ending, *1812* is far from the simple panegyric to

German nationalism that readers then and now might expect. In fact, the book considers both the difficulty of establishing a German community and the problems experienced by other national groups that fought for and against Napoleon.

As the novel opens, "a young German," Ludwig Rosen, is returning to Dresden from Italy in order to fulfill his duty to his mother and his "fatherland," both of whom are threatened by renewed French invasions.[38] Ludwig's familial obligation appears to be straightforward: his mother is a widow living with her daughter, and the two women could well fall victim to marauding soldiers should war break out again. What Ludwig owes the nation is far less clear, because the text immediately calls into question the categories "fatherland" and "German." If it were up to him, Ludwig would remain in Italy with its warm climate and friendly inhabitants, and he knows that Dresden will soon welcome Napoleon, with whom Saxony has long been allied. Yet, far from being disturbed by his countrymen's allegiances, Ludwig is an admirer of the French emperor, whom he views as the only possible solution to the German problem of small states and corrupt princes. Reluctant to be home, Ludwig decides that he can fight for Germany only by leaving, so he joins a Franco-Polish regiment whose officers he met during the journey from Italy. The news sends his sister into despair, and the reader encounters, in 1834, perhaps for the first time, an openly patriotic German woman.

Marie Rosen knows that her brother's absence will be hard for their mother to bear, but the prospect is even difficult for Marie to accept. Ludwig is aware that his sister has "a true German heart," but she, too, is torn by conflicting desires.[39] Marie has fallen in love with one of Ludwig's Polish officer friends, Count Rasinski, and he returns her affections. Indeed, he even offers to marry her once the war is over, despite their very different class and national backgrounds. Unlike the aristocratic heroines of earlier historical fiction, whose allegiances were more to caste than country and whose spheres of opportunity were decidedly domestic, Marie refuses. She even argues with Rasinski about politics, and the narrator takes great pains to explain her dilemma: "He was allied with people she could only view as the enemies of her fatherland; she could honor him as a noble man, love him as a generous friend, but never belong to him, fuse her whole being with his without neglecting duties whose sacredness completely pervaded her soul."[40] This is decidedly not the typical romantic heroine's musings here. In contrast to char-

CHAPTER 5

acters of that ilk, Marie Rosen has ventured far enough into the public sphere both to have an opinion on the day's burning issues and to accept the painful consequences of her beliefs. The choice she makes is difficult and groundbreaking. Renouncing romance was traumatic for anyone coded female in nineteenth-century fiction, and by choosing the German nation over domestic bliss, Marie essentially accepts the nation's masculine values. She also begins the process of modeling a form of happiness that can occur only within a single ethnic community. Unfortunately for Marie as a character, and even more unfortunately for the novelist, the heroine's decision raises innumerable narratological problems. In essence, by allowing Marie Rosen to break the narrative convention of female passivity in national issues, Rellstab severely limits his options for writing a plausible happy ending. In fact, *1812* requires all manner of contortions to end at all.

One might, however, forgive an author a great deal for daring to let women pose serious questions in his fiction. For example, although it strains the reader's credulity to believe that Ludwig Rosen would encounter, help rescue, and fall in love with a beautiful woman along the road over the Simplon Pass, later to be saved by her from the flames of Moscow, only to discover that she is really the long-lost sister of his best friend and therefore a German commoner rather than a Russian aristocrat, the woman does raise the issue of nature versus nurture with regard to national identity. Similarly, the Polish countess who meets Marie Rosen at a spa and offers to protect her from the French secret police turns out to be Count Rasinski's sister, Micielska; she also makes a sympathetic, personal case for Polish national feelings that clash sharply with Marie's German convictions. In short—and there are far more startling coincidences than those just listed—if one overlooks such improbabilities, Rellstab's novel can demonstrate just how complicated the issues of national identity had become for the author and his readers. His utterly unrealistic plot permits three female characters to become involved in very real dilemmas, each having to do with a different aspect of national identity. Moreover, the two German women ultimately join their male counterparts in a domestic idyll that serves as a model for the nation in progress.

At first glance, a historical novel devoted to the German struggle against Napoleonic France might seem like a strange place to encounter a sympathetic treatment of Polish nationalism. After all, Prussia and Austria had both participated, along with Russia, in the dismemberment of Poland at the end of the eighteenth century, and the Poles rebelled against Russia in 1830–31, just three years before Rellstab wrote his novel. Polish resentment against Germans, while not as fierce as that directed against Russians, was understandably high. Yet, despite the incompatibility of Polish and German nationalisms, Ludwig Rosen declares himself happy to have joined a Polish regiment, because he regards the Poles' struggle as "unquestionably just" (*unbestreitbar gerecht*, 121), and the cause gains genuine nobility through the figure of Countess Micielska. The narrator describes her as having a "tall, majestic physique" (*von hohem, majestätischem Wuchs*, 119); a page later her terms her "tall and noble" (*hoch und edel*, 120). She also fares surprisingly well when compared with the very German Marie:

> The countess showed an active, intellectual interest in public affairs; . . . she read the newspapers and the day's political tracts eagerly; she was familiar with the history of events, followed them with acumen, and was able to connect distant incidents intelligently with the fate of her fatherland. Marie by contrast simply loved her home and the people to whom she belonged above all else; her language and mode of thought made her a German. . . . Once the fatherland was liberated, her interest in public affairs would disappear or at least recede into the distance as it did for all women.[41]

The "all women" at the end of this passage contradicts what the reader has been led to believe about Countess Micielska, and it is particularly troubling as an assessment of the role of women in the German nation. On the one hand, the passage reflects an underlying patriarchal attitude, while on the other hand, it shows how difficult it was for writers to deal with strong women, particularly when they expressed an interest in politics. Since Poland, despite the nobility of both its cause and supporters, is not freed in the Wars of Liberation, since the countess cannot settle for the diminished life available to her in Europe after 1815, and since she is denied a heroic death in the conflict that claims her brother, Countess Micielska simply walks into the novel's final scene and announces that she is emigrating to America, where she hopes to die—soon, but nevertheless breathing the sweet air of freedom. Given her impassioned support for a doomed cause, it is as happy an ending as is possible.

Count Rasinski's death, by contrast, must mean Marie made the right choice in rejecting him. In fact, she eventually marries her brother's German friend, Bernhard, and the reader hears nothing more of her own patriotism. The nation's success probably pleases but at the same time disenfranchises Marie Rosen, and her fate is magnified in the story of the third major female character in Rellstab's novel. Ludwig knows her as Bianka, the mysterious figure who, as the novel gets under way, appears and disappears so frequently that she seems to haunt the young man's life like a ghost. Then, for the longest time Bianka is absent from the narrative, and the reader encounters in her stead a Russian countess, Feodorowna, who is unexpectedly critical of her own national origin. Although Russia became Germany's most important ally in the war against Napoleon, the novel presents Feodorowna's father as a particularly galling example of eastern barbarism. He is dishonest, treats his servants like cattle, and tries to marry his daughter to an odious but rich Russian prince. She rebels and even tells the family's German gardener to flee: "Woe to anyone who has to call [Russia] fatherland; blessed are they who have a different home!"[42] Despite those sentiments Feodorowna has resigned herself to accepting her Russian nationality. For her, national origin is an inescapable if also tragic fate.

Throughout Rellstab's novel identity exceeds political allegiance. Ludwig may volunteer to fight for Poland, but the national community modeled here is based on birth, that is, the kinship of blood. It is therefore not surprising, at least not to the attentive reader, that on her wedding eve the Russian Countess Feodorowna learns she was born German. In fact, she is none other than the long-lost sister of Ludwig's friend Bernhard. And if that rather startling coincidence were not enough, Feodorowna is revealed to be the beautiful Bianka, a character as pure (white) as her name has always suggested. Since they are no longer separated, either by caste or national identity, Bianka and Ludwig marry near the novel's end. Significantly, the book's two happy couples are both German. They have become eligible for a happy ending because there are no national encumbrances on their romances, which also means, both in narratological terms and for the model of Germany advanced here, that the two women can be relegated to lesser roles. The novel's penultimate chapter has both couples back in Germany, where the war is not quite over. In fact, it is only 1813, and the two men answer the fatherland's call to arms. Ludwig and Bernhard march off, this time as Germans in an ostensibly German army, while Marie and Bianka retreat to the countryside near Dresden. They, too, are German

THE GERMAN PEOPLE ARISE—AND MARRY

patriots, but as women they have to stay home, able only to observe, from a distance, the dreams of national unity and freedom that they share with their husbands.

To be sure, the two women fare far better than Countess Micielska, who has no choice other than exile and death, but the German fatherland has extracted a price from "his" female inhabitants too. For example, although Bianka's renunciation proves temporary, both she and Marie must reject the foreigners with whom they initially fell in love. German nationalism arranges their marriages; it brings them suitors rather than letting them range across Europe to find their own husbands. Perhaps as important for female readers of *1812*, neither Bianka nor Marie is as interesting or as fully developed a character as the Polish countess, and neither is as readily available as the book's male heroes as a focus for readers' identification. As women caught in the confines of conventional fiction they cannot act independently, and once they are back in Germany, they stop talking about conflicted identities and seem content to wait for their men to return home. For Rellstab, writing in the early 1830s, domestic tranquility apparently implied peace, prosperity, and passive female characters. At the same time, these women not only help found two new families, but they also participate in the process of redefining an imaginary German community after 1830. With them and their husbands, the family of true Germans now includes, indeed it centers upon, the bourgeoisie, where the feminine values of Queen Louisa increasingly hold sway.

Love, family, and the nation also play significant roles in Willibald Alexis's *Isegrimm* (1854), a sprawling work whose plot begins just after the Prussian defeat at Jena and ends sometime after the Revolution of 1848.[43] Here, too, courtship and marriage mirror versions of a future Germany. The novel's central character, Wolf von Quarbitz auf Ilitz, has three daughters who seem more interested in dancing with French officers than in seeing the enemy driven from their fatherland. In fact, except for the book's gnarled, grumpy, aristocratic patriarch, known as Isegrimm, Alexis's version of Prussia seems filled with men and women who are quite content to live with Napoleon's armies. At the bottom of the social scale a coachman declares that he would fight if called to arms, but since the king has made no demands, politics are really none of his business. He is less than enamored with the French, whom he mildly reproaches for being "windy and foggy" (*windig und dunstig*, 46), but quartering troops from Würtemberg, Bavaria, and Nassau was a far

CHAPTER 5

worse burden for the patriotic inhabitants of Prussia than having French soldiers in residence. Representing the middle classes, the town's mayor is stoic; he knows what is really important: "If the fatherland can't be saved, maybe we can save the horses."[44] Meanwhile, near the top of Prussian society, Isegrimm's distant cousin, the court counselor Baron Quarbitz auf Quilitz, hopes the French philosopher Voltaire will return to fashion. As he reasons, "the fatherland can become larger; it can encompass the entire civilized world."[45] A universal empire under Napoleon could profitably replace the Prussian state or even a German nation. In short, the nationalist fervor readers might expect from a fictional treatment of the French occupation is conspicuously absent from *Isegrimm*.

Patriotism rears its muddled head mainly in the conflict between the country's ancient aristocracy, of which Isegrimm is a prime example, and the politically powerless bourgeoisie. Isegrimm fancies himself a loyal if sorely disappointed vassal of Prussia's weak king. Indeed, he is so loyal to the idea of the monarchy that he argues against a popular uprising to save the present occupant of the throne. Involving the people would threaten the old order Isegrimm champions. As he succinctly puts it, "The rabble have no say," and he is particularly adamant in his opposition to bourgeois officers.[46] Since Alexis wrote in the wake of the unsuccessful Revolution of 1848, which called for, among other things, a national guard with elected officers, such comments were not simply retrospective judgments about the best means of ridding Prussia of Napoleon's armies. He must have been asking, as almost every novel about this period does, whether Germany's aristocracy or its bourgeoisie represented the nation and could lay the foundation for a future national community. Of note here is that Alexis was skilled enough as a writer to make the answer anything but easy for himself, his characters, or, ultimately, his readers.

Isegrimm's plot twists, turns, and stalls for a while before the reader becomes aware of the stakes, but the book poses the national question when two implausible lovers ride onto the scene. The one, a beautiful countess who can outride any man, claims to be the niece of a French general; the other is Isegrimm's ne'er-do-well nephew, Theodor. That young man, for all of his failings, remains the apple of his aunt's and, more important, his cousin Amalie's eyes. However, Amalie announces their love has died when she learns that her cousin is so smitten by the French countess that he is willing to quit the Prussian army and join the enemy. She cannot abide the idea of him renouncing king and fatherland, but not for patriotic reasons. His changing sides would break her father's heart and bring lasting shame to the whole family. As this point a chance encounter reveals the French countess as a fraud, and she disappears from the narrative on the arm of an officer who knew her first as the daughter of a Berlin fruit monger and then as a dancer in the opera. Meanwhile, Theodor regains his German orientation, only to embark on an ill-fated attack on the local French garrison. The adventure lands him in the dungeon of Isegrimm's castle, where he awaits execution, while his fate places the whole family on the horns of a dilemma.

Theodor's incarceration brings three other suitors into Isegrimm's household, each with his own drawbacks for the family's fiercely protective paterfamilias. More important, these three men allow Alexis to discuss almost every variation of the future German family. To begin, the youngest daughter, Amalie, is sorely in need of consolation over the impending death of her cousin. She finds a supportive shoulder attached to Albert Mauritz, a theology student who is living with the family while he waits for a position as a pastor. Predictably, the two fall in love, and, just as predictably, Isegrimm vehemently rejects the match. The father is particularly unhappy because he believes Amalie shares his aristocratic prejudices. Although Isegrimm accepts Mauritz's counsel in family matters and respects the young man's patriotic leanings, he regards the son of a craftsman an impossible match for the daughter of a baron. Meanwhile, his eldest daughter, Wilhelmine, raises the opposite set of objections. The man who courts her, Baron Eppenstein, is a wealthy nobleman, but his money and title are too new. Besides, as the name Eppenstein none too subtly suggests, he may be Jewish, and Wilhelmine despises him. She nevertheless offers to marry the baron in order to pay off a mortgage on the family estate, but Isegrimm will have no truck with such commerce. Better to face bankruptcy than accept a tainted parvenu into the family. Finally, the middle daughter, Karoline, presents Isegrimm with an even more intractable problem. She has fallen for the French colonel quartered in the castle. On the one hand, the man represents foreign invaders who have upended the system of ancient rights and privileges that Isegrimm regards as God-given. He is also Catholic. On the other hand, this particular colonel is a brilliant horseman, an accomplished soldier, and the scion of an ancient noble family. Isegrimm enjoys his conversations with the young man and even suspects they share some ancestors by way of the Huguenot colony in Berlin. The

CHAPTER 5

scene is ripe for melodramatic confrontation, and the critical juncture arrives as lightning strikes an outbuilding at the very moment Isegrimm has finished an argument by throwing the theologian out of his study. The damage would be largely symbolic except that Isegrimm's younger son and namesake hangs trapped atop a dovecote, screaming in terror as flames lick at his heels.

"Son?" asks all but the dimmest reader incredulously. "Younger son, implying an older one?" We take this opportunity to leave the boy in peril for a moment and ask where Isegrimm's sons have been all along in a novel devoted to an aristocrat's concern with the future of his family and country. Sons, and sons alone, can inherit property, carry on the family name, and join the forces fighting to free Prussia and Germany from the Napoleonic yoke. Yet, after the briefest of introductions, these sons have been missing for hundreds of pages, and when one of them finally reappears he is a frightened boy awaiting rescue. He seems unlikely to embody the nation's future, impossibly so if he dies. However, despite his quarrel with the boy's father, Amalie's theology student finds a ladder and begins climbing, but to no avail. The flames flare, and the boy cowers just beyond them, maddeningly, but perhaps also symbolically, just out of Mauritz's reach. One imagines a weekly installment breaking off at this point, when narrative tension has reached its highest pitch. Then, a week later, just as consumers snatch the next issue from their local newsstand or the hands of the mailman, who should ride by but Baron Eppenstein, resplendent in his hunting garb. The baron mounts the tower, tosses the boy to the ground, and then rides off because Wilhelmine has rejected him yet again. Isegrimm's son limps for the rest of his life, which might prefigure some national difficulty, while Alexis still faces the difficult problem of using this family to model a future for Germany.

Isegrimm's eldest daughter eventually marries an imperial count, but the man has long been a thorn in her father's side. His family lost their status as sovereign rulers of a tiny principality during the Napoleonic era, so when he regains the right to maintain a private army of twelve men at the Congress of Vienna, the restoration of ancient perquisites appears more ridiculous than triumphant. Besides, the count makes no bones about his probable descent from farmers and craftsmen. Worse yet, in Isegrimm's eyes, the count's sister marries Eppenstein, transforming the hated parvenu into a relative, however distant. Meanwhile, Isegrimm's middle daughter elopes with her French colonel and converts to his fanatic Catholicism. Isegrimm also learns that the Frenchman's ancient pedigree is false, so when the restored king of France later makes him a count, the gesture adds insult to injury. Finally, after the Wars of Liberation, the youngest daughter receives her father's permission to wed Mauritz, and Isegrimm appoints this newest member of the clan pastor at the local church. By now Isegrimm should be resigned to the match, or even happy, because the clergyman served with such distinction in the German cause that he was awarded the Iron Cross. In addition, Mauritz's fellow soldiers elected him their commanding officer, but the vote makes Isegrimm irate at the loss of aristocratic rights. The reader is well prepared for Isegrimm's principled rejection of meritocracy, because the novel contains long passages in which characters, including the preeminent Prussian reformer, Baron vom Stein, argue for and against bourgeois officers. But by undermining his daughter's happiness, Alexis's curmudgeonly hero is once again jousting at windmills and in the process undercutting the book's patriotic premises. Ultimately, Isegrimm remains endearingly blunt, but his family offers little hope for a national future. One senses that for all of his trouble Alexis was unable to imagine convincing versions of a united Germany, so he allows his central character to destroy or diminish every solution to the national question. Only the pastor's children resemble their grandfather, and the novel explicitly refrains from telling their tale. The narrator concedes that the omission might disappoint his readers, but he asks forbearance for the strictures history places on literature. Reversing Fontane's criticism of *Keeping Calm Is the Citizen's First Duty*, Alexis's narrator claims it is not his fault that history paints a darker picture of reality than literature. After the failures of 1848, he prophesizes only disappointment for those who hope, in fiction or in fact, for "complete awakening of the German people and the rebirth of the fatherland."[47] Although Alexis had toyed with almost every option, in 1854 imagining the nation's future proved too daunting a task.

Such problems never stopped or even slowed Louisa Mühlbach. Her sixteen-volume work *Napoleon in Germany* appeared in 1858, and four of those volumes deal with the Wars of Liberation.[48] Mühlbach again chose to focus on a single individual from the upper reaches of society, but here she seems far less interested than in her earlier novels in using the hero as a vehicle to broaden her focus. Blücher, the Prussian general who commanded allied forces from 1813 through the Battle of Waterloo in 1815, was the most popular hero in the wars against the

CHAPTER 5

French, but he was scarcely a commoner. Then, too, he was already seventy years old and could scarcely marry and father a family. In other words, the general is not particularly useful for sketching a future German society. Mühlbach does take great pains to give her hero a common touch, but she writes only supporting roles for the people who surround her hero. In Mühlbach's hands Blücher becomes wise and approachable, an uncle to the German people and a leader in the manner of Old Fritz, but those he leads lack all depth and interest. A single example illustrates the book's shortcomings.

The time is December 1812. Blücher frets during an uneasy retirement at his country estate. Although the general had already turned seventy, Napoleon still forced King Frederick William III to dismiss him from Prussian service. Grumpy and isolated, his few visitors consist of a series of even older men who claim to have captured him in 1760, when Blücher was a young officer in the Swedish army. They are all seeking favor—and lying—until an eighty-year-old hussar recounts his version of the tale. Blücher senses that this man is honest, and the two of them reminisce while sharing a bottle of wine. Of course, the hussar has an ulterior motive, but an honorable one. He asks Blücher to help his grandson: "He wishes to become a soldier, and help *you* drive out the French."[49] The general replies that he no longer commands any regiments. Despite the old man's implied prediction, Blücher remains certain that he will not be part of the next war. However, at that very moment, General Scharnhorst arrives to inform Blücher of Napoleon's Russian debacle. Scharnhorst comes from the king, but Mühlbach's readers know that the people spoke first. But, having spoken his few lines, the old hussar and his grandson leave the stage for good. Mühlbach, an otherwise democratic author, has reserved all the main roles in this cycle of novels for generals and ministers; her prescient hussar provides only a fleeting bit of color. Without some more fully developed supporting characters, like those who played such prominent roles in both the Frederick and Queen Louisa cycles, Mühlbach cannot create a national family or foreshadow a German future. Instead, this novel blunders along in its predictable hero worship and need detain us no longer.

Fritz Reuter chose a diametrically opposite tack in his *From the Time of the French* (1859).[50] In contrast to Mühlbach, Reuter's authorities remain a distant, almost invisible presence in this comic tale of hapless villagers dealing with French troops in Mecklenburg in 1812. The book begins as seven French marauders appear in Reuter's hometown of

Stavenhagen. The town's leading official comes up with the remarkable strategy of defending themselves by having a local miller drink the band's officer under the table. Meanwhile, the town's watchmaker, who hails from a formerly Prussian, French-speaking canton in Switzerland, is to don his old French uniform and threaten the six soldiers with prosecution for desertion. The plan succeeds until the next day, when regular French troops arrive and their officer talks about arresting everyone involved in the scheme. Needless to say, complications abound, and many of the town's difficulties offer implications for the book's vision of Germany. First, the watchmaker can barely make himself understood in German, and the narrator captures the man's linguistic and national confusion when he claims that this erstwhile Prussian-Swiss-Frenchman changed nationalities by marrying a local widow: "Germany is now his fatherland" (*Allemangne* sei nun seine *patrie*). In fact, the man is ready to do "everything for the fatherland" (*tout* für die *patrie*, 26, emphasis original). The reader is left wondering about the role of birth, language, and individual choice in determining national identity. Second, the miller is both a hero and a bankrupt drunk. Reuter allows him to vilify a Jewish moneylender, but the book is clear about the miller's inability to conduct his business profitably. He is also involved in an interminable lawsuit with a cousin over some inherited property. The miller could end the dispute by allowing his daughter to marry the cousin's heir, which the two young people devoutly wish, but he is too stubborn. Although he is German, the miller remains unattractive to the end. Third, and finally, the commander of the regular French troops is revealed to be a German from Westphalia. Unlike the watchmaker, who moved voluntarily from one linguistic and cultural community to another, while maintaining his dynastic loyalty, the officer swears allegiance to whatever nation the current ruler of his homeland favors. In 1812 Napoleon's brother Jerome occupied the throne in a newly created Kingdom of Westphalia, so the officer declares himself French. However, in a coincidence that strains credulity but raises the stakes in the nationalist debate, the town's highest official is an old friend of the officer's father; he believes that the young man "can only be a good German."[51] Disciplining the inhabitants of Stavenhagen therefore becomes, among other things, a matter of conflicting notions of national identity. Despite the book's comic tone, this particular town's problems resemble difficulties experienced throughout Germany.

Unlike so many novels and histories of the Wars of Liberation,

CHAPTER 5

From the Time of the French includes a long scene devoted to the volunteer militia that figured so prominently in the myth of Germany's renewal. However, their behavior is anything by heroic. Reuter assembles a column of inept and badly led townspeople, who are only too glad to discover that the French have already left the region. After a strenuous march that lasted almost a whole day, they can return home, only to find themselves embroiled in another bizarre scheme, this time hatched by the miller and a town councilor. The two men have sold grain entrusted to the miller and paid his debts with the proceeds, basing their action on an obvious mistake in the miller's agreement with some farmers. Having avoided bankruptcy, the miller can once again prevent his daughter's marriage, but only until higher authorities void the offending section of the contract. The miller still avoids default, because the French or, depending on one's point of view, good German officer entrusts the marauders' booty to his father's old friend so that he, in turn, can give it to the miller's daughter. Actually, the loot passes through several other hands, in keeping with a novel that contains more complications than fit into this summary. But the book ends in reconciliation and presages a happy ending for Germany. Although the cousin disappears for several years to fight for the fatherland, he returns to marry his beloved, and they start a solidly German family. By that time, in an oddly feminist turn, the miller's daughter has taken over the business, and the mill is prospering. The Westphalian officer appears at the wedding with his own wife, but the narrator nevertheless identifies him as "the French colonel," a label that does not disqualify him from participating in the postwar community, which also includes the watchmaker and his "little French brats."[52] One might wonder which side the colonel fought on, once Napoleon's brother decamped from Westphalia, and why the watchmaker's children remained outsiders. The reader never learns the answer, perhaps because Reuter, like the rest of Germany's writers and its leaders, still could not produce a convincing definition of Germany or the Germans. Still, romance provided far more opportunity to construct a myth of German renewal than battle, and Reuter paints a picture of a German future in which peasants and tradespeople unite under the benevolent but barely competent oversight of the authorities. Although the book's domestic focus is absolutely unremarkable, its comic tone makes Reuter's novel a rare if not unique treatment of the Wars of Liberation, one that also contains a fair measure of cynicism about the nationalist project and its intellectual underpinnings.

THE GERMAN PEOPLE ARISE—AND MARRY

Jews as German Patriots

By contrast, Julius von Wickede's *Tall Isaack* (1863) is a remarkably serious book, but one that remains obscure despite its being one of the few philo-Semitic works of nineteenth-century fiction.[53] This rare but rewarding novel recounts the lives of a patriotic German father and his two daughters; its characters pose the question of national identity in particularly poignant fashion merely by being Jewish, but they are scarcely passive or flat. Isaack is a peddler, plying his trade in the countryside around Lüneburg in 1813. His already difficult existence—trekking from farm to farm selling needles, knives, and fabric—has become even more arduous because war, taxes, and the cost of quartering French troops have taken their toll on the area's once prosperous farmers. One day the peddler knocks at the door of the proud but downwardly mobile Bruhn family, where he hears a profoundly mixed greeting: "Really and truly, Isaack, to be sure you are only a Jew, and I actually can't stand Jews, but there is not a man in all of Hannover who has a more honest heart in his chest than you do."[54] Isaack responds by claiming to have made his most recent foray not for business reasons but "so that he could render an important service to the fatherland."[55] His occupation provides cover while he gathers crucial information about the movement of the French army and relays it to the German population and the allied troops who are just beginning to defend them. Since he regards Germany as his fatherland, Isaack is willing to risk his life and fortune for those who despise him. His youngest daughter occupies an even more ambiguous position.

Rebekka lives in Lüneburg in a house that the narrator describes with faint and demeaning praise as "unusually clean for Jews."[56] Among her home's furnishings are busts of Schiller, Lessing, and Mendelssohn, which mark her as a lover of high culture. In fact, it was Rebekka's maternal grandfather, a learned rabbi, "who first revealed the rich treasures of our best German authors" to her, and Rebekka can scarcely read enough of her favorite writers.[57] She also longs for someone, presumably a man as intelligent and as well read as she is, so the two of them can talk about literature. When she offers to nurse a wounded Prussian officer back to health, she initially thinks her prayers have been answered. Rich, noble, and patriotic, Fritz von Dassow appears to be the ideal romantic hero, and he is also fresh from the university, which means, presumably, he is a reader. Although the irony may be unintentional, the narrator terms Rebekka's care "true Christian charity, a purer and nobler example

CHAPTER 5

could not be found on earth," and Rebekka hopes to hasten both the young man's recovery and their relationship by reading aloud to him from Goethe, Schiller, and Klopstock.[58] The scene is too good to be true, especially, as skeptical readers will note, when it comes this early in a three-volume novel. The beginning of volume 2 is no place for a happy ending.

As a character, Rebekka anticipates almost all the tensions and difficulties associated with German-Jewish assimilation throughout the nineteenth and into the twentieth century; she allows Wickede to explore a strategy that was open to question, even in 1863, more than seventy-five years before the Holocaust. Rebekka is educated, beautiful, sensitive, and more committed to German culture than are most Germans. She is also identified with traits such as cleanliness and charity that the novel codes as both Christian and German, as if these two labels were one. Although she refuses to renounce the religion of her forebears, Rebekka eagerly reads a New Testament that a theology student friend has given to the wounded officer. Despite her taste in literature, Rebekka wonders why Jews support Germany when most Germans reject them as compatriots. Wickede uses her to show how Germans like Fritz von Dassow and his bourgeois friends regarded this remarkable woman and her father—first, foremost, and only—as Jews whose German patriotism remains incomprehensible. While the Jews are unable to fashion either an acceptable or a coherent identity, neither can they understand the Germans' unyielding rejection of their German-Jewish orientation. *Tall Isaack* is a prophetic examination of the small tragedies that presaged Germany's greatest disaster, and the book's troubled philo-Semitism is particularly remarkable in an overtly patriotic treatment of the Wars of Liberation.

Fritz von Dassow is grateful for the care he receives but bored by the German classics Rebekka reads to him. And she learns to her dismay that their literary preferences run to polar opposites: "The books that the young lieutenant ordered from a lending library in the city during the course of his gradual recuperation, books that best suited his taste, were either so trivial or also so suggestive that [Rebekka] scornfully threw them aside after reading only a few pages."[59] Luckily for these would-be lovers, the contrast almost ceases to matter. As the son of an ancient noble family, Fritz knows that unbridgeable caste differences separate him from the daughter of a Jewish peddler, while Rebekka has long since lost interest in her dashing dolt, except when he talks of doing battle with the French:

> In his moments of military enthusiasm the lieutenant appeared to the Jewish woman again in the ideal light in which she had first seen him after he was wounded. . . . [and it] remained an inexplicable mystery to her that the same man who was open to such noble emotions, who continually showed himself ready to shed his heart's most intimate blood gladly for the liberation of the fatherland, would also show so little interest in every higher intellectual calling, indeed, would exhibit a taste for trivialities to which she was indifferent or even contemptuous. But Rebekka also felt the bitterest pain at defeats suffered by the allies, and she, too, loved her great German fatherland, for although she was a Jew, she was, at the same time, a true and genuine German.[60]

The issue at the center of this passage is what it meant to be German. The book questions the concept of a national cultural community (*Kulturnation*) by asking to what extent Germany's vaunted high culture linked the vast majority of its inhabitants, including German aristocrats who neither read nor understood the nation's artistic heritage, and the narrative voice also doubts the sufficiency of patriotic enthusiasm as a foundation for the national project. Most important, Wickede's novel wonders who the real Germans are, and whether the category could include women and Jews.

The question of national identity appears in a different guise when one of the local noblewomen, who had earlier turned down an offer of marriage from a solidly German farmer, is forced to marry a French officer. She finds herself isolated in occupied Hamburg, where she reluctantly visits the German-speaking mistress of the French military governor. For an aristocrat, even one whose husband could use a few favors, calling on this fallen woman and notorious Jew is a bitter pill to swallow, and her dismay is complete when she recognizes her hostess as Isaack's older daughter, Sara. Although French officers had carried her off in 1806, Sara seems to have made the best of a bad situation. She is as intelligent and as cultured as her sister, Rebekka, and, according to rumor, has had an affair with Napoleon himself. In effect, Sara represents one of

CHAPTER 5

the few choices available to a strong female character other than a submissive marriage, but for her, the wages of freedom include, first, a reputation for immorality; second, the hatred of her German compatriots, because she is both a traitor and a Jew; and, third, the scorn of her father and sister. Sara's only friend, if one can use the term so loosely, is the French officer's wife, for although the two women despise each other immediately and instinctively, neither of them has a better option. While readers are probably not disturbed by the sad fate accorded to an opportunistic and not particularly intelligent German countess, Sara's failure to find happiness proves troubling. In narratological terms, the author has no alternative. Renouncing France and freedom, even if it earned Sara a reconciliation with her father, would simultaneously entangle her in the same dilemma that Rebekka faces: where to turn in the multifaceted conflict between German high culture, crude forms of patriotism, and anti-Semitic prejudice. Neither sister has an answer.

The war and her father's absence force Rebekka to lodge with a slovenly aunt, a woman whose lack of household skills apparently make her more Jewish in one of the book's few slips into caricature. Despite the squalor, Rebekka sits with her favorite book, Lessing's *Nathan the Wise*. Its famous ring parable suggests that the Muslim, Christian, and Jewish religions are equally valid variations on a single theme, but Rebekka is to be sadly disappointed if she expects her reality to conform to what this classic text from the German Enlightenment espouses. When she and Fritz's theologian friend fall deeply in love, their relationship proves hopeless in the sense that neither can marry without one of them converting—presumably Rebekka, whose gender marks her as weaker. Although drawn together by common intellectual interests, mainly their love of German literature, these two characters are simultaneously repelled by their deeply held religious convictions. Here, too, Wickede stages a confrontation that is all the more telling because the text indicates he shared Lessing's enlightened perspective but was unwilling or unable to concoct the kind of implausible happy ending that preserved the playwright's idealism. Whereas Lessing reveals his play's young lovers to be siblings of such mixed parentage that the question of religion is obviated, while marriage is impossible, Wickede refuses to stoop to such coincidences. Whether he employed this high-mindedness to stake his own claim on literary quality is probably beside the point, even though the book raises the issue of high culture so relentlessly that it has to be reflecting on its own status along with the political questions that it poses. In any case, just as he is about to march off to fight the French, the theologian tells Rebekka that he will marry her after the war if she converts to Christianity. She refuses, saying, "God's will ordained that I was born a Jew. . . . if I had been born a Christian, I would certainly have become a true adherent of your religion."[61] In essence, Wickede portrays religious preference as an accident of birth, not unlike nationality, and the student, for all of his Protestant convictions, has no choice but to respect Rebekka's decision. The only question is what will or, in structural terms, what can happen to these ill-matched lovers.

It takes a great deal of plot before the two are reunited, but Rebekka eventually learns that her beloved theologian has been mortally wounded in the allies' victory over Napoleon at Leipzig. He wants to see her one last time before he dies, so Rebekka hurries off to the hospital. No one should be surprised that he expires in her arms, and, just as predictably, Rebekka succumbs to her own feverish nerves and dies, but at home, in Isaack's warm embrace. Even so, the melodrama is not quite complete; it still needs the narrator's final, lame assessment: "The souls of the two lovers were now in that better, eternal beyond, where no religious difference could ever separate them."[62] But as pathetic as this sounds, allowing religious difference to be overcome anywhere, even in an integrated heaven, is progressive on Wickede's part, and it is difficult to see what else he could have done with these characters. The student might have lived happily ever after with some patriotic German woman, but Rebekka's plight is as irresolvable as that of her namesake, Rebecca, in Sir Walter Scott's *Ivanhoe*. In an introduction that Scott wrote in 1830, a dozen years after the novel first appeared, he answered critics who thought that he should have married her to the hero: "But, not to mention that the prejudices of the age rendered such a union almost impossible, the Author may, in passing, observe that he thinks a character of a highly virtuous and lofty stamp is degraded rather than exalted by an attempt to reward virtue with temporal prosperity."[63] Wickede could scarcely contradict the master. In addition, the conflict between the two lovers gives the novel considerable narratological interest. Had Rebekka simply been a staunchly supportive German, she could hardly have played a larger role than the book's stalwart farmers' daughters. They appear once, simply to let the reader know of their existence; they then suffer some minor tragedy or threat that shows their prospective husband, who is invariably a soldier, in a favorable light; and in the final

CHAPTER 5

chapter they marry. *Tall Isaack* involves two such women whose virtual invisibility, for which they are rewarded, contrasts starkly with Rebekka's central position in the novel. She dies not only because of her religious convictions but also because there is not yet an acceptable role either for strong female characters or for partially assimilated Jews. One cannot imagine Rebekka heading off into exile, converting, or becoming a housewife. She has to die, and Germany, which cannot accept her divided loyalties, kills her.

Having eliminated his heroine, Wickede still has a few loose ends to tie up. Isaack, not surprisingly, dies alone, revered by the Bruhn family and rewarded for his service to the fatherland but a tragic figure nonetheless. The novel memorializes the fictional figure of Isaack, but one of the book's issues is the extent to which such legacies could survive in reality. If men such as Isaack existed, they would remain unmentioned in conventional histories, but he fares no better in the fictional Germany that Wickede constructed: "In the course of time the memory [of Isaack] disappeared completely."[64] The loss is particularly poignant because it deprives the novel's Germans of their Jewish brethren. Isaack is gone, and Rebekka dies unmarried, which leaves Sara as the only hope for German-Jewish reconciliation. Father and daughter meet again when she rescues him from imprisonment and death in Hamburg, but Sara pays a heavy price for her independence. She too dies, unmarried and childless. Sara's sin is not simply disloyalty to her father and the fatherland but her active sexuality, which offends against both parties. As the conscious mistress of her own body, Sara has made herself ineligible for a traditional happy ending. German men would reject her on religious, ethnic, and moral grounds, while marriage to a Frenchman would fly in the face of everything that novels of the Napoleonic wars profess. Having freed her father and, more important, having seen the consequences of her actions, Sara resolves to renounce future sins and end her relationship with Hamburg's French military governor. The reader sees her for the last time as she takes charge of a home for orphaned girls in Strasbourg. Hers is a better fate than Rebekka's, but doing penance on the border between France and Germany, far from her father and far from the privileged life she once led, is scarcely a reward.

The aristocrat's daughter, who is just as guilty as Sara, initially fares much better than her Jewish counterpart. After the woman's first husband dies, she marries into a family from the old French nobility, moves to Paris, and turns militantly French and Catholic. Of course, these choices preclude domestic bliss, and the book ends with an indirect condemnation of border-crossing unions when her corpulent mother chokes to death on too large a serving of Strasbourg liver pâté. The book's other aristocrats suffer similar ends, and the novel is filled with asides lamenting those German princes who live in wasteful splendor and, worse yet, side culturally and politically with the French rather than pursue policies intended to benefit their unhappy subjects and the larger cause of Germany. Yet despite its antiaristocratic subplots, Wickede's novel is scarcely republican in tenor. At one point a minor character calls for German unity under a Prussian king, a remarkably prescient view in 1863, some eight years before it came to pass, and fourteen years after 1849, when Frederick William IV rejected the German throne.[65] Of course, Wickede had no way of knowing how quickly such wishes would turn into political reality. More important, in the larger narrative context the Prussian monarchy functions not as the pinnacle of an aristocratic order but as a guarantee that the old order of merchants, craftsmen, and yeoman farmers would survive. Thus, the Bruhn family, whose members frequently appear in small roles, takes on a kind of clandestine centrality. Here the novel mixes tropes of exclusion with those of inclusion, ultimately deciding for the latter. On the one hand, Isaack's sad odyssey begins and ends at the Bruhn farm; on the other hand, Wilhelm and Gretchen Bruhn are the only characters in the book who marry successfully. After a few false starts and some considerable heroism on Wilhelm's part, they both marry Germans, presumably to raise large families of patriotic children. Wilhelm's bride is a rich farmer's daughter who recognized her prospective husband's "true worth as an officer" at their first meeting; she realizes Wilhelm earned his rank instead of being born to it.[66] Gretchen also marries an officer. The man's title could present a problem, but Colonel von Ihlow served with Gretchen's father in the more egalitarian volunteer corps and accepted the old man's gruff style of leadership. Unlike Fritz von Dassow, Ihlow is willing to wed outside his class. Meanwhile, the elder Bruhn sacrificed a hand saving the poet Theodor Körner and lost his younger son at the Battle of Waterloo, but at the novel's end the old farmer looks confidently into the future. The French are gone, and Wilhelm has returned to take over the family property. He will need Isaack's capital to rebuild, but the reader finishes this novel confident that two truly German families have emerged to embody Wickede's goals for the nation he wrote about: "Although, in the history of our fatherland, the remarkable year 1813 and the sacrifices so eagerly made by most of the German people will forever outshine our own bland, materialistic era, class differences were then incomparably sharper, and it was much rarer and more difficult to overcome them than is the case today. The spirit of the age has leveled such differences immeasurably in the last fifty years, and it will certainly continue to do more in the future, so that fifty years from now only a weak remnant of the German nobility will remain."[67]

Unfortunately, Wickede's narrator proves himself far less prescient about the status of the aristocracy in German society than he was about the position the Prussian monarchy would occupy in a united Germany. Wilhelm and Gretchen Bruhn remained exceptions, but the book's failure to predict the future by no means undercuts marriage as the model Wickede ultimately used to sketch his vision of Germany. For all of its progressive sentiment, *Tall Isaack* remains caught up in the prejudices of its times. Neither Rebekka nor Sara can marry into a future German community, both because they were Jewish and because, in their very different choices, they were each too forceful to become good German wives and mothers. Women from the nobility also lacked the qualities necessary to found a new German family; their fault was that they too easily fell victim to the temptation of French decadence. In sum, Wickede's novel represents the new Germany as a slight variation on the old order. Yeoman farmers marry the daughters of other yeoman farmers, while their sisters can marry outside of that class provided their husbands accept the values of the old middle class. The Bruhns represent an ordered organic community whose heroism justifies their rise to the status of national model, and Wickede entrusts Queen Louisa's benevolent heirs with the task of guaranteeing the entire German family's acceptance of these new national norms. He also shows how costly that solution would be, both to the resultant German nation and to some of those who aspired to membership in the new Germany.

Turning Back the Clock

George Hesekiel's *Stillness Before the Storm,* which also appeared in 1863, is just as interested in promoting Prussia and the country's royal family, but unlike Wickede's critical narrative, Hesekiel's novel champions the Prussian nobility as the best hope for a future German state.[68] *Stillness Before the Storm* completes the twelve-volume cycle of novels Hesekiel devoted to the period 1806–13. Its three volumes include some of the same characters we encountered in *Before Jena,* but the reader need not slog through the intervening six volumes in order to appreciate the final three. In fact, one could skip the entire series if Hesekiel had not appeared with Janke, one of the era's most prominent publishers of historical fiction, and edited Berlin's most influential newspaper. However, the author's prominence and his book's very different rendering of the myth of German renewal mean we should take a look at this aristocratic version of Germany's national family.

The novel's main character, Robert von Rouvroh, is the descendant of French Huguenots, but, unlike the hero of Fouqué's *The Refugee* from chapter 2, Rouvroh harbors no doubts about his loyalties. He speaks constantly of his devotion to Prussia and thinks of himself as German only to the degree that Prussians represent the nation's natural leaders. Readers first encounter Rouvroh as he flees from a detail of French soldiers, whom he outruns, but not before shooting the horse out from under their officer just as the Frenchman takes aim at Rouvroh. This masterful shot leaves the French officer unhorsed but also uninjured, and the deed so impresses its victim that he twice allows Rouvroh to escape more determined pursuers. Both men's gestures hark back to an age of chivalry, but unfortunately for Hesekiel and his narrative, these heroic individuals remain trapped in the more democratic and therefore uncertain politics of the Wars of Liberation. Neither the populus nor King Frederick William III proves up to the task of freeing the nation from French oppression: "The Prussian people do nothing without their king; that is their strength and also their weakness."[69] In a stance typical of German conservatives, Hesekiel chooses to defend the ancient virtues of the aristocracy against both the king and his ordinary subjects, but his wooden superhero turns out to be just as ill-suited as the book's other contenders for the job of national savior.

Part of the narrative difficulty seems to have been the necessity of garnering male and female readers by presenting them with a mixture of swashbuckling adventure and romance. However, Rouvroh, despite shooting and other skills that match Old Shatterhand's, can scarcely win the Wars of Liberation single-handedly. In fact, he is unable to do more than engage in a few successful skirmishes, and the novel ends in February 1813, just as Prussians answer their king's call to arms. In addition, Hesekiel flounders in depicting his hero's overly complex romantic entanglements, and background information frequently overwhelms the plot. For example, while waiting for the war to begin, Rouvroh falls instantly in love with, and almost as quickly rejects, Sophie Ostertag, the

CHAPTER 5

foster child of a tavern keeper, only to learn that she stands to inherit an immense fortune and an old noble name. He could marry her after all, and the reader expects it. Why else would the narrator spend so much time explaining who Sophie is, why her parents moved to Portugal, of all places, and how she returned to Brandenburg an orphan? Since Sophie and the rest of the female characters remain uninvolved in the nationalist narrative, the plot stalls until Rouvroh returns from Russia, where he has disappeared for hundreds of pages. But the hero no more than crosses the border into Prussia when he falls ill and staggers to an isolated farmhouse. There, the farmer's two stalwart daughters nurse him back to health, and the reader's appetite for action is whetted when the narrator remarks, "there is also heroism in bed."[70] Unfortunately, the reference is to the young man's struggle with a dread disease rather than romantic conquests. It is a relief when Rouvroh rides off to Berlin, but once he arrives, French soldiers open fire and kill him. Sophie eventually marries someone else, and the novel ends, leaving the reader puzzled about its message.

It is tempting but too easy to attribute the novel's peculiar conclusion to the author's lack of talent. One would have to argue that Hesekiel filled shelves in commercial lending libraries and the homes of conservative aristocrats without being able to resolve a fairly straightforward plot. Yet, even granting that proposition, to stop analyzing at this point is to leave questions the novel raises unanswered. Internal evidence indicates just how concerned Hesekiel was with the reputation of Prussia's aristocracy, because the story of their participation in the Wars of Liberation could determine their suitability to lead Prussia from the constitutional crisis that the country faced in the early 1860s, when he was writing. Without Bismarck's abrogation of the constitution, Prussia might have turned democratic, and the fact that both Wickede and Hesekiel wrote about aristocratic claims on power in 1863 indicates that the debate over the character of the country's ruling elite reached beyond newspapers into the more open sphere of popular literature. In view of the stakes involved in any portrayal of aristocratic claimants on political power, there could well be more than a lack of skill involved in Hesekiel's failure to have his hero marry and found a new German family.

If we regard marriage or its absence as the novel's central trope, both Rouvroh's death and a maddening string of plot digressions begin to make sense. They indicate just how troubling the issue of legitimate

THE GERMAN PEOPLE ARISE—AND MARRY

political inheritance had become. At one point, for example, an old pastor and his wife lament their son's union with the beautiful daughter of the local baker. Presumably the young man followed his heart in good bourgeois fashion, but the act has unfortunate consequences for the elderly couple and their parish. Some interloper rather than their son now inhabits the parsonage, and in an affront to the entire community and the old order it represents, the new pastor's wife sings songs that the couple regards as "too secular" (*zu weltlich*, 2: 234). In other words, the book portrays love as a dangerous passion. During this same aside the reader also learns that Sophie's grandfather was a republican and a crank infected with French ideas. Moreover, like so many intellectuals in his day, her grandfather frequented Jewish salons in Berlin and joined the Freemasons. No wonder, then, that Sophie's acquaintances describe her as "soulless"; they also describe her outwardly pleasant personality as "uncanny" (*unheimlich*), using a term that translates literally as "undomestic" (3: 101). They therefore believe she will never marry, which would turn this novel of Germany's national triumph into tragedy.

Of course, the book must end happily, but simply showing how Germans ousted the French would not solve the hero's problems, nor would it answer any questions about the nation's future. Like so many other works that frustrate the naive reader's expectation of dramatic military scenes, Hesekiel's book locates the important conflict on the home front. Sophie, the pastor's son, Rouvroh, and half a dozen other characters struggle not with French invaders but with two competing forms of desire. Theirs is "a difficult battle that pits strong and noble inclination [*Neigung*] against befooling and ensnaring love [*Liebe*]."[71] While this dichotomy and the pages of digression it inspires make for boring reading, Hesekiel nevertheless makes a telling point. In the world of his novel, and, by implication, in the nation it attempts to model, inclination with its controlled commitment to the old order must triumph. Romantic love remains the stuff of bourgeois fiction, liberal imaginations, and the French. Inclination, by contrast, respects and maintains a form of social order beyond the individual; it is also, at least by implication, solidly German. Once again *Gemeinschaft* clashes with *Gesellschaft* over the soul of a future Germany. Rouvroh's inability to choose sides makes him unfit to marry and unworthy of a place in the nation's future. His death, which comes just before the Russians arrive in Berlin, takes on positive overtones because it marks the end of German stillness in the book's title. By killing Rouvroh, the French clear the way for more worthy opponents and move inexorably toward the storm awaiting them just over the horizon.

No storm ensues, but the novel has not quite ended. Rouvroh has died, but Sophie is still alive and unwed. In the book's final chapter she marries an older man, Count von Mespelbrunn, who was once in love with her mother. One might expect the match to produce tragic consequences on the order of those suffered by Effi Briest in Fontane's eponymous novel, but that would be to introduce modern concerns into a thoroughly premodern parable. Once Mespelbrunn proposes, he leaves it to his father and his father's sometime-rival and comrade, General von Ihlow, to negotiate a settlement that unites these two noble families and their considerable fortunes. Renewal rather than a storm waits over this particular horizon, but the book's patiently awaited happy ending has still not quite arrived. Although Sophie exudes happiness, her emotions remain shallow, deepening only when she bears a son. The birth takes place in the Mark Brandenburg, the ancient heart of Prussia, in an idyllic landscape far from the Wars of Liberation, and it seems to herald the beginning of a new era. By placing his heroine in the hands of an older aristocrat, Hesekiel completes his vision of conservative regeneration at the level of the family. Along with a son, Sophie receives the one thing bourgeois love could not offer: inclination has given her a soul. Thus, in the space of a single short chapter the novel has taken its readers from the stillness before the storm to the stillness it proposes as Germany's future. Strange as it may seem, to finish his tale, Hesekiel had to distance his protagonists from battles that supposedly set the stage for the nation's unification, once again showing the centrality of marriage rather than war in this portion of Germany's national myth.

A Feminist National Utopia?

Louisa von François's *The Last von Reckenburg* (1871) also ends with a marriage and the heroine's inheritance of a vast feudal estate, but unlike Hesekiel's aristocratic vision, this happy couple represents a compromise between aristocratic privilege and bourgeois propriety.[72] The two sides unite in their shared sense of duty, albeit in a thoroughly patriarchal order. How François arrives at this mixed conclusion requires minimal unpacking of her multigenerational plot with its series of twists, turns, and coincidences. Eberhardine von Reckenburg knows full well that she is the last member of a rich and powerful family, but to protect a friend's reputation this generous noblewoman refuses to deny a damning rumor.

As a result, a ne'er-do-well soldier, August Müller, dies, mistakenly believing himself a secret Reckenburg rather than the neglected son of Dorothee Müller, a cooper's daughter. The soldier's child, Hardine Müller, shares her supposed grandmother's first name and, for the longest time, her father's illusion about its meaning. Only gradually do Hardine and the reader learn the truth behind this deception. They also come to understand her putative grandmother's vision for the Reckenburg estates, which I read as another model German community.

The novel's action spans the period from the French Revolution in 1789 to 1837, so the Wars of Liberation provide the backdrop for only part of the plot. They are nevertheless crucial to an understanding of Eberhardine von Reckenburg and the role she envisions for Hardine Müller. Although the conflict rages well outside her domain, this last Reckenburg enters into what she describes as "a sort of connection with the patriots who were secretly spinning their webs in Prussia and Austria"; she also allows a considerable portion of "the abundant resources at my disposal to flow towards the highest aims."[73] Afterward she rebuilds her mini-state, twice calling herself "Fritzian" (*fritzisch*), in an obvious reference to Frederick the Great's reconstruction of Prussia following the Seven Years' War (385, 391).[74] François made this character, who narrates her own life, proud and headstrong, but the last Reckenburg's descriptions betray a certain reticence, both to claim credit for her achievements and to deal the contradictory roles that voluntary spinsterhood forced upon her. She chooses not to marry, because as the sole ruler of a territorial anachronism, she deals with potential suitors on an equal footing, "between man and man" (*zwischen Mann und Mann*) and refuses to exchange that power for the subordinate position of a wife (397). At the same time, this purposeful and energetic woman faults herself for lacking feminine feelings. Under her watchful eye Reckenburg had become prosperous and virtuous, but it was also "a colony devoid of joy and love."[75] She softens only when she takes Hardine Müller into her household, and the younger woman brings bourgeois and female virtues into this aristocratic world. Though too gruff to voice her admiration for the changes, the old lady has melted. She gradually cedes control and watches contentedly as the old ethos gives way to a new order.

At first it seems odd that the last Reckenburg decides neither to adopt her foster daughter nor to tell Hardine she will inherit the Reckenburg territories. However, this freedom from future wealth,

CHAPTER 5

power, and responsibility allows Hardine Müller to marry in good bourgeois fashion for love. Her husband is the accomplished son of a local pastor rather than the neighboring count. The latter would have been only too glad to marry an heiress, even one with an adopted title, but such arranged marriages belong to an earlier age. More important, under bourgeois influences, the best of the old world still flourishes: "The periodic gala parties have come to an end, but young people in the castle and village sing and dance around the Maypole and under the harvest wreath; the tavern raises its welcoming sign into the air; bowling balls roll; and mugs of beer clack, albeit in moderation."[76] Although filled with happy inhabitants, Reckenburg is still a colony; the idyll François who has been sketched remains thoroughly premodern, protected from the incursions of technology and capitalism by its newly feminized patriarchy. Unfortunately, Hardine Müller purchases this wildly implausible scene by renouncing her foster grandmother's independence. The pastor's wife might sponsor teas or visit the sick, but she will no longer run the estate. Love conquering all means that bourgeois sentimentality disenfranchises an energetic woman's equally strong helpmate and heir. The novel remains vague about how Hardine Müller accomplished the estate's transition from feudal gloom to bourgeois bliss and why, except for conventional notions about romantic love, she would want to give up her position as Reckenburg's guiding hand.

Contrary to what modern readers might have expected, a woman author's favoring marriage over warfare does not make for feminist fiction. Indeed, none of the model Germanies discussed thus far was open to women's participation in the nationalist struggle. Even Eberhardine von Reckenburg can manage only "a sort of connection with the patriots"; while the other wives and daughters that populate historical fiction are lucky if their family histories, whether bourgeois or noble, allow them to appear for more than a page or two before the narrator forces them into a subordinate position. Except as wives—and then mothers, should their parentage prove suitable—the fatherland offered women little scope for development. Far from being a feminist exception, François's reluctant heroine supports male domination by illustrating the price women pay when they take on men's roles. The book's sole progressive element is its renunciation of inherited position, but even that stance rests upon notions of romantic love, the subordinate position of the happy wife as helpmate to her active husband, and the belief that with a little help from above, craftsmen can maintain the idyllic world of the old middle class. Even in fiction the struggle for power in a future Germany remained a male preserve.

Is Austria German?

After 1871 the question of who was German took on new urgency. Whether the Prussian-dominated empire could legitimately claim the title "Germany" remained an open question. Far from all of the people who thought of themselves as Germans were comfortable with membership in the new empire, just as others were uncomfortable at being left outside it. The question of Germany's size—*kleindeutsch* versus *großdeutsch*—remained open, so it is scarcely surprising that Karl Frenzel's *Lucifer* (1873) foregrounds the opposition between Prussia and Austria.[77] Almost everyone in the novel is Austrian, but some of the book's characters aspire to the label "German." Weighing in at five volumes, *Lucifer* offers plenty of room for complication. For my purposes its major source of interest concerns the patriarch of an old noble family, Count Ulrich von Wolfsegg; his stunning niece, Antoinette de Gondreville; and a plain, bourgeois woman from Vienna, Magdalene Armhart, later revealed to be Wolfsegg's illegitimate daughter. Since this, too, is a novel about marriage, the two women require two suitors, who set the stage for a confrontation between competing identities. The first contestant is an Austrian knight incongruously named Zambelli; the second is Egbert Heimwald, whose name translates as "home forest," indicating that he is likely to be the tale's hero. Given the long-standing mystical connection between Germans and trees, Heimwald also seems destined to represent an authentic Germany, but what Germany means to him, the narrator, and, ultimately, the book's readers remains an open question for nearly one thousand pages.

Of course, the two women stand for more than a straightforward choice between Austria and Germany. Antoinette's father hails from the border between France and Germany, and he has served at the French court. Moreover, while in France Antoinette's mother became such a devout partisan of the royal family that she named her daughter after France's infamous queen, Marie Antoinette. Like the queen, who was born a Hapsburg, the upper echelons of the Austrian nobility seem drawn to prerevolutionary France, which disqualifies them as potential Germans. At first Magdalene also seems tainted, because she believes her father to be a secretary in some Austrian ministry, where he spies for the French. In reality, Wolfsegg sired her during a liaison with a singer in

CHAPTER 5

Vienna, but it takes four volumes of the novel for the young woman to learn about and then act upon her real roots. However, in a hopeful sign, Magdalene starts the novel estranged from her purported father. She then rents a room in the Heimwald home, befriends Egbert's sister, and falls in love with the hero. Yet, for all of their potential as characters, neither Antoinette nor Magdalene actually says or does anything of consequence; the novel confines them simply to existing as one thing or another: an aristocrat or a commoner, a habitué of balls or a potential mother, an admirer of French ideals or a passive example of the simplicity increasingly identified as German. Clever readers suspect Magdalene will make the better wife, while Antoinette will propel the more interesting plot developments.

The two men also represent more than the alternative between a larger and a smaller version of Germany. Zambelli characterizes himself as "a subject of the house of Hapsburg by birth," adding, in a telling phrase, "I hope to be and remain a good Austrian, dead or alive."[78] As unambiguous as his statement might sound today, what the word "Austrian" meant in 1873 requires interpretation. Zambelli stems not from Austria proper but from Trent, a Hapsburg territory in what is now northern Italy. His orientation is therefore dynastic rather than national. Moreover, as the younger son of an impoverished nobleman, Zambelli owes ultimate loyalty to whoever pays the bills, and he regards Napoleon, born on the formerly Genoese island of Corsica, as a fellow countryman. As a result, he eagerly follows Austria into the arms of the new French emperor. Of course, he fancies Antoinette, the Austrian aristocrat linked to France, and it is worth noting that, like Zambelli, who craves the security granted by genuine nobility, Napoleon spends much of the book hoping to marry into the Austrian imperial family. He lands a Hapsburg princess, while Zambelli struggles for five volumes in his quest for Antoinette, no doubt keeping some readers on the edges of their chairs.

Zambelli's opponent, Egbert Heimwald, could scarcely present a more thorough contrast. Born in Vienna to a wealthy doctor and another singer, Egbert identifies with German culture but begins the book undecided about a career and uninterested in politics. Complex plot developments gradually push him into the anti-Napoleonic camp, but Egbert's diffidence and artistic nature raise doubts about his suitability as a husband and, more important, as a German. Not surprisingly, Antoinette's beauty enflames him, but Egbert fails to impress her; she

THE GERMAN PEOPLE ARISE—AND MARRY

complains, "He looks like a fairy-tale hero but speaks as shyly as a girl."[79] Antoinette's mother regards the match as akin to the French Revolution. In her view, the son of a Freemason and a doctor has no business wooing a noblewoman. Unlike the young woman's mother, Antoinette's uncle has become a German patriot. He therefore views his niece's prospective husband positively: "The bourgeoisie has value to me; it is the core of the German people. It is our duty to inspire this heretofore sluggish mass and fill it with the holy fire of love for the fatherland."[80] However, if Wolfsegg succeeds in inspiring Egbert to patriotic deeds, he makes it less likely that the young man will remain interested in or of interest to the decidedly French Antoinette.

The plot thickens as patriotic Germans use Egbert's reputation as an apolitical artist as cover to send him on a secret mission to France. There he encounters Napoleon, who vows to defeat the Germans even though he admits the superiority of German culture: "We will have to import artists from Germany. Wieland and Goethe are the century's greatest poets."[81] At the same time, Napoleon rails against Germany's youth and its universities: "What a shame that [students] have been infected with false ideas and their susceptibility to dreams and crank notions has been increased. What would these young people accomplish under my banner! As it stands, Germany has no natural scientists, no mathematicians, no inventors."[82] Instead, German students are about to begin swarming to the nationalist cause. Napoleon is made all the more angry when, during the same encounter, Antoinette asks him to pardon her brother, who was involved in some intrigue. She receives the favor from Napoleon but reaps contempt from Egbert. He sees her as selfish in relation to the larger cause of Germany, while the narrator, as has often been the case in this novel, sneers at women involved in politics. After Egbert is wounded defending the German cause from Zambelli's machinations, the real heroine nurses him back to health. By the end of volume 4, Egbert has proposed to Magdalene, and they seem destined for a happy ending. The reader might wonder about the point of the novel's final volume.

The hook that keeps the story going is Magdalene's discovery of her illegitimacy. She deems herself unworthy of Egbert's affections, and the marriage cannot take place until Count Wolfsegg returns from Tyrol to set things right. He had been fighting as an anonymous partisan alongside Andreas Hofer in one of the first sustained uprisings against Napoleon. Once back in Vienna, Wolfsegg adopts Magdalene, which

CHAPTER 5

should pave the way for her union with Egbert, except that the hero then declares himself unfit for marriage. Still plagued by his girlish voice and lack of interest in Germany, Egbert decides he must prove himself worthy of Magdalene. It seems like only padding in an already long novel, but Frenzel was writing in the tradition of the German Bildungsroman. Thus, his novel is ultimately concerned with tracing Egbert's development toward manhood, with one important difference. Unlike protagonists from earlier eras, this hero's progress takes place within the explicit context of German nationalism: "He had worked his way up from the narrow limitations of a life inimically divided from the masses, where he regarded the intellectual contemplation of the self as the only purpose of existence. Fighting, he paid his debt to the fatherland and realized that the fate of the individual is inextricably connected to the life of the state and the larger community that bore him and give him language, education, and customs."[83] Having finally become both a man and a German, Egbert is ready to start a family, and the novel treats his decision to marry Magdalene as explicitly patriotic. For example, Wolfsegg acknowledges Magdalene as his daughter by calling her "a German, modest, good middle-class girl" (*ein deutsches, bescheidenes, gutes Bürgermädchen,* 5: 75)—in that order. In the nationalist idiom, that string of adjectives was becoming redundant, in part through portrayals such as Frenzel's.

Meanwhile, after spending time as Napoleon's mistress and Zambelli's fiancée, Antoinette perishes in a fire. Her death comes at a ball to celebrate the French emperor's marriage to Marie Louisa of Austria, and various characters use the event to predict a similar conflagration for the French forces that will soon face Germans. Zambelli has also died but not before the novel links him to Prince Metternich, the man who ruled the Hapsburg domains from 1815 to 1848. Significantly, the narrator describes Metternich's politics in a manner that effectively discredits Austria's intentions up to the time Frenzel published his novel. "For [Metternich,] Germany is a name, a geographic term, with no resonance in his heart. If he can warm to anything, it is to his own status and a state that is exclusively Austrian."[84] Thus, in contrast to Metternich/Zambelli's dynastic conception of the world, both Egbert's maturation and his choice of a German wife implicitly endorse the nationalist answer to the German question, an outcome that demanded, in the era's idiom, Prussian hegemony in a smaller German state. One need not imagine Egbert and Magdalene moving to Berlin to conclude that good

Germans ought to look north for further developments in the national saga.[85]

Nobles, Prussians, and Germans?

As luck would have it, the quintessentially Prussian author Theodor Fontane wrote the next novel in this chronological survey. At first glance, his *Before the Storm* (1878) fits easily into the pattern of long courtship, competing brides and bridegrooms, followed by a marriage that presages a potential German nation.[86] As the novel opens, Lewin von Vitzewitz, a young nobleman from the heart of Brandenburg Prussia, is as good as betrothed to his Polish cousin Kathinka Ladalinski, while his sister, Renate, pines for Kathinka's brother, Tubal. These two romances cross national boundaries but respect those of caste and, as a result, are fraught with tension. Meanwhile, the good German, but utterly lower-class orphan Marie Kniehase secretly loves Lewin but believes him impossibly distant. The stage is set for a romantic conflict that pits nationalism against social class. In other words, does Lewin marry Kathinka or Marie? By now, you may suspect who is likely to marry whom, but if all that happened in the course of this, for Fontane, uncharacteristically long novel, were the expected marriage, there would be little reason to discuss the book further. However, Fontane complicates his conventionally nationalistic plot in a manner that warrants closer attention.

To begin, *Before the Storm* takes direct aim at the heroic myth of a popular uprising. In Fontane's version of events the people conspicuously fail to rise, although, to be fair, neither do the country's leaders cover themselves with glory. The government dithers and delays, while the king, who is supposed to embody the bold legacy of Frederick the Great, refuses every call to action. Surrounded by lethargy, the nobility regards itself as the nation's sole hope, but the book's aristocrats cannot reconcile their loyalty to the idea of monarchy with the disloyalty that dire circumstances and an incompetent king demand. Fontane's complex array of characters mirrors the tensions in a situation without providing easy answers. Rather than taking sides, the novel pits competing interests against one another and asks, first, who represents the nation and, second, on what basis its representatives might act.

On the one hand, the narrator uses a description of the Vitzewitz's home village to stake a claim for popular sovereignty. "Soltwedel Castle [actually Salzwedel, the cradle of the Prussian state under Albrecht the

CHAPTER 5

Bear (1100–70)] is ancient, but silent. [Frederick the Great's] Sanssouci speaks, but is as young as any parvenu. Only our village churches present themselves to us as the bearers of our *entire* history; by demonstrating the interplay of various centuries, they both possess and express the magic of historical continuity."[87] At a time when history dominated intellectual discourse and provided the basis for political legitimacy, deciding that peasants' churches rather than the residences of the Hohenzollern monarchs best represented the nation's past was no small matter. Yet, while unschooled peasants and their architecture appear to embody the nation, the novel's central character, Lewin's father, Berndt, simultaneously understands and mistrusts the widespread discontent he sees in Prussia. "The current government's measures, which ignore the people's judgment, inoculate the people with disobedience. The people rebel not because they want to, but because they must."[88] The elder Vitzewitz is willing to advocate, join, and, if necessary, lead the people's disobedience, but he also knows that a popular uprising would spell the end of his caste's domination of Prussian politics and society. Although he hesitates for hundreds of pages before drawing the logical conclusion from his statement, at some level Berndt von Vitzewitz recognizes the connection between his impassioned "must act" and the people's broader right to participate in the affairs of state. He represents a sea change in attitudes that Fontane probably wanted to see in the German nobility of his own day, but the character is complex enough to fear the consequences of his own and his creator's position. Justifiable or not, a popular uprising could reproduce in Germany the frightful results of the French Revolution, and Prussian traditions, including the shared sense of historical continuity, would perish along with the aristocracy.

On the other hand, speaking for the Prussian nobility, Berndt von Vitzewitz asserts its right to independent action, with or without the people, by claiming a more ancient bond to the fatherland than the Hohenzollern dynasty's connection, which dates only to the early fifteenth century. As his friend General von Bamme says, "*We* were here *before* the Hohenzollerns."[89] The implication is twofold: first, that the king should answer to the nobility instead of commanding it and, second, that "here"—by which Bamme means something like the nation, with its cultural, historical, and linguistic loyalties rather than mere geography—justifies his call to arms. As Berndt puts it, "We are responsible for the country" (*Land,* and we also guarantee it, in the double meaning of *einstehen*).[90] He therefore stands "*with* the king as long as possible, *without* him if necessary."[91] That position might ally him with the people, but it simultaneously highlights the difficult relationship between any aristocracy and the nation. When Berndt von Vitzewitz claims to represent the national interest, caste complicates sovereignty. Moreover, by invoking the general will to justify action for those who would themselves act if only they were cognizant of their own real interests, the elder Vitzewitz puts himself dangerously close to Robespierre. Knowing how treacherous his argument has become, ideologically as well as politically, he hesitates for most of the novel.

Berndt is finally drawn into action when Lewin forces his hand. Until then, nothing much happens. The French occupy Prussia without meaningful resistance. No one seems capable of removing them, nor is anyone willing to attempt the task—no one except Lewin, whose quixotic attack on the local French garrison fails, leaving him guilty of treason and facing summary execution. In short, for all of its abstract justification, this particular, not very popular uprising, led by an inept and reluctant nobility, flops. The only military success in the novel comes when Berndt rescues his son, but even that small victory exacts a terrible price. Renate's beloved Tubal dies, mortally wounded while returning to save the Vitzewitz family dog. His sacrifice mixes tragedy with farce. More important, Tubal's death and Lewin's escapade do nothing to resolve the issues raised by the French occupation and lack of meaningful German resistance. Not coincidentally, the book ends "before the storm," in other words, before the supposedly heroic Wars of Liberation, which were, it suggests, equally meaningless. To be sure, the 1813–15 conflict drove out the French, but it neither replaced them with a German nation-state nor answered the question of who embodied the nation.

One of Fontane's few concessions to the myth of German heroism appears in an oblique aside in the novel's final chapter, when Lewin returns home, presumably from the campaign in France, with a saber scar on his forehead but without his "soft streak" (*der weiche Zug*, 709). Although she says nothing about its cause, Renate finds the scar becoming. Marie merely notes the change in Lewin's personality. The passage forms part of a single short paragraph; otherwise, the events of 1813–15 remain unmentioned. In fact, except for the assumptions of conventional wisdom, there is no reason to believe that Lewin's wound was the result of bravery rather than a foolhardy accident. Fontane's reticence might also signal his mistrust of heroism, for after juxtaposing Lewin's rescue with Tubal's death, his return coincides with and is overshadowed by the unveiling of another man's tombstone. Although the marker commemorates the heroic death of a bourgeois volunteer, the event occupies only half a sentence in a chapter devoted to showing how Lewin's ill-fated attack came undone. Fontane has little truck with heroes.

In part, he was following a well-established genre convention. As we have repeatedly seen, novels about the Wars of Liberation frequently end before the fighting begins, or they remain on the sidelines, ignoring what naive readers would regard as the main event. We expect tales of swashbuckling adventure, but in novel after novel the plot stops dead or leaps from early 1813 to mid-1815, when the male protagonists return home to marry. Like so many other novels, *Before the Storm* meets our expectations for narrative (and romantic) closure, and in so doing, it proves once again that marriage is more important than war in Germany's national narrative. The book therefore scores some telling points as various characters discuss the significance of Lewin and Marie's union. At first Lewin's father is reluctant to consent, but he ultimately agrees and, in the process, makes an argument for the abolition of inherited caste distinctions. "One thing I know for sure, she will spoil the family tree but not our profile, not our profile and not our convictions. And those two are the best things the nobility has."[92] In fact, Marie cannot spoil beliefs this old aristocrat has already reversed and turned modern, if not wholly democratic. By claiming appearance and attitude as the nobility's foremost attributes, Berndt effectively discounts its claim on power. So too does General von Bamme question his caste's pretensions, reluctantly upping the ante by saying, "There is nothing to this notion of two sorts of people. . . . I am not impressed by these French windbags, but there is a grain of truth in all their foolishness. Nothing will come of their fraternity, or freedom, but there is something to be said for the word between those two [equality]. Ultimately, it just means, people are people."[93] And if the novel makes Lewin and Marie equals, their status has ramifications, both for the German nation and for politics in Prussia at the time Fontane was writing.

Aside from questioning the role of the nobility, *Before the Storm* raises another, even more dangerous complication for Bismarck's empire: it questions the connection between Prussia and Germany. Indeed, various characters spend a great deal of time debating the notion of Germany as a linguistic and cultural community and arguing about the

THE GERMAN PEOPLE ARISE—AND MARRY

content of national identity. Here, too, Fontane refuses to take sides. Instead, he seems willing to disrupt the comfortable assumption that the struggle for Germany's soul began in 1813 and ended in 1871. *Before the Storm* first raises the issue when two minor characters debate local archeological finds. One of them, Pastor Seidentopf, doggedly claims "not only that the ancient origins of the Mark Brandenburg were German, but also that the territory *remained* so through every subsequent century."[94] Disregarding the large number of Slavic names and remnants of Slavic settlements in Prussia, Seidentopf considers his homeland fundamentally Germanic. His opponent, county attorney Turgany, describes himself as an "Apostle of Pan-Slavism."[95] For him, the Germans who occupied Brandenburg in an earlier era were barbarians, little more than cavemen, dependent on the local Slavic population, the Wends, for every cultural advance. The two men's argument lasts the entire book, ending only at Seidentopf's grave, when Turgany declares, "Now, without contradiction, I can proclaim this area Wendish, but I would rather not."[96] Deference to an old friend mixes with Turgany's abiding skepticism. He was always more interested in disputing the idea of cultural superiority than in claiming victory for the Slavs. He also rejects the notion of sole ownership and pure races in a landscape where Germans and Slavs had mingled for centuries. Giving Turgany the last word might indicate Fontane's preference, or it could simply show how difficult it was to make convincing nationalist claims in a Prussian state that contained a substantial Wendish-speaking population and that even Bismarck admitted was part Polish.

What it means to be Polish is another question this book raises, while it simultaneously probes the nature of both Prussian and German identities and their relationship to French values. For example, Tubal and Kathinka's father, Count Ladalinski, entered Prussian service in 1792, when the final partition of Poland eliminated his homeland. As we have seen in chapter 2, his act would not be remarkable in a culture characterized by mobile aristocrats, but here the narrator speaks of Ladalinski's "more Prussian- than Polish-oriented nature," suggesting that what the culture termed Prussian adhered to individuals by their own choice rather than devolving by birth to groups linked by blood. Thus, the narrator continues, "Soon [after entering the bureaucracy, Count Ladalinski] was more Prussian than the Prussians themselves."[97] By contrast, Tubal calls himself a moderate Prussian, whose affection for this adopted homeland "comes more from observation than from

CHAPTER 5

blood."[98] Like the Huguenots from whom Fontane descended, Tubal and his father represent the possibility of becoming Prussian or German rather than being born one or the other. Kathinka represents a third option: Prussia's allure never captures her. After wavering for a while, she decides not to marry Lewin. Instead, she elopes with Count Bninski, whom Lewin's aunt calls "a Pole from head to foot."[99] This aunt, meanwhile, although born in the Prussian heartland, is an outspoken Francophile, who reveals herself not only by speaking French and preferring French food, parlor games, and literature, but also by disparaging no less a national symbol than Schiller. No one would care, except that the following exchange between Berndt and his sister shows just how high the stakes are in the novel's extended discussions of poetry: "Pardon me, sister, you know nothing about the people and the fatherland; you only know the court and society, and your heart, if you ask yourself honestly, is with the enemy." To which she answers, "Not with the enemy, but with that at which he exceeds us."[100] One could cite such examples at considerable length. Here, the point is to demonstrate how carefully Fontane's novel treats the problem of identity. It admits neither a biological essence nor the primacy of language and culture. Instead it poses serious questions and undercuts every easy answer.

This strength connects to what some readers might see as the book's chief weakness: a multiplicity of characters and opinions embedded in a plot that almost ends without resolution and, more glaring as a fault during the nineteenth century, without much happening along the way.[101] Lewin marries, presumably to live happily ever after, while Renate lives out her life as a spinster when Tubal's death leaves her without a romantic interest. However, this summary sells Renate short. She enters a convent to do good works, but not because some man consigned her to a nunnery in the fashion of Hamlet's command for Ophelia. Renate is far more active than the typical heroine of historical fiction, and she is only one of five female characters who play large roles in this novel. They range from Renate's aristocratic aunt to an engaging and opinionated dwarf, Hoppenmarieken. Two of the five are bourgeois, and one of them, Marie Kniehase, does live happily ever after. Except for the hopelessness of the Polish cause, Kathinka's life might also end positively, but the reader never learns her fate. At least, and uncharacteristically for the genre, Fontane does not kill her for choosing the wrong side or for breaking with her father and brother. Thus, as formulaic as *Before the Storm* might be in its portrayal of marriage as the ultimate arbiter of national identity, it nevertheless lets both its male and female characters make choices and then shows the cost of their decisions. Like so many of the authors who preceded him, Fontane did not fabricate a simple myth of Germany's rise to national consciousness. Once he loosed his book's large cast of characters, the complexity of his own and historical reality mitigated against the linear tale his readers probably expected. In all likelihood, they were also not prepared for the novel's egalitarian message and its lack of a heroic high point, but if they persevered, Fontane rewarded them with a good read and a critical examination of the ideology behind the Wars of Liberation. One could scarcely ask for more.

Harlequin Nation

More, however, was precisely what readers got if they turned to Gustav Freytag's *Ancestors*.[102] The first of that novel's six volumes appeared in 1873, five years before Fontane's *Before the Storm,* but the narrative did not arrive at the Wars of Liberation until its final installment in 1881. As we saw in the previous chapter, *From a Small Town* opens in 1805, just before the Prussian defeat at Jena, and its action continues until after the Revolution of 1848. Although the book contains a wealth of characters and action, readers familiar with the plots of Harlequin romances will recognize the simple narrative structure that Freytag employed to create his vision of an ideal Germany; for when all is said and done, the novel revolves around a woman, Henriette Senior, who is torn between two suitors. Early on, she accepts an offer of marriage from the wrong man, forcing the right man to spend several hundred pages encouraging her to rectify the mistake. She ultimately marries the hero, and the book might be forgettable, except that in the present context, instead of two competitors vying for some damsel's hand, France does battle with Germany for the right to marry a pastor's daughter. Thus, despite the predictable plot, the stakes remain high.

The nobility plays almost no role in Freytag's tale. Instead, his narrative pits a German doctor, Ernst König, against a French officer named Dessalle. The two men first meet when König asks Dessalle to surrender in the midst of a skirmish. Although wounded and surrounded by two dozen German volunteers, Dessalle refuses. He thereby proves himself braver than the German militiamen, who need a civilian doctor to help them capture the officer. Ironically, König binds wounds that the Frenchman received while rescuing the heroine from a party of deserters.

CHAPTER 5

Only later will he learn that the two of them are competing for Henriette's love. Here, without quite knowing why, König finds himself respecting the Frenchman while simultaneously despising his cause. Dessalle is just as ignorant of these future plot complications and says he hopes to encounter König again, but on the same side in the coming conflict. He argues that France and Napoleon both value talent and would happily reward König as a man of skill, courage, and principles. Each of the two appreciates the other's culture. König had studied in Paris, and Dessalle, for reasons that become clear only in the novel's epilogue, speaks German, albeit with an accent. No wonder Henriette has difficulty making a choice between them.

Freytag builds an enormous edifice on the foundation of this simple triangle, two sides of which become far more complicated than the above summary indicates. For example, when French soldiers threaten the pastor's property and Henriette's virtue, assigning guilt should prove easy. However, Freytag's French marauders are actually Germans serving in Napoleon's army, and not only are Germans villains in this scene, but it is also none other than the Frenchman Dessalle who rescues the heroine. Thus, it is scarcely surprising that König feels grudging respect for Dessalle. Just as unsurprising is the response of Henriette's father. He declares her champion a "handsome man, [who arrived in the nick of time] as if he came from heaven."[103] Dessalle drives the intruders away and ensures Henriette's continued safety by claiming her as his own, saying, "You dogs, how dare you touch the fiancée of a French officer."[104] When the evil Germans call him a liar, he forces them to witness his engagement, including an exchange of rings with Henriette. She remains silent, almost unconscious, during the scene, but her gratitude is understandable. Moreover, she had not yet met König and was unsure if Dessalle would ever return from what promises to be a long war. The Frenchman's ring both protects her and injects tension into the narrative, for neither party is willing to break the engagement without the other's consent.

König learns of Henriette's plight during his second visit to the parsonage, when Henriette's father relates the tale of her engagement. The pastor's story explains the ring König noticed on Dessalle's finger; it also forces him to reconsider the secret plans he made after falling in love with Henriette—at first sight, as the genre demands. Knowing she needs Dessalle's permission to marry him, König says nothing of his intentions, with the unintended consequence that Henriette wonders

THE GERMAN PEOPLE ARISE—AND MARRY

why he remains silent. In part to forget his anguished love, König joins the rebellion against the French, only to have Napoleon personally order his arrest. Luckily, Henriette learns of the danger, warns him, and then collapses in his arms. Uncharacteristically, the romantic portion of Freytag's plot advances through the woman's action rather than the man's. Henriette has decided to return Dessalle's ring, but since the Frenchman is fighting guerrillas in Spain, getting it back to him involves delay and potential heartbreak. The postal service is unreliable, and although she dare not hope it on moral grounds, Dessalle may already be dead, a casualty of the fighting in Spain. Worse yet from her perspective, he may come back, hold a grudge against König, and imperil what would otherwise be a happy ending. Caught between two suitors, Henriette's position resembles that of Germany, where French troops once again threaten to overwhelm the nation's aroused but still impotent young men. Lest there be any doubt about the symbolic burden Henriette bears, the narrator explicitly conflates her struggle with Germany's: "The woman [*das Weib*, singular] who struggled to break unbearable chains, the men who armed themselves for battle with the enemy, all the peoples of a continent who rose up against the tyranny of a hated nation, would hope again in vain. . . . Guard yourselves, German hearts, that your courage does not disappear or the tender shoots of your love are not trodden beneath the ironclad heel of cold, hard, malicious egotism that a foreign nation and its god-forsaken master direct against you."[105]

In similar fashion, König represents the nation's young men. Just as he dithers while awaiting encouragement from Henriette, so too does Germany long for "the liberating word that would press weapons in the hands of an angry people."[106] The French debacle in Russia comes and goes in the space of a few pages, and Dessalle returns, wounded but ready to make good his promise of matrimony. Finally, the doctor must act. He can either bind his enemy's wounds once again, fulfilling his medical and humanitarian obligations, or he can let the man die and clear the path to happiness for himself and Henriette. As a product of Freytag's lingering liberalism, his hope for a future Germany, and the genre's need for an unblemished hero, König behaves ethically, while Dessalle, once he learns of Henriette's wishes, declares the doctor his mortal enemy. The Frenchman returns to his regiment, and König rejoins a company of German volunteers. The reader expects man-to-man conflict, but like almost every other novel treated here, the book

CHAPTER 5

satisfies only its romantic promise, not its adventurous possibilities. After the French defeat at Leipzig, Henriette receives an envelope containing her ring and a letter from Dessalle. In essence, the nation rather than König forced him to do the right thing. And it is doubly significant, given the nationalist baggage that Henriette carries with her through the tale, that he relents after the very battle historians usually portray as a turning point in the Wars of Liberation. Wearing the thin disguise of a happy couple, Germany emerges victorious.

At last, the two protagonists can marry and start a family, portending happiness for the fatherland and its potentially united inhabitants. In fact, most Germans did live in the Prussian-dominated German empire in 1881, when *From a Small Town* appeared, and Freytag could have used the newly wed König family to show how the Wars of Liberation laid a foundation for the nation's subsequent greatness. Instead, this family's postwar history mirrors the disruptions and disappointments Germans experienced in the thirty-five years after 1815. Many of the prewar states were restored at the Congress of Vienna, and the economy of German-speaking Europe remained underdeveloped, locked in outmoded forms of production. Since Freytag became prominent with *Debit and Credit* (1855), a novel that examined the economic potential of capitalism, his critical view of the 1830s and 1840s should scarcely be surprising, but the critique he voices here runs deeper. The Königs name their firstborn Viktor to mark the German triumph over Napoleon, but the boy embodies the nation's hubris, wasted potential, and tendency toward dilettantism rather than mastery. Viktor dabbles in the theater, joins a fraternity, fights a duel, earns a doctorate in philosophy, and nearly dies during the Revolution of 1848. In short, nothing he does is respectable, nor has he found a way to become a useful member of society. Only a severe wound and the threat of imprisonment force Viktor into journalism, where Freytag's own success began. He then marries into an aristocratic family that has finally given up its prejudice against the middle class, thus paving the way for an all-German happy ending, one that bridged some of the class divisions that still troubled Freytag's contemporaries.

Having at long last realized the promise of 1815, the book ends with a surprise. Doctor König inherits some papers from a distant relative and learns that Dessalle was his cousin. The familial connection explains the Frenchman's ability to speak German, and it might have contributed to his willingness, however reluctant, to relinquish Henriette. After all, good Germans recognize the value of marriage based on romantic attachment, because such relationships underscore the bourgeois values behind late-nineteenth-century nationalism. This final plot twist also shows how the Napoleonic wars initially tore families and the nation apart, but those same conflicts also cleared the way for genuinely German unions. Without the battle of Leipzig neither Germany nor the König family could have existed. Love may not have conquered all, but it roused enough reader interest to permit dozens of model Germanies.

No More Happy Endings

After 1871, when Prussia had unified most of German-speaking Europe, the Wars of Liberation became less central to German popular history. Sedan Day, which marked the Prussian victory over the French in 1870, was imposed on the new empire as a national holiday, while the profusion of Bismarck columns set a new focus in the construction of a national mythology.[107] Karl May's *The Love of a Cavalry Officer* (1883–85) typifies the shift in emphasis in fiction. Although some of this five-volume scandalous tale takes place during 1813–15, plot complications from that era mainly motivate events during the 1870–71 German occupation of Paris.[108] Perhaps surprisingly, May's novel suggests the possibility of Franco-German reconciliation, because both of its German heroes marry French women, proving once again that marriage remained a dominant trope in tales of adventure. However, including novels devoted to the Franco-Prussian War would take this already long chapter too far a field. Instead, I close with Friedrich Spielhagen's *Noblesse oblige* (1888) and Hermann Sudermann's *The Cat's Bridge* (1889), because both of these novels, like Wickede's *Tall Isaack*, refuse to end happily, and in so doing they summarize both the tensions and the potential for discussion that still resided in novels about the Wars of Liberation.[109]

Spielhagen is another of those nineteenth-century novelists whose work failed to resonate once the era of nation building ended.[110] Nostalgic readers had no time for his often critical voice, while literary modernism pushed highbrow tastes in directions other than toward realism; but during his lifetime, 1829–1911, Spielhagen was esteemed and widely read. He set *Noblesse oblige* in Hamburg, perhaps using the city as an example of lingering local patriotism, and he, like so many of the authors dealt with in this chapter, placed a middle-class woman with

CHAPTER 5

two suitors in the center of the book's plot. Minna Warburg has fallen in love with the Marquis Hypolit d'Héricourt, but the year is 1812, and it finds him at Napoleon's side in Russia. Minna's father intercepts and withholds the young man's letters, mainly because he would prefer to see his daughter married to Theodor Billow, a prominent local businessman. Although he married a French-speaking woman from Belgium and raised his family to treasure French culture, the elder Warburg now teeters at the edge of bankruptcy and needs a rich son-in-law. Minna, who knows the score, is willing to sacrifice herself for the good of the family—besides, she has doubts about Héricourt: "The love of her heart was and still remains an enemy of her fatherland."[111] Unfortunately for her, the German contender also has faults, and Spielhagen uses Billow to let his readers wonder about the patriotism that they might otherwise have associated with the Wars of Liberation.

Billow puts business above all other considerations; he is more interested in one side or the other winning and making the world safe for commerce than in whether the Germans or the French prevail. Aside from Minna and her brother Georg, the only real German patriot is Samuel Hirsch, a Jewish businessman who was born in Russia. When Billow expresses surprise at his beliefs, Hirsch questions Billow's presuppositions, albeit in broken German: "Because Hirsch a Jew is . . . and the Jew has no fatherland?"[112] Hirsch is proud to support the nation that harbored him as a young man, allowed him to be successful, and later permitted him to bring his beloved Sara from Russia to Hamburg. Unlike Billow, Hirsch is ready to use his network of business connections to help the German cause. For example, he aids Georg Warburg, who, like General Yorck, has left Napoleon's army and joined the Russians. Billow, by contrast, treats Georg as a dangerous nuisance, a man who could never be trusted in business: "His hatred of all Frenchmen and everything French makes him irresponsible."[113] Although Minna does not know as much about Billow's beliefs as the reader, her reluctance to ally herself with him is understandable. She sums up his character by saying, "He had no heart; he was an egoist to the core of his being and a coward to boot."[114] The prospects for a happy conclusion seem dim indeed.

As usual in such novels, a great deal happens; it must, because the plot originally filled three hefty volumes; it weighs in at over five hundred pages in later editions. Minna and Billow marry and she bears him a son, while Hamburg lives through several uprisings. Napoleon's armies

THE GERMAN PEOPLE ARISE—AND MARRY

lose, win, and lose again. By the time we get to volume 3, Minna has shamed her husband by being active in the patriots' cause, and Héricourt is back in Hamburg as part of an occupying army. When the French take forty hostages, including her father, to ensure that the city will contribute to the war effort, Minna goes to their commandant and offers herself as a replacement. Her action is one more example of the novel's French title, *Noblesse oblige*, which refers to the nobility of Minna's sentiments and the duty she feels to help others rather than to obligations associated with high birth. By this time she has read Héricourt's letters to her and nursed him back to health after he dueled to defend her honor; she also realizes what a bad bargain she made in marrying Billow. She contemplates divorce but finally tells Héricourt, "[you cannot marry me] without being untrue to yourself and your nation, your fatherland."[115] He agrees because, despite her feelings for him, Héricourt knows not only that Minna regards the French as her hereditary enemies but also that the French, "through years of tyranny, through the thousands of wounds that they inflicted on Germany, have made themselves worthy of thousandfold hatred."[116] In a better world or in a trashier novel, love would somehow unite these two characters, but for an author struggling to define what it meant to be German, and for a readership that must have demanded plausible endings in works dealing with serious topics, reconciliation seems out of the question. Instead, with a plot twist that is almost as melodramatic as the happy ending that Spielhagen refused to deliver, Héricourt dies while attempting to rescue Billow from a shipwreck. In the end, with both her husband and her French suitor dead, Minna retires to Holstein, where she opens her home to the poor: *Noblesse oblige*.

Actually, the book still is not quite finished. Minna is left hoping for a world beyond nationalities. As she once pleaded with her brother, "Oh, leave me the illusion that I could have lived with my beloved [Héricourt] without having the terrible thought: Which side will your children be on when the two nations from which their parents hale once again slaughter one another?"[117] The book's final page attempts an answer. It finds Minna rereading Héricourt's letters, and she happens onto a passage in which he asks if the time will ever come "when a person will be able to exist without being asked to be inhumane in the name of love of family, welfare of the fatherland, [or] honor of the nation?" Minna thinks for a moment, smiles sadly, and concludes, "Never, beloved friend, whispering softly, never."[118] Besides, the son Minna bore

Billow is long since dead; Spielhagen leaves his readers with more fear than hope about the future of Germany.

If anything, Hermann Sudermann was even more pessimistic. Although he began his writing career as a combination journalist and novelist, Sudermann was once well known as the author of successful plays. Like the rest of his work, *The Cat's Bridge* now gathers dust on library shelves, but it went through over forty editions by 1900, that is, in just more than a decade after its initial publication.[119] More baffling than the book's present obscurity is its original popularity, for in an age that we, perhaps mistakenly, characterize by the appearance of excessive and unreflected patriotism, Sudermann's novel must have offended many readers. Not only do the protagonists, Boroslav von Schranden and Regine Hackelberg, not marry, but before the two of them even meet, the hero's father has also forced the heroine to serve as his maid and mistress. That burden, which adds immorality and the potential for a kind of incest to a wide social gap, makes Boroslav and Regine one of the least likely couples imaginable. In addition, Regine dies at the novel's end, murdered by her own drunken father. Boroslav dies too, albeit offstage, while two groups of patriotic militiamen compete to outdo each other in the categories of dishonor, drunkenness, and deceit. Moreover, the village pastor is a vicious hypocrite, while a crooked tavern keeper represents the state in his role as town mayor. Indeed, so off-putting are the traditional positive figures that Sudermann's novel might well be an attempt to eliminate the Wars of Liberation from the national myth. Still, the novel's strange plot and peculiar cast of characters show how contentious, difficult, and, nevertheless, important the conflict still was to Germans struggling with the idea of a shared history at the end of the nineteenth century. They simply could neither forget nor ignore the unfulfilled hopes of 1813–15.

Indeed, not forgetting functions as this novel's central topos. An event from the plot's prehistory remains seared in every character's memory, and everything that happens stems from that signal occurrence. In 1807 Boroslav's father directed French troops across the so-called cat's bridge, through his own property, and then behind the local garrison's defenses, with predictable results: dead Prussian soldiers and ignominy for the Schranden family. Actually, Baron von Schranden ordered Regine to perform the dastardly deed, one in a long series of degradations, yet she remains faithful to him even after townspeople burn the baron's castle and refuse him burial in the town's cemetery. The reader

THE GERMAN PEOPLE ARISE — AND MARRY

first sees Regine digging her oppressor an illicit grave in the vain hope of laying him and his poisonous past to rest, but she is unable to dispose of either his body or his legacy. Memory proves too powerful.

Meanwhile, Boroslav has been living peaceably with an aunt in Königsberg, when rumors of his father's actions make him a pariah. Forced to leave the university, he moves to Lithuania and loses touch with Helene Götz, his childhood sweetheart and the local pastor's daughter. Long estranged from his father and now distant from his homeland too, Boroslav eventually experiences an epiphany based on his own inability to forget. "The love of the fatherland that had slumbered quietly and self-confidently in his heart became a torturing force . . . He came close to blaming himself for Prussia's misfortune."[120] But to ensure that some good comes from the family, Boroslav adopts a pseudonym, joins the struggle against Napoleon, and distinguishes himself as the elected commander of a company of militiamen. True to the genre's form, none of these actions take place within the novel. Instead, the text begins with the hero parting from his comrades. He leaves for home before they can identify him as the son of such a disreputable father, knowing full well he cannot keep the secret for long. Once the truth comes out, Boroslav will have to take sides. No longer shielded by anonymity, he will have to choose between family and fatherland. Arriving conveniently at midnight to find Regine secretly burying his father, he must act. He can either join in her defiance, reclaim his patrimony, and attempt to expiate the old man's sins, or he can disavow his father and, with any luck, live happily ever after with Helene. Inexplicably, at least to this reader, Boroslav declares those who hated his father his own enemies, which forces him into Regine's arms. Together, they attempt the impossible: these two unlikely allies die, trying to undo an unforgivable and, in the economy of the novel, unforgettable act. The myth of 1813–15 almost dies with them.

Having forced his two main characters to take on the rest of society, Sudermann then lets his plot roll toward its inevitably tragic conclusion. What happens is less interesting than the array of patriotic villains who force the issue; for not only do the protagonists' deaths rob the novel of the standard model marriage, but the confrontation between Boroslav's misguided family loyalty and the unexpectedly reprehensible evil of Prussian society would seem to leave no hope for the future. For example, after describing a judge sent from the capital as someone who genuinely deserved his reputation as a defender of the fatherland, the

CHAPTER 5

narrator adds, "The vices of success, vanity and selfishness, soon appeared. What had begun as honest sacrifice gradually turned into a pedestal for his own personality, a monument dedicated to promulgating his fame to the world."[121] Acting as an honorable civil servant, the judge awards Boroslav the Iron Cross, while, unofficially, the man behind the office refuses to shake his hand, thereby emboldening the town's patriotic rabble. All they need is someone to draw first blood. At this point, one might expect the pastor to intercede, especially since he has known Boroslav for decades and must also be aware of his daughter's affection for the hero. Instead, he sides with his misguided parishioners and attempts to have Boroslav banished. Not content to show him behaving badly, Sudermann's narrator savages the pastor: "He stood, with his vulturelike profile and tiny, glowing eyes, like a bird of prey that wants to pounce on its catch." Harsh words, but not enough: "Scorpions sprang from the mouth of this man of Christian charity."[122] Fate, rather than justice or mercy, intervenes when Boroslav learns that Napoleon has left Elba. The fatherland again needs his services, and the young hero drops everything to rally the townspeople to the national cause. They refuse, unwilling to serve under a tainted commander. Indeed, the mayor/tavern keeper's son vows to die in a duel before he would rejoin the militia under such leadership. His insubordination precipitates Regine's murder, and the book's final chapter reads in its entirety as follows:

> We know little of Boroslav's fate.
> In light of the mutiny, the leadership viewed it as advisable to return him to his old regiment.
> Although the militia of East Prussia remained in the ancient provinces, he received the enviable authorization to return to the battlefield without delay.
> He is supposed to have fallen at Ligny [two days before Waterloo].[123]

Deceptively laconic, the ending demands unpacking. To begin, in this and every novel, readers never know more than the narrator chooses to tell them; he must therefore have reasons for his refusal to elaborate here. For example, since all that is known about Boroslav's demise is that he is "supposed to have fallen at Ligny," for all the reader knows, he could just as easily have succumbed to illness or some misadventure.

Rather than dying heroically, he could have fallen victim to others' or his own incompetence, to friendly fire or, more likely, to an unwarranted rashness that invited death. Moreover, since Napoleon's forces defeated the Prussian army at Ligny, Boroslav perishes before Germany triumphs. His end comes at what could have been as bleak a moment as Jena, and although he answers the fatherland's call, nothing remains to draw him home again. Without Regine he cannot overcome old hatreds and caste divisions. Defeated and unworthy, Boroslav will not found the new German family that marches confidently into the future, and neither, according to Sudermann's account, will anyone else. The Prussian militia remains at home, denied the glories of Waterloo, while representatives of the army, the crown, the clergy, and the middle class are all disqualified. Far from retrospectively justifying German unification, the novel's ending calls the whole national enterprise into question, with no alternatives in sight. Sudermann might have been reacting to dashed hopes during the three-emperor year of 1888, when William I's liberal heir, Frederick III, died after just ninety-nine days on the throne and was replaced by his loopy son William II. The novel could also reflect the pressures of continued social and economic turmoil in an agrarian society that became an industrial giant in little more than a generation, while still wracked with seemingly unbridgeable territorial, religious, and class divisions; for by the end of the century political positions had hardened beyond compromise, presaging the impossibility of lasting coalitions in the Weimar Republic, and in the 1890s the younger generation turned its back on the nation's complacent founders and began communing with nature. Hiking and health food replaced at least some of the patriotic bombast of the imperial era. Without making too much of that shift in outlook, *The Cat's Bridge* suggests that the search for a common past remained difficult.

Variations on the German Family

Sudermann's exceptionally unhappy ending should not lead anyone to believe that every writer and every reader viewed Germany with renewed skepticism in 1889. Questioning, critique, and an inability to agree on the content, form, or shape that a German nation state would assume had long marked the search for a unifying national myth. The inability to settle on one national narrative did not prevent people from acting as if they had achieved consensus; Germany's unity—political, social, and cultural—was simply more apparent than real. Still, key elements of the national narrative had changed in the years since 1830. First, the nuclear family had become the dominant model for the nation. Although Hesekiel, François, and, to a lesser degree, Alexis wrote of parent guardians, only the founding of new, independent, single-generation families could show readers how to imagine a unified Germany. Marriages could unite historically separate classes, regions, and religious groupings, as new generations made their own choices. Characters broke from the past and moved beyond the world their parents inhabited; they crossed previously insuperable boundaries and wed people their parents considered unacceptable. Often, perhaps to ease the transition, one or both members of the couple was an orphan or of unclear origins. As a result, the heroes and heroines of these novels used nationality to measure the suitability of a partner's ancestors rather than social class, religion, regional affiliation or even legitimacy. And even the failures, most notably in Wickede and Sudermann, raised the issue of nontraditional unions and left the reader feeling that Germany would be a better place had those novels' potential marriages proven possible. For if the nation was based on language, custom, ethnicity, shared values, and a common past, then every German male represented a potential husband for each of the nation's females, while all the women in Germany should have been eligible to wed any German man. The sole, and not inconsequential, difficulty was putting the broad-based promise of this collection of novels into practice.

Second, arranged marriages, those remnants of an earlier age and social order, gave way to the bourgeois norm of romantic love and companionate unions. Except for Hesekiel's soulless heroine, no one lets his or her elders choose a spouse. Isegrimm rails against his daughters' suitors, but they ultimately make their own decisions—sometimes, like their fellow heroes and heroines, disastrously. By definition, orphans obviate any role for their parents, but also for the legitimate offspring in these novels marriage is never about property and seldom revolves around class. Although characters frequently have to overcome lingering social prejudices when their desires transcend traditional borders, marrying the wrong person is invariably a matter of nationality. In those rare instances, mainly in chapter 2, when people love across national lines, the protagonists eventually see the error of their initial inclinations and marry within the version of Germany they are helping to construct. Love almost always triumphs, because the nation trumps all else. In fact, most of these novels posit the bridging of an inherited gap as the means of founding the new national family. Loving partners can overcome their parents' outmoded ideals and unite the *Volk* that earlier norms and values had kept from realizing its full potential. Within the nation only religious differences remain unbridgeable, as they were in German society for most of the nineteenth century. Thus, Isegrimm's one daughter ends unhappily not only because she marries a Frenchman but also because she adopts his fanatic Catholicism and leaves her family behind. So, too, do Tall Isaack's two daughters die unfulfilled, with far greater consequences for the nation. Yet even there, the problem resides in the larger society rather than in a father's meddling with his children's plans, as would have been the case in an earlier age.

Third, in novels set during the Wars of Liberation, history functions more as background than as a necessary element in the national saga. In contrast to nonfiction books and novels about both Frederick the Great and Jena, works that deal with the period 1813–15 contain surprisingly little history. The historians in this chapter struggled less successfully than the novelists with what to represent. Depictions of battles could only answer the question of *how* Germans freed themselves; they could never reveal *who* the Germans were. Including the militia might help, but in Germany's emerging national narrative the Wars of Liberation acquired a task that transcended the myth of national renewal. The conflict's mythic significance lay in its atypical elements, in engagements fought by volunteers and irregulars, which were outside the bounds of traditional history. In fact, much of the conflict consisted of conventional warfare, but the historical record mattered little in the larger enterprise of national mythmaking. What armies did was of little use in the task of inventing Germany. By contrast, every couple in these novels represented a vision of the nation that was either not yet realized or whose realization was still imperfect. Authors could use fictional families in an attempt to set the national agenda or criticize the nation's current course. Thus, although recounting the course of events involved no such stakes, 1813–15 offered an ideal backdrop for anyone hoping to define Germany. Since they were not looking for national heroes or assessing blame for the nation's mistakes, writers of historical fiction could make use of the genre's decided advantages over academic and popular history and concentrate on the ordinary men and women who would constitute the new entity called Germany.

Fourth, as necessary as it was to include women in any marriage,

CHAPTER 5

these novels frequently depict men returning home as heroes and then choosing a wife or at least attempting to marry. Ludwig Rosen rescues his beloved Bianka from her mistaken identity and then leaves her with his sister while he and his friend march off to battle. Fritz Reuter lets the miller's daughter run the family business, but she stays at home in the mill. Other happy brides spend their time offstage, presumably knitting or embroidering their trousseaus. Even Hardine Müller retreats from her responsibilities after a suitable husband appears. In contrast to those frail females waiting patiently by the national hearth, the fatherland rewards active women with a kiss of death. Regine Hackelburg is murdered for her troubles; the rest die unhappily as spinsters—some young, for example, Rebekka, her sister Sara, and Minna Warburg; others as old as Countess Micielska or the last Reckenburg. The focus on domesticity as the realm of national fulfillment included a demand for thoroughly domestic women even when women authors created them. In other words, the Wars of Liberation freed only half the population.

Finally, neither unity of purpose nor a shared theme could overcome differing views about the outcome of the national struggle. Authors might agree about the need to define the German people, and embark on that task in fiction or nonfiction, while simultaneously differing about membership in the new nation. Whether the aristocracy could or should join with the middle class in the project of nation building remained an open question in nineteenth-century German society, so representations of the nation's history also disagreed about the role and function of both the nobility and the bourgeoisie. Including peasants and the working class proved difficult politically after 1871, particularly as the Social Democratic Party grew in strength; no wonder it proved almost impossible for fictional aristocrats and professionals to marry that far beneath their station. Lewin von Vitzewitz had to overcome considerable objections, and his wife was a respectable orphan. Boroslav von Schranden could only bury his betrothed in the grave she had dug for his father. And these were both matches set in the safe distance of the past. As *Delusions Confusions* (1887) indicates, even Fontane was unable to imagine such matches in the Germany of his own day.

Germany and the Germans continued to represent different things to different people. Before 1871, authors were skeptical about the prospects for national unity, although they often tried to imagine what the new Germany would look like; after 1871 they were skeptical about the results. Whether the nobility really was part of the nation; whether the German *Volk* included Jews, Catholics, and Austrians; and whether national reconciliation would bridge the gap between the middle class and the poor were all questions that neither history nor fiction could answer, at least not until the society in which they were based achieved more than just political unity. Writers could raise these issues and use representations of the past only to propose imaginary solutions in an ongoing debate about the nation and its future. They helped stage the debate, set its terms, and test a variety of solutions. For that purpose depictions of the Wars of Liberation provided writers and the German reading public with an ideal vehicle.

Conclusion:
The Myth of a Common Past

People who follow German affairs know what an important role history plays in the national culture. In no other country in the world would a dispute about the outbreak of World War I land in Parliament, and nowhere else would controversy over interpretations of the Holocaust twice occupy the nation's press for months, in the latter instance making Daniel Jonah Goldhagen, one of German culture's leading detractors, into a media star and pundit.[1] More recently, discussions of the Berlin Republic revolve around the meaning of that city's past for its current and future inhabitants: for example, should the Hohenzollern's palace be rebuilt and the German Democratic Republic's capital building be torn down? Is it appropriate to house today's ministries in Nazi-era structures, and should the new American Embassy conform to eighteenth-century height and setback restrictions? Most important, does Berlin need a Holocaust memorial, and what statement should the monument make to the country's citizens and to the world?[2] Far from being dead or bunk, Germany's history is not even past.

German history remains controversial because Germans have not yet agreed upon the meaning of the present, although if they had achieved consensus about the past, many of today's problems would never have arisen. Instead, as new citizenship laws finally shift official attention from blood to residence, and as a once apparently homoge-

CONCLUSION

neous population becomes multicultural, what it means to be German continues to occupy society at every level, from the legislature to barroom philosophers. In the absence of both a common past and an agreed-upon sense of mission, and with a constitution that automatically grants citizenship to people whose families have lived in Russia, Rumania, or Argentina for centuries—but not to German-speaking Turks born in Berlin—the question of German identity remains unanswered.

In essence, this book argues that contemporary Germany's preoccupation with the past has its own long history. Inventing the nineteenth-century nation involved issues that were just as intractable and stakes that were just as high as today's. Nineteenth-century Germans were unable to reach consensus about their present because they, too, struggled to define a shared version of the past. As a result, history was never simply academic; the past always matters. Similarly, present values did not merely color developments in the discourse of history; rather, questions about the present lay behind both the choice of objects to be studied and the impact of historical explanations. Historians working both inside and outside the academy, in factual and fictional genres, asked where the nation was located, who its heroes and villains were, and what mission would take Germany into the future. Like the larger society, historians of various stripes and occupational categories failed to agree upon answers. It would take World War I to unite Germans, even temporarily, behind a national cause, as on August 4, 1914, Emperor William II declared, hoping it was true, "I no longer recognize parties; I recognize only Germans." However, by 1918 William had abdicated, and the struggle to come to terms with the nation's multiple pasts broke out with renewed vigor and seriousness. Questions posed in the nineteenth century arose again, and they remain controversial to the present day.

One caveat: saying that Germany's common past was mythical does not undercut the power of the idea. Most nineteenth-century Germans probably believed that they shared a single history with their fellow citizens. As Hermann Bausinger has written about the same issue today: "One knows to be sure that 'the Germans' do not exist, but that fact has not hindered anyone from believing them to be unmovable, nature-loving, zealously businesslike, disciplined, serious, and deep."[3] More important, that century's academic and extra-academic historical discourse reveals gradual agreement on certain issues. For example, Frederick II

CONCLUSION

moved beyond Prussian history and became the nation's favorite uncle. He achieved almost universal acceptance, because, except for Austria, regional divisions lessened. Print language ushered in the beginnings of a decline in dialects, while local customs became ever more antiquated, irrelevant to ordinary life, and, concomitantly, less distinct. As Alon Confino argues, the nation became a local metaphor: nostalgia for an intact peasant or artisan past gradually replaced particularism, while generic antimodernism became national. Indeed, nationalism promoted notions of a golden age in the nation's history, because that residue and simultaneous longing enabled the modernization that the nation promised and demanded. In this sense, Germany's mythical idyllic past played a crucial role in the nation's present, a role that required an exaggerated if not entirely false view of the past, but one that appeared to be held in common.

Germany's national narrative should have spoken to a single, unified public, but it mainly addressed and was sustained by the bourgeoisie. If this seems difficult to reconcile with the mythic significance of Frederick II and Prussia's Queen Louisa, the explanation lies not so much in their positions in politics and society as in the values they came to represent. Thus, anecdotes about the Prussian king invariably stress not only his courage and wisdom but also his approachability, common touch, and disdain for the dress, ceremony, and intrigue of the court. The burnished image of Old Fritz almost always shows him in a well-worn uniform as he involves himself not in the affairs of state but in the concerns of ordinary citizens and soldiers. Distinctly unmajestic, the Frederick of Germany's emerging national narrative interacted with his subjects as a stern but loving patriarch, the head of the national family. Whether seated in the park at Sanssouci, next to some campfire, or astride a favorite horse, Frederick rendered wise judgments and then blended perfectly into an idyllic, rural Germany that was as imaginary and as necessary to the myth as the king's avuncular qualities. Despite his admiration for France's literature, philosophy, art, and language, Frederick came to symbolize humble German virtues that were increasingly associated with the nation's old middle class, its yeoman farmers, artisans, and small-town professionals. Frederick's initial ascendance in the national imagination coincided with a decline in the cultural prestige of French fashion, gardens, and palaces and their replacement with German equivalents. Frederick II remained relevant because the bourgeoisie adopted these new norms as their own and linked the Prussian

CONCLUSION

king with simpler, more natural, and increasingly national tastes in dress, landscape, and princely housing. Moreover, his image flowed neatly into that of Prussia's legendary queen.

Gender complicated Louisa's situation, but her femininity provided mythmakers with new opportunities. Like Frederick, Louisa was depicted as preferring simple German pleasures. Authors reported that she ate fewer courses and lived in less elaborate circumstances than her predecessors; she also remained free from Napoleon's imperial pretensions. More important, the focus on Louisa shifted national attention from the public to the domestic sphere and then back again. Stories of Louisa's life helped sanction companionate marriage and the nuclear family as private virtues at the same time as these tales transformed the queen's values into national norms. Clearly, the shift had begun long before tales of Louisa's concern for her weak husband and innocent children garnered national attention. Bourgeois notions fill the pages of Lessing's tragedies, Goethe's *Sturm und Drang* novels, and all of those other books that people read instead of the classics. Lessing's Emilia Galotti, Werther's beloved Lotte, and the heroines of romance novels all helped insert middle-class ideas into the public sphere, but depictions of Louisa's life helped inject bourgeois norms into the national narrative. Needless to say, the ideals Louisa rejected were French, while those she embraced became German. Indeed, after Louisa, German and bourgeois almost became synonyms, for although the aristocracy continued to dominate politics, society, and the military, aristocrats' values increasingly coincided with those of the bourgeoisie.[4] For example, only one of the heroines of the Wars of Liberation enters into an arranged marriage; almost all of the other male and female characters marry and found German families based on their belief in values such as love, piety, and simple domesticity, values that Louisa appeared to champion in every account of her life. By representing Louisa in this fashion, authors changed the definition of what it meant to be German, and the queen became as important as Frederick in transmitting the national agenda. She, too, became German rather than Prussian.

Similarly, the sheer number of texts devoted to Jena and the Wars of Liberation demonstrates the importance of those conflicts in the national discourse about the past. Authors disagreed over what these events meant, but such disagreements should not obscure their centrality in almost every attempt to come to terms with German history. Like Frederick II and Queen Louisa, 1806 and 1813–15 belonged to an originally Prussian framework for understanding what became German history. Unfortunately for the mythmakers, Jena's heroes were rare, in part because less than a decade separated disaster from triumph. Since some people blamed profligate aristocrats for the national catastrophe, they could scarcely turn the villains of 1806 into heralds of the national future in 1815. Others saw such widespread moral turpitude that they believed national renewal demanded a cleansing fire. From that perspective the nation needed a new, not yet discovered set of champions, but authors and, presumably, their readers had a difficult time agreeing whom to include in the new German family. And since membership in the German "us" remained contested, writers devoted little effort to defining a foreign "them." The French functioned as adversaries in almost every rendering of the larger national saga, but they mainly acted offstage. With some Germans constituting the national other, hating the French became superfluous. Yet, even without an external enemy, the internal dynamics of Jena and the Wars of Liberation provided ideal locations for a discussion of the German nation—what it stood for and who it included. Accounts of military campaigns against the French could add little of importance to the larger task of narrating the nation.

The simultaneous emergence of professional and popular, frequently fictional history both fostered and took advantage of this partial consensus. New forms and new publishing possibilities allowed debates about history to resonate widely in an increasingly literate public, while new sensibilities about history lent impact to the disputes. In addition, the lack of a sanctioned public sphere turned the reading and writing of history into one of the few arenas available for discussions about the shape and substance of the German nation: Where else was it possible to discredit the aristocracy or the bureaucracy, to argue about the role of women, peasants, and Jews, or to explore alternatives to unsatisfactory political developments? Where else but in the safely distant past could noblemen marry commoners? And where else among this nation of passionate amateur historians—that is, among people like Fontane's characters Czako and Rex—could readers come to understand what it would mean to share a past with a nation of their fellows? Thus, despite its factual absence, Germans' belief in their shared history permitted them to use the discourse of history to come to terms with the present. At some level, the authors of history and historical fiction, as well as the prospective Germans in their audience, knew that the present demanded agreement about the past. If ordinary readers and the authors who precipitated, modeled, and reflected national debates nevertheless failed to decide what Germany meant, that failure is instructive both for the light it sheds on an intractable controversy and for its overturning of the myth that the Napoleonic wars, the triumph of 1871, or any subsequent event resolved the issue of German identity. Working in a variety of factual and fictional genres, authors who wrote about German history struggled mightily to invent Germany—in other words, to come up with and then disseminate one simple, agreed-upon, national narrative—but the task, whose context included German cultural, political, and social reality, proved too daunting. With some notable exceptions, writings about German history succeeded only in setting the parameters within which the debate could continue. Authors' inability to achieve consensus about the details, particularly about winners and losers in the Wars of Liberation, meant that for them and their readers the term "Germany" remained multivalent. The German nation signified different things to different people, while membership *in* and the orientation *of* Germany remained open questions throughout the nineteenth and into the twentieth century. Indeed, until the Federal Republic decides what to make of the Holocaust and the heritage of the German Democratic Republic, fundamental disagreement over what Germany is seems likely to persist. At least we know that such controversies have a long history.

Notes

Introduction

1. See Thomas W. Gaehtgens, *Anton von Werner. Die Proklamierung des Deutschen Kaiserreiches: Ein Historienbild im Wandel preußischer Politik* (Frankfurt am Main: Fischer, 1990), and Peter Paret, *Art as History: Episodes in the Culture and Politics of Nineteenth-Century Germany* (Princeton, NJ: Princeton University Press, 1988), 165–80.
2. Deutsches Historisches Museum, *Bismarck: Preussen, Deutschland und Europa* (Berlin: Nicolai, 1990), esp. Leonore Koschnick, "Mythos zu Lebzeiten—Bismarck als nationale Kultfigur," 455–82; and Rolf Parr, *"Zwei Seelen wohnen, ach! in meiner Brust!": Strukturen und Funktionen der Mythisierung Bismarcks* (Munich: Fink, 1992).
3. For a summary of the political narrative, see Liah Greenfeld, *Nationalism: Five Roads to Modernity* (Cambridge, MA: Harvard University Press, 1992), 272–395. Other recent attempts at understanding German nationalism include Harold James, *A German Identity: 1770–1990* (New York: Routledge, 1989); Stefan Berger, *The Search for Normality: National Identity and Historical Consciousness in Germany since 1800* (Providence, RI: Berghahn Books, 1997); and Hagen Schulze, *Germany: A New History*, Deborah Lucas Schneider, trans. (Cambridge, MA: Harvard University Press, 1998). For the eighteenth century, see Hans-Martin Blitz, *Aus Liebe zum Vaterland: Die deutsche Nation im 18. Jahrhundert* (Hamburg: Hamburger Edition, 2000).
4. Ernest Renan, "What Is a Nation?" in Homi K. Bhabha, ed., *Nation and Narration* (London: Routledge, 1990), 11.
5. Homi Bhabha, "Introduction," *Nation and Narration*, 5. The German counterpart to Bhabha's collection is *Grenzfälle: Über neuen und alten*

NOTES TO INTRODUCTION

Nationalismus, Michael Jeismann and Henning Ritter, eds. (Leipzig: Reclam, 1993).

6. Alon Confino, "Collective Memory and Cultural History: Problems and Method," *American Historical Review* 102.5 (December 1997): 1390. For the classic statement of how human memory works in a collective context, see Maurice Halbwachs, *On Collective Memory,* 1941/1952, Lewis A. Coser, trans. (Chicago: University of Chicago Press, 1992); see also Nora Gedi and Yigal Elam, "Collective Memory—What Is It?" *History and Memory* 8 (1996): 30–50. See also Alon Confino and Peter Fritzsche, eds., *The Work of Memory: New Directions in the Study of German Society and Culture* (Urbana: University of Illinois Press, 2002), esp. 1–21.

7. To be fair, one could also look at the history taught in schools. See M. J. Maynes, *Schooling in Western Europe: A Social History* (Albany: State University of New York Press, 1985), and Marjorie Lamberti, *State, Society, and the Elementary School in Imperial Germany* (New York: Oxford University Press, 1989). Another intriguing focus, historical artifacts and museums, is treated in Susan A. Crane, *Collecting and Historical Consciousness in Early Nineteenth-Century Germany* (Ithaca, NY: Cornell University Press, 2000).

8. "Ja Czako, das weiß ich ja alles. Das steht ja schon im Brandenburgischen Kinderfreund" (Theodor Fontane, *Der Stechlin* [1899], in *Werke und Schriften,* Walter Keitel and Helmuth Nürnberger, eds., [Frankfurt am Main: Ullstein, 1991], vol. 19, 103–4). Unless otherwise noted, all translations from German texts are my own.

9. The text in question is Friedrich Wilmsen, *Kinderfreunde: Der Brandenburgische Kinderfreund: Ein Lesebuch für Volksschulen, 1. Aufl. 1800* (Berlin: Georg Decker). *Der Deutsche Kinderfreund: Ein Lesebuch für volksschulen, 1. Aufl. 1802* (Berlin: Realschulbuchhandlung; reprint, Holger Rudloff, ed. [Cologne, Weimar, Vienna: Böhlau, 1992]).

10. In the United States, debates over a national history curriculum or the contents of an exhibit on the airplane that dropped the first atomic bomb raise roughly the same issues about national identity that were posed for Germans in the "historians' controversy" (*Historikerstreit*), the discussion of Daniel Jonah Goldhagen's book *Hitler's Willing Executioners* and proposals for a Holocaust memorial in Berlin.

11. Reprinted in the Rudloff edition, n.p.; "Bei dieser neuen Ausgabe ist die Geschichte Brandenburgs eingeschaltet worden, damit dieser Kinderfrund den Namen des Brandenburgischen mit Recht führen, die Jugend frühe mit den Schicksalen und Thaten der biederen und kräftigen Vorfahren bekannt werden, und desto treuer und inniger das Vaterland lieben möge." By 1824 the book was already in its fourteenth edition; it claims to be "unchanged," presumably since the eighteenth edition.

NOTES TO INTRODUCTION

12. "Solche Rekapitulation stärkt einen immer historisch und patriotisch" (Fontane, *Der Stechlin*, 188).
13. Rudy Koshar, *From Monuments to Traces: Artifacts of German Memory, 1870–1990* (Berkeley: University of California Press, 2000), 31.
14. Aleida Assmann, *Arbeit am nationalen Gedächtnis: Eine kurze Geschichte der deutschen Bildungsidee* (Frankfurt am Main: Campus, 1993), 51. For a discussion of monuments and their relationship to the national project, see Kirsten Belgum, "Displaying the Nation: A View of Nineteenth-Century Monuments through a Popular Magazine," *Central European History* 26.3 (1993): 457–74; Thomas Nipperdey, "Nationalidee und Nationaldenkmal in Deutschland im 19. Jahrhundert," in his *Gesellschaft, Kultur, Theorie: Gesammelte Aufsätze zur neueren Geschichte* (Göttingen: Vandenhoeck and Ruprecht, 1976), 133–73; and Wolfgang Hardtwig, *Geschichtskultur und Wissenschaft* (Munich: DTV, 1990), especially 224–301.
15. In a chapter on "The Cultural Establishment and Its Critics," James J. Sheehan labels one of the subsections "The Triumph of History," *German History 1770–1866* (Oxford: Oxford University Press, 1989), 542–55. See also Carl Schorske, *Thinking with History: Explorations in the Passage of Modernism* (Princeton, NJ: Princeton University Press, 1998).
16. See Anthony D. Smith, "National Identity and Myths of Ethnic Descent," *Research in Social Movements: Conflict and Change* 7 (1984): 95–130.
17. See Claus Ahlzweig, *Muttersprache—Vaterland: Die deutsche Nation und ihre Sprache* (Opladen: Westdeutscher Verlag, 1994), esp. 154–82, and Wolfgang Frühwald, "Die Idee kultureller Nationbildung und die Entstehung der Literatursprache in Deutschland," in Otto Dann, ed., *Nationalismus in vorindustrieller Zeit* (Munich: Oldenbourg, 1986), 129–41.
18. E. J. Hobsbawm, *Nations and Nationalism since 1789: Programme, Myth, Reality* (Cambridge: Cambridge University Press, 1990), 60–61.
19. Ahlzweig, *Muttersprache—Vaterland*, 156.
20. Schulze calls the shift from a population in which 15 percent could read and write in 1770 to one with a literacy rate of roughly 50 percent in 1840 "a true revolution" (119). That growth is especially impressive because at more or less the same time, between 1815 and 1848, the population of the German Confederation increased by over 50 percent, from 22 to 35 million.
21. Slavoj Žižek, *For They Know Not What They Do: Enjoyment as a Political Factor* (London: Verso, 1991), 20.
22. Like Schiller's sentimental poet, these readers longed for an intact past, without knowing as he did that history is often a projection. See Friedrich Schiller, "Über naïve und sentimentalische Dichtung," in *Sämtliche Werke,*

NOTES TO INTRODUCTION

Gerhard Fricke and Herbert G. Göpfert, eds. (Munich: Hanser, 1980), 5: 730.

23. Compare the happy endings discussed below with novels set in their authors' present, e.g., Georg Weerth's *Fragment eines Romans* (1843–47), Louise Otto-Peter's *Schloß und Fabrik* (1846), and Max Kretzer's *Meister Timpe* (1888).
24. Benedict Anderson, *Imagined Communities: Reflections on the Origin and Spread of Nationalism* (London: Verso, 1983, revised edition, 1991), 74.
25. See Hartmut Eggert, *Studien zur Wirkungsgeschichte des deutschen historischen Romans, 1850–1875* (Frankfurt am Main: Klostermann, 1971); and Alberto Martino, *Die deutsche Leihbibliothek: Geschichte einer literarischen Institution (1756–1914)* (Wiesbaden: Harassowitz, 1990). For a look at identity formation through the popular press, see Kirsten Belgum, *Popularizing the Nation: Audience, Representation, and the Production of Identity in* Die Gartenlaube, *1853–1900* (Lincoln: University of Nebraska Press, 1998); and for accounts of the Wars of Liberation, see Ferdi Akaltin, *Die Befreiungskriege im Geschichtsbild der Deutschen im 19. Jahrhundert* (Frankfurt am Main: Verlag Neue Wissenschaft, 1997), 213–78.
26. The phrase "deutsche Nationaloper" is from Bernhard Wördehoff, "National nach Noten," *Die Zeit* (International Edition) 51.28 (July 12, 1996): 6–8; see also Thomas S. Grey, "Wagner's *Die Meistersinger* as National Opera (1868–1945)," in Celia Applegate and Pamela Potter, eds., *Music and German National Identity* (Chicago: University of Chicago Press, 2002), 78–104. For a survey of the studies on poetry, see Walter Hinderer, ed., *Geschichte der politischen Lyrik in Deutschland* (Stuttgart: Reclam, 1978); Lorie Ann Vanchena's *Political Poetry in Periodicals and the Shaping of German National Consciousness in the Nineteenth Century* (New York: Peter Lang, 2000) contains a convincing overview and a well-indexed collection of 950 such poems.
27. See Willi Jasper, *Faust und die Deutschen* (Berlin: Rowohlt, 1998); on drama in general, see Walter Hinck, ed., *Geschichte als Schauspiel* (Frankfurt am Main: Suhrkamp, 1981), and Helmut Scheuer, ed., *Dicter und ihre Nation* (Frankfurt am Main: Suhrkamp, 1993).
28. See Hans Belting, *The Germans and Their Art: A Troublesome Relationship*, Scott Kleager, trans. (New Haven, CT: Yale University Press, 1998).
29. I have also excluded book reviews, because I believe that opinions about quality and adherence to various norms are of less impact than the narratives contained in the texts themselves. The authors' focus on a national discourse of history is clear to me whether or not critics highlighted the tendency in contemporary reviews.
30. See Markus Reisenleitner, *Die Produktion historischen Sinnes: Mittelalter-*

rezeption im deutschsprachigen historischen Trivialroman vor 1848 (Frankfurt am Main: Peter Lang, 1992). In an era of censorship, historians frequently relocated discussions of Austro-Prussian rivalry to the less dangerous terrain of German involvement in medieval Italy.

31. Wilhelm Hauff, *Lichtenstein: Romantische Sage aus der württembergischen Geschichte* (1826; Stuttgart: Reclam, 1988). The subtitle, *A Romantic Saga from the History of Württemberg,* indicates the book's provincial rather than national orientation. Belgum and Confino both argue that provincial images were frequently vague enough to conjure up scenes of Germany in general—its small towns, lush scenery, and happy peasants. I contend the argument applies far better to writing at the end of the century than to the material I discuss in chapter 2, which treats the period 1815–30, when caste and local identities trumped nationalism.

32. See Günther Hirschmann, *Kulturkampf im historischen Roman der Gründerzeit, 1859–1878* (Munich: Fink, 1978).

33. See Jürgen Link and Wulf Wülfing, eds., *Nationale Mythen und Symbole in der zweiten Hälfte des 19. Jahrhunderts: Strukturen und Funtionen von Konzeptionen nationaler Identität* (Stuttgart: Klett-Cotta, 1991), and Wulf Wülfing, Karin Bruns, and Rolf Parr, *Historische Mytholgie der Deutschen, 1798–1918* (Munich: Fink, 1991). New material, much of it popular, appeared in 2001 to mark the three hundredth anniversary of Prussia's becoming a kingdom rather than an imperial electorate. In the present context, see, for example, Günter de Bruyn, *Preußens Luise: Vom Entstehen und Vergehen einer Legende* (Berlin: Siedler, 2001), and Philipp Demandt, *Luisenkult: Die Unsterblichkeit der Königen von Preußen* (Cologne: Böhlau, 2003).

34. For an appreciation of both the conflict and the connection between region and nation, see Celia Applegate, *A Nation of Provincials: The German Idea of Heimat* (Berkeley: University of California Press, 1990), which concentrates on the Pfalz in southwest Germany; Alon Confino, *The National as a Local Metaphor: Württemberg, Imperial Germany, and National Memory, 1872–1918* (Chapel Hill: University of North Carolina Press, 1997); and Abigail Green, *Fatherlands: State-Building and Nationhood in Nineteenth-Century Germany* (Cambridge: Cambridge University Press, 2001), which deals with Hanover, Saxony, and Württemberg.

35. A. Smith, "National Identity," 100–105. To a degree, Smith's focus on "ethnic myths" overlaps with the recent search for "sites of memory," but to my mind his model demands a more coherent narrative and is therefore more useful for mapping national identity. The "sites" movement comes from Pierre Nora, ed., *Realms of Memory: The Construction of the French Past,* Lawrence D. Kritzman, ed., Arthur Goldhammer, trans. (New York:

Columbia University Press, 1996), 3 vols.; the German version is *Deutsche Erinnerungsorte,* Etienne François and Hagen Schulze, eds. (Munich: Beck, 2001), 3 vols.

36. Schulze, *Germany,* reports that in 1831 Berlin had eighty bookstores compared with forty-three in Vienna; in "1884 Berlin alone had more bookstores than the whole of Austria" (117).

37. Hans-Ulrich Wehler, *Deutsche Gesellschaftsgeschichte* (Munich: Beck, 1989), 1: 525.

38. See Patricia Herminghouse and Magda Mueller, *Gender and Germanness: Cultural Productions of Nation* (Providence, RI: Berghahn Books, 1997).

39. Italo Calvino, *If on a Winter's Night a Traveler,* trans., William Weaver (New York: Harcourt Brace Jovanovich, 1979), 5.

40. Janice A. Radway, *A Feeling for Books: The Book-of-the-Month Club, Literary Taste, and Middle-Class Desire* (Chapel Hill: University of North Carolina Press, 1997), 102–4. The attraction of such literature continues in Oprah Winfrey's book club, even if Jonathan Franzen now regrets having said as much. I am indebted to Lynne Tatlock for reminding me to consider the issue in these terms.

41. Max Horkheimer and Theodor W. Adorno, *Dialectic of Enlightenment,* John Cumming, trans. (New York: Continuum, 1969).

42. See, for example, Raymond Williams, *Culture and Society, 1780–1950* (New York: Harper & Row, 1958). The divide is neither national nor unbridgeable. Writing at roughly the same time as Williams and apparently unaware of Horkheimer and Adorno, British scholar Richard Hoggart, in *The Uses of Literacy: Changing Patterns in English Mass Culture* (Fair Lawn, NJ: Essential Books, 1957), laments "the creation of mass culture," calling it "in some important ways less healthy than the often crude culture it is replacing" (23–24).

43. The key text in this movement is Gilles Deleuze and Félix Guattari, *Kafka: Toward a Minor Literature,* Dana Polan, trans. (Minneapolis: University of Minnesota Press, 1986). Of course, Kafka's writings are everything but trivial. Whether his work is popular or middlebrow remains unclear, but can it really be considered *minor*? Culturally and linguistically, Kafka's German-Jewish roots put him in the minority in Prague, but his work nevertheless offers an odd foundation for any discussion of what most people regard as minor literature.

Chapter 1

1. Michael Riffaterre, *Fictional Truth* (Baltimore: Johns Hopkins University Press, 1990). See also Burghard Damerau, *Literatur und andere Wahrheiten: Warum wir ohne Bücher nicht sein wollen* (Berlin: Aufbau, 1999).

NOTES TO CHAPTER 1

2. Lennard J. Davis, *Factual Fictions: The Origins of the English Novel*, 2nd ed. (Philadelphia: University of Pennsylvania Press, 1996), argues that the distinction between fact and fiction was far less clear as the novel developed. Many, if not most, eighteenth-century novels purported to be true, *Robinson Crusoe* and Goethe's *Werther* being among the prominent examples. And the conceit continues; Laurie King claims to have found papers left behind by Sherlock Holmes's wife, while the "Flashman papers" provide the basis for George MacDonald Fraser's eponymous series of historical novels.
3. "Die Dichtung hat andere Wahrheitsgesetze als die Geschichte" (Theodor Fontane, "Willibald Alexis," in *Erinnerungen: Ausgewählte Schriften und Kritiken*, ed. Walter Keitel and Helmuth Nürnberger, *Aufsätze und Aufzeichnungen: Aufsätze zur Literatur*, ed. Jürgen Kolbe [Frankfurt am Main: Ullstein, 1979], 253). For another view of the larger problem, see Lionel Grossman, *Between History and Literature* (Cambridge, MA: Harvard University Press, 1990), especially chapter 8, "History and Literature: Reproduction or Signification."
4. Gordon Craig, "Fontane als Historiker," in Theodor Fontane, *Der Krieg gegen Frankreich, 1870–1871* (1873–76; Zurich: Manesse, 1985), xvii.
5. "Der Dichter ist Herr über die Geschichte" (Gotthold Ephraim Lessing, "Briefe, Die neueste Literatur betreffend" Dreiundsechzigster Brief, in *Werke II: Kritische und philosophische Schriften* [Munich: Winckler, 1969], 882); "Der Roman ist aus Mangel der Geschichte entstanden" (Novalis, *Fragmente und Studien, 1799–1800*, in *Schriften*, Richard Samuel, ed., [Stuttgart: W. Kohlhammer Verlag, 1960], 3: 668). Novalis was the pen name for Friedrich von Hardenberg.
6. "Seltsame Grille des volkes! Es verlangt seine Geschichte aus der Hand des Dichters und nicht aus der Hand des Historikers. . . . Sie geben derselben ganz treu, und sei es auch durch selbsterfundene Gestalten und Umstände" (Heinrich Heine, "Italien, 1828," *Reise von München nach Genua*, in Wolfgang Preisendanz, ed., *Werke II: Reisebilder, Erzählende Prosa, Aufsätze* [Frankfurt am Main: Insel, 1968], 251–52).
7. "Zeiten, welche der Dichter leichter versteht, als der Historiker" (Gustav Freytag, *Die Ahnen*, vol. 1, *Ingo und Ingraben*, 1873 [Leipzig: Hirzel, 1906], n.p.).
8. Theodor Fontane, *Schach von Wuthenow: Erzählung aus der Zeit des Regiments Gensdarmes*, 1883, in *Werke und Schriften*, ed. Walter Keitel and Helmuth Nürnberger (Frankfurt am Main: Ullstein, 1992), vol. 8., *A Man of Honor*, trans. E. M. Valk, in *Theodor Fontane: Short Novels and Other Writings*, ed. Peter Demetz (New York: Continuum, 1982).
9. Carlo Ginzburg, *The Cheese and the Worms: The Cosmos of a Sixteenth-Century Miller*, trans. John and Anne Tedeschi (Baltimore: Johns Hopkins

NOTES TO CHAPTER 1

University Press, 1980), and Steven Osment, *The Burgermeister's Daughter: Scandal in a Sixteenth-Century German Town* (New York: St. Martins, 1996). On the *Monumenta,* see G. P. Gooch, *History and Historians in the Nineteenth Century,* 3rd ed. (Boston: Beacon, 1959), 60–71.

10. Friedrich Jaeger and Jörn Rüsen, *Geschichte des Historismus* (Munich: Beck, 1992), 1. The classic account is Georg G. Iggers, *The German Conception of History: The National Tradition of Historical Thought from Herder to the Present* (Hanover, NH: Wesleyan University Press, 1968, 1983).

11. Franz Kugler and Adolph Menzel, *Geschichte des Friedrichs des Grossen* (Leipzig: Verlag der J. J. Weber'schen Buchhandlung, 1840). For a discussion of the book, see chapter 3 of the present text.

12. Professor Franz Kugler published novels under a pseudonym; Felix Dahn was also a professor, as were the novelists Georg Ebers and Adolf Hausrath. Gustav Freytag's career as a novelist began when he was unable to secure a professorship, but he nevertheless published numerous popular histories.

13. Hayden White, "The Burden of History," in *Tropics of Discourse: Essays in Cultural Criticism* (Baltimore: Johns Hopkins University Press, 1978), 43; emphasis original. As a sign that things might now be changing, if ever so slightly, see Simon Schama, *Dead Certainties (Unwarranted Speculations)* (New York: Knopf, 1991), a self-conscious mixture of history and historical fiction written by an eminent historian. Not only does Schama turn to fiction, but he has also gone beyond realist representation. As he writes in an afterword: "In keeping with the self-disrupting nature of the narratives, I have deliberately dislocated the conventions by which histories establish coherence and persuasiveness" (321).

14. Robert C. Holub, *Reflections of Realism: Paradox, Norm, and Ideology in Nineteenth-Century German Prose* (Detroit: Wayne State University Press, 1991); Lilian R. Furst, *All Is True: The Claims and Strategies of Realist Fiction* (Durham, NC: Duke University Press, 1995); Martin Swales, *Epochenbuch Realismus: Romane und Erzählungen* (Munich: Schmidt, 1997); Eric Downing, *Double Exposures: Repetition and Realism in Nineteenth-Century German Fiction* (Stanford, CA: Stanford University Press, 2000); and Todd Kontje, ed., *A Companion to German Realism, 1848–1900* (Rochester, NY: Camden House, 2002). See also Klaus-Detlef Müller, ed., *Bürgerlicher Realismus: Grundlagen und Interpretationen* (Königstein: Athenäum, 1981), and Hugo Aust, *Literatur des Realismus,* 2nd ed. (Stuttgart: Metzler, 1981).

15. A few titles nevertheless merit mention: Hugo Aust, *Der historischer Roman* (Stuttgart: Metzler, 1994); Hans Vilmar Geppert, *Der 'andere' his-*

torische Roman: Theorie und Struktur einer diskontinuierlichen Gattung (Tübingen: Niemeyer, 1976); Gerhard Kebbel, *Geschichtengeneratoren: Lektüren zur Poetik des historischen Romans* (Tübingen: Niemeyer, 1992); and Osman Durrani and Julian Preece, eds., *Travellers in Time and Space/Reisende durch Zeit und Raum: The German Historical Novel/Der deutschsprachige historische Roman* (Amsterdam: Rodopi, 2001), *Amsterdamer Beiträge zur neueren Germanistik*, vol. 51.

16. I admit to the same vice, which provides an opportunity to illustrate how novelists play with the boundary between fiction and fact. Hillary Tamar, the narrator of Sarah Caudwell's novel *The Shortest Way to Hades* (New York: Dell, 1984) and a professor of history, laments the constraints her profession places on what she claims, within the world of the novel, to be factual: "Would that the historian might be permitted to have regard to Art rather than Truth and so enliven the narrative with descriptions of scenes known only by hearsay or speculation" (2).

17. The classic statement of this position is Erich Auerbach, *Mimesis: The Representation of Reality in Western Literature*, trans. Willard R. Trask (Princeton, NJ: Princeton University Press, 1953). For an account of realism in art, see Linda Nochlin, *Realism* (New York: Penguin, 1971). Swales calls mimesis a breathtaking swindle in which the creative process of human perception is reduced to writing; the lack of textual awareness is realism's greatest fiction (132).

18. Charles Dickens, *David Copperfield* (New York: Modern Library, n.d. [1850]), 179.

19. "Dem Dichter ist es indes zuweilen vergönnt, eine andre Sonde in die Brust zu senken, wie er ja auch Geister und Träume zitiert, wo er der Vermittler zwischen dem Reich des Unsichtbaren und des Sichtbaren bedarf" (Willibald Alexis, *Ruhe ist die erste Bürgerpflicht* [1852; Frankfurt am Main: Ullstein, 1985], 27).

20. See Anthony Grafton, *The Footnote: A Curious History* (Cambridge, MA: Harvard University Press, 1997). It is worth noting that Grafton first published this book in Germany, where its title was "the tragic origins of the German footnote."

21. Thomas G. Pavel, *Fictional Worlds* (Cambridge, MA: Harvard University Press, 1986), 16.

22. Norbert Otto Eke, "Eine Gesamtbibliographie des deutschen Romans, 1815–1830. Anmerkungen zum Problemfeld von Bibliographie und Historiographie," in *Zeitschrift für Germanistik* Neue Folge 2 (1993): 301. More recently, Günter Mühlberger and Kurt Habitzel give the nod to Christian Traugott Voigt's *Athelin von Brutthow oder der Kreuzzug: Ein historischer Roman* (1794), in "The German Historical Novel from 1780 to 1945: Utilising the Insbruck Database," Manfred Nikolussi, trans., in

Durrani and Preece, *Travellers in Time*, 18.
23. Dennis Sweet, introduction to Naubert's "The Cloak," in Jeannine Blackwell and Susanne Zantrop, eds., *Bitter Healing: German Women Writers, 1700–1830* (Lincoln: University of Nebraska Press, 1990), 204.
24. Eggert, *Studien zur Wirkungsgeschichte*, 213–46.
25. For a complete bibliography and a brief interpretation of Mühlbach's life and work, see my article in the *Dictionary of Literary Biography*, vol. 133, *Nineteenth-Century German Writers to 1840*, ed. James Hardin and Siegfried Mews (Detroit: Gale Research, 1993), 204–10. There is also a very useful introduction to Mühlbach in "Clara Mundts Briefe an Hermann Costenoble: Zu L. Mühlbach's historischen Romanen," William H. McClain and Lieselotte E. Kurth-Voigt, eds., *Archiv für Geschichte des Buchwesens* 22 (1981): 917–52.
26. I think the case for Mühlbach's radicalism is somewhat overstated; the early novels all pull back from the political positions with which they start. Compare Renate Möhrmann, *Die andere Frau: Emanzipationsansätze deutscher Schriftstellerinnen im Vorfeld der Achtundvierziger-Revolution* (Stuttgart: Metzler, 1977), esp. 60–84.
27. These so-called double-, triple-, and quadruple-deckers kept the libraries' patrons coming back for more, and they also circulated more rapidly (and more profitably) than thick, one-volume editions.
28. Eggert, *Studien zur Wirkungsgeschichte*, 212. There were three editions in 1857, and one each in the years 1858, 1859, 1862–64, and 1882.
29. Martino, *Die deutsche Leihbibliothek*, 404, 410. On Mühlbach's American career, see Lieselotte E. Kurth-Voigt and William H. McClain, "Louise Mühlbach's Historical Novels: The American Reception," *Internationales Archiv für Sozialgeschichte der deutschen Literatur* 6 (1981): 52–77.
30. The complete cycle includes *Friedrich der Große und sein Hof* (Berlin: Janke, 1853), trans. Mrs. Chapman Coleman and her daughters as *Frederick the Great and His Court: An Historical Romance* (New York: Appleton, 1866); *Berlin und Sanssouci oder Friedrich der Große und seine Freunde* (Berlin: Simion, 1854), trans. Mrs. Coleman and her daughters as *Berlin and Sans-souci: or, Frederick the Great and His Friends: An Historical Romance* (New York: Appleton, 1867); *Friedrich der Große und seine Geschwister* (Berlin: Janke, 1855), trans. by Mrs. Coleman and her daughters as *Frederick the Great and His Family: An Historical Novel* (New York: Appleton, 1867); and *Deutschland in Sturm und Drang: Historischer Roman* (Jena: Costenoble, 1867–68). The first four volumes of *Deutschland in Sturm und Drang* are titled *Der alte Fritz und seine Zeit*, trans., Peter Langley as *Old Fritz and the New Era* (New York: Appleton, 1868), but Frederick doesn't actually die until the fifth volume of the series, the one entitled *Fürsten und Dichter*, trans. Chapman Coleman, as

NOTES TO CHAPTER 1

Goethe and Schiller: An Historical Romance (Akron, OH: New Werner, 1867). Unless otherwise noted, I quote from *The Works of Louisa Mühlbach in Eighteen Volumes* (New York: Collier, 1902), which is a reprint of the Appleton edition.

31. Although Grafton demonstrates how dependent Ranke was on earlier scholars, for all practical purposes the Berlin historian remains the father of modern academic history. See Grafton, 62–93.
32. "Blos zeigen, wie es eigentlich gewesen" (Leopold von Ranke, *Geschichten der romanischen und germanischen Völker von 1494 bis 1514*, 1824, in *Sämmtliche Werke* [Leipzig: Duncker und Humblot, 1874], 33: vii).
33. Walter Scotts Werke "trugen hauptsächlich dazu bei, die Theilnahme an dem Thun und Lassen der vergangenen Zeiten zu erwecken.... und ich las mehr als eins dieser Werke mit lebendiger Theilnahme" (Ranke, "Aufsätze zur eigenen Lebensbeschreibung: 4. Diktat vom November 1885," in *Sämmtliche Werke*, 54: 61). The offending novel was Scott's *Quentin Durward*.
34. "Ich war gleichsam beleidigt im Namen der alten Fürsten.... Ich empfand Widerwillen gegen den historischen Roman" (Ranke, "Am neunzigsten Geburtstag, 21. Dezember, 1885," in *Sämmtliche Werke*, 52: 596).
35. "Ich studierte Commines und die gleichzeitigen Berichte, die den neuen Ausgaben dieses Autors beigelegt sind, und überzeugte mich, daß ein Karl der Kühne, ein Ludwig XI., wie sie bei Scott geschildert wurden, niemals existirt hatten. Das wußte der würdige und gelehrte Autor wohl auch selbst; aber ich konnte ihm nicht verzeihen, daß er in seine Darstellungen Züge aufgenommen hatte, die vollkommen unhistorisch waren, und sie doch so vortrug, als glaubte er daran. Bei der Vergleichung überzeugte ich mich, daß das historisch Ueberlieferte selbst schöner und jedenfalls interessanter sei, als die romantische Fiction. Ich wandte mich hierauf überhaupt von ihr ab und faßte den Gedanken, bei meinen Arbeiten alles Ersonnene und Erdichtete zu vermeiden und mich streng an die Thatsachen zu halten" (Ranke, "Lebensbeschreibung," in *Sämmtliche Werke*, 54: 61). The French historian Philippe de Commines (1445–1511) was a contemporary of Charles the Bold and Louis XI; his memoirs were so evenhanded that some consider him, not Ranke, the first modern historian.
36. "Ich leugne nicht, daß mich diese Erwägungen in der kritischen Methode befestigten, welche dann als das Kennzeichen meiner Werke betrachtet worden ist; das heißt, bei dem stehen zu bleiben, was wörtlich überliefert ist, oder was sich daraus mit einer gewissen Sicherheit entwickeln läßt"; "[Daß] alles vermieden werden muß, was von der beglaubigten Ueberlieferungen der Thatsachen wesentlich abweicht" (Ranke, "Am neunzigsten Geburtstag," in *Sämmtliche Werke*, 52: 596).

NOTES TO CHAPTER 1

37. "Das Volk muß seine Helden nicht blos durch die Thaten, durch die historischen Begebenheiten, die sich an ihr leuchtendes Dasein anknüpfen, kennen lernen, . . .es muß hinter dem Helden auch den Menschen sehen und begreifen. Es muß seine Helden nicht blos bewundern mit dem Kopfe, sondern sie auch lieben mit dem Herzen." I found the advertisement in the inside back cover of George Hesekiel, *Stille vor dem Sturm* (Berlin: Janke, 1863), vol. 2. For a discussion of Hesekiel's novel, see chapter 4 of the present text.
38. "In den Räumen des venezianischen Archivs verweilt man mit Erstaunen und Vergnügen. . . . Deutlich wieder zu erkennen ist doch allein derjenige Theil des Lebens, der in Schriften aufbewahrt worden." (1831; Ranke, "Die Verschwörung gegen Venedig im Jahre 1618: Mit Urkunden aus dem venezianischen Archiv," in *Sämmtliche Werke*, 42: 172–73). In spite of everything written about Ranke and the question of objectivity in history, few have looked at the issue of selection or choice. An exception is Gunter Berg, *Leopold von Ranke als Akademischer Lehrer: Studien zu seinen Vorlesungen und seinem Geschichtsdenken* (Göttingen: Vandenhoeck and Ruprecht, 1968), esp. 180–99. See also, among his many useful essays, Jörn Rüsen, "Ranke's Historiography: A Theoretical Approach," in Gisela Brude-Firnau and Karin J. MacHardy, eds., *Fact and Fiction: German History and Literature, 1848–1924* (Tübingen: Franke, 1990), 41–56.
39. "Es kann nur darauf ankommen, eine Gesammtanschauung der politischen Handlungen Friedrichs und seiner kriegerischen Thaten zu gewinnen und der Nation vorzulegen" (Ranke, "Friedrich II. König von Preußen," in *Sämmtliche Werke*, 51: 359).
40. "Die allgemeine Bewegung ist das eigentlich Lebendige in der Geschichte; wahre Bedeutung hat der Staatsmann nur in sofern, als er sie an seiner Stelle fördert und vielleicht leitet" (Ranke, "Hardenberg und die Geschichte des preußischen Staates von 1793–1813," in *Sämmtliche Werke*, 46: vi).
41. "Die Disciplin des Schreckens stählte die Seele Friedrichs, die dadurch doch nicht unterjocht wurde" (Ranke, "Friedrich II. König von Preußen," in *Sämmtliche Werke*, 51: 361). Of course, popular historians were much guiltier of psychologizing beyond the evidence; for a typical example from *Die Gartenlaube*, see Belgum, 22.
42. Ranke, "Friedrich II. König von Preußen," in *Sämmtliche Werke*, 51: 362; that sentence reads: "Frederick retreated to his country home at Rheinsberg and occupied himself with his music and books; he took the studies of earlier years seriously, and they raised him far above the intellectual horizon of his father." ("Dann aber zog er sich auf seinen Landsitz Rheisberg zurück, um sich mit seiner Musik und seinen Büchern zu beschäftigen; mit den Studien der früheren Jahre machte er nun Ernst; sie

erhoben ihn über den geistigen Horizont seines Vaters.")
43. Again, the phrase is Theodor Scheider's.
44. See Hayden White, *Metahistory: The Historical Imagination in Nineteenth-Century Europe* (Baltimore: Johns Hopkins University Press, 1973).
45. For want of a better term, I reluctantly use Riffaterre's phrase, but I differ from his usage. Riffaterre seems content to label as true those works that are internally consistent, while I make a claim for historical fiction that parallels the truth claim made by historians for their work.
46. "Es fällt mir gar nicht ein, gegen solche gelerht thuende Krittler den historischen Roman, oder mich selber zu vertheidigen. . . . weil ihre Geschichtskenntniß so mangelhaft ist, daß sie jene Thatsachen nicht wußten" (Mühlbach, "Vorwort," *Deutschland im Sturm und Drang*, Teil I, *Der alte Fritz und die neue Zeit*, vi-vii, "The Historical Romance," in Mühlbach, *Old Fritz and the New Era*, Mrs. Chapman Coleman, trans.[New York: Collier, 1902], 1–5).
47. For Georg Lukács, it is the use of history as "mere costumery" that separates genuine historical novels from potboilers that happen to be set in the past. See *The Historical Novel*, trans. Hannah and Stanley Mitchell (Lincoln: University of Nebraska Press, 1983), 19. It is worth noting that practitioners seem to have found it difficult to make the distinction. For example, in the "Nachwort" to her *Graf Ernst von Mansfeld und seine Zeitgenossen: Seitenstück zu Friedrich dem Fünften, König von Böhmen und Churfürsten von der Pfalz* (Leipzig: Lauffer, 1825), Wilhelmine von Gersdorf writes: "I have remained as faithful as possible to the truth . . . and I have only, now and again, used literary invention [*Dichtung*] for help in adding living colors to the solemn background out of consideration for those readers who read more for entertainment than for historical instruction" (226–27).
48. Mühlbach, *Old Fritz*, 1; "Was ist aber dieses große, dieses erhabene Ziel des historischen Romanschriftstellers? Es ist dieses: die Geschichte zu illustriren, sie populär zu machen; die großen Gestalten, wie die großen Thatsachen, welche in den Büchern der Geschichte dem Gelehrten, dem höher Gebildeten sich enthüllten, aus der stillen Studierzimmer hinaus zu tragen auf den Markt des Lebens und zum Gemeingut Aller zu machen, was bis dahin nur das Gut des Gelehrten war" (Mühlbach, *Der alte Fritz*, viii).
49. Mühlbach, *Old Fritz*, 2; "Der strenge Geschichtschreiber hat es mit den Thatsachen zu thun, er darf nur nach strengster äußerlicher Wahrheit das niederschreiben und verzeichnen, was sich äußerlich begeben hat" (Mühlbach, *Der alte Fritz*, ix).
50. Mühlbach, *Old Fritz*, 2, italics original; "Der Gelehrte zeigt Euch das äußere Angesicht, die mächtige Gestalt der Geschichte, der historische

Roman soll Euch das Herz der Geschichte zeigen, und so Euch menschlich lieb nahe bringen, was sonst Euch hoch und fern gestanden" (Mühlbach, *Der alte Fritz*, ix).

51. Mühlbach, *Old Fritz*, 2; "muß mit seinem ganzen Geist und seinem ganzen Denken sich hingeben an das Studium der Zeitepoche, welche er schildern will, so daß er mit ihr lebt, mit ihr fühlt" (Mühlbach, *Der alte Fritz*, ix).
52. R. G. Collingwood, *The Idea of History* (Oxford: Oxford University Press, 1946).
53. Erich Auerbach comments on the common practice of fictitious speeches in antique history, using Tacitus as an example, *Mimesis*, 39–42.
54. Mühlbach, *Old Fritz*, 3, Again the translator softens Mühlbach's polemic by omitting the portion in square brackets; "Die Erhellung des Dunkels der Geschichte, welches die Historiker nothwendiger Weise übrig lassen müssen, weil nicht immer die Quellen dazu da sind, und der strenge Historiker nur aus den Quellen schöpfen darf" (Mühlbach, *Der alte Fritz*, x).
55. Mühlbach, *Old Fritz*, 2; "die schöpferische Phantasie des Dichters" (Mühlbach, *Der alte Fritz*, x).
56. Mühlbach, *Old Fritz*, 3; "Die Erhellung der Triebfedern, welche die einzelnen geschichtlichen Personen zu großen historischen Handlungen geführt, und aus den äußerlich unbedeutend erscheinenden Ereignissen ihres Lebens sich ihr innerstes Denken und Sein klar zu machen und es Andern klar hinzustellen" (Mühlbach, *Der alte Fritz*, xi).
57. Mühlbach, *Old Fritz*, 3; "auf dem Fundamente der Geschichte das Gebäude der Poesie aufzuführen, das dennoch ganz durchleuchtet und durchdrungen ist von der Wahrheit der Geschichte" (Mühlbach, *Der alte Fritz*, xii).
58. Mühlbach, *Old Fritz*, 3–4; "daß es dabei durchaus nebensächlich ist, ob die in dem historischen Romane handelnden historischen Personen dieses oder jenes Wort wirklich gesprochen, diese oder jene nebensächliche Handlung so gethan; es kommt nur darauf an, daß diese Worte und diese Handlungen in dem Geist und Charakter jener historischen Personen gehalten sind, und daß man ihnen nichts andichtet, was sie nicht gesprochen oder gethan haben könnten" (Mühlbach, *Der alte Fritz*, xii).
59. For a survey of the issues and the dilemmas any criteria raise, see Jochen Schulte-Sasse, *Literarische Wertung*, 2nd ed. (Stuttgart: Metzler, 1976).
60. See Peter Uwe Hohendahl, *Building a National Literature: The Case of Germany, 1830–1870,* trans. Renate Baron Franciscono (Ithaca, NY: Cornell University Press, 1989). Ruth-Ellen Boetcher Joeres has taken a new look at the exclusion of woman from the canon in her *Respectability and Deviance: Nineteenth-Century German Women Writers and the*

NOTES TO CHAPTER 1

Ambiguity of Representation (Chicago: University of Chicago Press, 1998), esp. 35–77.

61. Mühlbach, *Frederick the Great and His Court,* 341; "Die Zeit der trägen Ruhe ist vorüber, und es wird endlich Leben und Bewegung in diese rostige und knarrende Maschine der Staaten kommen" (Mühlbach, *Friedrich der Grosse und sein Hof,* 81).

62. Mühlbach, *Frederick the Great and His Court,* 340; "Alles war vorhergesehen, Alles vorbereitet, und es handelt sich nur um die Ausführung der Entwürfe, die ich seit langer Zeit in meinen Kopfe bewegt habe" (Mühlbach, *Friedrich der Große und sein Hof,* 3: 82).

63. "Man darf nicht bezweifeln, daß der Entwurf dazu, der zu den geheimsten Papieren gehörte, die von Fürst auf Fürst übergingen, dem neu eintretenden König bekannt geworden ist" (Ranke, "Friedrich II," in *Sämmtliche Werke,* 51: 364).

64. Mühlbach, *Berlin and Sans-Souci,* 144; "Und glaubst du denn, daß ich dafür kein Herz und kein Empfinden habe, weil ich ein König bin? Geh'! Ich habe obwohl dein König, doch die Augen und die Nase eines Menschen, und bin empfänglich für die Schönheit und den Blumenduft!" (Mühlbach, *Berlin und Sanssouci,* 2: 55).

65. Mühlbach, *Berlin and Sans-Souci,* 197; "Er hat kein Herz. Er kann niemals lieben, und Schmach und Schande über das Weib, welches liebt, ohne geliebt zu werden. Er liebt nichts als sein Preußen, seinen Ruhm und seine Größe" (Mühlbach, *Berlin und Sanssouci,* 2: 142).

66. Mühlbach, *Berlin and Sans-Souci,* 201; "Ich darf nicht thun, was jeder Mann an meiner Stelle thun würde. Ich nicht, denn—ich bin der König!" (Mühlbach, *Berlin und Sanssouci,* 2: 150).

67. Mühlbach, *Berlin and Sans-Souci,* 212; "Sie werden bleiben, sagte er, ich befehle es Ihnen! Ich, nicht der König, sondern ich" (Mühlbach, *Berlin und Sanssouci,* 2: 170).

68. Mühlbach, *Berlin and Sans-Souci,* 360; "Man verzeihe es, wenn wir von der Freiheit des Dichters Gebrauch machend, diese vier Jahre überspringen, und diesen vierten Band mit dem Jahre 1750 beginnen, mit demjenigen Jahre, welches die Geschichtschreiber gewohnt sind, als das glücklichste und sonnenhellste Jahr in dem Leben König Friedrich's des Zweiten zu bezeichnen.—Aber man weiß wohl, daß das Glück immer nur der schönen Purpurrose gleicht, welche trotz ihrer Schönheit, mit der sie uns erfreut, doch immer auch ihre Dornen hat, mit denen sie uns verwundet" (Mühlbach, *Berlin und Sanssouci,* 4: 7).

69. "Es ist mir um die innere Charaterentwicklung dieses großen Mannes zu thun gewesen, den Viele nur als den kühnen Helden, Viele als den weisen Gesetzgeber, den selbstregierenden König, sehr Wenige aber als den edlen, zartfühlenden, weichen Menschen kennen, der er wirklich war. Ich

NOTES TO CHAPTER 1

wollte Friedrich als den Menschen zeichnen, und aus seiner Seele und seinem Herzen heraus sein Leben entwickeln." The passage was omitted from the English translation; Eggert quotes it as if it were from *Friedrich der Große und sein Hof* (3: ix), but the whole cycle exists in a maddening array of editions, which were sometimes issued or bound together. The version to which I have access includes *Friedrich der Große und seine Geschwister* as part of that former work, and the quotation is from the Dritte Folge, Zweite Abteilung, Band I, ix.

70. Mühlbach, *Berlin and Sans-Souci*, 313; "Der König hat Dir gezürnt, der Bruder will mit Dir weinen. Komm, Amelia, komm an ein treues Bruderherz!" (Mühlbach, *Berlin und Sanssouci*, 3: 165).

71. Mühlbach, *Berlin and Sans-Souci*, 314; "Ich habe in dieser Stunde eine Schwester verloren, und ich habe sie sehr geliebt. Nun denn, Denen, die man liebt und die uns gestorben sind, pflegt man ein Denkmal zu setzen, ein Denkmal der Erinnerung und der Liebe. Arme, gestorbene Schwester, ich will Dir ein Denkmal setzen. Der König hat seine Schwester unglücklich machen müssen, dafür soll der König versuchen, sein Land glücklich zu machen, und wenn es denn kein Gesetz giebt, welches eine Prinzessin gegen den König anrufen kann, so soll es wenigstens für alle meine Unterthanen Gesetze geben, die sie schützen, und der Vernunft, dem Recht und dem göttlichen Gleichheitsprinzip der Menschen entsprechen! Ja, ich will meinem Lande ein neues Gesetzbuch, ich will meinem Volke ein allgemeines Landrecht geben. Das, Amalie, sei das Denkmal, welches ich Dir in meinem Herzen errichte" (Mühlbach, *Berlin und Sanssouci*, 166).

72. Ranke, "Friedrich II. König von Preußen," in *Sämmtliche Werke*, 51: 383–86.

73. Johann Gustav Droysen, *Historik: Historisch-kritische Ausgabe*, ed. Peter Leyh (Stuttgart, Bad Cannstatt: Frommann-Holzboog, 1977). Droysen held these lectures repeatedly during his long tenure in Berlin, principally in the years 1857, 1858, and 1882.

74. Johann Gustav Droysen, *Das Leben des Feldmarschalls Grafen Yorck von Wartenburg* (Berlin: Veit, 1851–52); and Fontane, "Was soll ich lesen?" in *Aufsätze zur Literatur*, 372–74.

75. "[P]oetische Wahrheit," Droysen, *Historik*, 239.

76. "Ranke hat die Kunst der Charakterzeichnung recht in den Vordergrund gestellt, nicht bloß die intellektuellen, sondern auch die moralischen Eigenschaften der Personen liebt er zu schildern, ja er geht dann wohl so weit, auch die Äußerlichkeiten der Kleidung, der Stimme, der äußeren Bewegung mit heranzuziehen, so daß man die Menschen wie leibhaftig vor sich zu sehen meint. . . . Allerdings nähert sich so die Erzählung der Anschaulichkeit eines historischen Romans" (Droysen, *Historik*, 239).

77. "Denn daß Friedrich auf der Flöte blies oder Caesar einige grammatische Schriften verfaßt hat, ist zwar sehr interessant, aber für die große geschichtliche Tätigkeit beider äußerst gleichgültig" (ibid., 243).
78. "Ich leugne nicht, daß ich die größte Scheu vor dieser Art von Anschaulichkeit habe; je länger ich mit Menschen lebe, desto bedenklicher werde ich, ihren Charakter mit Sicherheit zu erfassen, und je länger ich Geschiccte studiere, desto mehr erscheint es mir höchst bedenklich, Personen, von denen ich nur Urteile anderer habe, mir so auszumalen, daß ihre Persönlichkeit kongruent mit dem erscheint, was sie getan" (ibid., 239).
79. "Ich für mein Teil kann mich nicht bekehren zu diesem faschen Realismus" (ibid., 240).
80. "Wir bedürfen einer Darstellungsform, in der nicht die Erzälhung die Hauptsache ist" (ibid., 249).
81. "Nie hat sich ein Staat aus tieferem Sturz schneller und stolzer erhoben als Preußen nach dem Tage von Jena" (Droysen, *Das Leben Yorcks*, 1.
82. "Ohne alle Frage befand sich die Armee in einem Zustande taktischer Vollkommenheit. . . . Aber in Mitte dieser Ueberreife in kleinen Dingen begann man mit einer gewissen Unruhe inne zu werden, daß man in eben den Richtungen, denen Bonaparte seine wachsende Glorie bedankte, im hohen Maas unreif sei, daß man weder die Ideen, noch die Charactere, noch die Leidenschaft besaß, welche die Größe bedingen" (ibid., 118).
83. "Yorcks ganze Art konnten diese Dinge nicht anders als in hohem Maas peinlich sein" (ibid., 119).
84. "Es liegen keine Materialien vor, aus denen zu entnehmen wäre, wie Yorck in diesen peinlichen Monaten die Lage Preußens auffaßte. Man wird kaum irren, wen man annimmt" (ibid., 136).
85. See Craig, "Fontane als Historiker"; Craig speculates that in an era of excessive patriotism, Fontane's evenhandedness when dealing with the French might have cost him readers.
86. I rely here on the editorial apparatus in the German edition of *Schach*, particularly 144–50 and 165–67.
87. Fontane, *Man of Honor*, 20; "die Verkörperung jener preußischen Beschränktheit" (Fontane, *Schach*, 24).
88. Ibid.; "Er ist durchaus Zeiterscheinung. . . . Der sich in dieser Art und Weise nur in Seiner Königlichen Majestät von Preußen Haupt- und Residenzstadt, oder, wenn über diese hinaus, immer nur in der Reihen unsrer nachgeborenen friderizianischen Armee zutragen konnte, einer Armee, die statt der Ehre nur noch den Dünkel, und statt der Seele nur noch ein Uhrwerk hat—ein Uhrwerk, das bald genug abgelaufen sein wird" (Fontane, *Schach*, 130).
89. "Die Darstellung jener Epoche politischer Unfähigkeit, hohlen Dünkels

und sittlichen Falls. Daß ich persönlich über jenen ganzen Zeitabschnitt *viel* milder denke . . . W. Alexis sah die Dinge so an; Hunderttausende mit ihm; die große Geschichtsschreibung nicht minder" (Fontane, "Willibald Alexis," 248).

90. "Die Studien allein machen es freilich nicht, ein historischer Blick und ein rückwärts gewandtes prophetisches Ahnungsvermögen müssen hinzukommen. Aber diesen Blick und dies Ahnungsvermögen haben echte Poeten fast immer" (Fontane, "Josef Viktor von Scheffel," in *Erinnerungen: Ausgewählte Schriften und Kritiken*, 207).
91. Fontane, *Man of Honor*, 4; "Alles, was zum welfischen Löwen oder zum springenden Roß hält, will sich nicht preußisch regieren lassen. Und ich verdenk' es keinem. Für die Polen reichten wir allenfalls aus. Aber die Hannoveraner sind feine Leute" (Fontane, *Schach*, 8).
92. Fontane differs from Alexis, who calls historians "windbags" (*Windbeutel*) with no respect for tradition; Alexis also terms Ranke's critical method "conjecture" (*kritischen Konjekturen*). *Isegrimm* (Leipzig: Hesse and Becker, n.d. [1854]), 369, 384.
93. Fontane, *Man of Honor*, 44; "'Oder glauben Sie wirklich, daß der Odem Gottes im Spezialdienste des Protestantismus, oder gar Preußens und seiner Armee steht?' 'Ich hoffe, ja'" (Fontane, *Schach*, 48).
94. "Im letzten immer nur unsre eigene Kraft auch unsre Sicherheit, beziehungsweise unsre Rettung sein werde" (Fontane, *Schach*, 63).
95. Alexis's repsonse comes in an afterword to his novel *Isegrimm*, where he pleads helplessness "when history paints a darker image of things than literature." ("Wenn nun aber die Geschichte die geschehenen Dinge noch schwärzer malt als die Dichtung!" 723).
96. *Historik*, 217–83, where Droysen differentiates between "erzählende," "untersuchende," and "didaktische" Darstellungen.
97. "Der große Historiker müsse immer auch Poet sein" (Fontane, "Scheffel," 207).
98. Again, see Assmann and Lamberti, as well as Fontane's *Der Stechlin*.
99. "Der Verfasser dieses Buches will unserem Volke und insbesondere der vaterländischen Jugend geschichtlich treu, aber im leichten Gewande der Erzählung, einen bedeutungsvollen Abschnitt . . . zeigen" (Franz Otto [Spamer], *Der Große König und Sein Rekrut: Lebensbilder aus der Zeit des Siebenjährigen Krieges* [Leipzig: Spamer, 1873], v).
100. "Was ich will, dessen wenigstens bin ich mir klar bewußt: dem deutschen Volke seine Geschichte in angenehmer Form populär und lieb machen, ihm Liebe und Freude für seine Specialgeschichte einflößen, . . . [und] ihm Thatsachen der Geschichte zu einem wirklichen Stück Leben umzuwandeln" (Mühlbach, *Der alte Fritz*, viii). Here, the English translation mistakenly substitutes "our national history" for "the German people" (2).

NOTES TO CHAPTER 2

Chapter 2

1. "Lieber Gott, daß ich ein Mensch bin, dafür preise ich dich und freue mich! Auch dafür, daß ich ein Deutscher bin! Aber auch dafür, daß ich ein Preuße bin!" (Friedrich de la Motte Fouqué, *Der Refugié oder Heimat und Fremde: Ein Roman aus der neueren Zeit* [Gotha und Erfurt: Hennings'sche Buchhandlung, 1824], reprinted as vol. 10 of *Sämmtliche Romane und Novellenbücher,* Wolfgang Möhrig, ed. [Hildesheim: Olms, 1989]), here 2: 53 (vol. 10 is divided into three parts to correspond to the three volumes of the original novel).
2. "Preußenthum kann eben nur Deutschthum seyn! Und im Deutschthum soll das Preußenthum verschwinden!" (Fouqué, *Refugié,* 2: 54).
3. For example, Arndt's "Was ist des Deutschen Vaterland" (1812), Körner's "Lützows wilde, verwegene Jagd" (1814), and Kleist's *Katechismus der Deutschen* (1809).
4. Otto W. Johnston, *The Myth of a Nation: Literature and Politics in Prussia under Napoleon* (Columbia, SC: Camden House, 1989), argues that concerted nationalist efforts orchestrated by Baron vom Stein in 1807–15 collapsed after the end of the Wars of Liberation.
5. James J. Sheehan, "State and Nationality in the Napoleonic Period," in John Breuilly, ed., *The State of Germany: The National Idea in the Making, Unmaking, and Remaking of a Modern Nation-State* (London: Longman, 1992), 48.
6. See Eke and Martino. Martino lists August Lafontaine, August von Kotzebue, and Karl Gottlob Cramer as the most widely held authors in lending libraries for the period 1815–25; for 1815–48, as an indication of the popularity of historical fiction, Walter Scott became the second most widely held author, behind Lafontaine and ahead of Kotzebue. Of the authors dealt with in this chapter, Julius von Voß was ninth on the list of "Erfolgsautoren 1815–25," while Fouqué was eleventh, and Christoph Hildebrandt was twentieth. For 1815–48, Voß had fallen to sixteenth place, Fouqué to thirtieth, while Hildebrandt had risen to eleventh. The latter list also includes H. E. R. Belani (no. 26), Wilhemine von Gersdorf (no. 49), and Willibald Alexis (no. 97). C. J. Oldendorp and E. Auerbach each authored a single book and were therefore unlikely to show up in statistics based on the number of volumes held by libraries. See Martino, 27–78.
7. "Die Eule der Minerva beginnt erst mit der einbrechenden Dämmerung ihren Flug" (Georg Wilhelm Friedrich Hegel, *Grundlinien der Philosophie des Rechts,* Helmut Reichelt, ed. [1821; Frankfurt am Main: Ullstein, 1979], 14).
8. See Harry E. Shaw, *The Forms of Historical Fiction: Sir Walter Scott and His Successors* (Ithaca, NY: Cornell University Press, 1983), 19–50; and

NOTES TO CHAPTER 2

Herman J. Sottong, *Transformation und Reaktion: Historisches Erzählen von der Goethezeit zum Realismus* (Munich: Wilhelm Fink, 1992), 9–18.
9. See Hartmut Steinecke et al., *Deutschsprachige Romane 1815–1830 in der Fürstlichen Bibliothek Corvey: Probleme der Erforschung—Bestandsverzeichnis* (Stuttgart: Belser Wissenschaftlicher Dienst, 1991), which lists 612 titles, roughly 60 percent of what was published during the period. It is a broad cross-section of popular and more elite reading matter and includes hundreds of historical novels. I would like to thank Professor Steinecke, his coworkers, and the National Endowment for the Humanities (Summer Stipend, FT-38484-93) for making it possible for me to visit the Corvey collection and to read the material I analyze here.
10. Anderson, *Imagined Communities*, 74.
11. Hinrich C. Seeba, "'Germany—A Literary Concept': The Myth of National Literature," *German Studies Review* 17.2 (1994): 354.
12. "Braven deutschen Jungen" and "französischen Firlefanz" (Fouqué, *Refugié*, 1: 25, 27).
13. "Ehemalige Landsleute" (ibid., 2: 280).
14. "Immer bleicher und bleicher ward Robert Gautier . . . sein Fechten für die schöne, deutsche Sache kam ihm doch auf Einmal wie eine Art von schauerlichem Selbstmord vor" (ibid., 3: 151–52).
15. "O mein schönes Stammland, wir können Dich ja nicht anders erretten, als mit Feuer und Schwerdt! Und ein Sohn soll dazu seine Hand mit leihen? . . . Ein vom Frankenlande gemißhandelter Sohn, heimkehrend auf dieser Weise" (ibid., 3: 342).
16. "Er, dessen leuchtendes Ehrenbild uns jetzt wieder zum Kampf leitet" (ibid., 2: 422).
17. "Wenn Er ein ächter Refugié'ssohn ist, so beweis Er es mit der That, und dräng Er sich rüstig durch die Welt" (ibid., 2: 332).
18. Wilhelmine von Gersdorf, *Das Complott, oder Verrath und Treue. Aus der zweiten Hälfte des achtzehnten Jahrhunderts* (Leipzig: Wilhelm Lauffer, 1830). In addition to being credited with writing the first historical novel in German, *Aurora: Gräfin von Königsmark* (1817), Gersdorf (1768–1847) was one of the most prolific authors of historical fiction in the early years of the century; her name appears twenty-one times in the Corvey catalog of works, and her subject matter ranged from an Armenian woman shipwrecked off the coast of Ireland to a tale of Jacobean England.
19. "Er war der der Eroberer, der Besieger, der Unterdrücker Seines blühenden Vaterlandes, mit dem Recht des Stärkern gab er dort Seinem Volke Gesetze, wo Sein angeerbter, geliebter Fürstenstamm sonst für Sein Wohlergehen sorgte!" (Gersdorf, *Das Complott*, 123–24).
20. "Fliege, eile, dort ruht der König, dort schützen Gottes Engel dem

NOTES TO CHAPTER 2

Gesalbten des Herrn . . . ihm gieb diese Briefe, und du wirst das Werkzeug Gottes seyn, ihm zu retten und diesem Land einen wichtigenen Dienst zu erzeigen" (ibid., 164).

21. C[hristian] J[ohannes] Oldendorp, *Unglück und Rettung oder Jugendschicksale eines Offiziers aus der Zeit Friedrichs des Großen: Eine humoristische Erzählung* (Leipzig: Wilhelm Lauffer, 1826).
22. It is difficult to translate both accurately and ungrammatically: "E wohrer Handelsmann muß glück verkofe's Hemde vom Leib weg, wenn er kann mache e Profitche, aach 'ner so klein" (ibid., 162).
23. "Es ist num eine Gerechtigkeit und Ordnung im Lande. Hören Sie, gnädiger Junker, unser König ist ein Mann" (ibid., 215).
24. "[Erzählungen erregten] bei mir den Wunsch und die Begierde, Soldat zu werden, und so, wie diese ehrwürdigen Männer, mein Leben meinem Könige und Vaterlande zu widmen" (ibid., 228).
25. "Was ich bei allem, was ich sah und hörte, empfand, kann ich unmöglich beschreiben" (ibid., 238).
26. [Johann Andreas] C[hristoph] Hildebrand[t], *Die Familie von Manteufel: Ein historisch-romantisches Gemälde aus den Zeiten des siebenjährigen Kriegs* (Leipzig: Christian Ernst Kollmann, 1826). It is unclear why Hildebrandt spells Manteufel with one "f" rather than two, which was the real family's spelling. In the later nineteenth century, the family's most notable member was Field Marshall Edwin von Manteuffel, one of the heroes of the Franco-Prussian War. Hildebrandt (1764–1848) was another extraordinarily productive author of historical novels. The Corvey catalog lists seventeen of his multivolume works on subjects ranging from tenth-century Huns to a fifteenth-century Albanian uprising against the Turks, as well as three novels set during Frederick's reign.
27. "Der Gang der Geschichte ist bekannt" (Hildebrandt, *Die Familie von Manteufel,* 1: 205).
28. "[Er hatte] für seinen König Friedrich und für sein Vaterland seinen Fuß hingegeben" (ibid., 1: 5).
29. "Was sehr viel sagen will, da das treffliche Regiment fast ganz aus Ungarn und Polacken, also aus geborenen Reitern bestand" (ibid., 1: 200).
30. "Auch ihnen, als treuen Pommern, war die Nachricht [von Roßbach] viel werth" (ibid., 2: 109).
31. "Schwärme von Ungeheuern, die außer der Gestalt nichts Menschliches an sich hatten" (ibid., 2: 178).
32. "[Er] schauderte bei den Gedanken, vielleicht auf seinen Freund zu stoßen; das Herz sprach stärker als der Dienst; Freundschaft herrschte über Dienstverhältniß" (ibid., 2: 12–13).
33. "'Gern würde ich diese Verbindung sehen,' sagte der Graf Harrasch, 'wenn Manteufel die preußische Dienste verläßt und in unsere Heer tritt'" (ibid.,

NOTES TO CHAPTER 2

3: 136).
34. "Ein braver Mann bleibt immer brav und es ist einerlei, ob er auf der Satteltasche Friedrich Rex oder Maria Theresia hat . . . es bleibt ja nicht immer Krieg! Die großen Herren werden der Katzbalgerei auch satt" (ibid., 3: 154).
35. "Meinen König und mein Land verlasse ich nie. Beide haben zu viel an mir gethan als daß ich ihnen mit Undank lohnen könnte" (ibid., 3: 156).
36. "Nimm die beiden Güter und bleib Preuße von nun an bis in alle Ewigkeit!" (ibid., 3: 159).
37. Sottong, 115–27.
38. [Johann Andreas] C[hristoph] Hildebrand[t], *Das Merkwürdigste Jahr aus dem Leben eines alten Kriegers: Ein Historischer Roman aus den Zeiten Friedrichs II. und der Maria Theresia* (Halberstadt: Friedrich August Helm, 1830).
39. "Auch Sie, mein Sohn, werden im Laufe des Krieges in feindlichen Herre manchen trefflichen Mann kennen lernen, bei dem Sie gern Rock und Feldzeichen vergessen und blos das Herz achten" (ibid., 1: 166).
40. "Dergleichen Auswüchse des kriegerischen Standes" (ibid., 2: 143).
41. "Ich kannte die Feindschaft, den Nationalhaß der Preußen gegen alles, was Kaiserlich war" (ibid., 2: 198).
42. "'Cartel! auf ein halbe Stunde Cartel! meine Herren!' sagte er. 'Wenn Sie sonst nichts dawider haben, so setzen wir Paar Mann den Krieg beiseite! Wir werden so über Schlesiens Besitz nicht entscheiden!'" (ibid., 2: 129).
43. E. Auerbach, *Der Zigeunerraub, oder: Das Vaterhaus. Eine Erzählung aus dem Rettungsjahr 1813* (Braunschweig: G. C. E. Meyer, 1825).
44. "Jeder redliche Deutsche [sah] den Befreiern des Vaterlands mit Sehnsucht im Stillen entgegen" (ibid., 12–13).
45. "[Wir wurden] von den österreichischen Panduren und Croaten bis aufs Hemde ausgeplündert" (ibid., 25).
46. "Was ist unser hoher Gast für ein herrlicher, solider Mann!—so deutsch, so gerade weg, als wär' er wahrhaftig unser eins!" (ibid., 187).
47. H. E. R. Belani [Karl Ludwig Häberlin], *Die Demagogen: Novelle, aus der Geschichte unserer Zeit* (Leipzig: A. Wienbrack, 1829). This is one of sixty-four novels published by Karl Ludwig Häberlin (1784–1858) during his long, productive, and largely pseudonymous career—the latter perhaps a result of his having spent time in prison for embezzlement. See the entry by F. Spehr on Häberlin in the *Allgemeine Deutsche Biographie,* where one can read the fairly typical judgment of his works in literary terms: "Since they were conceived and written in great haste to earn his bread, these works lack all deeper meaning" (10: 280). I would argue that while they may not be art, there is nevertheless something at stake, perhaps even

NOTES TO CHAPTER 2

something deep in his and all the other popular depictions of German history.

48. "Aber seitdem ich Deutschland durchwandert bin und mich überall, in jedem Dorfe, in jedem Städchen überzeugt habe, daß Bauer und Bürger seine Fürsten und den Frieden liebt, halte ich es für unmöglich, daß die im ganzen kalte und vernünftige Masse des deutschen Volkes jemals in Revolutionszustand versetzt werden könnte" (Belani, *Die Demagogen,* 2: 174).
49. Julius von Voß, *Der deutsche Donquixott* (Berlin: J. W. Schmidts Wittwe und Sohn, 1819), and Willibald Alexis [Wilhelm Häring], *Die Geächteten: Novelle* (Berlin: Duncker und Humblot, 1825).
50. "Das erste Buch, welches er fertigte, hieß der ächtdeutsche Jüngling, das zweite die ächtdeutsche Jungfrau, das dritte der ächtdeutsche Mann, das vierte der ächtdeutsche Greis, so hatter er es stets mit ächter Deutschheit, sie war immer ein Ideal, das ihm vorschwebte. . . . Allein er gab diese Schriften nicht in den Buchhandel, studierte sie nur selbst, zu eigner Erbauung" (Voß, *Der deutsche Donquixott,* 141–42).
51. "Unbieder sey es, und deutschem Volkssinn nicht angemessen, einen Nachbar mit Krieg zu überziehn" (ibid., 142).
52. "Daß es in Deutschland mit deutschem Sinn noch nicht so steht, als ich es hoffte" (ibid., 256).
53. "Aber wie können Sie auf den irreligiösen Despoten sich berufen, den kleinen noch groß nennen?" (ibid., 353).
54. "Hüte sich Jeder in Deutschland mit Wahrheit und Vernunft aufzutreten" (ibid., 370).
55. "Er stritt gegen sein Vaterland" (Alexis, *Die Geächteten,* 105).
56. "Wer das Vaterland liebt, [kann] nichts weiter lieben" (ibid., 47–48).
57. "Dies Vaterland war eine schöne Idee, und die Wirklichkeit ein albernes Gemisch von Thorheit, Eitelkeit, Eigennutz, nicht werth die Anstrengungen eines Edlen" (ibid., 197).
58. "Vergessen wie jetzt die Namen der Helden, die . . . für Religion, Vaterland, Freiheit, eigene Sprache—die letzten—stritten und sanken" (ibid., 172).
59. "Die Schrecken langer Jahre sind verschwunden, die furchbaren Namen sind verklungen, und von jener Zeit ist nicht mehr als die Erinnerung eines Traumes geblieben" (ibid., 316).
60. Ludwig Rellstab, *1812: Ein historischer Roman* (1834; Leipzig: Brockhaus, 1914).
61. "An einem lauen Aprilabende des Jahres 1812 traf Ludwig Rosen, ein junger Deutscher, eben mit der sinkenden Sonne vor dem Städchen Duomo d'Ossola am Abhang des Simplon ein" (ibid., 1).

Chapter 3

1. "Daß einige Schriftstellerinnen von Genie dem großen Friedrich ein halbes Dutzend Liebesabenteuer angedichtet haben, alles nur, wie sie ganz richtig fühlten, daß es ohne dergleichen eigentlich nicht geht" (Theodor Fontane, *Unwiederbringlich* [1891; Frankfurt am Main: Ullstein, 1987], in *Werke und Schriften,* ed. Walter Keitel and Helmuth Nürnberger, vol. 15, 170).
2. Schieder's argument is contained in his essay "Friedrich der Große: eine Integrationsfigur?" For collections of anecdotes see, for example, Friedrich Nicolai, *Anekdoten von König Friedrich II. von Preußen, und von einigen Personen, die um Ihm waren* (Berlin and Stettin: 1789, 1792), and the anonymous work *Anekdoten und Karakterzüge aus dem Leben Friedrich des Zweiten,* which exists in an English translation, *Characteristic Anecdotes, and Miscellaneous Authentic Papers, Tending to Illustrate the Character of Frederick II, Late King of Prussia* by B. H. Latrobe (London: 1788).
3. "Zu kleinen Stils und überhaupt etwas zu wenig" (Fontane, *Unwiederbringlich,* 168).
4. "Einen privaten und einen historischen Standpunkt durchaus unterscheiden müsse" (ibid., 169).
5. The English versions are quoted from *Jenny Treibel,* trans. Ulf Zimmermann, *Theodor Fontane: Short Novels and Other Writings* (New York: Continuum, 1982), here 195; "Mir gilt in der Geschichte nur das Große, nicht das Kleine, das Nebensächliche" (Theodor Fontane, *Frau Jenny Treibel* [1892; Frankfurt am Main: Ullstein, 1984], in *Werke und Schriften,* ed. Walter Keitel and Helmuth Nürnberger, vol. 16, 70).
6. Zimmerman, *Short Novels,* 195; "Daß der Alte Fritz am ende seiner Tage dem damligen Kammergerichtspräsidenten, Namen hab' ich vergessen, den Krückstock an den Kopf warf, und, was mir noch wichtiger ist, daß er durchaus bei seinen Hunden begraben sein wollte, weil er die Menschen, diese 'mechante Rasse' so gründlich verachtete—sieh, Freund, das ist mir mindestens ebensoviel wert wie Hohenfriedburg oder Leuthen" (Fontane, *Frau Jenny Treibel,* 69).
7. Zimmerman, *Short Novels,* 195; "Das Nebensächliche, soviel ist richtig, gilt nichts, wenn es bloß nebensächlich ist, wenn nichts drin steckt. Steckt aber was drin, dann ist es die Hauptsache, denn es gibt einem dann immer das eigentlich Menschliche" (Fontane, *Frau Jenny Treibel,* 70).
8. "Eine reine Skandinavin" (Fontane, *Unwiederbringlich,* 169).
9. Ibid., 308.
10. Wilhelmine Lorenz, *Friedrich's II. einzige Liebe: Roman* (Leipzig: Verlag von A. Wienbrack, 1846).
11. On Lorenz, see Sophie Pataky, *Lexikon deutscher Frauen der Feder,* 1898 (Bern: H. Lang, 1971), 519–20.

NOTES TO CHAPTER 3

12. For a discussion of Frederick's sexual orientation, along with a reflection on what it would mean to impose such twentieth-century concepts as "gay" on the eighteenth century, see Simon Richter, "Winckelmann's Progeny: Homosocial Networking in the Eighteenth Century," in Alice Kuzniar, ed., *Outing Goethe and His Age* (Stanford, CA: Stanford University Press, 1996), esp. 34–37.
13. Countess Orzelska, who was born about 1707 and died in 1769, is an oddly recurrent figure in nineteenth-century historical fiction; just enough is missing from her biography to make her the perfect heroine for a historical novel. She is close enough to major figures to be used plausibly to show great men up close, while the gaps in her life history let writers fill in whatever seems appropriate to their narratives. H. E. R. Belani (Karl Ludwig Häberlin) cast her as a forest nymph before marrying her off to her one true love, Prince Moritz of H . . . stein. See Belani, *Gräfin Orzelska: Historische Novelle aus dem ersten Viertheil des vorigen Jahrhunderts* (Braunschweig: G. C. E. Meyer, 1827). The prince appears to be the same man she married so reluctantly in Lorenz's novel—and in real life too—the Duke of Holstein-Sonderburg-Beck. Countess Orzelska also makes a brief appearance in the fifth volume of Gustav Freytag's *Die Ahnen: Die Geschwister* (1878; Leipzig: Hirzel, 1905), where Freytag uses her to portray the decadence and arbitrary nature of the Saxon court (5: 369–99).
14. "In den weichen Lauten der Muttersprache Anna's, der gewöhnlichen Sprache an August's Hofe, floß die Unterhaltung dahin, und je weiter sie floß, und sich von der Natur über Kunst und Literatur verbreitete, um so lebhafter und interessanter ward sie" (Lorenz, 22).
15. "Unmerklich, doch süß durch alle Nerven bebend, drückte Friedrich den Finger der Gräfin, der leicht in den zwei Fingern lag mit denen er ihn zierlich gefaßt; wie es Sitte wenn ein Cavalier hohen Standes eine Dame zu führen verpflichtet war" (ibid., 33).
16. "Scheiden muß ich von Ihnen herrliche Gräfin, von Ihnen die Alles in sich vereint, was mir als höchstes Ideal edler Weiblichkeit in Engelsglorie schwebt vor meiner glühendec Phantasie" (ibid., 43–44).
17. "'Sagen Sie daß Sie mir verzeihen, daß Sie meiner denken wollen in Freundschaft, in . . . Ach ich darf ja nichts weiter sagen,' rief er in tiefem Schmerze: 'ich bin Sohn eines Königs!'" (ibid., 45).
18. Der Ring "sei mir das Unterpfand, daß Sie stets Ihres Volkes edler Vater sein werden" (ibid.).
19. "Anna sendet dieses Pfand einer seligen Minute dem Manne zurück, den noch ihr letzter Seufzer in hoher Verehrung segnen wird" (ibid., 183).
20. "Balsam auf die ewig blutende Wunde meines Herzens!" (ibid.).
21. "Als Andenken an sie der Sie so teu ergeben, an mich, der sie so rein geliebt. Geliebt wie er nie wieder lieben kann" (ibid.).

NOTES TO CHAPTER 3

22. "Für solchen Schmerz darf einem Fürsten nicht Raum bleiben" (ibid.).
23. "Aber diese Großthaten, Herrschermühen und Herrschersorgen ließen ihn das Mädchen vergessen das seine erste und einzige Liebe gewesen" (ibid., 185).
24. "Drohend rollte sein großes Flammenauge" (ibid., 189).
25. Except for the "Nachwort" (afterword), I quote from a reprint edition, Leipzig: Reprint-Verlag, n.d.; the text is identical to that of the first edition.
26. See Peter Paret, *Art as History: Episodes in the Culture and Politics of Nineteenth-Century Germany* (Princeton, NJ: Princeton University Press, 1988). Kugler, the historical novelist, seems unknown. I encountered him in an advertisement for his book *Der letzte Wendenfürst: Novelle aus der Zeiten der Gründung Berlins* (Berlin: Alexander Dunker, 1837), which was bound into a work by Julius Bacher. Kugler wrote fiction under the pseudonym F. Th. Erwin, but the ad identifies the real author in parenthesis.
27. The third edition, which appeared quickly, was part of its publisher's "historical home library" (Leipzig: Lorck, 1843); other popular editions followed in rapid succession, at least for so large and expensive a volume, e.g. (Leipzig: Mendelsohn, 1856).
28. "Wir legen Euch in diesem Buche die Geschichte eines Mannes vor, bei dessen Namen das Herz eines jeden Bürger im preußischen Staate, das Herz eines jeden Deutschen höher schlägt" (Kugler, *Geschichte Friedrichs*, v).
29. Paret says the book "helped confirm Frederick as a popular figure of middle-class culture in northern and central Germany," and he cites Fontane as having said "it was largely Kugler and Menzel who had made Frederick a popular hero" (59).
30. In addition to Paret, see Françoise Forster-Hahn, "Adolph Menzel's 'Daguerreotypical' Image of Frederick the Great: A Liberal Bourgeois Interpretation of German History," *Art Bulletin* 59.2 (1977): 242–61; Jost Hermand, *Adolph Menzel Das Flötenkonzert in Sanssouci: Ein realistisch geträumtes Preußenbild* (Frankfurt am Main: Fischer, 1985), esp. 13–22; and *Adolph Menzel, 1815–1905: Between Romanticism and Impressionism*, ed. Claude Keisch and Marie Ursula Riemann-Reyher (New Haven, CT: Yale University Press, 1996).
31. "Sie war einige Jahre älter als Friedrich; ihr schöner Wuchs, ihr adliger Anstand, die feine Bildung ihres Geistes, die heitere Laune, von der sie beseelt war, gaben ihr etwas unwiderstehlich Anziehendes. Nicht selten erschien sie in Mannskleidern, die aber nur dazu dienten, den Reiz ihrer Erscheinung zu erhöhen. Friedrich fühlte sich bald von glühender Leidenschaft ergriffen, und seine Wünsche fanden bei der Gräfin kein

NOTES TO CHAPTER 3

abgeneigtes Gehör" (Kugler, *Geschichte Friedrichs,* 41).
32. "In dieser Zeit dichtete der Kronprinz seine ersten Lieder, die den Reizen der Gräfin Orzelska gewidmet waren" (ibid., 44).
33. "Anekdoten, die wohl geeignet sind, die Charakergröße des seltnen Königs in eigentümlichem Lichte zu zeigen" (ibid., 266).
34. "Sein steter Morgengruß war: Guten Tag, Kinder! und stets tönte es zurück: Guten Tag, Fritz!" "alle seine Soldaten [redeten ihn] gern mit seinem bloßen Vornamen an: 'Fritz,' oder, mit einem liebkosenden Beiworte: 'Alter Fritz'" (ibid., 455, 451).
35. "Schlaf mein Kind, schlaf leis / Da draußen geht der Preuß" (Ludwig Pfau, "Badisches Wiegenlied," *Klassenkampf: Ein Lesebuch zu den Klassenkämpfen in Deutschland, 1756–1971,* ed. Hans Magnus Enzensburger et al. [Darmstadt: Luchterhand, 1972], 239–40).
36. "Siegreich um Preußens und um Deutschlands Rettung" (Kugler, *Geschichte Friedrichs,* 446).
37. See, for example, Friedrich Jaeger and Jörn Rüsen, *Geschichte des Historismus* (Munich: Beck, 1992), 86–92.
38. "In Deutschland aber, selbst bei den Gegnern Friedrichs, war fast allgemeiner Jubel über den Sieg bei Roßbach . . . Von jetzt an loderte das schon im Stillen genährte Feuer der Begeisterung für den deutschen Helden mächtig empor. . . . Der Deutsche fühlte endlich wieder den Stolz, ein Deutscher zu heißen" (Kugler, *Geschichte Friedrichs,* 349).
39. There is scattered anecdotal evidence of the popularity of such images. For example, volume 6 of Gustav Freytag's *Die Ahnen,* which is set in Silesia, reports that the province's inhabitants came to revere Frederick, "and his portrait hung in most living rooms"(2). George Hesekiel's *Stille vor dem Sturm* refers to Gustav Kühn's series of cheap prints, which provided the chief decorations in the servants' quarters of the hero's castle. The pictures he mentions show Frederick sharing his tobacco with ordinary soldiers, etc. (1: 124–25).
40. Fontane reports trying to buy one with well-printed illustrations in a letter to Wilhelm Hertz, December 8, 1861. See Theodor Fontane, *Briefe an Wilhelm und Hans Hertz, 1859–1898,* ed. Kurt Schreinert and Gerhard Hay (Stuttgart: Klett, 1972), 62–63.
41. The list of authors is from Hermand, 14–15. To expand on one example, Johann David Erdmann Preuß published a five-volume biography, *Friedrich der Große* (Berlin: Nauck, 1832–34), as well as *Friedrich der Große mit seinen Freunden und Verwandten* (Berlin: Dunker und Humblot, 1838) and *Friedrichs des Großen Jugend und Thronbesteigung,* with the same publisher in 1840.
42. Mühlbach, *Frederick and His Court,* 3; "eine Königen bleibt immer doch ein Weib" (*Friedrich und sein Hof,* 1: 4).

NOTES TO CHAPTER 3

43. Mühlbach, *Frederick and His Court*, 3; "Das war in der That eine königliche Toilette! Millionen Thaler, welche ihre Tage in zinsloser Ruhe verpaßten, und die müßig und verachtungsvoll den schweisgebadeten Menschen zuschauen durften, welche sich abmühten um ihre arme, kummervolle, bedrückte Existenz. Sophia Dorothea dachte nicht daran" (*Friedrich und sein Hof,* 1: 4).
44. Mühlbach, *Frederick and His Court*, 6; "würde lieber den ärmsten und niedrigsten Mann heiraten, wenn ich ihn liebe, als den reichsten Königssohn, der mir gleichgültig ist" (*Friedrich und sein Hof,* 1: 7–8).
45. Mühlbach, *Frederick and His Court*, 6; "Sind wir nicht alle dazu da, wie eine Waare verhandelt und an den Meistbietenden losgeschlagen zu werden?" (*Friedrich und sein Hof,* 1: 7).
46. Mühlbach, *Frederick and His Court*, 60; "Ich werde einen Namen haben, ich werde mir Ruhm erwerben, denn ich werde ein Schriftsteller und ein Dichter, ein Autor, der seine Stelle einnimmt in der Republik der Geister und keiner Königskrone bedarf, um in den Büchern der Geschichte verzeichnet zu werden" (*Friedrich und sein Hof,* 1: 80).
47. "Der erste Diener, der erste Arbeiter und Verwalter eines Volkes und eines Landes" (Mühlbach, *Friedrich und sein Hof,* 1: 171). In the English version the passage misses this point; see *Frederick and His Court*, 124.
48. Mühlbach, *Frederick and His Court*, 125; *Friedrich und sein Hof,* 1: 172.
49. Mühlbach, *Berlin and Sans-Souci*, 264; "ich will Euch mein halbes Brod geben! Das ist aber auch Alles, was ich für den König thun kann!" (Mühlbach, *Berlin und Sanssouci,* 3: 77).
50. Mühlbach, *Berlin and Sans-Souci*, 262; "Ja, est ist ein blutiger Sieg gewesen, ein mörderischer Bruderkampf! Der Deutsche hat gegen den Deutschen gekämpft, der Bruder gegen den Bruder! . . . Arme Königin Elisabeth Christine! Dein Gemahl hat gesiegt! Aber Ihr Beide habt den Sieg theuer bezahlt! . . . Sein ist der Ruhm und die Ehre! Du, arme Königin, Du hast nur neuen Kummer gewonnen! Dein sind die Thränen und der Schmerz!" (Mühlbach, *Berlin und Sanssouci,* 3: 73).
51. Mühlbach, *Frederick and His Court*, 51; "der Prinz liebt nur seine Flöte" (Mühlbach, *Friedrich und sein Hof,* 1: 65).
52. Mühlbach, *Frederick and His Court*, 70; "Ephraim verneigte sich stumm und wandte sich langsam der Thür zu. Des Kronprinzen Augen folgten ihm mit einem gütigen, sinnenden Ausdruck. Dann trat er rasch zu dem Tisch und nahm die Flöte. Ephraim war schon durch die offene Thür in das Vorzimmer eingetreten, als er hinter sich die leisen schmelzenden Töne der Flöte vernahm. Auf den Zehen durchschlich er das Vorzimmer, aber drüben an der Ausgangsthür blieb er stehen und lauschte. Der Kronprinz hatte den Lauscher, der sich drüben hinter der Thür zu verbergen suchte, wohl bemerkt, aber er spielte doch wieter; eine so

NOTES TO CHAPTER 3

schmelzende, so empfindungsvolle, so zarte Musik entlockte er seiner Flöte, daß Ephraim, von Entzücken und Wehmuth durchschauert, seine Hände faltete wie zum Gebet" (Mühlbach, *Friedrich und sein Hof,* 1: 94–95).

53. Mühlbach, *Frederick and His Court,* 65; "'Mein Prinz,' sagte er dann muthiger, 'ich bin ein Jude, das heißt, ein geächteter, geschmäheter und verfolgter Mensch, oder vielmehr kein Mensch, sondern ein Geschöpf, welches man wie einen Hund mit Füßen stößt, wenn es arm und elend ist, welchem man kaum Menschenrechte zugesteht, wenn es Geld und Schätze besitzt. Der Hund hat's besser, wie der Jude in preußischen Landen'" (Mühlbach, *Friedrich und sein Hof,* 1: 90).
54. Mühlbach, *Frederick and His Court,* 72; "Und nun fort mit den Sorgen und dem Ernst des Lebens. Wir wollen heute dein Fest feiern, glanzstrahlende Göttin der Freude" (Mühlbach, *Friedrich und sein Hof,* 1: 97).
55. Mühlbach, *Frederick and His Court,* 72; "die kleine Morien . . . diese flatternde, leichte Gazelle, dieses übermüthige jauchzende Frühlingsleben, diesen Tourbillon von Liebe, Herz, Leidenschaft, Leichtsinn und Uebermuth" (Mühlbach, *Friedrich und sein Hof,* 1: 97).
56. Mühlbach, *Frederick and His Court,* 73; "eine unüberwindliche Kluft zwischen ihnen Beiden" (Mühlbach, *Friedrich und sein Hof,* 1: 98).
57. Mühlbach, *Frederick and His Court,* 82; "er drückt mir zuweilen verstohlen die Hand, er flüstert mir dann und wann einige zärtliche, sehnsuchtsvolle Worte in's Ohr, er hat mich gestern, als ich ihm zufällig ganz allein im dunklen Korridor begegnete, sehr feurig umarmt und meine Lippen mit so glühenden und strürmischen Küssen bedeckt, daß ich fast erstickte" (Mühlbach, *Friedrich und sein Hof,* 1: 111).
58. Mühlbach, *Frederick and His Court,* 340; "Alles war vorhergesehen, Alles vorbereitet, und es handelt sich nur um die Ausführung und Entwürfe, die ich seit langer Zeit in meinem Kopfe bewegt habe" (Mühlbach, *Friedrich und sein Hof,* 3: 80).
59. Mühlbach, *Frederick and His Court,* 369; "daß die Fürsten dazu verurtheilt sind, ein einsames, freudloses Leben zu führen" (Mühlbach, *Friedrich und sein Hof,* 3: 125).
60. Louisa Mühlbach, "Der alte Fritz," in *Novellen: Federzeichnungen* (Berlin: Schweigger'sche Hofbuchhandlung, 1865), 5–35.
61. "Daß ein alter Mann kein Flötenspieler sein kann" (Mühlbach, "Der alte Fritz," 5).
62. "Ich bin dazu da, daß ich die Klagen und Beschwerden meiner Unterthanen anhöre und ihnen wo möglich Hülfe bringe" (ibid., 11).
63. "Der König heftete noch immer seine strahlenden Adleraugen auf das Antlitz Deesen's und ein freundliches Lächeln flog jetzt über seine Züge" (ibid., 12).

64. "Das Feuerauge des Königs richtete sich mit einem flammenden Blitz auf das Angesicht des Castellans" (ibid., 18).
65. "Aus seinen großen blauen Augen mit sanften Blicken"; "Der König hielt immer noch seine großen blauen Augen fest auf sie gerichtet" (ibid., 27, 29).
66. To the extent that his eagle-like gaze becomes a semantic marker that writers invariably associate with Frederick and his mythic powers, Wulf Wülfung, Karen Bruns, and Rolf Parr would term it a "Mytheme." See their *Historische Mythologie der Deutschen, 1798–1918* (Munich: Fink, 1991), 3.
67. Julius Bacher, *Die Brautschau Friedrich's des Großen* (Berlin: Alexander Dunker, 1857).
68. "So lange dem Prinzen das vertrackte französische Wesen in dem Kopf spukt, . . . wird nichts Gescheutes aus ihm. Er muß vor Allem Deutsch werden, an Jagd und einem derben Mahl Vergnügen finden" (ibid., 26).
69. According to the king, the German manner of living remained superior: "[Es] erhält die Mannheit, und Saft und Kraft bleibt gesund." He hopes Frederick will lead "ein geordnetes, vernünftiges Leben," and learn "wie wohl es thut, sich in Forst und Feld umher zu tummeln" (ibid., 27–31).
70. "Das glatte, falsche Franzosenthum"; "die Einem den Glauben an Gott und unsern Herrn Jesus rauben möchten" (ibid., 28).
71. "So ist er also doch zur Einsicht gelangt, daß deutsches Wesen besser ist" (ibid.).
72. Michael Jeismann, *Das Vaterland der Feinde: Studien zum nationalen Feindbegriff und Selbstverständnis in Deutschland und Frankreich, 1792–1918* (Stuttgart: Klett-Cotta, 1992), 16.
73. Slavoj Žižek, "Eastern Europe's Republics of Gilead," *New Left Review* 183 (September/October 1990): 57.
74. Anne Norton, *Reflections on Political Identity* (Baltimore: Johns Hopkins University Press, 1988), 53.
75. "Die deutsche Literatur war zu jener Zeit auf der tiefsten Stufe des Verfalles" (Kugler, *Geschichte Friedrichs*, 24).
76. Mühlbach, *Frederick and His Court*, 2; "Was sollte Preußen mit diesem empfindsamen Knaben Friedrich, mit diesem Modehelden, der wie ein französischer Stutzer sich kleidete" (Mühlbach, *Friedrich und sein Hof*, 1: 2).
77. "Französischen Unsinn, . . . welcher ihn denn auch zuletzt zu manchen Dummheiten verleitete" (Bacher, *Die Brautschau Friedrich's des Großen*, 185).
78. "Die innere Werth der Prinzessin nahm ihn ganz für dieselbe ein. . . . die einzelnen Gesichtszüge verriethen gerade nicht viel Verstand und Geist, konnten auch nicht schön genannt werden; jedoch war der allgemeine

Eindruck, den ihre Erscheinung machte, ein höchst angenehmer" (ibid., 108–9).

79. Typically, Bacher's novel includes what its narrator describes as the authentic text of a letter from Frederick William I addressed to "my dear son Fritz" (194–96). Actually, the letter is slightly false, in the sense that the narrator admits it was written "at roughly the same time" but not necessarily in the precise context that it occupies in the novel; its truth is therefore at the level of verisimilitude, an authentic document in a plausible situation. Its inclusion demonstrates once again the tension between the authors of historical fiction and their academic counterparts.

80. "Ich wünschte, der Prinz würde ein ächter deutscher Fürst; daher gebe ich ihm Zeit, sich in Küstrin zu sammeln" (Bacher, *Die Brautschau Friedrich's des Großen*, 186).

81. See Lothar Schirmer, "Friedrich der Große als Theaterheld," *Preußen: Versuch einer Bilanz*, vol. 4, *Preußen: Dein Spree-Athen* (Reinbeck bei Hamburg: Rowohlt, 1981), 232, 248. As an indication of Frederick II's popularity on the stage, Schirmer lists sixty-six titles of plays about him that were performed between 1850 and 1900, including, among other oddities, "Old Fritz and the Jesuits" and "Frederick the Great as a Doctor" (248–49).

82. Franz Otto [Spamer], *Der große König und sein Rekrut: Lebensbilder aus der Zeit des Siebenjährigen Krieges (Unter theilweiser Benutzung eines historischen Romans von A. H. Brandrupp, für Volk und Heer, insbesonder für die reifere Jugend bearbeitet)* (1865; Leipzig: Otto Spamer, 1873, 4th ed.). The extended subtitle and Spamer's introduction make reference to A. H. Brandrupp, *Das Glockenspiel der Garnisonkirche zu Potsdam*. Eggert mentions Brandrupp's book in his bibliography (217) with a publication date of 1855, but I have been unable to find any record of the book.

83. Franz Otto Spamer, *Aus dem Tabakskollegium und der Zopfzeit: Wie man vor 150 Jahren lebte und es trieb.* (Leipzig: Otto Spamer, n.d.); and *Das Buch vom Alten Fritz: Leben und Thaten des großen Preußenkönigs Friedrich II., genannt der Einzige, des Helden des achtzehnten Jahrhunderts. Der Jugend und dem Volke erzählt* (Leipzig: Otto Spamer, 1877).

84. "Glänzend war der Sieg, welcher bei Leuthen in 5 Stunden erkämpft ward; mit einem kleinen Herre von 30000 Mann schlug Friedrich die fast 90000 Mann starke österreichische Armee, welche bloß an Gefangenen 21,500 Gemeine und 307 Offiziere einbüßte. Unter der Beute waren 59 Fahnen und 134 Kanonen" (Wilmsen, *Kinderfreunde*, 242).

85. "Das Volk war seinem großen Könige mit der heißesten Liebe ergeben" (ibid., 241).

86. "[Friedrich] entbehrte lebenslang die Freuden des Familienvaters" (ibid., 239).

87. "Seine Augen waren groß und blau, sein Blick durchdringend" (Spamer, *Der große König*, 1: 31).
88. "Friedrich der Große hatte die Stellung der feindlichen Armee genau besichtigt und sein Genie sogleich das rechte Mittel gefunden, mit seiner kleinen Armee gegen die dreifach stärkere feindliche erfolgreich vorzugehen" (ibid., 1: 137).
89. "Unser Held" (ibid., 1: 121). Spamer's repeated use of the possessive "our" when referring to Felix is an attempt at encouraging young readers' identification with the king's recruit; it draws them into the narrative.
90. "Ich bin zufrieden mit Dir, Feldwebel Wunderlich! Hörst Du? Feldwebel bei der Garde!" (ibid., 1: 154).
91. "Im Grunde fehlt Dir freilich viel zu einem echten Diplomaten, doch wirst Du so viel, als Du brauchst, von Geschäften begreifen, zu denen nur Menschenverstand und Besonnenheit gehört" (ibid., 1: 159).
92. Shaw, *Forms of Historical Fiction*, 159.
93. Hans von Zollern, *Ein politischer Schachzug Friedrich's des Großen*, 2 vols. (Dresden: Minden, 1883).
94. "Der junge Diplomat würzte das Mahl mit einer Menge der herrlichsten Anecdoten der neusten Erfindungen von dem großen Friedrich, welche in diesen entfernten, etwas ländlichen Kreisen glücklicher Weise noch unbekannt waren und dem Erzähler duch ein frohes beständiges Gelächter lohnten" (ibid., 1: 133).
95. "Denn man betrachtete damals Oesterreich noch als den Erbfeind Preußens und Deutschlands" (ibid., 1: 28).
96. "Aus seiner Haltung sprach noch immer das Bewußtsein des mächtigen Herrschers; sein Adlerblick beherrschte mehr wie jemals zuvor seine ganze Umgebung" (ibid., 1: 2–3). Frederick's eagle-like gaze (*Adlerblick*) occurs twice more as the novel introduces him (12, 17).
97. Hirschmann, *Kulturkampf im historischen Roman der Gründerzeit*.
98. "Echt preußische Scene" (Zollern, *Ein politischer Schachzug*, 1: 67).
99. "Der großen deutschen Mission des mit Vorliebe nur französisch sprechenden und schreibenden Monarchen" (ibid., 1: 133).
100. "Ihr denkt deutsch, Messieurs, und wehret Euch doch so beharrlich dagegen, in vollem Sinne ein Glied jenes von Euch gerühmten deutschen Körpers zu werden, denn was ist Preußen anders als die Vormacht des deutschen Reichs im Osten" (ibid., 1: 24).
101. "Der stärkste Fels und Hort des Deutschen Reiches und der deutschen Mission im Osten gegen die Gelüste eines habgierigen Slaventhums" (ibid., 2: 367).
102. "Überall, wo Deutschland oder Preßen ist, das ist unser Heim" (ibid., 2: 158).
103. For a useful summary of current ethnographical literature, which is where

I first encountered this use of naturalization and legitimization, see M. Jaffe's *H-German* review (July 7, 1996) of Sharon Macdonald, ed. *Inside European Identities: Ethnography in Western Europe* (Providence, RI: Berg, 1993).
104. "So wäre es für den gemeinen Menschen besser, wenn er ein gut Stück preußisches Brot und Fleisch hätte, als die langen trockenen Fasten des Danziger Magistrats" (Zollern, *Ein politischer Schachzug,* 1: 313–14).
105. "Zum Schutze der Thürme meiner alten Vaterstadt sage ich 'Schach dem Könige.'" "Nun denn, damit meine guten Berliner nicht ungeduldig werden wegen dieser eigensinnigen Diva, muß ich meinen Vertrag schon sofort unterzeichnen" (ibid., 2: 358).
106. Hagen Schulze, *Germany: A New History,* trans. Deborah Lucas Schneider (Cambridge, MA: Harvard University Press, 1998), 117.
107. Levin Schücking, *Der Panduren Oberst: Historischer Roman aus dem Zeitalter Friedrichs des Großen* (Berlin: Oestergaard, n.d.). The novel appears to be one of two volumes from Schücking's *Aus den Tagen der Großen Kaiserin* (Vienna: 1858).
108. Two novels from chapter 2—Oldendorp's *Misfortune and Rescue* and Hildebrandt's *The Most Remarkable Year in the Life of an Old Soldier,* which both use "the Age of Frederick" in their subtitles—are further examples of the tendency.
109. "Im Deutschen heißt es Liebe zum Vaterlande; im Magyarischen drückt es mehr Haß aus" (Schücking, *Der Panduren Oberst,* 204).
110. Heinrich von Treitschke, *Treitschke's History of Germany in the Nineteenth Century,* trans. Eden and Cedar Paul (New York: McBride, Nast: 1915–19), and *Deutsche Geschichte im Neunzehnten Jahrhundert* (Leipzig: Hirzel, 1879–94).
111. Treitschke, *History,* 1: 57; "das Bild eines Helden gesehen, zu dem die gesammte Nation bewundernd emporblickte" (Treitschke, *Deutsche Geschichte,* 1: 49).
112. Treitschke, *History,* 1: 58, 61; "Königin von Ungarn" (Treitschke, *Deutsche Geschichte,* 1: 50, 53).
113. Treitschke, *History,* 5: 461; " Das Adlerauge des großen Königs blickte aus den Wolken, und aus weiter Ferne erklang schon der Schlachtendonner von Königgrätz" (Treitschke, *Deutsche Geschichte,* 4: 397). There are parallels in the world of art. For example, Hermann Julius Schlösser's 1867 painting *The Apotheosis of William I* shows that Prussian king being led into the Cathedral of Peace after defeating Austria in 1866. A goddess of victory in her chariot rolls behind him while Frederick the Great and the Great Elector watch from the clouds (Wuppertal, Von der Heydt-Museum. *Preußen: Versuch einer Bilanz,* vol. 1, *Ausstellungsführer* [Reinbeck bei Hamburg: Rowohlt, 1981], 479.) Queen Louisa occasion-

ally looks down at those who revenged the Prussian defeat at Jena during the Wars of Liberation.
114. Treitschke, *History,* 1: 92–97; (Treitschke, *Deutsche Geschichte,* 1: 80–84).
115. Treitschke, *History,* 1: 57; "Der springende Punkt in dieser mächtigen Natur bleibt doch die erbarmungslos grausame deutsche Wahrhaftigkeit" (Treitschke, *Deutsche Geschichte,* 1: 49).
116. Treitschke, *History,* 1: 62; "Doch er zeigt auch darin sein deutsches Blut, daß er die feurige Thatenlust von frühauf zu bändigen weiß durch kalte, nüchterne Berechnung" (Treitschke, *Deutsche Geschichte,* 1: 53).
117. Treitschke, *History,* 1: 69–70; "der Schirmherr des Protestanismus ... Die Befestigung der protestantisch-deutschen Großmacht war die schwerste Niederlage, welche der römische Stuhl seit dem Auftreten Martin Luthers erlitten; König Friedrich hat wirklich, wie der englische Gesandte Mitchell von ihm sagte, für die Freiheit des Menschengeschlechts gefochten" (Treitschke, *Deutsche Geschichte,* 1: 60–61).
118. Treitschke, *History,* 1: 64; "dem deutschen Leben entfremdet durch die erbliche Verbindung mit Frankreich wie durch die Härte katholischer Glaubenseinheit" (Treitschke, *Deutsche Geschichte,* 1: 55).
119. Treitschke, *History,* 1: 69, 61; "dieser lothringische Mehrer des Reichs" and "die wilde Meute . . . die moskowitischen Barbaren" (Treitschke, *Deutsche Geschichte,* 1: 59, 53).
120. The Kugler original is in note 28 above; "Ueberdies ist unser Buch nicht nur für preußische Leser allein geschrieben: es will auch der preußischen Nachbarschaft oder allen guten Deutschen [die Zeit Friedrichs vorführen]" (Spamer, *Der Große König un sein Rekrut,* xiv).
121. Franz Mehring—after Marx, the Social Democrats' most prominent historian—repeatedly demolished claims that Frederick was anything but a despot. Mehring's Frederick is devoid of Enlightenment principles except when they served his narrow self-interest. See, for example, "Friedrichs aufgeklärter Despotismus," in Franz Mehring, *Aufsätze zur Preussischen und Deutschen Geschichte* (Leipzig: Philipp Reclam jun., 1986), 122–36.
122. For an interpretation that pierces the disguise and discusses William's repressed homosexuality, see John C. G. Röhl, "The Emperor's New Clothes: A Character Sketch of Kaiser Wilhelm II," in Röhl and Nicolaus Sombart, eds., *Kaiser Wilhelm II: New Interpretations* (Cambridge: Cambridge University Press, 1982, 23–61). The picture of William dressed as Frederick is on p. 49.

Chapter 4

1. Sheehan, *German History,* 233.
2. Fanny Lewald, *Prinz Louis Ferdinand* (Berlin: Deutsche Buch-Gemeinschaft [1849]), and *Prince Louis Ferdinand,* trans. Linda Rogols-

NOTES TO CHAPTER 4

Siegel (Lewiston, NY: Mellen, 1988). On Lewald, see Irene Stocksieker Di Maio's article "Fanny Lewald," in James Hardin and Siegfried Mews, eds. *Dictionary of Literary Biography*, vol. 129, *Nineteenth-Century German Writers, 1841–1900* (Detroit: Gale, 1993), 202–13.

3. Lewald, *Prince Louis Ferdinand*, 107; "Was ist in diesen hundert Jahren geleistet! Welche Männer, welche Taten hat das Vaterland gesehen! Und jetzt! Diese Verblendung, diese schmachvolle Schwäche!—und ich stehe da, tatenlos, gefesselt, unfähig zu helfen! Ich—" (Lewald, *Prinz Louis Ferdinand*, 10).

4. Lewald, *Prince Louis Ferdinand*, 334; "Dabei sind diese Kerle Juwelen im Vergleich zu den geckenhaften Offizieren und den alten Generalen. Heldrich erählte mir, daß der Chef seines Regiments sich auf dem Pferde des Reitknechtes immer eine Fußbank nachbringen lasse, weil er zu dick geworden ist, ohne diese auf und ab zu steigen" (Lewald, *Prinz Louis Ferdinand*, 281). Sheehan reports that of 142 generals in the Prussian army in 1806, half were over sixty years old; thirteen were on the far side of seventy; four were in their eighties. Lewald appreciates that these officers, who had fought under Frederick II, were loath to meet the Napoleonic challenge; changing a military structure that had served them and their state so well appeared to be an unnecessary risk (*German History*, 295).

5. Lewald, *Prince Louis Ferdinand*, 227; "Die Begeisterung aber, welche sich an das Genie eines Fürsten knüpft, geht überall mit dem Tode des Genies unter" (Lewald, *Prinz Louis Ferdinand*, 152–53).

6. Lewald, *Prince Louis Ferdinand*, 335; "Das Heer besteht aus Landeskindern, und diese lieben ihr Land, diese sind treu und werden selbstbewußt das Recht ihrer Nationalität zu erhalten wissen, wenn man sie ihnen rauben wollte" (Lewald, *Prinz Louis Ferdinand*, 283).

7. Lewald, *Prince Louis Ferdinand*, 335; "Haben Ihre Ahnen an das Recht der Nationalität geglaubt, als sie Polen teilen halfen und dieses rein slawische Volk in Deutsche verwandeln wollten? Hat der Große Friedrich die Nationalität der Österreicher geachtet, als er die Schlesier zu Preußen machte . . . ?" (Lewald, *Prinz Louis Ferdinand*, 283).

8. In April 1808, in a letter to her father, Duke Karl of Mecklenburg-Strelitz, Queen Louisa of Prussia laments: "We fell asleep on top of [Frederick the Great's] laurels." The quotation was once famous enough to be included in the German "familiar quotations," Georg Büchmann's *Geflügelte Worte*.

9. At some level this chapter's middlebrow promoters of Queen Louisa worked in a sanctified and somewhat bizarre tradition begun in 1798 by Novalis. It was just a year after Frederick William III ascended to the throne that Novalis published his *Glaube und Liebe oder der König und die Königen* (Belief and Love or the King and the Queen). Its central premise

NOTES TO CHAPTER 4

was that the family, specifically the royal family, should serve as a model for the state.

10. Lewald, *Prince Louis Ferdinand*, 171; "So gebt mir die Freiheit, ein Bürger zu sein; gebt mir die Freiheit, die in der Gleichheit mit dem Menschen beruht! Laßt mich ein Weib nehmen nach meinem Herzen" (Lewald, *Prinz Louis Ferdinand*, 84).
11. Lewald, *Prince Louis Ferdinand*, 415; "Die wahnsinnigen Gesetze Ihres Landes, welche, uns auszutilgen von der Erde wie giftiges Gewürm, es nur zwei Kindern jeder jüdischen Familie gestatten, sich in der Vaterstadt zu verheiraten und anzusiedeln" (Lewald, *Prinz Louis Ferdinand*, 375).
12. Lewald, *Prince Louis Ferdinand*, 261; "Man schließt Augen und Ohren, will nicht sehen, was jenseits der Grenzen geschieht, will nicht hören, was die Stimme im Land fordert" (Lewald, *Prinz Louis Ferdinand*, 198).
13. Lewald, *Prince Louis Ferdinand*, 377; "In einen seidenen Schlafrock von persischen Stoffen gewickelt, das Halstuch losgeknüpft, das Jabot geöffnet und die Füße in wärmende Schuhe gehüllt, lag er" (Lewald, *Prinz Louis Ferdinand*, 33).
14. Lewald, *Prince Louis Ferdinand*, 385; "Er sah sich an der Spitze eines Heeres, die besten Männer des Vaterlandes strömten ihm zu, er zog Bonaparte entgegen, der Geist des Großen Friedrich schwebte über seinen Fahnen" (Lewald, *Prinz Louis Ferdinand*, 341).
15. Lewald, *Prince Louis Ferdinand*, 457; "Das Schicksal, welches ihm versagte, die Erhebung des Jahres 1813 zu erleben, hatte ihm wenigstens den Todesschmerz erspart über den, wie es damals schien, hoffnungslosen Fall des Vaterlandes" (Lewald, *Prinz Louis Ferdinand*, 422).
16. See Lynne Tatlock, "A Timely Demise: The Literary Reputation of Willibald Alexis and the *Reichsgründung*," *Monatshefte* 79.1 (1987): 76–88.
17. Fontane accuses Alexis of mistakenly representing Brandenburg as "Germany's promise" (*Verheißung*), while the liberal journalist Guido Weiß, writing in 1889, called him "the creator of the legend of Prussia's German mission." Both remarks are quoted in Christian Grawe, "Preußen 1803 bis 1813 im 'vaterländischen Roman': Willibald Alexis, George Hesekiel, Theodor Fontane," in Gerhard Schulz and Tim Mehigan, eds., *Literatur und Geschichte, 1788–1988* (Frankfurt am Main: Peter Lang, 1990), 156–57.
18. "Und's wäre auch zweifelhaft, ob selbst Friedrichs Genie imstande wäre, ihm überall zu parieren" (Alexis, *Ruhe*, 1: 39).
19. "Mit Theorien hätte auch Friedrich Schlesien nicht erobert; unsere Armee ist nun einmal so und nicht anders. . . . ob sie dann noch gut bleiben wird, wenn Ihr Rekrutierungssystem durchginge? Um Gottes willen keine neuen Flicken auf ein alt Kleid. Draußen Unruhe, aber Ruhe, Ruhe, Ruhe

NOTES TO CHAPTER 4

im Innern. Nichts angerührt!" (ibid., 1: 306–7).
20. "Wenn die entsetzlichste Ratlosigkeit wirklich zum Rat—und wenn zur Tat führte!" (ibid., 1: 442).
21. "Nach zehn Uhr wird nichts angenommen. Morgen früh um acht Uhr. Wenn's sehr wichtig ist, können Sie schon um sieben klingeln" (ibid., 1: 466).
22. "Mein Vater! Vergessen Sie auf einen Augenblick Ihren Sohn, dem Sie diese Schwelle verboten. Sehn Sie nur den Sohn des Vaterlandes. Es gilt dessen Ehre, vielleicht sein Dasein" (ibid., 1: 467–68).
23. "Gibt es Brauseköpfe wie du, Phantasten, Patrioten, leider sehr hohe und sehr gefährliche darunter, die das Schicksal des Staats auf eine Karte setzen möchten" (ibid., 1: 470).
24. "Wir sind nicht gerüstet, da hast du die Wahrheit, die man nicht aussprechen darf" (ibid., 1: 472).
25. "Sie sind ausgegeben, um den Schein, den äußern Anstrich von Friedrichs Heer zu erhalten. Poliert und frisch gestrichen ist alles, aber das Holz morsch und faul. . . . Unsre Festungen sind verfallen, unsre Generale Greise, unser Fuhrwesen verrottet, von unsren Truppen standen die wenigsten im Feuer, unser Exerzitium ist veraltet, und drüben steht ein Feind, flink wie der Wind" (ibid.).
26. "In elegantem Einband die neuesten werke der französischen Literatur. . . . *le classique est éternel!* Racine und Corneille" (ibid., 1: 59–62).
27. "Und dieser junge Mensch, der Monsieur Tic oder Tique, der mit seinen krausen Phantasien die Welt verkehrt machen will, glauben Sie, daß nach zehn Jahren noch ein Hahn nach ihm kräht?" (ibid., 1: 61–62).
28. "Damit man nicht dumm in der Gesellschaft ist. . . . Aber Tiedge, der sollte ja extravagante Ideen und die ganze junge Schule unsittliche Grundsätze predigen" (ibid., 1: 95).
29. "Den Hermann sollten sie doch ruhig auf seiner Bärenhaut schlafen lassen" (ibid., 1: 63).
30. "[Luise] glich der Erscheinung von Schutzgöttern des Vaterlandes" and "Landesmutter" (ibid., 2: 328–29).
31. "Diese Schlegel, Tieck, Novalis sind aber eine exzentrische Lektüre, welche das Blut erhitzt; keine für ein jünges Mädchen, das Herz und Geist zum Umgang mit rechtschaffenen Menschen ausbilden will" (ibid., 2: 330).
32. "Wie viele herzliche und frohe Stunden verdanken wir ihm, wie vielen Trost, wenn wir abends nach einem verdrießlichen Tage uns mit ihm auf dem Sofa vom Gewühl zurückgezogen" (ibid., 2: 331). For a contemporary assessment of Lafontaine's literary merit, see *Allgemeine deutsche Real-Encyclopädie für die gebildeten Stände (Conversations-Lexikon)* [*Universal German Encyclopedia for the Educated Classes*] (Leipzig: Brockhaus,

NOTES TO CHAPTER 4

1833–37). The article says that when "writing his bourgeois family portraits [Lafontaine] was less interested in artistic value than in entertaining in a pleasant and emotional manner. . . . If one has read some of his earlier works . . . the later ones can be skipped" (6: 441–42).

33. "Mich dünkt, des Dichters Aufgabe ist, die Menschen zu schildern, wie sie sind. Weil er Dichter ist, darf er das Schöne und Erhabene in seinem wunderbar geschliffenen Spiegel vergrößern und verschönen, und es mag ihm auch vielleicht erlaubt sein, das Häßliche und Schlechte noch etwas häßlicher zu machen. . . . [Lafontaine] weiß, wo wir alle schwach sind, und da versucht er uns zu streicheln, er drückt wehmütig die Hand, schlägt verführerische Akkorde an . . . und wenn wir wieder zu uns kommen, schämen wir uns darüber, denn er hat uns weich gemacht, wo wir stark sein sollten" (Alexis, *Ruhe,* 2: 332–33).

34. "Von wo entspringt alles das Unheil, an dem die Völker leiden? Aus den Beispielen, die wir unvorsichtig aus dem Altertum holen, aus der unverständigen Anwendung der Begriffe, die damals galten, auf die Verhältnisse von heut" (ibid., 2: 399).

35. "Der Soldat wird davon nicht animiert, daß man ihm die Geschichte des Siebenjährigen Krieges vorkrächzt. Hat etwa der Papa Gleim dem großen König zu seinem gewonnenen Bataillen verholfen? Laßt die Kerle sich selbst ihre Lieder von Schnaps und drallen Mädchen" (ibid., 2: 409).

36. "Es gab Männer, und Frauen auch, welche das Übel beim rechten Namen nannten. . . . Diese einigen waren die Kieselsteine, an denen der Stahl Funken schlagen sollte, aus denen der stille Brand ward, welcher später zum allmächtigen Feuer auflöderte. . . . Viele hat die Geschichte genannt, oder fängt jetzt an, ihre Namen zu nennen, aber wie viele sind schlummern gegangen, auf ihren Grabsteinen wächst Moos, und die Geschichte kratzt es nicht mehr ab. . . . Da darf die Dichtung, die soviel Trauriges und Schlimmes nicht verschweigen durfte, auch an die einzelnen Mutigen erinnern, und wo wir solche Bilder mutloser Zerschlagenheit aus der preußischen Hauptstadt hinstellen mußten, um wahr zu sein, wird es zur Pflicht, auch einiger Züge zu gedenken, die schon das ferne Wetterleuchten einer besseren Zeit am Horizont erscheinen" (ibid., 2: 508–9).

37. "Den Weg zum neuen Leben hatte sie ihm gezeigt—es gab nur einen—das Vaterland. . . . Dies Volk erwacht nicht wieder, es ist kein Volk.—Deutschland ist ein Traum der Dichter!" (ibid., 2: 200–201).

38. "Sie ist die Hoffnung oder die Puppe der Schwärmer für Deutschland. Sie hat ihn angetrieben, sie das Feuer geschührt. . . . keine Weiber zwischen uns. Die Königin muß fort" (ibid., 2: 449–50).

39. "Der Sonnenschein fiel durch die gelben Scheiben grade auf sein Gesicht, als Adelheid eintrat" (ibid., 1: 460). For an account of how the weather

NOTES TO CHAPTER 4

in nineteenth-century novels always cooperates to underscore the author's point, see F. C. Delius, *Der Held und sein Wetter: Ein Kunstmittel und sein ideologischer Gebrauch im Roman des bürgerlichen Realismus* (Munich: Hanser, 1971).

40. "Ein Sonnenstrahl, der durch die Baumwipfel auf ihren Scheitel fiel, setzte ihr eine goldene Krone auf" (Alexis, *Ruhe*, 2: 322).
41. "Ich sah meinen Gemahl, meine Kinder, die Thronfolge, alles, was mir lieb und wert war, in Gefahr. . . . Ja, ich hielt den Krieg für notwendig, und wenn das ein Verbrechen ist, so habe ich ihn gewünscht" (ibid., 2: 456–57).
42. See Wülfing, Bruns, and Paar, 59–111, and de Bruyn, 55–97.
43. Mühlbach, *Napoleon in Deutschland* (Berlin: Janke, 1858), *Rastatt und Jena*, 4 vols., trans. F. Jordan as *Louisa of Prussia and Her Times: An Historical Novel* (New York: Appleton, 1867); Mühlbach, *Napoleon und Königin Luise*, 4 vols., trans. F. Jordan as *Napoleon and the Queen of Prussia*. The German quotations are from the fourth printing of 1864, in which *Rastatt und Jena* is volume 1 and *Napoleon und Königin Luise* is volume 2.
44. Mühlbach, *Louisa of Prussia*, 59; "und da sie [die Hofdamen und Hofherren] gehört haben, wie Ew. Majestät aller Etikette zuwider im Gespräch mit Ihro Majestät der Königen Sich statt der französischen Sprache, welche doch überall in Deutschland die Hofsprache ist, oft der vulgären deutschen Sprache bedienen, so meinen sie auch berechtigt zu sein, zuweilen deutsch zu sprechen" (Mühlbach, *Rastatt und Jena*, 87).
45. Ibid.; "Unnatur und Ziererei" (Mühlbach, *Rastatt und Jena*, 87).
46. Ibid.; "in guter christlicher Ordnung" (Mühlbach, *Rastatt und Jena*, 89).
47. Another German couple, England's Queen Victoria and Prince Albert, embodied these same bourgeois norms and values for the Anglo-American middle class.
48. Whether the German middle class actually won the Revolution of 1848 by making German society bourgeois was the subject of a ferocious debate among historians during the 1980s. David Blackbourne and Geoff Eley launched the controversy with their book *The Peculiarities of German History: Bourgeois Society and Politics in Nineteenth-Century Germany* (Oxford: Oxford University Press, 1984) when it was published in Germany in 1980. See also Richard Evans, "The Myth of Germany's Missing Revolution," in Richard Evans, *Rethinking German History: Nineteenth-Century Germany and the Origins of the Third Reich* (London: Unwin Hyman, 1987), 93–122.
49. Mühlbach, *Louisa of Prussia*, 101–2; "daß seine Töchter nur die Erzeugnisse deutscher Industrie und die Arbeiten deutscher Handwerker tragen sollten, und daß kein Stück ihrer Aussteuer aus Frankreich entlehnt werden dürfe" (Mühlbach, *Rastatt und Jena*, 146).

NOTES TO CHAPTER 4

50. Mühlbach, *Louisa of Prussia*, 102; "wie glücklich bin ich, zu sehen, daß Deutschland wirklich ganz und gar Frankreichs entbehren und selbst allen seinen Bedürfnissen genügen kann!" (Mühlbach, *Rastatt und Jena*, 147).
51. Mühlbach, *Louisa of Prussia*, 105; "es geht uns, den reichen Jüdinnen, wie den armen Prinzessinnen, man verschachert uns an den Meistbietenden" (Mühlbach, *Rastatt und Jena*, 151). Women being unjustly denied the right to choose their own husbands is a recurrent topos with Mühlbach; Frederick the Great's sisters complain of the same treatment in Mühlbach's novels in chapter 3 of the present volume.
52. Mühlbach, *Louisa of Prussia*, 301; "Sie werden den Schein einer Religion von sich werfen, welche doch nicht mehr die Ihrige ist. . . Sie sind Ihrer Bildung, Ihren Gewohnheiten, Ihrer ganzen Lebensanschauung nach keine Jüdin mehr!" . . . "Niemals!" (Mühlbach, *Rastatt und Jena*, 423).
53. Mühlbach, *Louisa of Prussia*, 317; "Du sollst Vermittlerin sein zwischen der Aristokratie des Blutes und Stammbaums und der Aristokratie des Geldes, die Vermittlerin zwischen den Christenthum und den Judenthum" (Mühlbach, *Rastatt und Jena*, 445).
54. Mühlbach, *Louisa of Prussia*, 320; "Auch darin sollst Du unser geschmähtes Jedenthum vertreten, daß Du denen, welche uns verhöhnen und als Fremdlinge verachten, beweisest, daß wir geboren sind, und daß wir unser Jerusalem nicht im fernen Orient suchen, sondern in dem Vaterland, das wir mit allen andern Deutschen theilen" (Mühlbach, *Rastatt und Jena*, 448).
55. Mühlbach, *Louisa of Prussia*, 320; "gehörten nicht dem Roman, sondern der Wirklichkeit an" (Mühlbach, *Rastatt und Jena*, 449).
56. Mühlbach, *Louisa of Prussia*, 482; "Aber wo alle Männer zagten, wo sie alle scheu und feig ihren Schmerz und ihre Demüthigung herunterwürgten, da erhoben sich die Frauen in der echten kühnen Begeisterung ihres Schmerzgefühls. Sie konnten nicht drohen, nicht ihre Hand bewaffnen mit dem Schwert, wie die Männer, aber sie konnten flehen und bitten, und statt der Waffen in ihren Händen hatten sie die Thränen in ihren Augen" (Mühlbach, *Rastatt und Jena*, 676).
57. Mühlbach, *Louisa of Prussia*, 502; "kluge und besonnene" (Mühlbach, *Rastatt und Jena*, 704).
58. Mühlbach, *Louisa of Prussia*, 502–3; "prügelte den Soldaten das Ehrgefühl aus"; "Die Besonnenen hatten wohl Recht zu zagen; die Sorge, welche aus den düsteren Mienen des Königs sprach, hatte wohl ihre Berechtigung" (Mühlbach, *Rastatt und Jena*, 704–6).
59. Mühlbach, *Napoleon and the Queen*, 63; "'Ach, meine Söhne, Ihr seid schon in dem Alter, daß Euer Verstand die Ereignisse, welche uns jetzt heimsuchen, fassen und fühlen kann; ruft künftig, wenn Euer Mutter und Königin nicht mehr lebt, diese unglückliche Stunde in Euer Gedächtniß

NOTES TO CHAPTER 4

zurück; weint meinem Andenken Thränen, wie ich sie jetzt in diesem schrecklichen Augenblick dem Unsturz unseres Vaterlandes weine! Aber hört, fuhr die Königin fort,' und ihre Augen flammten auf in kühner Begeisterung, und sich aus ihren Sessel erhebend, stand sie groß und kühn wie eine strahlende Minerva da, 'begnügt Euch nicht mit Thränen allein. Handelt, entwickelt Eure Kräfte; vielleicht läßt Preußens Schutzgeist sich auf Euch nieder; befreit dann Euer Volk von der Schande, dem Vorwurf, der Erniedrigung, worin es schmachtet'" (Mühlbach, *Napoleon und Königin Luise*, 88).

60. Mühlbach, *Napoleon and the Queen*, 493; "Dieser Mann, der Morgen sein Vermählungsfest mit einer deutschen Prinzessin feiert, hat den Dolch in mein Herz gestoßen, an dem es verbluten wird" (Mühlbach, *Napoleon und Königin Luise*, 730).

61. A popular lithograph from 1810 shows the queen floating heavenward and bears the title *The Transfiguration [Verklärung] of Queen Louisa of Prussia* (Preußen: Versuch einer Bilanz, 1: 483). See also Wülfing, Bruns, and Parr, which includes two other images with the same title (80–81), along with a discussion of Louisa as the "Prussian Madonna" (85–89) and reports that interpreted the Wars of Liberation as Louisa's "rise from the dead" (*Auferstehung*, 94).

62. Max Ring, "Louise: Zur hunderjährigen Geburtstagsfeier der Mutter unseres Kaisers," *Die Gartenlaube* 24.1–4 (1876). In 1875 *Die Gartenlaube* claimed 382,000 subscribers; see Dieter Barth, *Zeitschrift für Alle: Das Familienblatt im 19. Jahrhundert: Ein sozialhistorischer Beitrag zur Massenpresse in Deutschland* (Diss., Westfälische Wilhelms-Universität, Münster, 1974) 437, and Belgum, *Popularizing the Nation*.

63. "Durch echt weibliche Tugenden, durch Sittenreinheit, selbstlose Liebe und hingebende Treue hat diese echt deutsche Fürstin einen unsterblichen Namen erworben" (Ring, "Louise," 4).

64. "Das durch französische Einflüsse zerrüttete Familienleben am Hofe wieder herzustellen, die vornehme Liederlichkeit zu unterdrücken und durch bürgerliche Einfachheit, strenge Sittlichkeit und Zucht Allen voranzuleuchten" (ibid., 7).

65. "Nur die Königin erkannte wiederum mit ihrem prophetischen Blick die Bedeutung dieser Volksbewegung" (ibid., 71).

66. "So war Louise, so lange sie lebte, die reinste deutsche Frau, die liebvollste Gattin und Mutter, der Genius der Familie, nach ihrem Tode aber war sie der Schutzgeist ihres Volkes, das sie noch immer wie eine Heilige verehrt und dem sie als das Ideal der reinsten Weiblichkeit unvergeßlich bleibt" (ibid., 72).

67. Heinrich von Treitschke, "Königin Luise" in *Historische und Politische Aufsätze* (Leipzig: Hirzel, 1920), 2nd ed., 4: 139–53.

68. "In der Erinnerung ihres dankbaren Volkes lebt sie fort wie eine Lichtgestalt, die den Kämpfern unseres Befreiungskrieges den Pfad weisend, hoch in den Lüften voranschwebt" (ibid., 139).
69. "[Es] blieb ihr verborgen, welche wüste, überfeinerte Unzucht ihr Wesen trieb in diesem Berlin . . . Die Glückliche ahnte nicht, wie alles morsch ward in dem Staate, wie das Auge des Großen Königs zürnend auf die Erben niederblickte" (ibid., 145).
70. "Mit jedem Heldengeiste gesegnet, dessen Hauch wir noch spürten in unserem jüngsten Kriege" (ibid., 139, emphasis added).
71. "Welche dem Ruhm und der Macht der Völker allein die Gewähr der Dauer geben" (ibid., 153).
72. Treitschke, *History*, 1: 175; "erst durch die heitere Herzensgüte der Königin Luise gewann das Verhältnis zwischen den Hohenzollern und ihrem treuen Volke jenen gemüthlichen Zug der Vertraulichkeit, der sich sonst nur in dem Stilleben der Kleinstaaten zeigt" (Treitschke, *Deutsche Geschichte*, 1: 151).
73. Treitschke, *History*, 1: 254; "haltlos den Einfällen seines unruhigen Kopfes" (Treitschke, *Deutsche Geschichte*, 1: 219).
74. Treitschke, *History*, 1: 258; "Allein die Nüchternheit des Königs bewahrte den Staat vor einem verderblichen Schritte" (Treitschke, *Deutsche Geschichte*, 1: 222).
75. Treitschke, *History*, 1: 261; "durch die Mißgriffe der beiden Kaiser" (Treitschke, *Deutsche Geschichte*, 1: 225).
76. Treitschke, *History*, 1: 276; "mit aufrichtigen Bedauern sah er jetzt das Reich zu Grunde gehen. . . . Der König glaubte kein Wort mehr von den glatten Schmeichelreden, womit ihn Napoleon noch während des Winter überschüttet hatte" (Treitschke, *Deutsche Geschichte*, 1: 237–38).
77. Treitschke, *History*, 1: 290; "der Verlust der Doppelschlacht wesentlich durch die Führung verschuldet war" (Treitschke, *Deutsche Geschichte*, 1: 249).
78. Treitschke, *History*, 1: 313; "[Es] schaarte sich mit einem Male ein neues Geschlecht um den Thron: mächtige Charaktere, begeisterte Herzen, helle Köpfe in unabsehbarer Reihe, eine dichte Schaar von Talenten des Rathes und des Lagers, die den literischen Großen der Nation ebenbürtig an die Seite traten" (Treitschke, *Deutsche Geschichte*, 1: 268).
79. Johann Gustav Droysen, *Vorlesungen über das Zeitalter der Freiheitskriege*, 2nd ed. (1846; Gotha: Perthes, 1886).
80. "Die Neugründung jenes protestantisch deutschen Staates" (ibid., 1: 12).
81. "Und die Wissenschaft der Geschichte hat keine höhere Aufgabe, als diesen Glauben zu rechtfertigen; darum ist sie Wissenschaft. Sie sieht und findet in jenem wüsten Wellengang eine Richtung, ein Ziel, einen Plan; sie lehrt uns Gottes Wege begreifen und bewundern" (ibid., 1: 4–5).

82. "Noch war Deutschland nicht tief genug erniedrigt; es mußte erst ganz zertreten und geschunden werden, ehe es sich erhob" (ibid., 2: 198).
83. "Jetzt war Preußen auf dem Plan" (ibid., 2: 199).
84. "Nie ist eine Niederlage vollständiger gewesen" (ibid., 2: 209). Droysen uses a similar formulation to describe Napoleon's meeting with Prussia's royal couple at Tilsit: "Never was a king more deeply humiliated and never was a queen more bitterly insulted than Frederick William and Louisa" ("Nie ist ein König tiefer gedemütigt, nie eine Königin bitterer gekränkt worden, als Friedrich Wilhelm und Luise in Tilsit," 2: 217).
85. "Ideen genug waren vorhanden, aber sie vermochten nirgens diesen Wust von Indolenz, Selbstgefälligkeit und Genußsucht, mit dem die im Dienste Graugewordenen das Kabinett und den Thron umgaben, zu durchbrechen. Bitterkeit, Zuchtlosigkeit und Excentrizität auf der einen, Schlaffheit, Unklarheit, Gemaschen- und Tabellenwesen auf der anderen Seite, und als Vereinigung beider die formelle Ehre des Standes, des Ranges, des preußischen Namens" (ibid., 2: 199–200).
86. "So schankte man zwischen Angriff und Verteidigung, hielt Veranstaltungen ohne Beschluß, manövrierte weiter ohne Plan" (ibid., 2: 208).
87. "Unter der verknöcherten Hülle des alten fridericianischen Staates [war] schon ein neues Preußen herangewachsen" (ibid., 2: 214).
88. Ludwig Häusser, *Deutsche Geschichte vom Tode Friedrichs des Großen bis zur Gründung des deutschen Bundes,* 2nd. ed.([1855–57], Berlin: Weidmannsche Buchhandlung, 1859).
89. Sheehan, *German History,* 844.
90. "Aber noch war die äußerste Gränze deutscher Erniedrigung nicht erreicht" (Häusser, *Deutsche Geschichte vom Tode,* 2: 592).
91. "Noch ahnte im Lande Niemand, wie morsch die überlieferten Ordnungen dieses Staates geworden waren. . . . Männer wie Stein dachten unter solchen Umständen vor Allem daran, die Regierungsmaschine zu bessern, die unzweifelhaft eine der Ursachen des Verfalles war" (ibid., 1: 593–95).
92. "Adelig-soldaische Uebermuth," "die Bewaffnung war . . . sehr mangelhaft," "so wird die Bekleidung der Soldaten als ganz elend geschildert," "Die neue Kriegskunst in ihrer Beweglichkeit und Vielsetigkeit ward kaum noch begriffen, geschweige denn nachgeahmt" (ibid., 2: 605–7).
93. "Man erkannte nicht, daß das System der preußischen Wehrverfassung sich überlebt hatte. Man glaubt, äußerte damals Kleist, wir brauchten uns nur blicken zu lassen, so gehen die Franzosen schon davon" (ibid., 2: 605–6).
94. Although German usage is not as strict as English in discouraging impersonal constructions, a sixteen-line paragraph that contains the word "one" (*man*) seven times is, by any measure, excessive and symptomatic of

NOTES TO CHAPTER 4

Häusser's difficulty in affixing blame (600). The text is also filled with the passive voice and its equivalents.

95. "[Er] nannte Rüchel einen Fanfaron, den Marschall Möllendorf einen abgestumpften Greis, den General Kalkreuth einen listigen Ränkeschneider" (Häusser, *Deutsche Geschichte vom Tode,* 2: 622).
96. "Der Erfolg dieses Planes hing freilich davon ab, daß man dem Feinde zuvorkam" (ibid., 2: 631).
97. "Der Besitz dieses Ortes entschied nun über den Ausgang der Schlacht" (ibid., 2: 640).
98. "Die ganze alte Monarchie war gesprengt" (ibid., 2: 641).
99. "Wo noch deutsche Scham und patriotische Empfindung lebte, fing man jetzt erst an, das unermeßliche Elend des Vaterlandes zu überschauen; der letzte Trug selbstgemachten Trostes war verschwunden . . . Die Nation selber mußte jetzt zeigen, ob sie ihrer Fortdauer werth war" (ibid.).
100. Gustav Freytag, *Bilder aus der deutschen Vergangenheit* (1859–62; Berlin: Knaur, 1927). For a survey of Freytag's life and work, which includes a publishing history, see Nancy Kaiser, "Gustav Freytag," in *Dictionary of Literary Biography,* vol. 129, *Nineteenth-Century German Writers, 1841–1900,* ed. James Hardin and Siegfried Mews (Detroit: Gale, 1993), 92–100. The best treatment of Freytag as a historian is Lynne Tatlock's "Realist Historiography and the Historiography of Realism: Gustav Freytag's *Bilder aus der deutschen Vergangenheit,*" *German Quarterly* 63.1 (1990): 59–74.
101. "Aus der Zeit der Zerstörung" (Freytag, *Bilder,* 2: 760–91); Gethe's autobiography begins on page 780.
102. "Das preußische Heer litt an denselben Mängeln, wie die Politik und Verwaltung des Staates. Auch hier war im einzelnen manches gebessert, vieles Alte ward sorgfältig beibehalten, was einst ein Fortschritt gewesen war, bestand jetzt zum Unheil" (ibid., 2: 776).
103. "Diese unglückliche Geschichte mußte in einem Lande, wo man noch gar nicht preußisch gesinnt war, die Gemüter empören. . . . und unsere preußische Justiz, wovon wir den Mund so voll genommen hatten, bekam einen häßlichen Flecken" (ibid., 2: 784–85).
104. "Jetzt war ihnen das voreilige Anerbieten leid geworden, und sie hatten keine Lust, ihm den Degen zu senden, weil sie bei ihm die Willfährigkeit, welche sie erwartet, nicht gefunden hatten. Was aus dem Degen geworden, habe ich nicht erfahren, man hielt die Sache geheim" (ibid., 2: 789).
105. Gustav Freytag, *Die Ahnen,* vol. 6, *Aus einer kleinen Stadt* [1880].
106. "Zustände, welche dergleichen möglich machen, sind tyrannisch und im schreienden Widerspruch gegen die Gebote der Humanität" (ibid., 6: 13).
107. For a recent analysis that looks at both the national question and the

NOTES TO CHAPTER 4

Kulturkampf, see Helmut Walser Smith, *German Nationalism and Religious Conflict: Culture, Ideology, Politics, 1870–1914* (Princeton, NJ: Princeton University Press, 1995).

108. George Hesekiel, *Vor Jena: Roman nach den Aufzeichnungen eines königlichen Officiers vom Regiment Gensd'armes* (Berlin: Janke, 1859), here *Vaterländische Romane*, vol. 1, 1865.

109. Fontane to Wilhelm Friedrich, November 5, 1882, in Fontane, *Schach* (161). For a discussion of the two men's personal connection, see Grawe. Fontane devotes a chapter to Hesekiel in the second installment of his memoirs, *Von Zwanzig bis Dreißig: Autobiographisches* (1898; Munich: DTV, 1973), 247–74.

110. Fontane, *Von Zwanzig bis Dreißig*, 254–55.

111. "Ihr armen Junker aber, ihr werdet immer ärmer, ihr kommt nicht mehr zurück, weil euch diese gottverfluchte Leibeigenschaft eurer Bauer wie ein Centnergewicht am Halse hängt . . . [und in den Städten] verdammtes Gemengel von schönen Redensarten, jüdischer Weisheit und französisch-revolutionärer Frechheit" (Hesekiel, *Vor Jena*, 138–39).

112. "[Elendigkeit] daß Groß und Klein an dem Gelde hängt und Gelderwerb und bequemes Leben als Zweck und Ziel des Strebens betrachtet" (ibid., 14).

113. "Die Juden [haben] überhaupt keine Neigung zu den Thieren, auch nicht die vernünftige, die rechtschaffen, keine Freude an Roß und Hund, kein Verständnis für die Natur. Wir freuen uns im rauschenden Wald, der Jude aber zittert" (ibid., 76).

114. "Die Juden und die Franzosen haben viel mehr Aehnlichkeiten miteinander, als man denkt . . . wir verlieren an jenen geistigen Spieltischen unsere deutsche Gedanken, unsere deutsche Gefühle, unsere Siegerinnen zwingen uns fremde, undeutsche Gedanken und Gefühle auf . . . die geistreichen Jüdinnen sind die Vorposten der revolutionären französischen Weltherrschaft in Berlin" (ibid., 77).

115. "Aufgefallen ist mir das lange, daß die Juden hier, mit wenigen Ausnahmen, nur Geld, aber viel Geld zu verdienen wissen, während die Jüdinnen sich in Besitz einer geistigen Herrschaft gesetzt haben, so hat das Judenthum hier eine doppelte Macht" (ibid., 76).

116. "[Sie] hatte das Unglück, daß Niemand ihr den schönen Namen ließ, den sie in der Taufe erhalten, der französelnde Deutsche, ihr Vater, nannte sie Babette, die Geheimrätin, eine Deutsch-Französin, engländerte gern und nannte sie Betty" (ibid., 26).

117. "Wie heißt? Stehlen? Gott soll mir schenken noch ein fünfzig Jährchen, dann werden wir sein in dieser Stadt die Edelleute und die Edelleute werden sein Gojim, die uns dienen!" (ibid., 180).

118. "Noch immer giebt es lieder Schriftsteller, welche sich nicht scheuen, die

NOTES TO CHAPTER 4

alten Unwahrheiten immer wieder auf's Neue aufzutischen und zu erzählen, die Junker und adligen Offiziere, die sie feig, albern und brutal nennen, hätten das Unglück des Vaterlantes herbeigeführt" (Hesekiel, *Stille vor dem Sturm,* 1: 156).

119. Fontane, *Man of Honor,* 47; "Welche Augen wohl König Friedrich gemacht habe würde, wenn man ihn den 'guten Friedrich' genannt hätte" (Fontane, *Schach,* 52).

120. Fontane, *Man of Honor,* 114, ellipses original; "Und die Tochter! Weiß wohl, weiß; armes Kind. . . . Aber enfin, müssen sie doch charmant gefunden haben. . . . habe mit der Königen darüber gesprochen; will Sie sehn; Frauenlaune" (Fontane, *Schach,* 117–18).

121. Fontane, *Man of Honor,* 116; "Wüßt' ich kaum etwas, was mir in diesem Augenblicke so lieb wäre, wie die Schlichtung dieses Streits und der Bund zweier Herzen, die mir füreinander bestimmt erscheinen. . . . Und nun eilen Sie heim, und machen Sie glücklich und werden Sie glücklich" (Fontane, *Schach,* 119).

122. Fontane, *Man of Honor,* 116; "so galt es denn für ihn, etwas ausfindig zu machen, was Gehorsam und Ungehorsam in sich vereinigte" (Fontane, *Schach,* 120).

123. In a description of the Louisa monument at Gransee, Fontane flatly denies the notion that the queen died from heartbreak over the fatherland's misfortune. He also says one would have to go back to medieval saints to find a similar icon, and he claims Louisa's admirerers did more damage to her reputation than anything her detractors could say (*Wanderungen durch die Mark Brandenburg: Die Grafschaft Ruppin, Das Oderland.* Helmuth Nürnberger, ed. [Munich: DTV, 1994], 1: 501–2).

124. Wilhelm Jensen, *Um die Wende des Jahrhunderts (1789–1806)* (Dresden: Reißner, 1899).

125. For a brief account of Jensen's and Raabe's friendship and its literary reverbations, see Jeffrey L. Sammons, *Wilhelm Raabe: The Fiction of the Alternative Community* (Princeton, NJ: Princeton University Press, 1987), 22–27.

126. "Ihre Füße hatten augenscheinlich nichts puppenhaft zierliches, sondern standen mit ihrer Größe, wie ebenso die unbehandschuten schöngeformten Hände in richtigem Verhältniß zu der ganzen körperlichen Gestaltung" (Jensen, 1: 24).

127. "Dabei führte er die nämliche halbfranzösische Sprache im Mund, wie die Nachahmer des Hofes von Versailles, nur klang sie auf seiner Zunge ganz anders, man dachte nicht an Fremdländisches dabei, sie weckte völlig das Gefühl, ein derbes, gradaus den Nagel auf den Kopf treffendes Deutsch zu sein" (ibid., 1: 143).

128. "Doch wer den Degen gegen seine Nation führt, ist ein Filou und Cujon.

Wenn Er in Frankreich gewesen ist, weiß Er, was das heißt. Aber ich will es Ihm auch in Seiner Muttersprache appliciren. Auf deutsch benennt man es einen Hundsfott" (ibid., 2: 122).
129. "Eine dumpfe Betäubung lag über dem deutschen Volk" (ibid., 2: 132).
130. "Mit ihm fiel Preußen" (ibid., 2: 210).
131. "Ich segne das böse Schwert, das Dich traf, denn es schuf mein Glück" (ibid., 2: 226).
132. Jochen Schulte-Sasse's *Literarische Wertung* is still, to my mind, the best statement of this position, but in the years since its publication the ground from which to launch an ideological critique has become shaky. In addition, despite earlier caveats about cultural study's search for progressive popular fiction, Jensen shows how bad novels can be progressive.

Chapter 5

1. Todd Kontje, *Women, the Novel, and the German Nation, 1771–1871: Domestic Fiction in the Fatherland* (Cambridge: Cambridge University Press, 1998), 6, where he invokes Theweleit's argument. To be fair, Kontje is contrasting Körner with women writers rather than making a grand claim about the content of the era's domestic fiction.
2. Christopher Clark, "The Wars of Liberation in Prussian Memory: Reflections on the Memorialization of War in Early Nineteenth-Century Germany," *Journal of Modern History* 68 (September 1996): 550. See also Jost Hermand, "Dashed Hopes: On the Painting of the Wars of Liberation," trans. James D. Steakley, in *Political Symbolism in Modern Europe,* ed. Seymour Drescher, David Sabean, and Allan Sharlin (New Brunswick, NJ: Transaction, 1982), 216–38. I am indebted to Kevin Cramer for bibliographical and other information concerning the name "Befreiungskriege."
3. Louise von François, *Geschichte der preußischen Befreiungskriege in den Jahren 1813 bis 1815* (Berlin: Janke, n.d. [1873]). So far as I have been able to learn, the book exists only in a single printing, nevertheless labeled a "people's edition" (*Volks-Ausgabe*).
4. "Russisch-deutscher Krieg von 1812–1815," *Allgemeinge deutsche Real-Encyklopädie für die gebildeten Stände* (Leipzig: Brockhaus, 1836), 9: 505–20.
5. "Noch gab er den Zweck nicht an, allein sein Volk verstand ihn, und mit nie gesehener Begeisterung kamen aus allen Gegenden Tausende nach den Sammelplätzen; Tausende, zu alt zum Kampf, gaben den letzten Sparpfennig" (ibid., 9: 511).
6. "Mit dem Namen der Freiheitskriege pflegen wir in Deutschland jene drei unvergesslichen Jahre zu bezeichnen, in denen, zum erstenmal nach Jahrhunderten, das deutsche Volk gemeinsam und in dem Hochgefühl

NOTES TO CHAPTER 5

seiner Einheit gekämpft und gesiegt hat" (Droysen, *Vorlesungen,* 1: 3).
7. "Welch ein Widerspruch zwischen dem Staat Frankreich und dem Volk der Franzosen. Als endlich Ludwig XVI, beide auszugleichen . . . versuchte, da stürzten ihm wie aus tausend Schleusen die Gedanken der Freiheit, der Menschenrechte, der Gleichheit entgegen" (ibid., 1: 8).
8. "Es geschah am 23.Juni; 'der zweite' polnische Krieg ist begonnen.' [Proklamation von Wilkowiski] Ein polnischer Krieg? Galt es die Herstellung Polens? . . . Der Kabinettskrieg schug um zum Volkskrieg" (ibid., 2: 402).
9. "Die ganze Herrlichkeit eines großen einigen Vaterlandes that sich den Blicken des deutschen Volkes auf. Wohl als ein erhebendes Vorbild mochte Preußen, König und Volk, erscheinen" (ibid., 2: 420).
10. "In der Nähe Berlins, bei Groß-Beeren, kam es zur entscheidenden Schlacht; Bülow wagte sie wider die Meinumg des Kronprinzen von Schweden; es waren die Preußen allein, die zur Schlacht kamen; es war der erste Ehrentag der Landwehren; ihre Kolbenschläge erzwangen den Sieg; Berlin war gerettet" (ibid., 2: 438).
11. "Was Hunderttausende auf die erste Kunde des russischen Verhängnisses in Stillen ergriffen hatte, die Ahnung, daß, wenn jemals, jetzt der Moment gekommen sei, die Ketten abzuschütteln, das war hier unerwartet geschehen; der Gedanke der Zeit war durch Yorck zur That geworden. Das ward weithin von Millionen gefühlt. Nicht in Preußen allein, . . . nicht nur in Oesterreich, . . . auch tief im Rheinbund . . . Und in Frankreich . . . man fühlte vollkommen, daß das nicht die isolirte That eines Einzigen, sondern ein erstes Symptom einer Erhebung der deutschen Völker war" (Häusser, *Deutsche Geschichte,* 4: 20–21).
12. "Wie man mit jungen Leuten aus den gebildeten und wohlhabenden Ständen, denen alle Dressur noch abging, etwas Tüchtiges herstellen könne. . . . Oekonomen und Referendarien, Studenten, Kaufleute und Justizräthe" (ibid., 4: 169).
13. "Die Bevölkerung vollends zeigte dem wärmsten Eifer und bei vielen Anlässen gab sich die Sympathie für die gute Sache in wahrhaft rührenden Zügen kund" (ibid., 4: 170).
14. "Wo es zum Handgemenge kam und das Gewehr versagte, gingen sie wie rechte Naturkinder des Krieges mit dem Kolben und die blutige Arbeit" (ibid., 4: 266–67).
15. Heinrich von Sybel, *Die Erhebung Europas gegen Napoleon I: Drei Vorlesungen, gehalten am 24., 27. und 30. März 1860* (Munich: Literarisch-artistische Anstalt der J. K. Cotta'schen Buchhandlung, 1860).
16. "Daß selbst Napoleons überragendes Feldherrngenie nicht im Stande gewesen wäre uns zu überwältigen—hätten wir uns nicht selbst gelähmt, nicht selbst bekämpft und besiegt" (ibid., 53).

17. "Indessen pflanzte sich die Erhebung und Begeisterung der Gemüther unaufhaltsam durch die Lande fort" (ibid., 113).
18. "Wie die Jugend so das Alter; Familienväter und Greise stellten sich, und mehr als ein Mädchen trat verkleidet in die Reihe der Männer, um dem Vaterlande Blut und Leben darzubringen" (ibid., 117).
19. "Ein Schäfer aus Anclam verkaufte seine Heerde, schaffte sich dafür Waffen und Uniform und ging zum Regiment" (ibid., 119).
20. "Ein alter preußischer Officier, der vier Söhne zum Heere gebracht, wurde von dem Könige gefragt, wie es ihm und den Söhnen gehe. 'Es geht uns gut,' antwortete er, 'und stockte einen Augenblick, meine Söhne sind Alle für Ew. Maj. Gefallen.' 'Nicht für mich,' rief darauf erschüttert der König, 'nicht für mich, wer könnte das ertragen, aber für das Vaterland'" (ibid., 142).
21. "Die leitenden Geister der Nation, die großen Dichter und Denker, waren der Ueberzeugung, daß der Patriotismus eine Beschränktheit und der ächte Mann lediglich zu ästhetischer Bildung und humanem Weltbürgerthum berufen sei" (ibid., 55).
22. Treitschke, *History*, 1: 479; "Der Kampf um die Befreiung der Welt blieb doch in erster Linie ein Kampf um die Wiederaufrichtung Preußens" (Treitschke, *Deutsche Geschichte*, 1: 408).
23. Treitschke, *History*, 1: 477–695; (Treitschke, *Deutsche Geschichte*, 1: 406–508).
24. Treitschke, *History*, 1: 507; "Neben den alten Soldaten empfand die gebildete Jugend den Ernst der Zeit am lebhaftesten; in ihr glühte die schwärmerische Sehnsucht nach dem freien und einigen Deutschland. Kein Student, der irgend die Waffe schwingen konnte, blieb daheim" (Treitschke, *Deutsche Geschichte*, 1: 431).
25. Treitschke, *History*, 1: 508; "Nur die Polen in Westpreußen und Oberschlesien theilten die Hingebung der Deutschen nicht; auch in einzelnen Städten, die bisher vom Heeresdienste frei gewesen, stießen die neuen Gesetze auf Widerstand" (Treitschke, *Deutsche Geschichte*, 1: 431–32).
26. Treitschke, *History*, 1: 509; "Nur der alte Goethe wollte sich zu der neuen Zeit kein Herz fasen" (Treitschke, *Deutsche Geschichte*, 1: 433).
27. Treitschke, *History*, 1: 511; "Der deutsche Befreiungskrieg war in seiner ersten, schwereren Hälfte ein Kampf Preußens gegen die von Frankreich beherrschten drei Viertel der deutschen Nation. . . . während der Süden erst zwei Menschenalter später des Glückes theilhaftig ward, für das große Vaterland zu kämpfen und zu siegen" (Treitschke, *Deutsche Geschichte*, 1: 434).
28. Treitschke, *History*, 1: 512; "Und etwas von den deutsch-patriotischen Gedanken, welche die bewaffnete Jugend der gebildeten Stände erfüllten,

drang doch allmählich bis in die niederen Schichten des preußischen Volkes herab" (Treitschke, *Deutsche Geschichte*, 1: 435).
29. Treitschke, *History*, 1: 511; "der alte deutsche Gott, zu dem sie [die Jugend] betete, war der Gott der Protestanten" (Treitschke, *Deutsche Geschichte*, 1: 434).
30. Treitschke, *History*, 1: 527 and 561; "eine jener aufgeblasenen Mittelmäßigkeiten, woran die diplomatische Geschichte der Mittelstaaten so reich ist," and "die Felonie der deutschen Fürsten" (Treitschke, *Deutsche Geschichte*, 1: 447, 478).
31. Treitschke, *History*, 1: 529; "Den Soldaten erschien er herrlich wie der Kriegsgott selber, wenn der schöne hochgewachsene Greis noch mit jugendlicher Kraft und Anmuth seinen feurigen Schimmel tummelte" (Treitschke, *Deutsche Geschichte*, 1: 450).
32. Treitschke, *History*, 1: 533, "ein echter Germane, nur germanischen Menschen ganz verständlich in der rauhen Größe" (Treitschke, *Deutsche Geschichte*, 1: 453).
33. Treitschke, *History*, 1: 531; "Die Kleinmeister entsetzten sich über den Jüngling im Greisenhaar, der noch zuweilen auf den Hofbällen mit den eleganten jungen Gardeoffizieren eine Quadrille tanzte; tiefere Naturen fühlten bald, daß dies ausgelassene Treiben nur der natürliche Ausdruck einer unbändigen überschäumenden Lebenskraft war" (Treitschke, *Deutsche Geschichte*, 1: 451–52).
34. Treitschke, *History*, 1: 596; "er sammelte aus dem reichen Schatze seines Wissens alle die historischen Erinnerungen und romantischen Bilder, deren er bedurfte um auf sein gelehrtes Volk zu wirken, und lebte sich ein in eine Anschauung, welche damals noch neu, bald eine treibende Kraft des Jahrhunderts werden sollte: in den Gedanken, daß am letzten Ende die Sprache und historische Eigenart der Nationen die Grenzen der Staaten bestimme" (Treitschke, *Deutsche Geschichte*, 1: 508).
35. Treitschke, *History*, 1: 555, "Die breite Kluft, welche das geistige Leben der Oesterreicher von den übrigen Deutschen trennte, wurde durch den Befreiungskrieg nicht überbrückt" (Treitschke, *Deutsche Geschichte*, 1: 472).
36. In addition to Ferdi Alkaltin, see Sandra Georgina Peterson, "The Treatment of the Napoleonic Wars in German Historical Fiction," Diss., Vanderbilt University, 1971. Unfortunately, Peterson is mainly interested in accuracy, which she measures by comparing novels to the accounts of historians. The latter she accepts without question.
37. Martin Swales, *Epochenbuch Realism: Romane und Erzählungen* (Berlin: Schmidt, 1997), 35–36.
38. "Ein junger deutscher . . . ihm bangte, sein unglückliches, entwürdigtes Vaterland zu betreten" (Rellstab, *1812*, 1.)

NOTES TO CHAPTER 5

39. "Das deutsche treue Herz" (ibid., 101).
40. "Er war im Bündnis mit denen, die sie nur als die Feinde ihres Vaterlandes betrachtete; sie konnte ihn als einen edlen Mann ehren, als einen großmütigen Freund lieben, niemals aber ihm angehören, ihr ganzes Wesen mit dem seinigen verschmelzen, ohne Pflichten zu verletzen, von deren Heiligkeit ihre Seele aufs tiefste durchdrungen war" (ibid., 111).
41. "Die Gräfin nahm einen tätigen, geistigen Anteil an dem Öffentlichen; . . . . Daher las sie mit Eifer die Zeitungen, die politischen Schriften des Tages; sie war mit der Geschichte der Ereignisse vertraut, verfolgte sie mit Scharfblick, brachte ferne Geschicke mit denen ihres Vaterlandes in denkende Beziehung. Marie hingegen liebte nur ihre Heimat, das Volk, dem sie angehörte, über alles; sie war durch Sprache und Denkweise eine Deutsche. . . . Mit der Befreiung ihres Vaterlandes wäre ihr Anteil am öffentlichen Leben erloschen, oder wenigstens so in die Ferne zurückgetreten wie bei allen Frauen" (ibid., 376).
42. "Wehe dem, der es Vaterland nennen muß; wohl dem, der eine andere Heimat kennt!" (ibid., 182).
43. Willibald Alexis, *Isegrimm: Vaterländischer Roman*, in *Vaterländische Romane*, ed. Ludwig Lorenz and Adolf Bartels, vol. 10 (Leipzig: Hesse and Becker, n.d. [1854]).
44. "Wenns Vaterland nicht zu retten ging, retten wir doch vielleicht die Pferde" (ibid., 161).
45. "Aber das Vaterland kann größer werden; es kann die ganze kultivierte Welt umfassen" (ibid., 156).
46. "Der Pöbel hat nicht mitzusprechen" (ibid., 337).
47. "[Leser, die ein Buch erwarten,] welches die vollständige Erhebung und Wiedergeburt des Vaterlands darstelle, werden sich getäuscht finden" (ibid., 722).
48. Louisa Mühlbach, *Napoleon in Deutschland*, vol. 3, *Napoleon und Blücher*, trans. F. Jordan as *Napoleon and Blücher: An Historical Novel* (New York: Appleton, 1867).
49. Mühlbach, *Napoleon and Blücher*, 103, emphasis added. The German version takes longer to engage Blücher in the grandson's plan, but they do eventually join to fight the enemy: "dabei will mein Christian helfen, will Soldat werden, und die Franzosen raus schmeißen helfen" (*Napoleon und Blücher*, 145).
50. Fritz Reuter, *Aus der Franzosenzeit [Ut de Franzosentid]*, trans. into standard German by Friedrich and Barbara Minssen, *Gezeiten des Lebens: Die Romane der Erinnerung* (Munich: Langen Müller, 1976).
51. "[Der Sohn] kann nur ein braver Deutscher sein" (ibid., 86).
52. "Der französische Oberst," "lütte französische Gören" (ibid., 161, 162).
53. Julius von Wickede, *Der lange Isaack: Historischer Roman aus der Zeit des*

deutschen Befreiungskrieges (Jena: Costenoble, 1863).
54. "Gewiß und wahrhaftig, Isaack, Du bist zwar ein Jude, und die Juden kann ich eigentlich nicht leiden, aber ein Kerl, der ein braveres Herz als Du in seiner Brust hat, lebt weit und breit nicht im ganzen hannover'schen Land" (ibid., 1: 49).
55. "Damit er der Sache des Vaterlands einen wichtigen Dienst zu leisten vermöge" (ibid., 1: 50).
56. "In einem für Juden ungewöhnlich sauberen Haus" (ibid., 1: 109).
57. "Der ihr zuerst auch die reichen Schätze unserer besten deutschen Schriftsteller eröffnet" (ibid., 1: 117).
58. "[Mit] wahrer christlicher Barmherzigkeit, wie sie auf dieser Erde nicht reiner und edler gefunden werden kann, pflegte Rebekka den verwundeten Offizier" (ibid., 2: 8).
59. "Die Bücher, aber, welche der Lieutenant sich bei seiner allmäligen Wiederherstellung aus einer Leihbibliothek in der Stadt hatte holen lassen, und die seinem Geschmacke am Besten zusagten, waren entweder so trivial oder gar auch zweideutig, daß sie solche schon nach dem Lesen einiger Seiten stets verächtlich wieder aus der Hand warf" (ibid., 2: 31).
60. "In solchen Augenblicken der kriegerischen Begeisterung erschien der Lieutenant wieder der Jüdin in dem ideellen Lichte, in dem sie ihn anfänglich nach seiner Verwundung gesehen hate. . . . es war und blieb ihr stets ein unerklärliches Räthsel, daß derselbe Mann, der so edlen Gefühlen zugänglich war, der sich stets bereit zeigte, sein innigstes Herzblut freudig für des Vaterlands Befreiung zu verspritzen, auf der anderen Seite wieder eine so geringe Neigung für jede höhere geistige Richtung zeigte und solchen Geschmack an Trivialitäten, die ihr gleichgültig, ja sogar selbst verächtlich erschienen, finden konnt. Aber auch Rebekka selbst fühlte den bittersten Schmerz über die Unfälle der verbundenen Waffen, auch sie liebte ihr großes deutsches Vaterland auf das Wärmste, denn wenn sie auch Jüdin, so war sie zugleich doch eine so wahre, echte Deutsche" (ibid., 2: 39–40).
61. "Gotteswille hat es so gefügt, daß ich als Jüdin geboren wurde. . . . Wäre ich als Christin geboren, sicherlich würde ich dann eine wahrhafte Anhängerin Eurer religion geworden" (ibid., 2: 321–22).
62. "So waren die Seelen der beiden Liebenden dann jetzt in dem bessern ewigen Jenseits, wo kein Unterschied der Religion sie von einander mehr zu trennen vermochte" (ibid., 3: 343).
63. Sir Walter Scott, *Ivanhoe* (1819; New York: Modern Library, 1997), xxiii.
64. "Im Laufe der Zeit ist auch sein Andenken allmälig dort gänzlich erlöschen" (ibid., 3: 345).
65. "Und wenn wir selbst vielleicht auch nicht mehr so erleben es doch sicherlich unsere Kinder oder Kindeskinder, daß dereinst noch die Kaiserkrone

NOTES TO CHAPTER 5

des einigen, freien Deutschlands das Haupt eines Königs von Preußen schmückt" (ibid., 2: 78).
66. "Wahre Würde als Offizier" (ibid., 2: 59).
67. "So sehr das in unserer vaterländischen Geschichte ewig denkwürdigen Jahr 1813 auch in der vollen warmen Opferfreudigkeit des großten Theils des deutschen Volkes hoch über unsere matte, nur materiell rechnende Gegenwart steht, so waren die Standesunterschiede damals noch ungleich schärfer, und eine Durchbrechung derselben viel schwieriger und seltener, als dies jetzt schon der Fall ist. Der Geist der Zeit hat hierin in den letzten fünfzig Jahren unendlich Vieles ausgeglichen, und wird dies sicherlich in Zukunft noch immer mehr thun, so daß nach späteren fünfzig Jahren kaum wohl noch ein schwacher Ueberrest des deutschen Adels vorhanden sein dürfte" (ibid., 2: 35–36).
68. Hesekiel, *Stille vor dem Sturm*.
69. "Das preußische Volk thut nichts ohne seinen König, das ist sein Stärke und auch seine Schwäche" (ibid., 1: 172).
70. "Es gibt auch ein Heldenthum im Bett" (ibid., 3: 157).
71. "Den schweren Kampf einer starken und edeln Neigung gegen eine bethörende und bestrickende Liebe" (ibid., 3: 127).
72. Louise von François, *Die letzte Reckenburgerin* (1871; Bonn: J. Latka Verlag, 1988).
73. "Trat ich auch in eine Art Verbindung mit den Patrioten, welche in Preußen und Österreich heimlich ihre Fäden spannen, und warum soll ich es verschweigen, daß manche von den Mitteln, die mir ja ausreichend zu Gebot standen, den höchsten Zwecken zugeflossen sind" (ibid., 391–92).
74. In *Louise von François and Die letzte Reckenburgerin: A Feminist Reading* (New York: Peter Lang, 1988), Thomas C. Fox draws an equally plausible link to the reforms championed by Stein and Hardenberg, emphasizing that they, too, involved an undemocratic revolution from above (129).
75. "Eine freude- und lieblose Kolonie" (François, *Die letzte Reckenburgerin*, 393).
76. "Die periodischen Galafeste haben aufgehört, aber im Schloß wie im Dorf singt und springt die Jugend unter dem Maibaum und Erntekranz; die Schenke streckt einladend ihren Arm in die Luft, die Kegel rollen, die Krüge klappen, wenn auch mit Maß" (ibid., 443).
77. Karl Frenzel, *Luzifer: Ein Roman aus der Napoleonischen Zeit* (Leipzig: Ernst Julius Günther, 1873), 5 vols.
78. "Ich bin ein geborener Unterthan des Hauses Hapsburg und hoffe lebend und sterbend ein guter Oesterreicher zu sein und zu bleiben" (ibid., 1: 17).
79. "Er sieht aus wie ein Held aus dem Märchen und redet so schüchtern wie

ein Mädchen" (ibid., 1: 160).
80. "Mir ist das Bürgerthum werth; es ist das Mark des deutschen Volkes. Unsere Pflicht ist es, diese bisher so träge Masse zu begeistern und mit dem heiligen Feuer der Vaterlandsliebe zu erfüllen" (ibid., 1: 158).
81. "Wir werden uns die Dichter aus Deutschland holen müssen. Wieland und Goethe sind die größten Poeten des Jahrhunderts" (ibid., 3: 97).
82. "Schade, daß man ihnen falsche Grundsätze einflößt und ihren Hang zur Träumerei und Grillenhaftigkeit vemehrt. Unter meinen Fahnen, was würde diese Jugend vollbringen! So hat Deutschland keine Naturforscher, keine Mathematiker, keine Erfinder" (ibid., 3: 101).
83. "Aus der engen Beschränktheit eines Lebens, das sich feindselig gegen das Allgemeine abschließen wollte und in schöngeistiger Selbstbescheulichkeit den einzigen Zweck des Daseins fand, hat er sich emporgearbeitet, kämpfend hat er dem Vaterland seine Schuld bezahlt. Innig und unlöslich ist das Geschick des Einzelnen mit dem des Staates und der großen Gemeinschaft verknüpft, in die ihn Geburt und Sprache, Erziehung und Gewöhnung gestellt" (ibid., 5: 186).
84. "Deutschland ist für ihn ein Name, eine geographische Bezeichnung, er hat kein Herz dafür. Wenn er sich für etwas erwärmen kann, so ist es für seine eigene Größe und einen ausschließlich österreichischen Staat" (ibid., 4: 115).
85. At the very end of the novel, Wolfsegg blames competition between Prussia and Austria for Germany's sad fate under Napoleon. However, if he regarded the project of German unity as incomplete, to make sense as a character he also would have demanded Austrian acceptance of the Prussian model.
86. Theodor Fontane, *Vor dem Sturm,* ed. Walter Keitel and Helmuth Nürnberger (1878; Munich: DTV, 1980).
87. "Burg Soltwedel ist uralt, aber schweigt. Schloß Sanssouci spricht, aber ist jung wie ein Parvenü. Nur unsere Dorfkirchen stellen sich uns vielfach als die Träger unserer *ganzen* Geschichte dar, und die Berührung der Jahrhunderte untereinander zur Erscheinung bringend, besitzen und äußern sie den Zauber historischer Kontinuität" (ibid., 37, emphasis original).
88. "Die Maßregeln unserer gegenwärtigen Regierung, indem sie das Urteil des Volkes mißachten, impfen ihm den Ungehorsam ein. Das Volk widerstreitet nicht, weil es will, sondern weil es muß" (ibid., 305).
89. "*Wir* waren *vor* den Hohenzollern da" (ibid., 287, emphasis original).
90. "Wir stehen ein für das Land" (ibid.).
91. "*Mit* dem König, solange es geht, *ohne* ihn, wenn es sein muß" (ibid., 218, emphasis original).
92. "Und eines weiß ich, sie wird uns freilich den Stammbaum, aber nicht die

Profile verderben, nicht die Profile und nicht die Gesinnung. Und das beides ist das Beste, was der Adel hat" (ibid., 703).
93. "Es ist nichts mit den zweierlei Menschen. . . . Ich mache mir nichts aus diesen Windbeuteln von Franzosen, aber in all ihrem dummen Zeug steckt immer eine Prise Wahrheit. Mit ihrer Brüderlichkeit wird es nicht viel werden, und mit der Freiheit auch nicht; aber mit dem, was sie dazwischengestellt haben, hat es was auf sich. Denn was heißt am Ende anders als: Mensch ist Mensch" (ibid., 706).
94. "[Es] stand für ihn unwandelbar fest, daß die Mark Brandenburg nicht nur von Uranfang ein deutsches Land gewesen, sondern auch durch alle Jahrhunderte hin *geblieben* sei" (ibid., 86, emphasis original).
95. "Apostel des Panslawismus" (ibid., 88).
96. "Nun kann ich diesen Landesteil unangefochten für wendisch erklären; aber ich tät' es lieber nicht" (ibid., 710).
97. "Seine mehr preußisch als polnisch angelegte Natur. . . . Er war bald preußischer als die Preußen selbst" (ibid., 328–29).
98. "Eine Liebe, die mehr aus der Betrachtung als aus dem Blute stammt" (ibid., 236).
99. "Pole vom Wirbel bis zur Zeh'" (ibid., 161).
100. "Aber verzeih, Schwester du weißt nichts von Volk und Vaterland, du kennst nur Hof und Gesellschaft, und dein Herz, wenn du dich recht befragst, ist bei dem Feinde." "Nicht bei dem Feinde, aber bei dem, was er von uns voraus hat" (ibid., 298).
101. See Otfried Keiler, "Vor dem Sturm," in Christian Grawe, ed., *Fontane Novellen und Romane* (Stuttgart: Reclam, 1991), esp. 34–42.
102. Freytag's *Pictures from the German Past* contains two chapters devoted to the Wars of Liberation. Here, too, his aim is to follow the course of events "not through outstanding personalities but to show how they were revealed in the lives of ordinary people." ("Nicht wie er in hervorragenden Personen sondern wie er im Leben des kleinen Mannes sichtbar wurde, soll hier dargestellt werden," 798). The novel mirrors this intention, but does so more successfully because the primary material such individuals left behind for Freytag the historian was not nearly as rich as the fictional possibilities in the author's imagination.
103. "Ein schöner Mann, wie von Himmel kam er" (Freytag, *Ahnen*, 6: 79). The situation reminds attentive readers of Kleist's *Marquise von O*, except that Freytag's savior doesn't rape the woman he rescues.
104. "Wagt es, ihr Hunde, die Braut eines französischen Officiers anzurühren" (ibid., 6: 79).
105. "Aber das Weib, welches darnach rang unerträgliche Fesseln zu lösen, die Männer, welche zum Kampf gegen den Feind rüsteten, alle Völker eines Weltheils, die sich gegen die Tyrannei einer verhaßten Nation empörten,

sollten noch eimal vergebens hoffen. . . . Hütet euch, deutsche Herzen, daß der Muth nicht schwinde und die grünende Saat eurer Liebe nicht niedergetreten werde unter dem gepanzerten Tritt kalter, harter, tückischer Selbstsucht, die eine fremde Nation und ihr gottverfluchter Meister gegen euch verüben" (ibid., 6: 209–10.

106. "Das erlösende Wort, welches die Waffen in die Hände des zornigen Volkes drücken sollte" (ibid., 6: 222).
107. Alon Confino's *The Nation as a Local Metaphor*, 73–93, offers a particularly good explanation of resistance to what was seen as a Prussian holiday in a nation that was more unified politically than culturally.
108. Karl May, *Die Liebe des Ulanen* (Dresden: Münchmeyer, 1901–2; facsimile edition, New York: Olms, 1972). May's text appeared originally in installments, from which the author attempted to distance himself; he was involved in a lengthy lawsuit to prevent republication in book form, because he feared damage to his reputation as a writer of children's books should the public learn about this "racy" text.
109. Friedrich Spielhagen, *Noblesse oblige* (1888; Leipzig: Verlag von V. Staackmann, 1905) and Hermann Sudermann, *Der Katzensteg* (Stuttgart: Verlag der Cotta'schen Buchhandlung, 1889). I quote from the fifteenth edition, n.d.
110. See Jeffrey L. Sammons, "Friedrich Spielhagen: The Demon of Theory and the Deline of Reputation," in Todd Kontje, ed., *A Companion to German Realism, 1848–1900* (Rochester, NY: Camden House, 2002), 133–57.
111. "Der Geliebte ihres Herzens war und blieb doch immer der Feind ihres Vaterlandes" (Spielhagen, *Noblesse oblige*, 105).
112. "Weil der Hirsch ist ein Jud'? erwiderte der alte Mann erregt, und der Jud' hat kein Vaterland?" (ibid., 56).
113. "Sein Haß gegen alles Französisch und alle Franzosen machte ihn unzurechnungsfähig" (ibid., 34).
114. "Er hatte kein Herz; er war ein Egoist bis in den Kern seines Wesens und ein Feigling dazu" (ibid., 272).
115. "Ohne Dir selbst untreu zu werden und Deiner Nation, Deinem Vaterlande" (ibid., 439).
116. "Durch Jahre der Tyrannei, durch die Tausend Wunden, die es Deutschland schlug, tausendfach hassenswert gemacht hat" (ibid., 442).
117. "O, laß mir die Illusion, ich hätte mit dem Geliebten leben können ohne den furchtbaren Gedanken: auf welcher Seite werden eure Kinder stehen, wenn die beiden Nationen, aus denen ihre Eltern stammen, sich abermals zerfleischen!" (ibid., 499).
118. "Ein Mensch wird sein können, ohne daß man im Namen der Familienliebe, der Wohlfahrt des Vaterlandes, der Ehre der Nation

Unmenschliches von ihm fordert? . . . Niemals, geliebter Freund, flüstert sie, niemals!" (ibid., 506).
119. Hermann Sudermann, *Der Katzensteg* (Stuttgart: J. G. Cotta'sche Buchhandlung, n.d. [1889]).
120. "Die Vaterlandsliebe, die früher ruhig und selbstsicher in seinem Herzen geschlummert hatte, war zu quälerischem Leben erwacht . . . Viel fehlte nicht, daß er sich selber die Schuld an Preußens Unglück zumaß" (ibid., 43).
121. "Dann stellten die Marodeure des Erfolges, Eitelkeit und Eigensucht, bei ihm ein. Was zum Beginne ein Werk lauterster Opferfreude gewesen war, wurde allgemach ein Postament für die eigene Persönlichkeit, ein Denkstein, um seinen Ruhm der Welt zu verkündigen" (ibid., 214).
122. "Wie ein Raubvogel, der auf seine Beute niederschießen will, so stand er da mit seinem Geierprofil und dem glühenden Aeuglein. . . . Ja, wahrlich, diesem Manne der christlichen Milde sprangen Skorpionen aus dem Munde" (ibid., 233, 239).
123. "Von den weitern Schicksalen Boroslavs weiß man nicht viel. In Anbetracht der stattgehabten Meuterei hielt das Kommando für geraten, ihn zu seinem früheren Regiment zurückzuversetzen. Während die ostpreußische Landwehr noch in den alten Provinzen zurückblieb, bekam er, viel beneidet, die Erlaubnis, sich ohne Verzug zum Kriegsschauplatz zu begegen. Bei Ligny soll er gefallen sein" (ibid., 350).

Conclusion

1. On the debate that followed Fritz Fischer's reinterpretation of WWI, see Imanuel Geiss, *Studien über Geschichte und Geschichtswissenschaft* (Frankfurt am Main: Suhrkamp, 1972), esp. 108–98. Richard J. Evans summarizes the first Holocaust controversy in *In Hitler's Shadow: West German Historians and the Attempt to Escape from the Nazi Past* (New York: Pantheon, 1989); see also Hans-Ulrich Wehler, *Entsorgung der deutschen Vergangenheit? Ein polemischer Essay zum "Historikerstreit"* (Munich: Beck, 1988). To get a sense of the storm Goldhagen unleashed, see Robert R. Shandley, ed., *Unwilling Germans? The Goldhagen Debate* (Minneapolis: University of Minnesota Press, 1998).
2. See Brian Ladd, *The Ghosts of Berlin: Confronting German History in the Urban Landscape* (Chicago: University of Chicago Press, 1997).
3. Hermann Bausinger, *Typisch deutsch: Wie deutsch sind die Deutschen?* (Munich: Beck, 2000), 159.
4. See Blackbourne and Eley, *Peculiarities*. The book's thesis, which I follow here, proved controversial; the introduction (1–35) provides a good summary of the stakes and players in the argument.

Bibliography

Primary

Alexis, Willibald. *Die Geächteten: Novelle.* Berlin: Duncker und Humblot, 1825.
———. *Isegrimm: Vaterländischer Roman.* In *Vaterländische Romane,* ed. Ludwig Lorenz and Adolf Bartels. Vol. 10. Leipzig: Hesse and Becker, n.d. [1854].
———. *Ruhe ist die erste Bürgerpflicht.* Frankfurt am Main: Ullstein, 1985.
Allgemeinge deutsche Real-Encyklopädie für die gebildeten Stände. Leipzig: Brockhaus, 1833–37.
Auerbach, E. *Der Zigeunerraub, oder: Das Vaterhaus. Eine Erzählung aus dem Rettungsjahr 1813.* Braunschweig: G. C. E. Meyer, 1825.
Bacher, Julius. *Die Brautschau Friedrich's des Großen.* Berlin: Alexander Dunker, 1857.
Belani, H. E. R. *Die Demagogen: Novelle, aus der Geschichte unserer Zeit.* Leipzig: A. Wienbrack, 1829.
———. *Gräfin Orzelska: Historische Novelle aus dem ersten Viertheil des vorigen Jahrhunderts.* 2 vols. Braunschweig: G. C. E. Meyer, 1827.
Calvino, Italo. *If on a Winter's Night a Traveler.* Trans. William Weaver. New York: Harcourt Brace Jovanovich, 1979.
Caudwell, Sarah. *The Shortest Way to Hades.* New York: Dell, 1984.
Dickens, Charles. *David Copperfield.* New York: Modern Library, [1850].
Droysen, Johann Gustav. *Das Leben des Feldmarschalls Grafen Yorck von Wartenburg.* Berlin: Veit, 1851–52.
———. *Historik: Historisch-kritische Ausgabe.* Ed. Peter Leyh. Stuttgart, Bad Cannstatt: Frommann-Holzboog, 1977.
———. *Vorlesungen über das Zeitalter der Freiheitskriege,* 2nd ed. 2 vols. Gotha:

BIBLIOGRAPHY

Perthes, 1886 [1846].

Fontane, Theodor. *Aufsätze und Aufzeichnungen: Aufsätze zur Literatur.* Jürgen Kolbe, ed. In *Ausgewählte Schriften und Kritiken,* ed. Walter Keitel and Helmuth Nürnberger. Frankfurt am Main: Ullstein, 1979.

———. *Briefe an Wilhelm und Hans Hertz, 1859–1898.* Ed. Kurt Schreinert and Gerhard Hay. Stuttgart: Klett, 1972.

———. *Der Krieg gegen Frankreich, 1870–1871.* 1873–76. Zurich: Manesse, 1985.

———. *Der Stechlin.* 1899. In *Werke und Schriften,* ed. Walter Keitel and Helmuth Nürnberger. Vol. 19. Frankfurt am Main: Ullstein, 1991.

———. *Frau Jenny Treibel.* 1892. In *Werke und Schriften,* ed. Walter Keitel and Helmuth Nürnberger. Vol. 16. Frankfurt am Main: Ullstein, 1984.

———. *Jenny Treibel.* Trans. Ulf Zimmermann. In *Theodor Fontane: Short Novels and Other Writings,* ed. Peter Demetz. New York: Continuum, 1982.

———. *A Man of Honor.* Trans. E. M. Valk. In *Theodor Fontane: Short Novels and Other Writings,* ed. Peter Demetz. New York: Continuum, 1982. Trans. of *Shach von Wuthenow.*

———. *Schach von Wuthenow: Erzählung aus der Zeit des Regiments Gensdarmes.* 1883. In *Werke und Schriften,* ed. Walter Keitel and Helmuth Nürnberger. Vol. 8. Frankfurt am Main: Ullstein, 1992.

———. *Unwiederbringlich.* 1891. In *Werke und Schriften,* ed. Walter Keitel and Helmuth Nürnberger. Vol. 15. Frankfurt am Main: Ullstein, 1987.

———. *Von Zwanzig bis Dreißig: Autobiographisches.* 1898. Munich: DTV, 1973.

———. *Vor dem Sturm.* 1878. Ed. Walter Keitel and Helmuth Nürnberger. Munich: DTV, 1980.

———. *Wanderungen durch die Mark Brandenburg: Die Grafschaft Ruppin, Das Oderland.* Helmuth Nürnberger, ed., Munich: DTV, 1994.

Fouqué, Friedrich de la Motte. *Der Refugié oder Heimat und Fremde: Ein Roman aus der neueren Zeit.* Gotha: Hennings'sche Buchhandlung, 1824. Reprinted as vol. 10 of *Sämmtliche Romane und Novellenbücher,* ed. Wolfgang Möhrig. Hildesheim: Olms, 1989.

François, Louise von. *Die letzte Reckenburgerin.* 1871. Bonn: J. Latka Verlag, 1988.

———. *Geschichte der preußischen Befreiungskriege in den Jahren 1813 bis 1815.* Berlin: Janke, [1873].

Frenzel, Karl. *Luzifer: Ein Roman aus der Napoleonischen Zeit.* 5 vols. Leipzig: Ernst Julius Günther, 1873.

Freytag, Gustav. *Bilder aus der deutschen Vergangenheit.* 1859–62. 2 vols. Berlin: Knaur, 1927.

———. *Die Ahnen.* 7 vols. 1873–81. Leipzig: Hirzel, 1905.

Gersdorf, Wilhelmine von. *Das Complott, oder Verrath und Treue. Aus der zweiten Hälfte des achtzehnten Jahrhunderts.* Leipzig: Wilhelm Lauffer, 1830.

BIBLIOGRAPHY

Gersdorf, Wilhelmine von. *Aurora Gräfin von Königsmark. Ein historischer Roman*. 2 vols. Quedlinburg: Basse Verlag, 1817.

——. *Graf Ernst von Mansfeld und seine Zeitgenossen: Seitenstück zu Friedrich dem Fünften, König von Böhmen und Churfürsten von der Pfalz*. Leipzig: Lauffer, 1825.

Goethe, Johann Wolfgang von. *Faust: A Tragedy, Part One*. Trans. Martin Greenberg. New Haven, CT: Yale University Press, 1992.

Hauff, Wilhelm. *Lichtenstein: Romantische Sage aus der württembergischen Geschichte*. 1826. Stuttgart: Reclam, 1988.

Häusser, Ludwig. *Deutsche Geschichte vom Tode Friedrichs des Großen bis zur Gründung des deutschen Bundes*. 4 vols. 2nd ed. Berlin: Weidmannsche Buchhandlung, 1859 [1855–57].

Hegel, Georg Wilhelm Friedrich. *Grundlinien der Philosophie des Rechts*. Ed. Helmut Reichelt. [1821]. Frankfurt am Main: Ullstein, 1979.

Heine, Heinrich. *Reise von München nach Genua*. Ed. Wolfgang Preisendanz. In *Werke II: Reisebilder, Erzählende Prosa, Aufsätze*. Frankfurt am Main: Insel, 1968.

Hesekiel, George. *Stille vor dem Sturm*. 2 vols. Berlin: Janke, 1863.

——. *Vor Jena: Roman nach den Aufzeichnungen eines königlichen Officiers vom Regiment Gensd'armes*. Berlin: Janke, 1859.

Hildebrand[t], [Johann Andreas] C[hristoph]. *Das Merkwürdigste Jahr aus dem Leben eines alten Kriegers: Ein Historischer Roman aus den Zeiten Friedrichs II. und der Maria Theresia*. Halberstadt: Friedrich August Helm, 1830.

——. *Die Familie von Manteufel: Ein historisch-romantisches Gemälde aus den Zeiten des siebenjährigen Kriegs*. 3 vols. Leipzig: Christian Ernst Kollmann, 1826.

Jensen, Wilhelm. *Um die Wende des Jahrhunderts (1789–1806)*. Dresden: Reißner, 1899.

Kugler, Franz. *Der letzte Wendenfürst: Novelle aus der Zeiten der Gründung Berlins*. Berlin: Alexander Dunker, 1837.

Kugler, Franz, and Adolph Menzel. *Geschichte des Friedrichs des Grossen*. Leipzig: Verlag der J. J. Weber'schen Buchhandlung, 1840.

Lessing, Gotthold Ephraim. "Briefe, Die neueste Literatur betreffend." In *Werke II: Kritische und philosophische Schriften*. Munich: Winckler, 1969.

Lewald, Fanny. *Prinz Louis Ferdinand*. Berlin: Deutsche Buch-Gemeinschaft, [1849].

——. *Prince Louis Ferdinand*. Trans. Linda Rogols-Siegel. Lewiston, NY: Mellen, 1988.

Lorenz, Wilhelmine. *Friedrich's II. einzige Liebe: Roman*. Leipzig: Verlag von A. Wienbrack, 1846.

May, Karl. *Die Liebe des Ulanen*. Dresden: Münchmeyer, 1901–2. Facsimile edition, New York: Olms, 1972.

BIBLIOGRAPHY

Mehring, Franz. "Friedrichs aufgeklärter Despotismus." *Aufsätze zur Preussischen und Deutschen Geschichte.* Leipzig: Philipp Reclam jun., 1986.

Mühlbach, Louisa. *Berlin and Sans-souci: or, Frederick the Great and His Friends: An Historical Romance.* Trans. Mrs. Coleman and her daughters. New York: Appleton, 1867. Trans. of *Berlin und Sanssouci oder Friedrich der Große und seine Freunde.* Berlin: Simion, 1854.

[Mühlbach, Louisa], "Clara Mundts Briefe an Hermann Costenoble: Zu L. Mühlbach's historischen Romanen," ed. William H. McClain and Lieselotte E. Kurth-Voigt. *Archiv für Geschichte des Buchwesens* 22 (1981): 917–52.

Mühlbach, Louisa. "Der alte Fritz." *Novellen: Federzeichnungen,* 5–35. Berlin: Schweigger'sche Hofbuchhandlung, 1865.

———. *Deutschland in Sturm und Drang: Historischer Roman.* Jena: Costenoble, 1867–68. Vols. 1–4. *Old Fritz and the New Era.* Trans. Peter Langley. Trans. of *Der alte Fritz und seine Zeit.* New York: Appleton, 1868.

———. *Deutschland in Sturm und Drang: Historischer Roman.* Jena: Costenoble, 1867–68. Vol. 5. *Goethe and Schiller: An Historical Romance.* Trans. Chapman Coleman. Akron, OH: New Werner, 1867. Trans. of *Fürsten und Dichter.*

———. *Erste und letzte Liebe.* Atona: Hammerich, 1838.

———. *Frederick the Great and His Court: An Historical Romance.* Trans. Mrs. Chapman Coleman and her daughters. New York: Appleton, 1866. Trans. of *Friedrich der Große und sein Hof.* Berlin: Janke, 1853.

———. *Frederick the Great and His Family: An Historical Novel.* Trans. Mrs. Coleman and her daughters. New York: Appleton, 1867. Trans. of *Friedrich der Große und seine Geschwister.* Berlin: Janke, 1855.

———. *Napoleon and Blücher: An Historical Novel.* Trans. F. Jordan. 4 vols. (New York: Appleton, 1867). Trans. of *Napoleon in Deutschland.* 16 vols. Berlin: Janke, 1858.

———. *Napoleon und Königin Luise.* 4 vols. Trans. F. Jordan as *Napoleon and the Queen of Prussia.* New York: Appleton, 1867.

———. *Rastatt und Jena.* 4 vols. Trans. F. Jordan as *Louisa of Prussia and Her Times: An Historical Novel.* New York: Appleton, 1867.

———. *The Works of Louisa Mühlbach in Eighteen Volumes.* New York: Collier, 1902.

Nicolai, Friedrich. *Anekdoten von König Friedrich II. von Preußen, und von einigen Personen, die um Ihm waren.* Berlin: 1789, 1792.

Novalis. *Fragmente und Studien, 1799–1800. Schriften.* Ed. Richard Samuel. Stuttgart: W. Kohlhammer Verlag, 1960.

Oldendorp, C[hristian] J[ohannes]. *Unglück und Rettung oder Jugendschicksale eines Offiziers aus der Zeit Friedrichs des Großen: Eine humoristische Erzählung.* Leipzig: Wilhelm Lauffer, 1826.

Pfau, Ludwig. "Badisches Wiegenlied." In *Klassenkampf: Ein Lesebuch zu den Klassenkämpfen in Deutschland, 1756–1971.* Ed. Hans Magnus Enzensburger et al. Darmstadt: Luchterhand, 1972.

Preuß, Johann David Erdmann. *Friedrich der Große.* Berlin: Nauck, 1832–34.

———. *Friedrich der Große mit seinen Freunden und Verwandten.* Berlin: Dunker und Humblot, 1838.

———. *Friedrichs des Großen Jugend und Thronbesteigung.* Berlin: Dunker und Humblot, 1840.

Ranke, Leopold von. *Sämmtliche Werke.* Leipzig: Duncker und Humblot, 1867–90.

Rellstab, Ludwig. *1812: Ein historischer Roman.* 1834. Leipzig: Brockhaus, 1914.

Reuter, Fritz. *Aus der Franzosenzeit [Ut de Franzosentid].* Trans. into standard German by Friedrich and Barbara Minssen. *Gezeiten des Lebens: Die Romane der Erinnerung.* Munich: Langen Müller, 1976.

Ring, Max. "Louise: Zur hunderjährigen Geburtstagsfeier der Mutter unseres Kaisers." *Die Gartenlaube* 24.1–4 (1876).

"Russisch-deutscher Krieg von 1812–1815." In *Allgemeinge deutsche Real-Encyklopädie für die gebildeten Stände.* Leipzig: Brockhaus, 1833–37.

Schiller, Friedrich. *Sämtliche Werke.* Ed. Gerhard Fricke and Herbert G. Göpfert. Munich: Hanser, 1980.

Schücking, Levin. *Der Panduren Oberst: Historischer Roman aus dem Zeitalter Friedrichs des Großen.* Berlin: Oestergaard, n.d.

Scott, Sir Walter. *Ivanhoe.* 1819. New York: Modern Library, 1997.

Spamer, Franz Otto. *Aus dem Tabakskollegium und der Zopfzeit: Wie man vor 150 Jahren lebte und es trieb.* Leipzig: Otto Spamer, n.d.

[Spamer], Franz Otto. *Der Große König und sein Rekrut: Lebensbilder aus der Zeit des Siebenjährigen Krieges.* 1865. (Unter theilweiser Benutzung eines historischen Romans von A. H. Brandrupp, für Volk und Heer, insbesonder für die reifere Jugend bearbeitet). 4th ed. Leipzig: Otto Spamer, 1873.

Spamer, Franz Otto. *Das Buch vom Alten Fritz: Leben und Thaten des großen Preußenkönigs Friedrich II., genannt der Einzige, des Helden des achtzehnten Jahrhunderts. Der Jugend und dem Volke erzählt.* Leipzig: Otto Spamer, 1877.

Spielhagen, Friedrich. *Noblesse oblige.* 1888. Leipzig: Verlag von V. Staackmann, 1905.

Sudermann, Hermann. *Der Katzensteg.* Stuttgart: Verlag der Cotta'schen Buchhandlung, 1889.

Sybel, Heinrich von. *Die Erhebung Europas gegen Napoleon I: Drei Vorlesungen, gehalten am 24., 27. und 30. März 1860.* Munich: Literarisch-artistische Anstalt der J. K. Cotta'schen Buchhandlung, 1860.

Treitschke, Heinrich von. *Deutsche Geschichte im neunzehnten Jahrhundert.*

Leipzig: Hirzel, 1879–94.

———. "Königin Luise." In *Historische und Politische Aufsätze*. Leipzig: Hirzel, 1920. 2nd ed., vol. 4: 139–53.

———. *Treitschke's History of Germany in the Nineteenth Century, 1879–1894*. Trans. Eden and Cedar Paul. New York: McBride, Nast: 1915–19.

Voß, Julius von. *Der deutsche Donquixott*. Berlin: J. W. Schmidts Wittwe und Sohn, 1819.

Wickede, Julius von. *Der lange Isaack: Historischer Roman aus der Zeit des deutschen Befreiungskrieges*. Jena: Costenoble, 1863.

Wilmsen, Friedrich. *Der Deutsche Kinderfreund: Ein Lesebuch für Volksschulen, 1. Aufl. 1802*. [Berlin: Realschulbuchhandlung]. Holger Rudloff, ed. Cologne, Weimar, Vienna: Böhlau, 1992. Reprint of *Kinderfreunde: Der Brandenburgische Kinderfreund: Ein Lesebuch für Volksschulen, 1. Aufl. 1800*. [Berlin: Georg Decker].

Zollern, Hans von. *Ein politischer Schachzug Friedrich's des Großen*. 2 vols. Dresden: Minden, 1883.

Secondary

Adolph Menzel, 1815–1905: Between Romanticism and Impressionism. Ed. Claude Keisch and Marie Ursula Riemann-Reyher. New Haven, CT: Yale University Press, 1996.

Ahlzweig, Claus. *Muttersprache—Vaterland: Die deutsche Nation und ihre Sprache*. Opladen: Westdeutscher Verlag, 1994.

Akaltin, Ferdi. *Die Befreiungskriege im Geschichtsbild der Deutschen im 19. Jahrhundert*. Frankfurt am Main: Verlag Neue Wissenschaft, 1997.

Anderson, Benedict. *Imagined Communities: Reflections on the Origin and Spread of Nationalism*. London: Verso, 1983, revised edition, 1991.

Applegate, Celia. *A Nation of Provincials: The German Idea of Heimat*. Berkeley: University of California Press, 1990.

Applegate, Celia, and Pamela Potter, eds. *Music and German National Identity*. Chicago: University of Chicago Press, 2002.

Assmann, Aleida. *Arbeit am nationalen Gedächtnis: Eine kurze Geschichte der deutschen Bildungsidee*. Frankfurt am Main: Campus, 1993.

Auerbach, Erich. *Mimesis: The Representation of Reality in Western Literature*. Trans. Willard R. Trask. Princeton, NJ: Princeton University Press, 1953.

Aust, Hugo. *Der historischer Roman*. Stuttgart: Metzler, 1994.

———. *Literatur des Realismus,* 2nd. ed. Stuttgart: Metzler, 1981.

Barth, Dieter. *Zeitschrift für Alle: Das Familienblatt im 19. Jahrhundert: Ein sozialhistorischer Beitrag zur Massenpresse in Deutschland*. Diss., Westfälische Wilhelms-Universität, Münster, 1974

Bausinger, Hermann. *Typisch deutsch: Wie deutsch sind die Deutschen?* Munich: Beck, 2000.

BIBLIOGRAPHY

Belgum, Kirsten. "Displaying the Nation: A View of Nineteenth-Century Monuments through a Popular Magazine." *Central European History* 26.3 (1993): 457–74.

———. *Popularizing the Nation: Audience, Representation, and the Production of Identity in* Die Gartenlaube, *1853–1900*. Lincoln: University of Nebraska Press, 1998.

Belting, Hans. *The Germans and Their Art: A Troublesome Relationship*. New Haven, CT: Yale University Press, 1998.

Berg, Gunther. *Leopold von Ranke als Akademischer Lehrer: Studien zu seinen Vorlesungen und seinem Geschichtsdenken*. Göttingen: Vandenhoeck and Ruprecht, 1968.

Berger, Stefan. *The Search for Normality: National Identity and Historical Consciousness in Germany since 1800*. Providence, RI: Berghahn Books, 1997.

Bhabha, Homi. *Nation and Narration*. London: Routledge, 1990.

Blackbourne, David, and Geoff Eley. *The Peculiarities of German History: Bourgeois Society and Politics in Nineteenth-Century Germany*. Oxford: Oxford University Press, 1984.

Blitz, Hans-Martin. *Aus Liebe zum Vaterland: Die deutsche Nation im 18. Jahrhundert*. Hamburg: Hamburger Edition, 2000.

Bruyn, Günter de. *Preußens Luise: Vom Entstehen und Vergehen einer Legende*. Berlin: Siedler, 2001.

Clark, Christopher. "The Wars of Liberation in Prussian Memory: Reflections on the Memorialization of War in Early Nineteenth-Century Germany." *Journal of Modern History* 68 (September 1996): 550–76.

Collingwood, R. G. *The Idea of History*. Oxford: Oxford University Press, 1946.

Confino, Alon. "Collective Memory and Cultural History: Problems and Method." *American Historical Review* 102.5 (1997): 1386–1403.

———. *The Nation as a Local Metaphor: Württemberg, Imperial Germany, and National Memory, 1871–1918*. Chapel Hill: University of North Carolina Press, 1997.

Confino, Alon, and Peter Fritzsche, eds. *The Work of Memory: New Directions in the Study of German Society and Culture*. Urbana: University of Illinois Press, 2002.

Crane, Susan A. *Collecting and Historical Consciousness in Early Nineteenth-Century Germany*. Ithaca, NY: Cornell University Press, 2000.

Damerau, Burghard. *Literatur und andere Wahrheiten: Warum wir ohne Bücher nicht sein wollen*. Berlin: Aufbau, 1999.

Davis, Lennard J. *Factual Fictions: The Origins of the English Novel*, 2nd. ed. Philadelphia: University of Pennsylvania Press, 1996.

Deleuze, Gilles, and Félix Guattari. *Kafka: Toward a Minor Literature*. Trans. Dana Polan. Minneapolis: University of Minnesota Press, 1986.

Delius, F. C. *Der Held und sein Wetter: Ein Kunstmittel und sein ideologischer Gebrauch im Roman des bürgerlichen Realismus.* Munich: Hanser, 1971.

Demandt, Philipp. *Luisenkult: Die Unsterblichkeit der Königen von Preußen.* Cologne: Böhlau, 2003.

Deutsches Historisches Museum. *Bismarck: Preussen, Deutschland und Europa.* Berlin: Nicolai, 1990.

Downing, Eric. *Double Exposures: Repetition and Realism in Nineteenth-Century German Fiction.* Stanford, CA: Stanford University Press, 2000.

Durrani, Osman, and Julian Preece, eds. *Travellers in Time and Space/Reisende durch Zeit und Raum: The German Historical Novel/Der deutschsprachige historische Roman. Amsterdamer Beiträge zur neueren Germanistik.* Amsterdam: Rodopi, 2001, vol. 51.

Eggert, Hartmut. *Studien zur Wirkungsgeschichte des deutschen historischen Romans, 1850–1875.* Frankfurt am Main: Klostermann, 1971.

Eke, Norbert Otto. "Eine Gesamtbibliographie des deutschen Romans, 1815–1830. Anmerkungen zum Problemfeld von Bibliographie und Historiographie." *Zeitschrift für Germanistik* Neue Folge 2 (1993): 295–308.

Evans, Richard J. "The Myth of Germany's Missing Revolution." *Rethinking German History: Nineteenth-Century Germany and the Origins of the Third Reich.* London: Unwin Hyman, 1987.

———. *In Hitler's Shadow: West German Historians and the Attempt to Escape from the Nazi Past.* New York: Pantheon, 1989.

Forster-Hahn, Françoise. "Adolph Menzel's 'Daguerreotypical' Image of Frederick the Great: A Liberal Bourgeois Interpretation of German History." *Art Bulletin* 59.2 (1977): 242–61.

Fox, Thomas C. *Louise von François and Die letzte Reckenburgerin: A Feminist Reading.* New York: Peter Lang, 1988.

François, Etienne, and Hagen Schulze, eds. *Deutsche Erinnerungs Orte.* 3 vols. Munich: Beck, 2001.

Frühwald, Wolfgang. "Die Idee kultureller Nationbildung und die Entstehung der Literatursprache in Deutschland." In *Nationalismus in vorindustrieller Zeit,* ed. Otto Dann. Munich: Oldenbourg, 1986. 129–41.

Furst, Lilian R. *All Is True: The Claims and Strategies of Realist Fiction.* Durham, NC: Duke University Press, 1995.

Gaehtgens, Thomas W. *Anton von Werner. Die Proklamierung des Deutschen Kaiserreiches: Ein Historienbild im Wandel preußischer Politik.* Frankfurt am Main: Fischer, 1990.

Gedi, Nora, and Yigal Elam. "Collective Memory—What Is It?" *History and Memory* 8 (Spring/Summer 1996): 30–50.

Geiss, Imanuel. *Studien über Geschichte und Geschichtswissenschaft.* Frankfurt am Main: Suhrkamp, 1972.

BIBLIOGRAPHY

Geppert, Hans Vilmar. *Der 'andere' historische Roman: Theorie und Struktur einer diskontinuierlichen Gattung.* Tübingen: Niemeyer, 1976.

Ginzburg, Carlo. *The Cheese and the Worms: The Cosmos of a Sixteenth-Century Miller.* Trans. John and Anne Tedeschi. Baltimore: Johns Hopkins University Press, 1980.

Gooch, G. P. *History and Historians in the Nineteenth Century,* 3rd ed. Boston: Beacon, 1959.

Grafton, Anthony. *The Footnote: A Curious History.* Cambridge, MA: Harvard University Press, 1997.

Grawe, Christian. "Preußen 1803 bis 1813 im 'vaterländischen Roman': Willibald Alexis, George Hesekiel, Theodor Fontane." In *Literatur und Geschichte, 1788–1988,* ed. Gerhard Schulz and Tim Mehigan. Frankfurt am Main: Peter Lang, 1990.

Green, Abigail. *Fatherlands: State-Building and Nationhood in Nineteenth-Century Germany.* Cambridge: Cambridge University Press, 2001.

Greenfeld, Liah. *Nationalism: Five Roads to Modernity.* Cambridge, MA: Harvard University Press, 1992.

Grossman, Lionel. *Between History and Literature.* Cambridge, MA: Harvard University Press, 1990.

Halbwachs, Maurice. *On Collective Memory.* 1941/1952. Trans. Lewis A. Coser. Chicago: University of Chicago Press, 1992.

Hardin, James, and Siegfried Mews, eds. *Dictionary of Literary Biography.* Vols. 129 and 133. Detroit: Gale, 1993.

Hardtwig, Wolfgang. *Geschichtskultur und Wissenschaft.* Munich: DTV, 1990.

Hermand, Jost. *Adolph Menzel Das Flötenkonzert in Sanssouci: Ein realistisch geträumtes Preußenbild.* Frankfurt am Main: Fischer, 1985.

——. "Dashed Hopes: On the Painting of the Wars of Liberation." In *Political Symbolism in Modern Europe,* trans. James D. Steakley, ed. Seymour Drescher, David Sabean, and Allan Sharlin. New Brunswick, NJ: Transaction, 1982. 216–38.

Herminghouse, Patricia, and Magda Mueller. *Gender and Germanness: Cultural Productions of Nation.* Providence, RI: Berghahn Books, 1997.

Hinck, Walter, ed. *Geschichte als Schauspiel.* Frankfurt am Main: Suhrkamp, 1981.

Hinderer, Walter, ed. *Geschichte der politischen Lyrik in Deutschland.* Stuttgart: Reclam, 1978.

Hirschmann, Günther. *Kulturkampf im historischen Roman der Gründerzeit, 1859–1878.* Munich: Fink, 1978.

Hobsbawm, E. J. *Nations and Nationalism since 1789: Programme, Myth, Reality.* Cambridge: Cambridge University Press, 1990.

Hoggart, Richard. *The Uses of Literacy: Changing Patterns in English Mass Culture.* Fair Lawn, NJ: Essential Books, 1957.

BIBLIOGRAPHY

Hohendahl, Peter Uwe. *Building a National Literature: The Case of Germany, 1830–1870*. Trans. Renate Baron Franciscono. Ithaca, NY: Cornell University Press, 1989.

Holub, Robert C. *Reflections of Realism: Paradox, Norm, and Ideology in Nineteenth-Century German Prose*. Detroit: Wayne State University Press, 1991.

Horkheimer, Max, and Theodor W. Adorno. *Dialectic of Enlightenment*. Trans. John Cumming. New York: Continuum, 1969.

Iggers, Georg G. *The German Conception of History: The National Tradition of Historical Thought from Herder to the Present*. Hanover, NH: Wesleyan University Press, 1968, 1983.

Jaeger, Friedrich, and Jörn Rüsen. *Geschichte des Historismus*. Munich: Beck, 1992.

Jaffe, M. Rev. of *Inside European Identities: Ethnography in Western Europe*, ed. Sharon Macdonald. Providence, RI: Berg, 1993. *H-German*, July 7, 1996.

James, Harold. *A German Identity, 1770–1990*. New York: Routledge, 1989.

Jasper, Willi. *Faust und die Deutschen*. Berlin: Rowohlt, 1998.

Jeismann, Michael. *Das Vaterland der Feinde: Studien zum nationalen Feindbegriff und Selbstverständnis in Deutschland und Frankreich, 1792–1918*. Stuttgart: Klett-Cotta, 1992.

Jeismann, Michael, and Henning Ritter, eds. *Grenzfälle: Über neuen und alten Nationalismus*. Leipzig: Reclam, 1993.

Joeres, Ruth-Ellen Boetcher. *Respectability and Deviance: Nineteenth-Century German Women Writers and the Ambiguity of Representation*. Chicago: University of Chicago Press, 1998.

Johnston, Otto W. *The Myth of a Nation: Literature and Politics in Prussia under Napoleon*. Columbia, SC: Camden House, 1989.

Kebbel, Gerhard. *Geschichtengeneratoren: Lektüren zur Poetik des historischen Romans*. Tübingen: Niemeyer, 1992.

Keiler, Otfried. "Vor dem Sturm." In *Fontane Novellen und Romane*, ed. Christian Grawe, 13–43. Stuttgart: Reclam, 1991.

Kontje, Todd. *A Companion to German Realism, 1848–1900*. Rochester, NY: Camden House, 2002.

———. *Women, the Novel, and the German Nation, 1771–1871: Domestic Fiction in the Fatherland*. Cambridge: Cambridge University Press, 1998.

Koshar, Rudy. *From Monuments to Traces: Artifacts of German Memory, 1870–1990*. Berkeley: University of California Press, 2000.

Kurth-Voigt, Lieselotte E., and William H. McClain. "Louise Mühlbach's Historical Novels: The American Reception." *Internationales Archiv für Sozialgeschichte der deutschen Literatur* 6 (1981): 52–77.

Ladd, Brian. *The Ghosts of Berlin: Confronting German History in the Urban*

BIBLIOGRAPHY

Landscape. Chicago: University of Chicago Press, 1997.

Lamberti, Marjorie. *State, Society, and the Elementary School in Imperial Germany*. New York: Oxford University Press, 1989.

Link, Jürgen, and Wulf Wülfing, eds. *Nationale Mythen und Symbole in der zweiten Hälfte des 19. Jahrhunderts: Strukturen und Funtionen von Konzeptionen nationaler Identität*. Stuttgart: Klett-Cotta, 1991.

Lukács, Georg. *The Historical Novel*. Trans. Hannah and Stanley Mitchell. Lincoln: University of Nebraska Press, 1983.

Martino, Alberto. *Die deutsche Leihbibliothek: Geschichte einer literarischen Institution (1756–1914)*. Wiesbaden: Harassowitz, 1990.

Maynes, M. J. *Schooling in Western Europe: A Social History*. Albany: State University of New York Press, 1985.

Möhrmann, Renate. *Die andere Frau: Emanzipationsansätze deutscher Schriftstellerinnen im Vorfeld der Achtundvierziger-Revolution*. Stuttgart: Metzler, 1977.

Müller, Klaus-Detlef, ed. *Bürgerlicher Realismus: Grundlagen und Interpretationen*. Königstein: Athenäum, 1981.

Nipperdey, Thomas. *Gesellschaft, Kultur, Theorie: Gesammelte Aufsätze zur neueren Geschichte*. Göttingen: Vandenhoeck and Ruprecht, 1976.

Nochlin, Linda. *Realism*. New York: Penguin, 1971.

Nora, Pierre, ed., *Realms of Memory: The Construction of the French Past*. 3 vols. Ed. Lawrence D. Kritzman. Trans. Arthur Goldhammer. New York: Columbia University Press, 1996–98.

Norton, Anne. *Reflections on Political Identity*. Baltimore: Johns Hopkins University Press, 1988.

Osment, Steven. *The Burgermeister's Daughter: Scandal in a Sixteenth-Century German Town*. New York: St. Martins, 1996.

Paret, Peter. *Art as History: Episodes in the Culture and Politics of Nineteenth-Century Germany*. Princeton, NJ: Princeton University Press, 1988.

Parr, Rolf. *"Zwei Seelen wohnen, ach! in meiner Brust!": Strukturen und Funktionen der Mythisierung Bismarcks*. Munich: Fink, 1992.

Pataky, Sophie. *Lexikon deutscher Frauen der Feder*. 1898. Bern: H. Lang, 1971.

Pavel, Thomas G. *Fictional Worlds*. Cambridge, MA: Harvard University Press, 1986.

Peterson, Sandra Georgina. "The Treatment of the Napoleonic Wars in German Historical Fiction." Diss., Vanderbilt University, 1971.

Preußen: Versuch einer Bilanz. 5 vols. Reinbeck bei Hamburg: Rowohlt, 1981.

Radway, Janice A. *A Feeling for Books: The Book-of-the-Month Club, Literary Taste, and Middle-Class Desire*. Chapel Hill: University of North Carolina Press, 1997.

Reisenleitner, Markus. *Die Produktion historischen Sinnes: Mittelalterrezeption im deutschsprachigen historischen Trivialroman vor 1848*. Frankfurt am Main:

BIBLIOGRAPHY

Peter Lang, 1992.

Richter, Simon. "Winckelmann's Progeny: Homosocial Networking in the Eighteenth Century." In *Outing Goethe and His Age*, ed. Alice Kuzniar. Stanford, CA: Stanford University Press, 1996, 33–46.

Riffaterre, Michael. *Fictional Truth*. Baltimore: Johns Hopkins University Press, 1990.

Röhl, John C. G. "The Emperor's New Clothes: A Character Sketch of Kaiser Wilhelm II." In *Kaiser Wilhelm II: New Interpretations*, ed. Röhl and Nicolaus Sombart, 23–61. Cambridge: Cambridge University Press, 1982.

Rüsen, Jörn. "Ranke's Historiography: A Theoretical Approach." In *Fact and Fiction: German History and Literature, 1848–1924*, ed. Gisela Brude-Firnau and Karin J. MacHardy, 41–56. Tübingen: Franke, 1990.

Sammons, Jeffrey L. *Wilhelm Raabe: The Fiction of the Alternative Community*. Princeton, NJ: Princeton University Press, 1987.

Schama, Simon. *Dead Certainties (Unwarranted Speculations)*. New York: Knopf, 1991.

Scheuer, Helmut, ed. *Dichter und ihre Nation*. Frankfurt am Main: Suhrkamp, 1993.

Schorske, Carl. *Thinking with History: Explorations in the Passage of Modernism*. Princeton, NJ: Princeton University Press, 1998.

Schulte-Sasse, Jochen. *Literarische Wertung*. 2nd ed. Stuttgart: Metzler, 1976.

Schulze, Hagen. *Germany: A New History*. Trans. Deborah Lucas Schneider. Cambridge, MA: Harvard University Press, 1998.

Seeba, Hinrich C. "'Germany—A Literary Concept': The Myth of National Literature," *German Studies Review* 17.2 (1994): 353–69.

Shandley, Robert R. *Unwilling Germans? The Goldhagen Debate*. Minneapolis: Minnesota University Press, 1998.

Shaw, Harry E. *The Forms of Historical Fiction: Sir Walter Scott and His Successors*. Ithaca, NY: Cornell University Press, 1983.

Sheehan, James J. *German History, 1770–1866*. Oxford: Oxford University Press, 1989.

———. "State and Nationality in the Napoleonic Period." In *The State of Germany: The National Idea in the Making, Unmaking, and Remaking of a Modern Nation-State*, ed. John Breuilly, 47–59. London: Longman, 1992.

Smith, Anthony D. "National Identity and Myths of Ethnic Descent." *Research in Social Movements: Conflict and Change* 7 (1984): 95–130.

Smith, Helmut Walser. *German Nationalism and Religious Conflict: Culture, Ideology, Politics, 1870–1914*. Princeton, NJ: Princeton University Press, 1995.

Sottong, Herman J. *Transformation und Reaktion: Historisches Erzählen von der*

BIBLIOGRAPHY

Goethezeit zum Realismus. Munich: Wilhelm Fink, 1992.

Spehr, F. "Karl Friedrich Huberlin." In *Allgemeine Deutsche Biographie*. Leipzig: Duncker and Humblet, 1875–1912, 10: 278–80.

Steinecke, Hartmut, et al. *Deutschsprachige Romane 1815–1830 in der Fürstlichen Bibliothek Corvey: Probleme der Erforschung—Bestandsverzeichnis*. Stuttgart: Belser Wissenschaftlicher Dienst, 1991.

Swales, Martin. *Epochenbuch Realismus: Romane und Erzählungen*. Munich: Schmidt, 1997.

Sweet, Dennis. Introduction to Naubert's "The Cloak." In *Bitter Healing: German Women Writers, 1700–1830*, ed. Jeannine Blackwell and Susanne Zantrop. Lincoln: University of Nebraska Press, 1990.

Tatlock, Lynne. "Realist Historiography and the Historiography of Realism: Gustav Freytag's *Bilder aus der deutschen Vergangenheit*." *German Quarterly* 63.1 (1990): 59–74.

———. "A Timely Demise: The Literary Reputation of Willibald Alexis and the *Reichsgründung*." *Monatshefte* 79.1 (1987): 76–88.

Vanchena, Lorie Ann. *Political Poetry in Periodicals and the Shaping of German National Consciousness in the Nineteenth Century*. New York: Peter Lang, 2000.

Wehler, Hans-Ulrich. *Deutsche Gesellschaftsgeschichte*. Munich: Beck, 1989.

———. *Entsorgung der deutschen Vergangenheit? Ein polemischer Essay zum "Historikerstreit."* Munich: Beck, 1988.

White, Hayden. "The Burden of History." *Tropics of Discourse: Essays in Cultural Criticism*. 27–50. Baltimore: Johns Hopkins University Press, 1978.

———. *Metahistory: The Historical Imagination in Nineteenth-Century Europe*. Baltimore: Johns Hopkins University Press, 1973.

Williams, Raymond. *Culture and Society, 1780–1950*. New York: Harper, 1958.

Wördehoff, Bernhard. "National nach Noten." *Die Zeit* (International Edition) 51.28 (July 12, 1996): 6–8.

Wülfing, Wulf, Karin Bruns, and Rolf Parr. *Historische Mythologie der Deutschen, 1798–1918*. Munich: Fink, 1991.

Žižek, Slavoj. "Eastern Europe's Republics of Gilead." *New Left Review* 183 (September/October 1990): 50–62.

———. *For They Know Not What They Do: Enjoyment as a Political Factor*. London: Verso, 1991.

Index

Adorno, Theodor, 25; *Dialectic of Enlightenment*, 24
Aesthetics, 47, 61, 62, 64
Ahlzweig, Claus, 10
Alexis, Willibald, 186, 187, 262; and Fontane, 31, 62, 64, 158, 162, 163; on invention, 37; *Isegrimm*, 219–23; *Keeping Calm Is the Citizen's First Duty*, 23, 31, 157–66; and Lewald, 161; and Mühlbach, 171; *The Outlaws*, 90, 92–94
Amadeus, Victor, 22
Amelia (Anna Amelia Hohenzollern), 54–55, 113
Ancestry, 17–18, 19, 77, 262
Anderson, Benedict, 13, 73
Anecdotes, 100, 101, 109, 110, 118, 131, 132, 139, 142
Anna, Countess Orzelska, 102, 103–5, 108, 109, 115
Anti-Semitism, 20, 21, 80, 139, 169, 185, 186, 187, 188, 230. *See also* Jews
Anti-Socialist Laws, 136
Aristocracy: in Alexis, 158, 220, 221, 223; in Belani, 89, 90; and caste, 215; in Droysen, 178; in Fontane, 189, 197, 245, 246, 247, 248; in Fouqué, 77; in François, 238, 239, 240; and Frederick the Great, 141; and French culture, 96; in Frenzel, 241, 242, 243; in Freytag, 183, 251, 254; in Häusser, 207; in Hesekiel, 185, 186, 188, 234, 235, 236, 238; in Hildebrandt, 84, 85, 86, 87, 88; and Jena, 196–97, 271; in Jensen, 192, 193, 194, 195; in Lewald, 154, 155; loyalty of, 70–71; and marriage, 201; and middle class, 264; in Mühlbach, 113, 114, 167, 170; and national identity, 94; and nationalism, 70–71; in Rellstab, 214; in Treitschke, 175; in Wickede, 229, 232, 233, 234. *See also* Courtiers; Society
Arndt, Ernst Moritz, 70, 201, 213
Arnold, Miller, 55
Assmann, Aleida, 8
Auerbach, E., *The Gypsy Theft*, 88–89
Auerstadt, battle of, 194
Austria: in Auerbach, 88; and Bismarck, 133; in Droysen, 177; and French culture, 241, 242; in Frenzel, 241, 242, 244; and

INDEX

Austria (*continued*)
  Germany, 17, 18, 88, 110, 133, 211, 213, 241; in Hildebrandt, 82, 83, 84, 86, 87; and Hungary, 138; and Metternich, 70; in Mühlbach, 115; and Prussia, 133, 241; in Sybell, 208; and Treitschke, 139, 140, 211; and Wars of Liberation, 204, 216

Bacher, Julius, 143; *Frederick the Great's Search for a Wife*, 119–25
Bausinger, Hermann, 268
Bavaria, 141, 208
Belani, H. E. R., *The Demagogues*, 89–90
Bhabha, Homi, 4
Biedermeier period, 70
Bildungsroman, 244
Biography, 57–60
Bismarck, Otto von, 36, 145; anti-Austrian unification of Germany, 133; as center of the imperial enterprise, 2; dismissal by William II, 99; empire of, 17; and Frederick the Great, 19; German acceptance of, 4; and Louisa, Queen of Prussia, 174; monuments to, 8, 255; Prussian identity of, 142–43; representations of, 1, 2–3, 15; and Silesia, 143; and Treitschke, 211, 213; in Werner, 2, 107
Blücher, Gebhard Leberecht von, 19, 202, 212, 213, 223–24
Bülow, General von, 62, 189, 205, 207

Capitalism, 24, 74
Caste, 11, 15; and aristocracy, 215; in Belani, 89, 90; in Fontane, 247; in Fouqué, 77, 78; in Hildebrandt, 83, 86, 87; and identity, 86–89; loyalty to, 71; in Mühlbach, 167; in Rellstab, 96, 214; and unity, 94, 200, 201; in Wickede, 228. See *also* Class; Society
Catherine the Great, 137, 172
Catholic Church, 86–87, 92, 122, 134, 141, 184, 211, 221. See *also* Christianity
Character, 63–64, 66, 98
Christianity, 227, 228, 231. See *also* Catholic Church; Protestants/Protestantism; Religion
Civil service, 182, 196–97
Clark, Christopher, 202
Class, 136, 221, 222, 245. See *also* Caste; Society
Clausewitz, Baron von, 180
Collingwood, R. G., 49
Colomb, Friedrich August Peter von, 207
Common people. See People/common people
Community, 74, 86; cultural, 229; in François, 239; in Hesekiel, 237; imagined, 13, 73, 211, 219; national, 220; in Rellstab, 216. See *also* Society
Confino, Alon, 4, 269
Courtiers, 86, 87. See *also* Aristocracy; Monarchy
Craig, Gordon, 30
Crauer, Carl, 2
Culture, 15, 24–25, 227, 228, 229, 230

Dahn, Felix, *Struggle for Rome*, 13
Danzig, 133, 134–36
Decline. See Myth; Society
Democracy, 197, 202, 248. See *also* Egalitarianism; Liberalism
Denmark, 17
Downing, Eric, 36
Droysen, Johann Gustav, 56, 110; biography in, 57–60; on fact, 58; and Fontane, 64; and Häusser, 179; hero in, 56; *Historik*, 56–57; history in, 57–58, 177; Jena in, 56, 57; *Lectures on the Age of Wars*

346

INDEX

of Liberation, 176–78, 204–6; *The Life of Field Marshal Count Yorck von Wartenburg,* 57, 58, 64–65; on motivation, 58; and Mühlbach, 59; and Ranke, 56, 57–58; and Treitschke, 177; truth in, 59–60
Dumas, Alexandre, 39

Egalitarianism, 96, 136, 251. *See also* Democracy; Liberalism
Eggert, Hartmut, 39
Eke, Norbert, 38
Elizabeth Christine of Brunswick-Wolfenbüttel, 17, 102, 115, 116, 118, 124, 125
Enlightenment, 86, 96, 117, 122
Ephraim, Benjamin Veitel, 187
Ephraim, Veitel Heine, 116–17
Ethnicity, 16–18, 76, 85, 88–89, 94, 214, 216, 218

Fact: in Droysen, 58; in Fontane, 61; in historical fiction, 8–9, 45–46; in historical fiction *vs.* history, 130, 131; as impersonal event, 98; importance of, 5; in Mühlbach, 47; in Ranke, 40–41, 51; as raw material, 98; in Spamer, 130. *See also* Truth
Fallersleben, Hoffman von, "Song of the Germans," 17
Family: in Alexis, 221, 222, 223, 262; in Auerbach, 88, 89; in Belani, 89, 90; in François, 262; and Frederick the Great, 119; in Hesekiel, 187, 238, 262; in Hildebrandt, 83, 86; ideal, 75; in Jensen, 193; and Louisa, Queen of Prussia, 172, 270; national, 17–18, 89, 200, 219, 224, 234, 263; in Rellstab, 215, 219; in Reuter, 226; in Sudermann, 258, 259, 261, 262; in Wickede, 234, 262, 263
Fatherland: in Alexis, 93, 164, 220; in Belani, 90; in Droysen, 205; in Frenzel, 243; in Gersdorf, 79; in Hildebrandt, 82; in Jensen, 195; in Oldendorp, 81; and Prussian, 145; in Rellstab, 215, 219; in Reuter, 226; in Sudermann, 260; in Sybell, 209; in Treitschke, 210, 211. *See also* Germany; Nation; Nationalism; Patriotism
Fiction. *See* Historical fiction
Fontane, Theodor: aims of, 65–66; and Alexis, 31, 62, 64, 158, 162, 163; aristocracy in, 189, 197, 245, 246, 247, 248; career of, 60; and Droysen, 64; fact in, 61; Frederick the Great in, 97–98, 99, 100, 101, 145, 189, 190; Germany in, 190, 246, 248–49, 250, 251; and Hesekiel, 184, 185, 187; and historical fiction, 60, 62, 101; on historical vision, 62–63; history in, 99–100, 100–101, 189; identity in, 249–50, 251; Jena in, 60, 61–62, 63, 64, 188, 189–91; Louisa, Queen of Prussia in, 190, 191, 197, 198; marriage in, 245, 248, 250–51; monarchy in, 97, 197, 245, 246–47; and Mühlbach, 63; past *vs.* present in, 63; Prussia in, 26, 31, 60, 61–62, 63, 64, 188, 189–91, 248, 249–50; readers of, 63, 97, 143; reception of, 22; renewal in, 197; and Scheffel, 62; society in, 31, 60, 188, 189–91, 245; truth in, 30, 31, 35, 45, 60, 61–62, 64; Wars of Liberation in, 26, 247, 251; women in, 31, 190, 250;
WORKS: *Before the Storm,* 30, 60, 245–51, 264; *Beyond Recall,* 97; *Delusions Confessions,* 264; *Frau Jenny Treibel,* 100; *A Man of Honor,* 31, 60–62, 63–64, 184, 188–91; *Der Stechlin,* 6, 7–8, 26, 30, 63; *Wanderings through the Mark Brandenburg,* 60
Förster, Friedrich, 111
Fouqué, Friedrich de la Motte, 84,

INDEX

Fouqué, Friedrich de la Motte (*continued*) 86, 162, 235; *The Refugee or Home and Abroad*, 69–72, 75, 76–79

France: in Alexis, 92, 93, 159; and aristocracy, 96; cooperation with, 201; Frederick the Great routs, 111; in Freytag, 251; and Germany, 17, 120, 121–24, 125, 199; in Häusser, 179; as pinnacle of civilization, 149. *See also* French culture

Francis I, Emperor of Austria, 142, 150, 175

François, Louisa von, 262, 264; *The History of the Prussian Wars of Liberation*, 202; *The Last von Reckenburg*, 238–41

Frederick Barbarossa, 16

Frederick the Great: in Alexis, 158–59; as anchor in change, 142; anecdotes about, 100, 109, 110, 118, 131, 132, 139, 142; and Anna, Countess Orzelska, 102, 103–5, 108, 109; as Antichrist, 79; and aristocracy, 141; in Bacher, 119–21, 122–23, 124, 125; benevolence of, 110, 118, 199, 269; and Bismarck, 19; as bully, 109; and commoners, 80, 96, 107, 119, 141, 142, 269; and conservatism, 144; in Droysen, 177; and duty *vs.* pleasure, 118; and Elizabeth Christine, 17, 115, 116, 118, 124, 125; emotions of, 108; and Ephraim, 116–17; as Everyman, 127; eyes of, 118–19, 127, 133; as fairy-tale monarch, 119; as fallible mortal, 112; and family, 119; and father, 80, 103, 105, 117, 118, 120, 123, 124, 125, 127; as father, 18, 109, 118, 127, 131, 137; and flute, 107, 112, 144; in Fontane, 97–98, 99, 100, 101, 145, 189, 190; in Fouqué, 78–79; in François, 239; and French culture, 98, 120, 121, 122, 123–24, 125, 141, 149, 155–56, 269; and friendship, 107; as German, 98, 120, 121, 123–24, 125, 132, 133, 134–35, 140–41, 142, 269; and German Customs Union, 140, 142; and German unity, 3, 111, 118, 140–41, 144; in Gersdorf, 79, 80; heirs of, 99; as hero, 78, 79, 80, 81, 120, 123, 141, 147; and heroic age, 94; in Hesekiel, 186; in Hildebrandt, 81, 82, 84; historical novels concerning, 18–19, 101–5, 112–39; in history, 18–19, 106–12, 139–42; and Hohenzollern dynasty, 163; homosexuality of, 108; human side of, 35, 108, 109; as integrative figure, 115; interest in, 100; in Jensen, 193, 194, 195; justice of, 55, 80, 81, 112, 133, 137, 141; as justification for present, 140; Katzbach victory of, 110; in Kugler, 106–12, 123, 143; in Lewald, 153, 155–56; and liberalism, 106, 107, 136, 144; as liminal, 123, 155–56, 167, 193; and location myth, 19; in Lorenz, 102–4, 105; and Louisa, Queen of Prussia, 167; and love, 97, 100, 102, 103, 104, 105, 108, 115, 116, 117, 118, 119, 124, 125, 128, 131, 142; and Maria Theresa of Austria, 87; marriage of, 102; memory of, 75–76; in Menzel, 107; and middle class, 96, 269; military activity of, 98, 106, 110–11, 128, 129, 131; as misanthrope, 108; mortality of, 118; in Mühlbach, 39–40, 43, 44, 52, 53–56, 112–13, 114–19, 130, 143–44, 171; and national consciousness, 130; and national family, 269; and nationalism, 136, 145; and national narrative, 44; in

348

INDEX

Oldendorp, 80–81; as Old Fritz, 19, 80, 96, 98, 101, 109, 110, 123, 133, 136, 137, 142, 145, 189; as oppressor, 112; as ordinary person, 119, 127, 129, 130; personal life of, 42, 43, 101; and prenationalist order, 81; private life of, 100, 130, 143–44; as protector, 112; and Prussia, 133, 142, 143, 145; and Prussian Uniform Code, 55; public actions of, 100; in Ranke, 42, 43, 44, 52–53; Rauch's equestrian statue of, 106; realism of, 141; and religion, 117, 141; as representing past, 80, 81; reputation/image of, 98–99, 101, 104, 106, 119–20; and Roßbach victory, 111; and Saxony, 110; in Schücking, 137, 138, 139; self-image of, 114; and Silesia, 33, 52, 118, 123, 139, 141; and soldiers, 107, 109, 110, 115, 141; in Spamer, 127–28, 129–30, 131, 143; subjects of, 109, 112; in Treitschke, 139, 140–41, 142, 144, 173–74; and victory over Napoleon, 110; and Voltaire, 107, 144, 149; in Voß, 91; and War of Bavarian Succession, 111, 132; as well-rounded, 109; and William II, 144–45; in Wilmsen, 126–27; as wise, 98, 109, 137; and women writers, 97–98, 142, 145; and Yorck von Wartenburg, 59; in Zollern, 132–33, 137

Frederick William I: in Bacher, 120, 122, 123, 125; in Lorenz, 102–5; in Mühlbach, 112, 113, 117, 118; and son, 80, 105, 117, 118, 120, 123, 124, 125, 127

Frederick William III: in Alexis, 163, 165, 220; "Appeal to My People," 202–3; in Droysen, 178, 205; in Fontane, 190; in Hesekiel, 235; in Lewald, 153, 154, 156; and middle class, 172; in Mühlbach, 166–67, 224; in Sybell, 209; in Treitschke, 174–75; weakness of, 148, 150, 151, 178, 270

Frederick William IV, 107, 148, 172

French culture: in Alexis, 159, 161–62, 164, 219; and aristocracy, 96, 155–56, 166–68, 193–94; and Austria, 241, 242; in Bacher, 120, 121, 122–23, 124; as corrupting, 122; in Fontane, 249, 250; in Fouqué, 76–79; and Frederick the Great, 98, 120, 121, 122, 123–24, 125, 141, 149, 155–56, 269; in Frenzel, 241, 242; in Freytag, 183, 252, 253; and Germany, 166, 201; and Jena, 196–97, 198; in Jensen, 192, 193, 194; in Lewald, 154, 155–56; and Louisa, Queen of Prussia, 172, 174, 270; in Mühlbach, 166, 167, 170; as progressive, 201; reform through, 201; in Spielhagen, 256; in Treitschke, 174. *See also* France

French Revolution, 16, 89, 122, 148–49, 155, 246, 247

Frenzel, Karl, *Lucifer*, 241–45

Freytag, Gustav, 22, 31; *Ancestors*, 13, 23, 31, 183, 251; *Debit and Credit*, 13, 254; *Portraits from the German Past*, 181–84; *From a Small Town*, 183–84, 251–55

Furst, Lilian R., 36

Garden Bower, The, 172–73

Gender, 21, 33, 216, 218–19, 240–41, 263–64. *See also* Women

Gentz, Friedrich, *Germany in Her Deepest Depredation*, 168

German Customs Union, 140, 142

Germania monument (Rüdesheim), 3

Germany: in Alexis, 158, 160, 164, 165, 223; in Auerbach, 88; and Austria, 17, 18, 88, 110, 133, 211, 213, 241; in Bacher, 120, 121, 122, 124; in Belani, 89; *Biedermeier*, 89; and Bismarck, 4,

INDEX

Germany (*continued*) 133; boundaries of, 135–36; and Catholic Church, 122, 134; common enemy of, 199, 200; common past of, 5; cooperation with France in, 201; creation of, 73; cultural community of, 229; decline of, 190; defeat of, 178; and Denmark, 17; discursive formation of, 4–5; disenchantment with, 92; in Droysen, 204, 205, 206; expansion of, 70; in Fontane, 190, 246, 248–49, 250, 251; and France, 17, 120, 121–24, 125, 199, 201; and Frederick the Great, 3, 98, 111, 118, 120, 121, 123–24, 125, 132, 133, 134–35, 140–41, 142, 144, 269; and French culture, 166, 201; French reorganization of, 149–50; in Frenzel, 241–42, 243; in Freytag, 184, 251, 253, 254; future of, 166, 183, 200, 219, 221, 224, 237; and gender, 21; in Häusser, 179, 180, 206; in Hesekiel, 186, 188, 237, 238; in Hildebrandt, 82, 84; and historical forces, 210; and history, 267; humiliation of, 179; identity of, 9–12, 120, 121, 122–23, 124, 241; as imagined community, 73, 211, 219; as inclusive, 25; independent states of, 18; invention of, 11, 12, 15, 26; and Jena, 19–20, 147, 270, 271; in Jensen, 192, 193, 194–95; kinship in, 214, 218; and Louisa, Queen of Prussia, 173; in Mühlbach, 168, 171; and Napoleon, 155, 156; Napoleon's conquest of, 149–50; national community of, 214, 218, 220; national myth of, 75; national narrative of, 15; and Protestantism, 121, 122; and Prussia, 3, 5, 17, 86, 110, 132, 134–36, 140–41, 142, 143, 158, 173, 179, 202, 205, 209, 210, 211, 241, 248, 254; redemption of, 160, 194; regeneration/renewal of, 20–21, 59, 147, 171, 172, 177, 180, 188, 193, 194–95, 197, 198, 199, 200, 209, 214, 226, 235, 238, 263; and religion, 121; in Rellstab, 95, 215, 216, 217, 219; in Reuter, 225, 226; and Revolution of 1848, 148; and Russia, 17, 218; in Schücking, 138, 139; and Sedan Day, 255; shared culture of, 121, 145, 199, 258; shared history of, 111, 267, 268, 269, 271; shared work of, 199; size of, 241; socio-political change in, 12–13; in Spielhagen, 257; as state and nation, 5; in Sudermann, 258, 261; superiority of, 74; in Sybell, 209; in Treitschke, 139, 140–41, 210, 211, 212; unity of, 70, 89, 110, 122, 133, 138, 139, 140–41, 158, 165, 168, 171, 177, 180, 184, 199, 200, 204, 206, 211, 223, 233, 261; and Wars of Liberation, 202, 203, 204, 205, 206, 207, 208, 209; in Wickede, 232, 233, 234; writing of, 12; in Zollern, 133, 134–35, 136. *See also* Fatherland; Nation; Nationalism

Gersdorf, Wilhelmine von: *Aurora Countess of Konigsmark*, 38; *The Conspiracy, or Treason and Loyalty*, 79–80

Gethe, Christoph Wilhelm Heinrich, 181–82, 183

Goethe, Johann Wolfgang von, 12, 30, 175; *Sorrows of Werther*, 114, 270

Great events, 82

Great men, 35, 56–60, 81, 124, 205, 206, 210

Greeks, 16, 34

Grossbeeren, battle of, 207

INDEX

Hapsburg Empire. *See* Austria
Hardenberg, Karl August von, 156, 175, 183
Hauff, Wilhelm, *Lichtenstein,* 14
Häusser, Ludwig, *German History,* 178–81, 206–8
Heine, Heinrich, 30–31
Hermann the German (Arminius), 16, 163
Hero: disjunctive, 129; in Droysen, 56; in Fontane, 56, 245, 247–48; Frederick the Great as, 78, 79, 80, 81, 120, 123, 147; and Jena, 195–96; in Jensen, 195; middle class as, 95–96; middling, 51, 56, 63, 96, 129, 213–14; mythic age of, 18; myth of, 147; in Sudermann, 261; in Wickede, 233, 234
Hesekiel, George, 184, 185, 187, 197, 262; *Before Jena,* 184–88, 191, 234; *Stillness Before the Storm,* 234–38
Hessen-Rotenburg, landgrave of, 22
Hildebrandt, Christoph, 84, 86, 93; *The Most Remarkable Year in the Life of an Old Soldier,* 86–88; *The von Manteufel Family,* 81–82, 87, 96
Hirschmann, Günther, 134
Historical fiction: characters in, 66; and character *vs.* event, 35; common people in, 12, 124; and consensus over past, 95; and contemporary situation, 134, 137, 254, 261; development of, 15–16; empathy in, 45, 46–47; fact in, 8–9, 45–46; in Fontane, 60, 62, 101; and Freytag, 181, 183; gender of authors, 34; great men's human side in, 35; and Häusser, 180; and history, 5–6, 8, 9, 16, 31, 32, 34–35, 38, 40–42, 43, 49, 66, 101, 130, 140; identity in, 72, 76, 271–72; intuition in, 45, 46–47; invention in, 37, 100–101, 130–31; Jena defeat in, 19; and Kugler, 108; legitimacy of, 44–45; medieval setting for, 14; modes of representation in, 47; Mühlbach on, 47–51, 54; and nationalism, 9, 46; and national narrative, 66; popularity of, 8; in post-Napoleonic era, 70; quality of, 52; Ranke on, 40–42; readability of, 35; readers of, 12–13, 43, 44, 72; realism in, 36, 37; speaking parts in, 50, 51; special truth of, 46; subject matter of, 73; as teacher, 66; and Treitschke, 140, 175, 176; truth in, 29–32, 35, 44–46, 46, 66; understanding in, 45, 46–47; Wars of Liberation in, 21, 73, 213–14, 248; women in, 85
History: as academic discipline, 8, 32–33; and Alexis, 163; appeal of, 12–18; as branch of literature, 30; character development in, 57; critical method of, 40, 41; in Droysen, 57–58, 177; factors in representations of, 47; in Fontane, 99–101, 189; Frederick the Great in, 18–19, 106–12; in Freytag, 31, 181, 182; gender in, 33–34; and German identity, 34, 267; in Hildebrandt, 85, 86; and historical fiction, 5–6, 8, 9, 16, 31, 32, 34–35, 38, 40–42, 43, 49, 66, 101, 130, 140; and identity, 32, 71–72, 267–68; individual in, 57, 58; intuition in, 53; Jena defeat in, 19; kinds of, 4–9; knowledge of, 63; local, 34; meaning in, 18; motivation in, 56, 58; in Mühlbach, 167; and nationalism, 9, 46; Nietzsche on, 6; politics in, 32–33; popular, 5–6, 12, 34, 106–12; popularity of, 13; power *vs.* greatness in, 174; quality of, 52; and Ranke, 16, 40, 41, 42–43; readers of, 12, 44; realism in, 35–38; in Rellstab, 95;

INDEX

History (*continued*)
representation in, 58; and Scheffel, 62; shared, 111, 267, 268, 269, 271; and society, 33, 163; in Sottong, 85; in Spamer, 129, 130; speech in, 50; and Treitschke, 140, 176; truth in, 1–2, 32, 44, 45, 46, 57; and Wars of Liberation, 21, 73, 255

Hobsbawm, Eric, 10

Hohendahl, Peter Uwe, 74

Holub, Robert C., 36

Holy Roman Empire, 150, 177, 201

Horkheimer, Max, 25; *Dialectic of Enlightenment*, 24

Hungary, 87, 138

Identity, 75; and aristocrats, 94; in Bacher, 120–21, 122, 123–24; in Belani, 89; of Blücher, 212; and bourgeoisie, 96; and caste, 86–89; disillusionment with, 94; examination of, 11–12; fictional mediation of, 75, 76; in Fontane, 249–50, 251; formation of, 11, 13, 21, 72, 76, 188; in Fouqué, 69–70, 76, 77, 78; and Frederick the Great, 123; in Frenzel, 241, 244; of Germany, 9–12, 120, 121, 122–23, 124, 241; in Hesekiel, 188, 235; in Hildebrandt, 82, 83; in historical fiction, 72, 76, 271–72; and history, 32, 34, 71–72, 267–68; and Jena, 271; in Jensen, 192, 193; and liminality, 123; and middle class, 94; national, 21, 65, 69–70, 71, 72, 75, 76, 77, 81–85, 94, 106, 120–21, 122, 123–24, 133–34, 225; reader's formation of, 13; regional, 15, 69–70, 106, 133–34; in Rellstab, 95, 214, 216, 219; in Reuter, 225; shared, 15; in Spamer, 65; in Spielhagen, 257; and us *vs.* them principle, 121, 122, 196; and Wars of Liberation, 70, 82, 271; in Wickede, 227, 228, 229; in Zollern, 136. *See also* Ethnicity; Nation; Nationalism

Individual, 50, 56, 57, 58, 206–7, 209, 213–14

Intuition, 45, 46–47, 53, 62–63

Jahn, Friedrich Ludwig, 20–21

James, G. P. R., 39

Jeismann, Michael, 121

Jena, battle of: in Alexis, 157, 158, 159, 160, 164, 166; and aristocracy, 271; as cleansing experience, 160, 172, 176; collective memory of, 75; and decline, 94, 147, 157; in Droysen, 56, 57, 176, 177, 178; as fall from grace, 19–20, 147; in Fontane, 26, 60, 61–62, 63, 64, 188, 189–91; and French culture, 198; in Freytag, 181, 182, 183; and future, 166, 183; and Germany, 19–20, 147, 270, 271; in Häusser, 178, 179, 180, 181; and heroes, 195–96; in Hesekiel, 187, 188; and identity, 271; in Jensen, 192, 193, 194; in Lewald, 157; in Mühlbach, 170, 171; as national myth, 157; and old Germany, 150; Prussian defeat at, 147–48, 150–51; and redemption, 195–96; and renewal, 199; in Sybell, 209; as transitory event, 176; in Treitschke, 174, 175, 176; and Wars of Liber-ation, 196; written treatments of, 148

Jensen, Wilhelm, 197; *Gradiva*, 191; *At the Turn of the Century*, 191–95

Jews: in Alexis, 221; assimilation of, 169, 228, 232; in German literature, 169; in Hesekiel, 185, 186, 187, 188, 197; and Holocaust, 24; and language, 187; in Lewald, 151, 154; in Mühlbach, 116–17, 168–69, 187; and myth of decline, 20; in Oldendorp, 80; in Reuter,

225; speech of, 117; in Spielhagen, 256; in Treitschke, 139; in Wickede, 21, 227–34. *See also* Religion

Joseph II, 137

Kleist, Heinrich von, 70, 161, 163, 179
Kock, Paul de, 39
Kontje, Todd, 200
Köppen, Carl Friedrich, 111
Körner, Theodor, 70, 200, 201, 233
Koshar, Rudy, 8
Kugler, Franz, 139, 143; *History of Frederick the Great*, 34, 106, 123

Lafontaine, August, 162, 163
Language, 10, 12, 13, 36–37, 143, 172, 187, 213, 252
Leipzig, battle of, 202, 209, 254, 255
Lenbach, Franz von, 3
Lessing, Gotthold Ephraim, 30, 37, 96, 270; *Nathan the Wise*, 230
Leuthn, battle of, 128, 131
Lewald, Fanny, 161, 186; *Prince Louis Ferdinand*, 151–57
Liberalism, 106–7, 118, 136, 144, 167, 202, 207, 237. *See also* Democracy; Egalitarianism
Libraries, 23, 72, 106
Liechtenstein, Prince von, 169
Liminality, 123, 155–56, 167, 193
Literature, 23, 24, 32, 57, 58, 74–75, 161–63, 175, 176. *See also* Historical fiction
Lorenz, Auguste Wilhelmine, 101, 132, 143; *Frederick II's Only Love*, 102–5
Louisa, Queen of Prussia: in Alexis, 162–63, 165, 166; and Bismarck, 174; as exemplary, 96; and expiation of sin, 197–98; and family, 270; in Fontane, 190, 191, 197, 198; and Frederick the Great, 167; and French culture, 172, 174, 270; in Jensen, 194, 195; in Lewald, 154, 156; and marriage, 270; as martyred saint, 199; as mediating figure, 167, 174; and middle class, 167, 168, 171, 172, 197, 270; as mother, 18, 174, 197, 199; in Mühlbach, 170, 171; and Napoleon I, 197; pan-Germanic status of, 3; and past, 173–74, 197; and regeneration, 198; representations of, 15; in Ring, 172–73; in Sybell, 209; in Treitschke, 173–76
Louis Ferdinand, 151–57, 164, 178
Love: in Alexis, 219, 220–21, 222–23; in François, 239, 240; and Frederick the Great, 97, 100, 102, 103, 104, 105, 108, 115, 116, 117, 118, 119, 124, 125, 128, 131, 142; in Frenzel, 241, 242, 243, 244; in Freytag, 251–55; in Hesekiel, 235–37, 238; in Hildebrandt, 83, 86; in Kugler, 108; in Lorenz, 102, 103, 104, 105; in Mühlbach, 113–14, 115, 116, 117, 118, 119; and nationalism, 262–63; in Rellstab, 215–16, 217–18; in Spamer, 131; in Spielhagen, 255–57; in Sudermann, 258, 259; in Wickede, 228, 230, 231. *See also* Marriage
Lower class, 96, 197
Loyalty: in Belani, 89; in Fouqué, 78; in Hildebrandt, 82–83, 83, 84, 85, 87; personal *vs.* ethnic, 87; in Rellstab, 96; in Reuter, 225; and Wars of Liberation, 70
Luther, Martin, 202

Maria Theresa of Austria, 33, 52, 86, 87, 138, 139–40, 142, 184
Marriage: in Alexis, 219, 222–23; and aristocracy, 201; arranged, 262; in Belani, 89, 90; emotional bonding in, 114; in Fontane, 245, 248, 250–51; in François, 238, 239, 240; in Frenzel, 241, 244; in Freytag, 251, 252, 254, 255;

353

INDEX

Marriage (*continued*)
in Hesekiel, 236–37, 238; in Hildebrandt, 84, 85; in historical fiction, 214; in Lewald, 154; in Lorenz, 102; and Louisa, Queen of Prussia, 270; in May, 255; in Mühlbach, 113, 114, 167; in Rellstab, 215–16, 217, 218; in Reuter, 225, 226; in Spielhagen, 256, 257; in Sudermann, 258, 259; in Wickede, 229, 230, 232, 233, 234. *See also* Love

Martino, Alberto, 39

May, Karl, *The Love of a Cavalry Officer*, 255

Mecklenburg, 92

Memoir, 75

Memory, 4, 5, 75–76, 93–94, 99, 189, 258, 259

Menzel, Adolph, 106–7, 109, 139; *History of Frederick the Great*, 34

Meritocracy, 151, 156

Metternich, Prince Klemens von, 70, 208, 244

Middle class: in Alexis, 220, 223; and aristocracy, 264; in fiction, 96; in Fontane, 189; in François, 238, 239, 240; and Frederick the Great, 96, 269; in Frenzel, 243, 244; in Freytag, 254, 255; in Häusser, 207; as heroes, 95–96; in Hesekiel, 237, 238; and identity, 96; Lessing on, 37; in Lewald, 153, 155, 156; and Louisa, Queen of Prussia, 167, 168, 171, 172, 197, 270; in Mühlbach, 114, 167, 168, 171; and national identity, 94; and national narrative, 269; and politics, 72; and public sphere, 72; and realism, 36; regeneration from, 197; in Rellstab, 95, 96, 214; in Sottong, 85; and unity, 201; in Wickede, 228. *See also* People/common people; Society

Military: in Alexis, 159, 160, 164, 223; in Fontane, 190; and Frederick the Great, 98, 106, 110–11, 128, 129, 131; French, 150, 159; and French culture, 201; in Freytag, 182, 183; in Häusser, 207; in Hesekiel, 185, 186; in Jensen, 193, 194, 195; in Kugler, 108; in Lewald, 152–53, 155; in Mühlbach, 170; in Oldendorp, 81; in Ranke, 42; in Rellstab, 218; in Sybell, 209; in Treitschke, 211; unity of, 206; and Wars of Liberation, 200, 202, 204. *See* Militia

Military officers: in Alexis, 223; in Fontane, 189, 197; in Freytag, 182, 183; in Hesekiel, 188, 197; in Hildebrandt, 83, 84, 85, 86, 87–88; identity of, 69–70; and Jena, 196–97; in Jensen, 194; in Lewald, 152, 153, 154, 156; and Rellstab, 96; in Sybell, 209; and unity, 201; in Wickede, 233

Militia, 200, 202, 205, 207–8, 226, 263

Mommsen, Theodor, 110; *Roman History*, 30

Monarchy, 97, 152, 197, 220, 234, 245, 246–47

Money, 115–16, 165, 185, 186, 221, 225

Monumenta Germaniae Historica, 33

Monuments, 8, 13, 34, 255

Morality: in Alexis, 158; decay of, 20; and Jena, 147; in Lewald, 151, 152, 154; and Louisa, Queen of Prussia, 172; and social decline, 31, 147, 151–52, 153–57, 158, 159, 161, 162, 175, 179, 180, 182, 188, 189–91, 192, 193, 194, 198, 258; in Sudermann, 258; in Wickede, 230

Mühlbach, Louisa, 143; on academic history, 47–51, 54; aims of, 65; and Alexis, 171; aristocracy in, 113, 114, 167, 170; common people in, 39–40, 43, 44, 114, 167,

INDEX

224; and Droysen, 59; and empathy, 49; experience of, 46; fact in, 47; and Fontane, 63; footnotes in, 50; Frederick the Great in, 39–40, 43, 44, 52, 53–56, 112–13, 114–19, 130, 143–44, 171; Frederick William I in, 112, 113, 117, 118; Frederick William III in, 166–67, 224; French culture in, 166, 167, 170; Germany in, 168, 171; and Hesekiel, 186; on historical fiction, 47–51, 54; historical reality in, 54; and historicity, 46; on history, 167; and individual *vs.* universal, 50; invention in, 51, 53; Jews in, 116–17, 168–69, 187; life of, 39; love in, 113–14, 115, 116, 117, 118, 119; on middle class, 114, 167; motivation in, 49, 53–56; Napoleon in, 170, 171, 224; personal details in, 43, 44; and poetry, 49; quotation in, 50, 53; and Ranke, 43, 49–50, 52–53; readers of, 65, 143; Silesian invasion in, 52; society in, 171, 223–24; sources of, 48–49; speech in, 50, 51; on sublime, 48; truth in, 45; and universality, 46; women in, 168, 169, 170; WORKS: *Berlin and Sans-Souci,* 54, 112; *First and Last Love,* 39; *Frederick the Great and His Court,* 39–40, 112–13; *Frederick the Great and His Family,* 54, 112; *Germany in Storm and Stress,* 112; *Goethe and Schiller,* 112; *Louisa of Prussia and Her Times,* 166, 168; *Napoleon and the Queen of Prussia,* 166; *Napoleon in Germany,* 166, 223–24; *Old Fritz and the New Era,* 47, 65

Mundt, Theodor, 39

Münster, 149

Myth: of ancestry, 17–18, 19; of decline, 18, 20, 195–96, 198, 200; of ethnicity, 16–18; in Fontane, 189; of hero, 245, 247–48; of heroic age, 18, 147, 200; of location, 17, 18, 19; meaning of, 18; of redemption, 195–96; of regeneration, 18, 20, 200; of renewal, 59, 235; of temporal origins, 16; in Treitschke, 213; of universal participation, 210

Napoleon I: in Alexis, 159, 164, 165; as commander, 150; conquest of Germany, 149–50; in Droysen, 178; and Frederick the Great, 110; in Frenzel, 243, 244; in Freytag, 252, 253; German admiration for, 155, 156; in Häusser, 179, 180; inability to resist, 31; in Lewald, 152; and Louisa, Queen of Prussia, 197; in Mühlbach, 170, 171, 224; in Rellstab, 215; and Russia, 224; in Treitschke, 175

Narrative, national, 18–26; debate over, 25; and family, 261–62; and Frederick the Great, 44; and historical fiction, 66; and invention of Germany, 15; Jena in, 147; marriage in, 248; and middle class, 269, 270; and nationalism, 73, 74; and Prussian seizure of control, 3, 4–5; success composing, 272; and Sybel, 208; Wars of Liberation in, 263; women in, 170

Nation: in Auerbach, 88, 89; in Belani, 89, 90; and family, 89, 200, 219, 224, 234, 263; in Fouqué, 77; Germany as, 5; in Hildebrandt, 83, 88; and language, 213; in Rellstab, 215, 216; in Wickede, 234. *See also* Fatherland; Germany

Nationalism: in Alexis, 92, 93, 220–21; and aristocracy, 70–71; in Bacher, 120–21, 122, 123–24; as belief, 10; disenchantment with, 92; examination of, 11–12; in Fontane, 245, 246, 247, 248, 249; in Fouqué, 76, 77, 78, 88;

355

INDEX

Nationalism (*continued*)
and Frederick the Great, 136, 145; in Frenzel, 243, 244; in Häusser, 207, 208; in Hesekiel, 236; in Hildebrandt, 85, 88; and historical fiction, 9; and history, 9; and history *vs.* fiction, 46; and Hungarians, 87; and identity, 21, 65, 69–70, 71, 72, 75, 76, 77, 81–85, 94, 106, 120–21, 122, 123–24, 133–34, 225; and Jena, 196; and Jensen, 197; in Lewald, 153; literary, 12; literature of, 74; and love, 262–63; in Mühlbach, 115; Polish, 216–17; in post-Napoleonic era, 150; and Prussia, 143; and regionalism, 133–34; in Rellstab, 214, 215, 216, 217, 219; in Reuter, 225; in Sudermann, 261; in Sybell, 209; in Treitschke, 175–76, 210, 211; trivialization of, 91; undeveloped myth of, 94; and urban elite, 91; in Voß, 90, 91, 92; and Wars of Liberation, 70, 72; in Wickede, 227, 229; in Zollern, 135, 136. *See also* Fatherland; Germany

Naturalism, 37
Naubert, Benedikte, 38–39
Nazis, 17, 24
New Prussian Newspaper, 185
Newspapers, 13, 73
Nietzsche, Friedrich, *Untimely Meditation: The Use and Abuse of History*, 6
Nobility. *See* Aristocracy
Nochlin, Linda, 38
Norton, Anne, 123
Novalis, 30, 162
Novel. *See* Historical fiction

Oettingen-Wallerstein Library, 22
Officers. *See* Military officers
Oldendorp, C. J., 93; *Misfortune and Rescue*, 80–81
Other, 122, 123, 133, 196. *See also* Identity

Palm (bookseller), 170, 177, 179
Past: consensus view of, 95; construction of, 78; continuity with, 173–74; in Fontane, 63, 189; Frederick the Great as representing, 80, 81; ideal, 75; in Lewald, 157; and Louisa, Queen of Prussia, 173–74, 197; shared, 17, 78, 94, 157, 267, 268, 269. *See also* History
Patriarchy, 217, 238, 240
Patriotism: in Alexis, 164, 220, 223; in Frenzel, 243, 244; in Freytag, 183; in Spielhagen, 256, 257; in Sudermann, 258, 260; in Wickede, 228, 229, 230, 233. *See also* Fatherland; Nationalism
Pavel, Thomas, 37
Peasantry, 246, 264
People/common people, 56–60; in Alexis, 164, 219; in Bacher, 124, 125; in Belani, 90; in Fontane, 189; and Frederick the Great, 80, 96, 107, 119, 141, 142, 269; in Häusser, 206, 207; in Hesekiel, 235; in historical fiction, 12, 124; identification with, 81; and Jena, 196, 197; in Jensen, 194, 195; in Mühlbach, 39–40, 43, 44, 114, 167, 224; in Rellstab, 216; renewal from, 167; in Sybell, 209, 210; in tragic drama, 96; in Treitschke, 210, 211, 212–13; and unity, 201; in Zollern, 136. *See also* Middle class
Pfau, Ludwig, "Baden Lullaby," 110
Plenzdorf, Ulrich, 45
Poland, 134, 143, 153, 204, 216–17, 218, 249
Politics: in academic history, 32–33; in Alexis, 161; in Belani, 90; change in, 12; as fraud, 90; in Freytag, 183; in Häusser, 180; in Hesekiel, 186; in Hildebrandt, 86;

356

INDEX

and Jena, 147; in Kuglar, 108; and middle class, 72; in Mühlbach, 114; and personal, 66; in Ranke, 42, 43; in Rellstab, 218; in Sybell, 209; upheaval in, 74; in Zollern, 136
Popular uprising, 173, 174, 202, 203, 204, 206, 210, 245, 246
Postmodernism, 36
Preuß, J. D. E., 111
Princely Library at Castle Corvey, 22
Protestants/Protestantism, 92, 121, 122, 137, 141, 184, 211. *See also* Christianity
Prussia: in Alexis, 31, 92, 158, 159, 160, 161, 166, 219–20; and Austria, 133, 241; and Bismarck, 3; boundaries of, 135–36; corruption of, 179, 180, 182; decline of, 152–55, 156, 157; defeat at Jena, 19–20, 147–48, 150–51; in Droysen, 177–78, 205; and fatherland, 145; in Fontane, 26, 31, 60, 61–62, 63, 64, 188, 189–91, 248, 249–50; and Frederick the Great, 133, 142, 143, 145; in Freytag, 182, 184; and Germany, 3, 5, 17, 86, 110, 132, 134–36, 140–41, 142, 143, 158, 173, 177, 179, 202, 205, 209, 210, 211, 241, 248, 254; in Gersdorf, 79; in Häusser, 179–80, 207; in Hesekiel, 186, 234, 235, 236, 238; in Hildebrandt, 82, 83, 84, 85; and Jena, 56, 271; in Jensen, 194; in Lewald, 152–55, 156, 157; and Louisa, Queen of Prussia, 173; moral decline of, 161, 162; in Mühlbach, 170, 171; and nationalism, 143; negative image of, 110; in Oldendorp, 81; in Pfau, 110; and Poland, 134; priority of, 86; redemption of, 160; renewal of, 172; and Sedan Day, 255; in Sudermann, 259; in Sybell, 208, 209; in Treitschke, 139, 210, 211, 212; and Wars of Liberation, 3, 157, 202, 205; in Wickede, 234; in Zollern, 133, 136
Prussian army: in Alexis, 164; in Freytag, 182; in Häusser, 207; in Jensen, 194, 195; in Lewald, 152–53, 155; in Mühlbach, 170; in Treitschke, 211
Prussian Uniform Code, 55
Publication, 86–87, 106, 137, 143, 271
Public sphere, 33, 72, 85, 216, 271

Raabe, Wilhelm, 35, 191
Radway, Janice, 23
Ranke, Leopold von: biography in, 57–58; and Droysen, 56, 57–58; facts in, 40–41, 51; Frederick the Great in, 42, 43, 44, 52–53; on historical fiction, 40–42; historical reality in, 54; history in, 16, 40, 41, 42–43; and individual *vs.* universal, 50; intuition in, 53; motivation in, 53; and Mühlbach, 43, 49–50, 52–53; politics in, 32; readers of, 44; reception of, 22, 23; rhetoric in, 53; Silesian invasion in, 52–53; on truth, 40–41; *Universal German Biography* entry, 42
Rauch, Christian Daniel, 106
Readers: in Alexis, 163; of Bacher, 124, 125, 143; children as, 126; and common people, 124; contemporaries as, 63; of Fontane, 63, 97, 143; in Germany, 137; of Hesekiel, 235; of Hildebrandt, 81; of historical fiction, 12–13, 72; of histories, 12–13; of history *vs.* fiction, 44; identification by, 43, 44, 64, 65, 81, 121, 182, 212, 214, 219; knowledge of, 63, 65, 67, 81; of Kugler, 106, 111; of Lewald, 157; of Lorenz, 143; middlebrow, 23; of Mühlbach, 65, 143; and personal aspects of heroes, 42; of Ranke, 44;

357

Readers (*continued*)
resemblance to characters, 98; of Spamer, 126, 128, 130, 131; of Spielhagen, 257; of Treitschke, 143; and truth, 44; of Wilmsen, 126, 127; women, 143; of Zollern, 143

Realism, 35–38, 57, 58, 214

Reform, 70, 152, 155, 175, 183, 197, 201, 223

Regeneration. *See* Germany; Myth

Region, 94, 96, 106, 133–34, 200, 201

Religion: in Fouqué, 78; and Frederick the Great, 117; in Freytag, 184; and Germany, 121; in Lessing, 230; in Treitschke, 211–12; unbridgeable differences in, 263; and unity, 201; and Wartburg festival, 202; in Wickede, 227, 228, 230, 231, 232. *See also specific religious groups*

Rellstab, Ludwig, 264; *1812*, 95, 214–19

Renan, Ernest, 4, 8

Reuter, Fritz, *From the Time of the French*, 224–26

Revolution. *See* French Revolution

Revolution of 1848, 110, 144, 148, 151, 207, 220, 251, 254

Riffaterre, Michael, 29

Ring, Max, "Louise," 172–73

Romans, 16, 34

Romanticism, 161, 175

Roon, Albrecht von, 1, 2, 4

Russia, 17, 202, 216, 217, 218, 224, 253

Saalfeld, battle of, 156, 164

Saxons, 139, 186, 204, 208

Saxony, 110, 211, 215

Scheffel, Josef Viktor von, *Ekkehard*, 13, 62

Scheider, Theodor, 98

Schiller, Friedrich, 12, 30, 175; *History of the Thirty Years War*, 164; "Song of the Bell," 74; *William Tell*, 74

Schlegel, August, 161, 162

Schlegel, Friedrich, 161, 162; *Lucinde*, 178

Schücking, Levin, *The Cavalry Colonel*, 137–39

Schulze, Hagen, 137

Scott, Sir Walter, 38, 39, 45, 46, 96, 213–14; *Ivanhoe*, 231; middling hero in, 51, 56, 63, 96; Ranke on, 40–42; *Waverley*, 72, 129

Second Empire, 36

Sedan Day, 255

Seeba, Hinrich, 74, 75

Self-reflection, 37

Self *vs.* other, 122, 123

Seven Years War, 79, 83, 129

Shaw, Harry, 129

Sheehan, James J., 71–72, 150

Silesia, 126, 141; and Bismarck, 143; and Frederick the Great, 33, 52, 118, 123, 139; in Hildebrandt, 87, 88; in Mühlbach, 115; seizure of, 115; in Treitschke, 143

Silesian Wars, 81, 82, 126, 138

Smith, Anthony D., 16, 20, 94

Socialism, 136, 144

Society: in Alexis, 31, 158–62, 163, 164, 165–66, 219–20; change in, 12; and confusion after Wars of Liberation, 94; in Fontane, 31, 60, 188, 189–91, 245; in François, 240; in Freytag, 182, 183; grand narrative shaping, 15; in Häusser, 179, 180; in Hesekiel, 185–88; and history, 33, 163; and Jena, 147; in Jensen, 192, 193, 194, 195; in Lewald, 151–52, 153–57; and Louisa, Queen of Prussia, 172; moral decline of, 31, 147, 151–52, 153–57, 158, 159, 161, 162, 175, 179, 180, 182, 188, 189–91, 192, 193, 194, 198, 258; in Mühlbach, 171, 223–24; in

INDEX

Ring, 172; in Sudermann, 258; in Treitschke, 175; unpheaval in, 74; in Wickede, 234. *See also* Aristocracy; Caste; Community; Middle class
Sohr, battle of, 115
Sottong, Hermann, 85
Spamer, Franz Otto, 65, 143; *The Great King and His Recruit*, 126, 127–31; *The Old Fritz Book*, 126; *The Tobacco College and the Age of the Powdered Wig*, 126
Spielhagen, Friedrich, *Noblesse oblige*, 255–58
Stein, Baron vom, 70, 71, 156, 175, 179, 183, 213, 223
Sudermann, Hermann, *The Cat's Bridge*, 255, 258–61, 264
Sue, Eugène, 39, 162
Swales, Martin, 36, 214
Sweet, Dennis, 38–39
Sybell, Heinrich von, 110; *Europe's Uprising against Napoleon I*, 208–10

Theweleit, Klaus, 200
Thirty Year's War, 14, 134
Thucydides, *History of the Peloponnesian Wars*, 49
Tieck, Ludwig, 161, 162
Treitschke, Heinrich von, 22, 30, 110, 143, 144, 177, 179, 213; Frederick the Great in, 139, 140–41, 142, 144, 173–74; *History of Germany in the Nineteenth Century*, 139–42, 174, 210–13; "Konigin Luise," 173–76
Trenck family, 137–38
Truth: in Droysen, 59–60; in Fontane, 30, 31, 35, 45, 60, 61–62, 64; in historical fiction, 29–32, 35, 44–46, 66; in historical representation, 1–2; historical *vs.* literary, 32; in history, 1–2, 32, 44, 45, 46, 57; and motivation, 66; in Mühlbach, 45; Ranke on, 40–41; and readers, 44; in Spamer, 65. *See also* Fact
Tsar Alexander, 165

Unity. *See* Germany
Universal German Encyclopedia for the Educated Classes, 202–3

Voltaire, 107, 144, 149
Voß, Julius von, *The German Don Quixote*, 90–92

War of Austrian Succession, 88
War of Bavarian Succession, 111, 132
Wars of Liberation, 6; actual *vs.* mythic participation in, 20–21; dynastic vs. voluntarist interpretation of, 202–4; in Alexis, 223; as background to fiction, 263; collective memory of, 75–76; definition of, 202–8; in Droysen, 204–6; in Fontane, 26, 247, 251; in Fouqué, 69, 78; in François, 239; in Freytag, 251, 254; and future, 200; in Hesekiel, 235, 236, 238; in Hildebrandt, 83; historical accounts of, 21, 73, 255; in historical fiction, 21, 73, 213–14, 248; and identity, 82, 271; and Jena, 196; in Jensen, 195; and Louisa, Queen of Prussia, 173; in May, 255; and military, 200, 202, 204; in Mühlbach, 167, 223–24; and national identity, 15, 70; and nationalism, 70, 72, 94; and perception of past, 73; as popular uprising, 173, 174, 202, 203, 204, 205, 206, 210; and Prussia, 3, 157, 202, 205; regeneration/renewal through, 20–21, 59, 94, 147; in Rellstab, 95; in Reuter, 224–26; social confusion after, 94; in Spielhagen, 256; in Sudermann, 258; in Sybell, 208–10; treatments of, 148; in Treitschke, 210–13; as unifying

INDEX

Wars of Liberation, (*continued*) background, 199; in Voß, 91; in Wickede, 227, 228, 229
Wartburg festival, 202–3
Wehler, Hans-Ulrich, 20
Werner, Anton von, *The Proclamation of the German Empire*, 1–2, 4, 107
Westphalia, 92, 149
White, Hayden, 45
Wickede, Julius von, 263; *Tall Isaack*, 21–22, 227–34, 255
William I, 8, 99, 118, 142–43, 145, 172
William II, 99, 144–45, 198
Williams, Raymond, 24
Wilmsen, Friedrich, 128; *The Brandenberg Children's Companion*, 6, 7–8, 15, 67, 126
Wittelsbach dynasty, 141
Women: in Alexis, 31, 162, 165; as authors, 38; in Fontane, 31, 190, 250; in François, 239; and Frederick the Great, 97–98, 142, 145; in Hesekiel, 186, 236; in Hildebrandt, 85, 86, 87; in historical fiction, 85, 240; history of, 33; and husband's identity, 21; invention by, 100–101; loyalty of, 85; in Mühlbach, 168, 169, 170; patriotic death of, 21; and public sphere, 85; as readers, 143; in Rellstab, 215–16, 217, 218–19; subordination of, 86; and Wars of Liberation, 263–64; in Wickede, 21, 229, 230, 232, 234. *See also* Feminism
Working class, 136, 144, 264

Xenophobia, 21, 188

Yorck von Wartenburg, 57, 58–59, 165, 202, 206, 208, 256
Young Germany Movement, 39

Žižek, Slavoj, 12, 122
Zollern, Hans von, 143, 144; *A Political Chess Move by Frederick the Great*, 132–37.